An Introduction to Shī'ī Law

An Introduction to Shī'ī Law

a bibliographical study

Hossein Modarressi Tabātabā'i

Ithaca Press London 1984

ISBN 0 86372 015 3

First published in 1984 by

Ithaca Press 13 Southwark Street London SE1 1RQ

Typeset by Barbara Daykin Gloucester

Printed & bound in Great Britain by

Biddles Ltd Guildford & King's Lynn

FOREWORD

The Shīʿī legal system, which is one of the two major divisions of Islamic law, is a developed integrated system with a long continuous tradition of innovation. As the system has always been open to new ideas, and as criticism and original contributions were welcome and encouraged, it grew into and continues to grow as a developed, thriving body of legal thought. Many Shīʿī jurists in the past were at the same time outstanding philosophers, and through them many elements from Islamic logic and philosophy were introduced into, and discussed in, Shīʿī law and jurisprudence. This process resulted, on the one hand, in the appearance of new and highly meticulous legal analyses in Shīʿī law and jurisprudence, and contributed, on the other hand, to the development of Islamic logic and philosophy. Shīʿī legal works, and in particular those of the last two centuries are, therefore, of significant value not only for their legal analyses but also for their evaluation and criticism of certain traditional points of view in logic and philosophy as studied in the Islamic world.

The intention of this work is to give the general outlines of Shīʿī law. It is arranged in two parts. In the first part a short description is given of the contents of Shīʿī law and jurisprudence, together with a brief discussion of its historical development. In the second part, a list of some Shīʿī comprehensive legal works and monographs is given to provide students of this legal system with essential information about references that should be consulted in any serious study of this subject.

The author would like to thank Professor W. Madelung, Professor A.K.S. Lambton and Mr. Albert Hourani who read the first part of this work and offered valuable suggestions for its improvement.

CONTENTS

Abbreviations

Transliteration

PART ONE

GENERAL STRUCTURE OF SHĪʿĪ LAW 1

Chapter One : THE SHĪʿĪ LEGAL SYSTEM AND ITS SOURCES 2

Chapter Two : GENERAL REMARKS ON SHĪʿĪ JURISPURDENCE 7

Chapter Three : THE OUTLINES OF SHĪʿĪ LAW 13

Chapter Four : THE PERIODS OF SHĪʿĪ LAW 23

PART TWO

MAIN WORKS ON SHĪʿĪ LAW 59

Chapter Five : SOME COMPREHENSIVE WORKS 62

A Systematic Legal Works 62

B Collections of *Fatwā*s 95

C Miscellaneous Works 100

Chapter Six : SOME MONOGRAPHS 114

A General 114

B On Acts of Devotion 120

C On Contracts 170

D On Unilateral Obligations 195

E On 'Rules' 199

BIBLIOGRAPHY 217

INDEX 239

ABBREVIATIONS

q	=	*hijrī qamarī*
sh	=	*hijrī shamsī*
k/K	=	*kitāb*
cat.	=	the catalogue of the library concerned
AB	=	Āghā Buzurg, *al-Dharī'a ilā taṣānīf al-Shī'a*
EI	=	*Encyclopaedia of Islam* (second edition)
Nash.	=	*Nashriyya-yi Kitābkhāna-yi Markazi-yi Dānishgāh-i Tehran dar bāra-yi nuskhahāy-i khaṭṭī*

References in footnotes are given by authors and, if necessary, by a short title of the work. The full titles are to be found in the bibliography under the author's name or under the short title if the work is anonymous. Likewise the libraries are referred in the second part by a short title and the full names and details of their catalogues are to be found in the bibliography.

TRANSLITERATION

The system used in the *Encyclopaedia of Islam* has been adopted, with the following exceptions:

ج	j
ق	q
چ	ch

There are two more points to be noted here:

(1) For well-known geographical names the common spellings have been preferred.

(2) The definite article has been omitted from the beginning of the names in all references in the footnotes, except where it is followed by an adjective with the article.

Part One
General Structure of Shī'ī Law

Chapter One

THE SHĪʿĪ LEGAL SYSTEM AND ITS SOURCES

As a doctrinal system, Shīʿism represents a particular tendency of Islam shaped by a chain of theologico-historical analyses. The *Ḥadīth al-Thaqalayn*, a tradition which was handed down by both Shīʿīs and Sunnīs from the Prophet, according to which the Prophet called on Muslims to follow the Qur'ān and his own Family after him,[1] was, along with a number of other traditions,[2] the root and original source of this tendency which was later strengthened by further theologico-philosophical and historical reasonings.

In religious matters, Shīʿism has generally based its views on the instructions of prominent members (Imāms) of the Prophet's family. The main difference between Sunnī and Shīʿī legal schools is the manner in which they received the Prophet's Tradition and in their legal sources. Whereas Sunnīs received Tradition as transmitted by the Prophet's companions, Shīʿīs received it through his Family. In another respect, whereas Sunnī legal schools follow the juridical opinions of some jurisconsults of Medina and Iraq, Shīʿīs follow the opinions of their Imāms, who were descendants of the Prophet. The Twelver Shīʿa which is now the

---

[1] See Ibn Saʿd, II, p. 194; Aḥmad, III, pp. 14, 17, 59, IV, p. 371, V, pp. 181-2; Muslim, II, pp. 237-8; Tirmidhī, II, pp. 219-20; Nasā'ī, p. 93; Dārimī, II, p 310; Bayhaqī, II, p. 148, VII, p. 30, X, p. 113; Ḥākim, III, pp. 109-10, 533; Khaṭīb, III, pp. 255, 258; Ṭaḥāwī, II, p. 307, IV, p. 368; Mundhirī, II, p. 199; Ṭabarānī, I, pp. 131, 135; al-Ḥakīm al-Tirmidhī, pp. 68-9; Baghawī, V, pp. 593, 600; Ibn al-Athīr, I, p. 187; Ibn al-Turkumānī, VII, p. 31; Qasṭalānī, VII, pp. 4-8; Haythamī, IX, pp. 164-5; ʿAsqalānī, IV, p. 65; Ibn ʿAsākir, I, p. 45; Maqrīzī, p. 38; Suyūṭī, *Iḥyā'*, pp. 11-30; Muttaqī, XV, pp. 91, 122-3. Independent works are written about this tradition, among them a treatise by Qawām al-Dīn al-Wishnawī (*Ḥadīth al-Thaqalayn*, Cairo, 1374q). Mīr Ḥāmid Ḥusayn al-Laknawī devoted a whole volume of his *ʿAbaqāt al-anwār* to the chains of authority of this tradition (see the Arabic translation of this book, Vol. I, in which the tradition is quoted from approximately two hundred Sunnī sources).

[2] See for instance Sharaf al-Dīn, pp. 42-51, 130-227.

prevalent Shīʿī school, follow the opinions of their twelve Imāms, especially the sixth, Abū ʿAbd Allāh Jaʿfar b. Muḥammad al-Ṣādiq, and for this reason their legal school is also known as *Jaʿfarī*.

* * *

The Qur'ān, Tradition (*sunna*), the consensus of the Shīʿī jurists (*ijmāʿ*) and reason (*ʿaql*)[1] form the sources of Shīʿī law.[2]

The Qur'ān, in its apparent literal sense, has shaped the spirit and foundation of Shīʿī law.

The Tradition, i.e. the statements, deeds and tacit consent of the Prophet and the Imāms, must be handed down be reliable narrators. In respect to this reliability, the doctrinal views of the transmitters are considered irrelevant. A tradition handed down by a reliable non-Shīʿī is viewed as sound and acceptable just as one transmitted by a veracious Shīʿī.

Ijmāʿ, i.e. the unanimity of the views of all Shīʿī jurists on a certain legal question, is not a source on its own, but it can become a means through which the opinions of the Imāms may be discovered. This function of *ijmāʿ* has been explained in various ways, up to twelve.[3] The most popular among these in contemporary Shīʿī law holds that since *ijmāʿ* is the unanimity of the views of 'all' Shīʿī scholars, it naturally includes the views of those scholars who lived in the time of the Imāms or the period quite close to it. Many of these were close companions of the Imāms and knew their opinions quite thoroughly. The consensus of these very early jurists, most of whom were absolute followers of the Imāms, normally demonstrates the view of the Imāms.

By 'reason' as a source[4] for Shīʿī law is meant categorical judgments

---

1 The common sources of the four Sunnī legal schools are: the Qur'ān, Tradition, *ijmāʿ* and *qiyās*. Opinions differ about a number of other sources which have been added by some of the schools to those four. *Ijmāʿ* is a source on its own in the Sunnī legal system. *Qiyās* is the application of the precept of a certain legal case to a similar one through analogical reasoning. The Shīʿīs maintain that such an application is possible only where there is a basic common denominator between the two cases inasmuch as one can be certain that the same reason which is behind the precept in the original case, covers the other case as well (see Karakī, *Ṭarīq istinbāṭ al-aḥkām*, p. 17).

2 It should be noted that these are the sources of the predominant *Uṣūlī* school of Shīʿī law. The *Akhbārī* school resorted only to Tradition. The earliest legal work in which the four sources above are mentioned with the same order is Ibn Idrīs al-Ḥillī's *al-Sarā'ir*, p. 3. The early Shīʿī *uṣūl* works did not usually mention reason as a source of law. See further Muẓaffar, II, p. 122.

3 See Muẓaffar, II, p. 107.

4 As will be explained later, reason, in Shīʿī law, is also employed as

drawn from both pure and practical reason. A clear instance is the judgment of practical reason that justice is good and injustice is evil.[1] In Shīʿī *uṣūl al-fiqh* there is a principle which states that whatever is ordered by reason, is also ordered by religion (*kull mā ḥakam bih al-ʿaql, hakam bih al-sharʿ*). In accordance with this principle, which is known as the 'rule of correlation' (*qāʿidat al-mulāzama*), religious rules may be inferred from the sole verdict of reason.[2] The correlation between the obligatoriness of an act and the obligatoriness of its prerequisites (*muqaddamat al-wājib*), or between prescribing something and prohibiting its opposite (*mas'alat al-ḍidd*), or, the impossibility of combining command and prohibition in a single case from a single standpoint (*ijtimāʿ al-amr wa'l-nahy*), are all rational precepts in the methodology of Shīʿī law and sources based on pure reason in the juridical efforts to discover legal rules.

* * *

The traditions handed down from the Prophet and Imāms, which constitute the most important source for Shīʿī law,[3] are assembled in special collections. The most renowned of these, which are the usual reference works for jurists, are the following:

1. *K. al-Kāfī*, by Abū Jaʿfar Muḥammad b. Yaʿqūb al-Kulaynī (d. 329/941)
2. *K. Man lā Yaḥḍuruh al-faqīh*, by Muḥammad b. ʿAlī b. Bābawayh al-Qummī, known as al-Ṣadūq (d. 381/991-2)
3. *Tahdhīb al-aḥkām*, by Muḥammad b. Ḥasan al-Ṭūsī, Shaykh al-Ṭā'ifa (d. 460/1067)
4. *al-Istibṣār*, by Muḥammad b. Ḥasan al-Ṭūsī

---

the means for thinking, in which sense it simply means rational argument. This sense of reason is described in the traditions of the Imāms as the only means to discover realities (see Karājakī, p. 70).

[1] See Muḥaqqiq, *Muʿtabar*, p. 6; Shahīd I, *Dhikrā*, p. 5; idem, *Qawāʿid*, p. 25; Miqdād, *Tanqīḥ*, fols. 2b-3a; Ṣāḥib al-Madārik, *Hidāyat al-ṭālibīn*, fols. 2b-3a; Qaṭīfī, *Kashf al-fawā'id*, p. 130.

[2] Muḥammad Bāqir al-Ṣadr maintains that 'reason' is a potential rather than an actual source for Shīʿī law. He says that although, according to the methodology of Shīʿī law, reason can on its own discover an injunction and guide toward a certain religious precept, this has never been actualized in practice and all religious commands which can be discovered through the categorical verdicts derived from reason are to be found in the Qur'ān and Tradition (Muḥammad Bāqir al-Ṣadr, *Fatāwā*, I, p. 98).

[3] This is because the traditions indicate duties in particular cases with details, whereas the Qur'ān usually has general rules.

5. *al-Wāfī*, by Muḥammad b. Murtaḍā al-Kāshānī, known as Muḥsin al-Fayḍ (d. 1091/1680)
6. *Wasā'il al-Shī'a*, by Muḥammad b. Ḥasan al-Ḥurr al-'Āmilī (d. 1104/1693)
7. *Biḥār al-anwār*, by Muḥammad Bāqir b. Muḥammad Taqī al-Majlisī (d. 1110/1699)
8. *Mustadrak al-Wasā'il*, by Ḥusayn b. Muḥammad Taqī al-Nūrī (d. 1320/1908)[1]

The first four of these books are collectively known as 'the four books' (*al-kutub al-arba'a*). In Shī'ī legal literature these four hold the same position that the six famous collections of Sunnī traditions (*al-kutub al-sitta*) have among Sunnīs. The most popular legal work of reference is *Wasā'il al-Shī'a* which gathers the legal traditions contained in the 'four books' and in many other sources, and since it is limited to traditions concerned with legal subjects, it is the most convenient reference handbook for every jurist.

The acceptability of any of the traditions of these books is subject to certain conditions.[2] The reliability and honesty of all the narrators of a chain of transmitters of a tradition must first be proved. This is done by a branch of scholarship known as *'ilm al-rijāl* (=*'ilm rijāl al-ḥadīth*) which investigates the narrators of the traditions and their biographies.[3] Traditions are graded and divided in accordance with the levels of their reliability,[4] on the basis of specific principles found in another branch of

---

[1] Some other major comprehensive collections of Shī'ī traditions are: *Jawāmi' al-kalim* by Muḥammad b. 'Alī al-Jazā'irī, *'Awālim al-'ulūm wa'l-ma'ārif* by 'Abd Allāh b. Nūr Allāh al-Baḥrānī, *Jāmi' al-ma'ārif wa'l-aḥkām* by 'Abd Allāh b. Muḥammad Riḍā Shubbar al-Ḥusaynī al-Kāẓimī and *Jāmi' aḥādīth al-shī'a* by Ḥusayn b. 'Alī al-Ṭabāṭabā'ī al-Burūjirdī.

[2] See Shahīd II, *Dirāya*, pp. 62-81; Abu'l-Qāsim b. Ḥasan Yazdī, I, pp. 44-61.

[3] The main Shī'ī works on this discipline are: *K. Ma'rifat al-rijāl* by al-Kashshī, *K. al-Ḍu'afā'* by al-Ghaḍā'irī, *K. al-Rijāl* by al-Najāshī, *K. al-Fihrist* and *K. al-Rijāl* by Muḥammad b. Ḥasan al-Ṭūsī. Some important later works are: *Ma'ālim al-'ulamā'* by Ibn Shahrāshūb, *Īḍāḥ al-ishtibāh* and *Khulāṣat al-aqwāl* by al-'Allāma, *K. al-Rijāl* by Ibn Dāwūd, *al-Taḥrīr al-Ṭāwūsī* by Ṣāḥib al-Ma'ālim, *Manhaj al-maqāl* by Muḥammad b. 'Alī al-Astarābādī, *Naqd al-rijāl* by al-Tafrīshī, *Majma' al-rijāl* by al-Quhpā'ī, *Ḥāwī al-maqāl* by 'Abd al-Nabī al-Jazā'irī, *Jāmi' al-ruwāt* by Muḥammad al-Ardabīlī, *Muntahā al-maqāl* by Abū 'Alī, *al-Fawā'id al-rijāliyya* by Baḥr al-'Ulūm, *Tanqīḥ al-maqāl* by 'Abd Allāh al-Māmaqānī, *Qāmūs al-rijāl* by Muḥammad Taqī al-Tustarī, and *Mu'jam rijāl al-ḥadīth* by al-Khu'ī. For other Shī'ī works on this subject see Āghā Buzurg, *Muṣaffā al-maqāl fī muṣannifī 'ilm al-rijāl* (Tehran, 1959).

[4] See Shahīd I, *Dhikrā*, p. 4; Ibn Fahd, *Muhadhdhab*, fol. 2b; Miqdād, *Tanqīḥ*, fol. 3a; Karakī, *Ṭarīq istinbāṭ al-aḥkām*, p. 10;

scholarship known, in Shīʿī literature, as *ʿilm al-dirāya* (= *ʿilm dirāyat al-ḥadīth*).[1] On these bases, many traditions of the above sources are not, in the view of the jurists, sound and reliable.

* * *

The inference of legal precepts, from the four aforementioned sources of Shīʿī law (the Qur'ān, Tradition, *ijmāʿ* and reason) is carried out through a kind of logical reasoning which, in Islamic terminology, is called *ijtihād*. According to Shīʿī teachings, it is always possible for scholars to practise this kind of rational argument in Islamic law, while Sunnīs restrict it to some scholars of the early centuries of Islam. In confronting any legal problem, every Shīʿī jurist must personally investigate these legal sources to take his own decision about it. Imitation of the opinion of a *mujtahid*, however great he is, by another *mujtahid* in legal matters is unlawful.[2]

Shahīd II, *Dirāya*, pp. 19-61; Ḥusayn b. ʿAbd al-Ṣamad, *Wuṣūl al-akhyār*, pp. 20-56; Ṣāḥib al-Madārik, *Hidāyat al-ṭālibīn*, fol. 5a; Bahā' al-Dīn al-ʿĀmilī, *Wajīza*, pp. 4-5; idem, *Mashriq al-shamsayn*, p. 269; Dāmād, *Rawāshiḥ*, pp. 115-204; Bihbahānī, *Taʿlīqāt*, pp. 5-9; Abu 'l-Qāsim b. Ḥasan al-Yazdī, I, pp. 3-44; Māmaqānī, *Miqbās*, pp. 35-105.

[1] Some main Shīʿī works on this subject are: *al-Dirāya* and *Sharḥ Risālat al-dirāya* by al-Shahīd al-Thānī, *Wuṣūl al-akhyār* by Ḥusayn b. ʿAbd al-Ṣamad, *al-Wajīza* by Bahā' al-Dīn al-ʿĀmilī, *al-Rawāshiḥ al-samāwiyya* by al-Dāmād, *Tawḍīḥ al-maqāl* by ʿAlī al-Kanī; *Miqbās al-hidāya* by ʿAbd Allāh al-Māmaqānī, and *Samā' al-maqāl* by Abu 'l-Hudā al-Kalbāsī. Also *Fawā'id-i shāfiya* by al-Farāhī, *Lubb al-Lubāb* by Muḥammad Jaʿfar al-Astarābādī, *Qawāʿid al-ḥadīth* by al-Gharīfī, and *Ḍiyā' al-dirāya* by Ḍiyā' al-Dīn al-ʿAllāma.

[2] All the above-mentioned principles are according to the Uṣūlī school of Shīʿī law. The Akhbārīs rejected *ijtihād* and prohibited the practice of rational argument in law. There are some objections to the practice of *ijtihād* in the traditions from the Imāms and in early Shīʿī works too. Most of these, however, refer to the Sunnī version of *ijtihād* which includes *qiyās* and *istiḥsān*.

Chapter Two

GENERAL REMARKS ON SHĪʿĪ JURISPRUDENCE

The inference and discovery of legal norms (*istinbāṭ*) from the aforementioned sources, which are in some cases contradictory, follow particular rules which are explained by a special branch of scholarship known as *uṣūl al-fiqh* (principles of law). This discipline is a collection of general rules and regulations on how to deduce positive precepts from the sources. Some of these rules and principles have been borrowed from other disciplines such as logic, philosophy, theology and philology.

In the early periods of Islam, Shīʿī scholars wrote treatises on some topics of *uṣūl al-fiqh*, as is mentioned in the sources.[1] But the oldest extant work on *uṣūl al-fiqh* by a Shīʿī scholar is *al-Tadhkira bi-uṣūl al-fiqh* by al-Shaykh al-Mufīd, Muḥammad b. Muḥammad b. al-Nuʿmān al-Baghdādī (d. 413/1022), a summary of which is included by al-Karājakī in his book *Kanz al-fawāʾid*.[2]

Next, there is a relatively voluminous work on this subject by al-Sharīf al-Murtaḍā, ʿAlī b. Ḥusayn al-Mūsawī (d. 436/1044), entitled *al-Dharīʿa ilā uṣūl al-sharīʿa*.[3] The book of Shaykh al-Ṭāʾifa Muḥammad b. Ḥasan al-Ṭūsī, *ʿUddat al-uṣūl*[4] is the most famous work on *uṣūl al-fiqh* of early periods. It was a text-book in Shīʿī centres of learning for a long time. Another rather old source is the relevant chapter of *al-Ghunya*

---

1 See Ḥasan al-Ṣadr, pp. 310-12. It will be seen later on in this work that a group of early Shīʿī jurists, who were contemporaries of the Twelve Imāms, used rational argument and thr rules of *uṣūl al-fiqh* in the inference of legal precepts.

2 Karājakī, pp. 186-94 (see also Shaykh, *ʿUdda*, p. 2; *Yādnāma-yi shaykh-i Ṭūsī*, III, p. 373; Brunschvig, pp. 201 ff).

3 Edited Tehran, 1967-9. Al-Murtaḍā had written independent treatises on almost all the topics of *uṣūl al-fiqh* (see his introduction to *al-Dharīʿa*, I, p. 2). He also discussed the *uṣūl* topic of *akhbār al-āḥād* in his *al-Dhakhīra*, formally a work of *kalām* theology (see Shaykh, *ʿUdda*, pp. 33-7).

4 Edited Tehran, 1313-14q and Bombay, 1312-18q.

by Ibn Zuhra al-Ḥalibī (d. 585/1189-90).[1] *K. al-Maṣādir fī uṣūl al-fiqh* by Sadīd al-Dīn Maḥmūd al-Ḥimmaṣī, the Shīʿī scholar of late 6th/12th century is not extant,[2] but some paragraphs of it are quoted in Ibn Idrīs's *al-Sarāʾir.*[3] Next, the works of al-Muḥaqqiq Jaʿfar b. Ḥasan al-Ḥillī (d. 676/1277) such as *Maʿārif al-wuṣūl*, and then those of al-ʿAllāma Ḥasan b. Yūsuf b. al-Muṭahhar al-Ḥillī (d. 726/1325) such as *Tahdhīb al-uṣūl, Mabādiʾ al-wuṣūl* and *Nihāyat al-wuṣūl* contributed to the evolution of this discipline.

Following this period, many commentaries (*sharḥ*) and annotations (*ḥāshiya*) appeared on the works of al-ʿAllāma, some of which are listed in Āghā Buzurg al-Ṭihrānī's *al-Dharīʿa ilā taṣānīf al-Shīʿa.*[4] Two of the most famous of these are the commentaries known as al-Ḍiyāʾī and al-ʿAmīdī[5] which had a notable influence on the development of Shīʿī *uṣūl al-fiqh*. Al-Shahīd al-Awwal Shams al-Dīn Muḥammad b. Makkī al-ʿĀmilī (d. 786/1384) assembled these two commentaries, together with some useful notes by himself, in a volume entitled *Jāmiʿ al-bayn.*[6]

Ḥasan b. Zayn al-Dīn al-ʿĀmilī (d. 1011/1602) paved the way for concentrated discussions on *uṣūl al-fiqh* by composing a systematic and well-arranged text as an introduction to his legal work *Maʿālim al-dīn*. Thereafter, numerous commentaries and annotations were composed on this text, which has been a text-book in Shīʿī centres of learning since the 11th/17th century.

During the 11th/17th century, the most significant *uṣūlī* views were put forward by Ḥusayn b. Rafīʿ al-Dīn Muḥammad al-Marʿashī al-Māzandarānī (d. 1064/1653-4), one of the authors of the commentaries to *Maʿālim*. *Zubdat al-uṣūl* by Bahāʾ al-Dīn al-ʿĀmilī (d. 1030.1621) and *Wāfiyat al-uṣūl* by ʿAbd Allāh b. Muḥammad al-Tūnī (d. 1071/1660-1) are among the best-known Shīʿī *uṣūl* texts of this century.

In the 12th/17th century, the *Akhbārī* school which repudiated the discipline of *uṣūl al-fiqh*, became predominant and inhibited its further

---

[1] Edited Tehran, 1276q (in the collection of *al-Jawāmiʿ al-fiqhiyya*, pp. 523-49).

[2] AB, XXI, p. 95.

[3] Ibn Idrīs, pp. 409-10.

[4] AB, VI, pp. 54-5; XIII, pp. 165-70; XIV, pp. 53-4.

[5] That is *Munyat al-labīb* by Ḍiyāʾ al-Dīn ʿAbd Allāh b. Majd al-Dīn Muḥammad al-Aʿrajī al-Ḥusaynī, and *Sharḥ al-Tahdhīb* by ʿAmīd al-Dīn ʿAbd al-Muṭṭalib b. Majd al-Dīn Muḥammad al-Aʿrajī al-Ḥusaynī. These two brothers were the neqphew of al-ʿAllāma, and both lived in the first half of the 8th/14th century (AB, XIII, p. 168).

[6] AB, V, pp. 43-4.

development. It was, however, revived with the appearance of a prominent scholar in the last third of the 12th/17th century, Muḥammad Bāqir b. Muḥammad Akmal al-Bihbahānī, known as al-Waḥīd (d. 1205/1791), who strove vigorously to combat the influence of Akhbārism and to propagate *uṣūl al-fiqh*. His students also devoted themselves to the same cause. Works such as *Qawānīn al-uṣūl* by Abu ʾl-Qāsim b. Ḥasan al-Gīlānī, known as al-Muḥaqqiq al-Qummī (d. 1231/1816), *al-Fuṣūl* by Muḥammad Ḥusayn b. Muḥammad Raḥīm al-Iṣfahānī (d. 1250-4/1834-9), *Hidāyat al-mustarshidīn* by Muḥammad Taqī b. Muḥammad Raḥīm al-Iṣfahānī (d. 1248/1833), *Mafātīḥ al-uṣūl* by Muḥammad b. ʿAlī al-Karbalāʾī al-Ṭabāṭabāʾī, known as al-Mujāhid (d. 1242/1827) and *Ḍawābiṭ al-uṣūl* by Ibrāhīm b. Muḥammad Bāqir al-Qazwīnī (d. 1262/1846), all of which were written by the pupils and followers of al-Bihbahānī's school, were instrumental in the progress and the spread of *uṣūlī* doctrine.

Shaykh Murtaḍā al-Anṣārī, the great scholar and legal theoretician (d. 1281/1864), systematically revised and reconstructed the methodology of Shīʿī law, and extended the horizons and dimensions of this discipline. The collection of his treatises on *uṣūl al-fiqh*, entitled *Rasāʾil* or *Farāʾid al-uṣūl* is still used as a text-book in traditional academies of Shīʿī law.

In the school of al-Anṣārī, which has continued up to the present date, the principles of *uṣūl al-fiqh* have been continuously subjected to scrupulous and minute examination by his disciples and followers. As a result of the emergence of great scholars such as Muḥammad Kāẓim al-Khurāsānī (d. 1329/1911) author of *Kifāyat al-uṣūl*, Muḥammad Ḥusayn al-Nāʾīnī (d. 1355/1936), Ḍiyāʾ al-Dīn al-ʿArāqī (d. 1361/1948) author of *Maqālāt al-uṣūl*, and Muḥammad Ḥusayn al-Iṣfahānī al-Kumpānī (d. 1361/1942) author of *Nihāyat al-dirāya*, and through their incisive intellectual efforts, Shīʿī *uṣūl al-fiqh* is now the most elaborate in Islamic scholarship, and is still subject to discussions and open to further development, changes and perfection.

* * *

As mentioned before, Shīʿī law has four basic sources: the Qurʾān, the Tradition, consensus and reason. The discipline of *uṣūl al-fiqh* aims to show how the legal norms can be deduced from those four sources. In some cases, however, the law cannot be directly discovered by resorting to these. Special general principles have therefore been laid down for such circumstances, and these are known in Shīʿī jurisprudence as *uṣūl ʿamaliyya* (procedural principles). Thus, Shīʿī *uṣūl al-fiqh* is divided into two parts; one part discusses the method of inference of legal norms from the four original sources; the other part examines the manner of reasoning with the above-mentioned principles.

In the first part of *uṣūl al-fiqh*, the rules of reasoning with the written code, the Qur'ān and the Tradition, are discussed. At first there is some semantic discussion relating to the nature of word-making, the use of words in their metaphorical sense, and similar subjects. Then there is general legal discussion about various implications of the imperative and the negative imperative, general law and exception, absolute and conditional laws, explicit and reverse implication, and ambiguous and clear designations. Next, the validity of the four original sources of Shīʿī law are investigated. Meanwhile the nature of law, legal judgments arrived at through pure reason, and the valid means for arriving at knowledge of legal obligations are discussed.

In the second part of Shīʿī *uṣūl al-fiqh*, the legal basis and the scope of validity of the procedural principles are examined. These are the four principles of *barā'a* (exemption), *iḥtiyāṭ* or *ishtighāl* (prudence), *takhyīr* (option) and *istiṣḥāb* (continuance). They cover all cases where the real obligation is not known. If the case has a precedence, the same law should continue according to the last principle. Otherwise the first principle excludes any legal obligation where it is not known if there is such an obligation. However, if there is a known obligation, but it is uncertain between two or more options, all must be followed according to the second principle if it is possible. But one option should be chosen according to the third principle if it is impossible to follow both or all. These four principles are very important in modern Shīʿī law. Considerable scholarly efforts have been devoted to elaborating the methods and the conditions of their application. Many logical and philosophical concepts are used and discussed to this end, and new logical and philosophical ideas are developed through these discussions. This part of *uṣūl al-fiqh* expanded significantly during the last century. In earlier Shīʿī works on *uṣūl al-fiqh*, up to the 10th/16th century, only a few pages or even lines were devoted to these principles.[1]

After the two parts mentioned above there is a chapter on conflict between laws, followed in most works by a chapter on the necessary qualific-

---

[1] See Mufīd, *Tadhkira*, pp. 192-3; Shaykh, *ʿUdda*, pp. 296-302, 303-4; Muḥaqqiq, *Maʿārij*, pp. 144-56; idem, *Muʿtabar*, pp. 6-7; ʿAllāma, *Mabādi'*, p. 56; idem, *Nihāya*, fols. 273a-277b; idem, *Tahdhīb*, p. 105; Karakī, *Ṭarīq istinbāṭ al-aḥkām*, pp. 16-17; Ḥusayn b. ʿAbd al-Ṣamad, *ʿIqd*, pp. 14-15, 23-5; Ṣāḥib al-Maʿālim, pp. 227-31; Bahā' al-Dīn al-ʿĀmilī, *Zubda*, pp. 48, 72.

ations of a jurisprudent who must exercise and follow his own decision in legal matters and of those of a jurisconsult whose legal decisions should be followed by the ordinary people who are not able to discover their obligations directly from the sources.

* * *

What follows is a selected bibliography of modern Shīʿī *uṣūl al-fiqh* developed during the last one hundred years. These are the most important works of the school of al-Anṣārī, given in chronological order:

AL-ANṢĀRĪ:
- *Maṭāriḥ al-anẓār* (his lectures complied by Abu ʾl-Qāsim al-Ṭihrānī), Tehran, 1308q
- *Farāʾid al-uṣūl = al-Rasāʾil*, edited many times (e.g. Tehran, 1296q)

AL-ĀSHTIYĀNĪ:
Baḥr al-fawāʾid (a commentary on al-Anṣārī's *Farāʾid al-uṣūl*), Tehran, 1300, 1314-15q

HĀDĪ AL-ṬIHRĀNĪ:
Maḥajjat al-ʿulamāʾ, Tehran, 1318-20q

ʿALĪ B. FATḤ ALLĀH AL-NAHĀWANDĪ:
Tashrīḥ al-uṣūl al-kabīr, Tehran, 1316-20q

AL-KHURĀSĀNĪ:
- *Kifāyat al-uṣūl*, Tehran, 1326-7q, 1341-2q, 1364q
- *Durar al-fawāʾid*, Tehran, 1315q, 1318q, 1343q.

ṢĀDIQ AL-TABRĪZĪ:
Al-Maqālāt al-Ghariyya, Tabrīz, 1317q

ʿABD AL-KARĪM AL-ḤĀʾIRĪ:
Durar al-fawāʾid, Tehran, 1337-8q, 1344q, 1355q, 1361q, 1372q

AL-NĀʾĪNĪ:
- *Ajwad al-taqrīrāt* (his lectures compiled by Abu ʾl-Qāsim al-Khuʾī), Tehran, 1348q
- *Fawāʾid al-uṣūl* (another collection of his lectures compiled by Muḥammad ʿAlī al-Kāẓimī al-Khurāsānī), Tehran, 1368q (vols. 1-2), Najaf, 1349-51q (vols. 3-4)

ḌIYĀʾ AL-DĪN AL-ʿARĀQĪ:
- *Maqālāt al-uṣūl*, Najaf, 1358q (vol. 1), Tehran, 1369q (vol. 2)
- *Nihāyat al-afkār* (his lectures compiled by Muḥammad Taqī al-Burūjirdī), Najaf, 1371-7q

MUḤAMMAD ḤUSAYN AL-IṢFAHĀNĪ AL-KUMPĀNĪ:
- *Nihāyat al-dirāya*, Tehran, 1343-71q
- *Al-Uṣūl ʿala ʾl-nahj al-ḥadīth*, Najaf, 1957

ABU ʾL-MAJD AL-IṢFAHĀNĪ:
Wiqāyat al-adhhān, [Iran], 1337 q

AL-BURŪJIRDĪ:
Nihāyat al-uṣūl (his lectures compiled by Ḥusayn ʿAlī al-Muntaẓirī), Qum, [1377 q?]

AL-KHUʾĪ:
- *Muḥāḍarāt fī uṣūl al-fiqh* (his lectures compiled by Muḥammad Isḥāq al-Fayyāḍ), Najaf, 1974-
- *Miṣbāḥ al-uṣūl* (another collection of his lectures compiled by Muḥammad

Sarwar al-Bihsūdī), Najaf, 1377-86q

AL-KHUMAYNĪ:
- *Tahdhīb al-uṣūl* (his lectures compiled by Jaʿfar al-Subḥānī), Qum, 1373-82q
- *Al-Rasāʾil*, Qum, 1385q

MUḤAMMAD RIḌĀ AL-MUẒAFFAR:
Uṣūl al-fiqh, Najaf, 1966

MUḤAMMAD BĀQIR AL-ṢADR:
- *Durūs fī ʿilm al-uṣūl*, Beirut, 1978
- *Taʿāruḍ al-adilla al-sharʿiyya* (his lectures compiled by Maḥmūd al-Hāshimī), Tehran, 1396q

Chapter Three

THE OUTLINES OF SHĪʿĪ LAW

The subjects of Islamic law (*fiqh*) have been classified in different forms. In Sunnī law, they are usually divided into two categories: *ʿibādāt* (acts of devotion) and *muʿāmalāt* (here meaning worldly affairs). Al-Ghazālī, the Shāfiʿī scholar (d. 505/1111) in his *Iḥyāʾ ʿulūm al-dīn*[1] divided all religious and moral injunctions into four groups, *ʿibādāt*, *ʿādāt* (ordinary affairs), *munjiyāt* (what ensures salvation) and *muhlikāt* (what causes perdition). This classification had some influence on later Shāfiʿī legal texts,[2] and inspired another procedure which divided legal subjects into four groups: *ʿibādāt*, *muʿāmalāt*, *munākaḥāt* (personal status) and *jināyāt* or *ʿuqūbāt* (penal law).[3] In order to justify this latter division, it is said that the subjects of *fiqh* concern either life in this world or life in the hereafter. The subjects related to the former state of being are divided into three parts: those which regulate human relationships (*muʿāmalāt*), those which preserve human kind (*munākaḥāt*) and those which protect both individuals and mankind (*jināyāt*). The subjects related to the latter state of being, i.e. the precepts which should bring happiness and welfare in the next life, are *ʿibādāt*.[4]

The oldest extant systematic codifications of Shīʿī law are found in some works of jurists of the 5th/11th century. Abu ʾl-Ṣalāḥ al-Ḥalabī (d. 447/1055-6) classified, in his *K. al-Kāfī fi ʾl-fiqh*, the legal subjects according to the religious precepts. He considered all religious dues to be of three kinds: *ʿibādāt*, by which he meant not only the common acts of devotion but all obligations including part of the category of *muʿāmalāt*,

---

1 Ghazālī, *Iḥyāʾ*, I, p. 3. See also Fayḍ, *Maḥajja*, I, pp. 4-5.

2 See for example Qaffāl, III, p. 382; Ghazzī, p. 598; Bājūrī, II, p. 332.

3 See Ḥaydar, I, p.15/Maḥmaṣānī, p. 24 quoting al-Anqarawī, *al-Fatāwā al-anqarawiyya* (Cairo, 1281q), I, p. 1.

4 Muḥammad al-Āmulī, *Nafāʾis al-funūn*, p. 146.

muḥarramāt (prohibitions) and *aḥkām* (rules). This latter term refers to all legal precepts which do not impose any religious duty (action or abstention) on Muslims, i.e. which cannot be included in the other two categories.[1]

Qāḍī ʿAbd al-ʿAzīz b. al-Barrāj (d. 481/1088) in his *al-Muhadhdhab* divided religious precepts into two categories, those which affect *all* the people and those which do not. The former are *ʿibādāt* which are general duties and for this very reason precede the rest of *fiqh*.[2]

Another Shīʿī jurist of the same period, Sallār b. ʿAbd al-ʿAzīz al-Daylamī (d. 448/1056-7) first classified *fiqh* in two sections: *ʿibādāt* and *muʿāmalāt*, then he divided the latter into *ʿuqūd* (contracts) and *aḥkām*,[3] and then divided *aḥkām* further into *jināyāt* and other types of rules.[4] Al-Muḥaqqiq, inspired by this method, classified *fiqh* in his *Sharāʾiʿ al-Islām* into four sections: *ʿibādāt*, *ʿuqūd* (here meaning bilateral obligations), *īqāʿāt* (unilateral obligations) and *aḥkām*.[5] This method was accepted by jurists who succeeded him.[6] Al-Shahīd al-Awwal justified this classification in his *al-Qawāʿid* by arguing that religious precepts are concerned either with life on earth or life in the hereafter. The former fall under *muʿāmalāt* and the latter under *ʿibādāt*. This first category, the *muʿāmalāt*, is in turn divided into two parts since these are precepts which either concern the undertakings of individuals themselves or those which are not related to the undertakings of individuals. These latter are known as *aḥkām* and include all judicial, penal and inheritance rules, etc. Undertakings too are of two kinds since some are bilateral (*ʿuqūd*) and others unilateral (*īqāʿāt*).[7] Al-Shahīd offers the same explanation in his *Dhikrā* with the exception that in this book, the basic difference between *ʿibādāt* and other categories is that acts of devotion must be practised in order to obey God and move closer to him, whereas other categories do not carry this obligation.[8] Some other scholars

---

[1] Ḥalabī, *Kāfī*, fols. 1-2. See also his *Taqrīb al-maʿārif*, fol. 96a, in which he classified all religious duties into actions and abstentions.

[2] Ibn al-Barrāj, *Muhadhdhab*, fol. 123b.

[3] Sallār, p. 28.

[4] Ibid., p. 143.

[5] Muḥaqqiq, *Sharāʾiʿ*, I, pp. 19, 163, II, pp. 53, 135.

[6] See for example ʿAllāma, *Taḥrīr*, I, pp. 1, 158, II, pp. 52, 123. See also Nāʾīnī, I, p. 33.

[7] Shahīd I, *Qawāʿid*, p. 4. See also Miqdād, *Tanqīḥ*, fols. 3b-4a; *Sharḥ qaṭrat al-baḥrayn*, fol. 1b.

[8] Shahīd I, *Dhikrā*, pp. 6-7. See also Jawād al-ʿĀmilī, IV, p. 2; Kalbāsī, fol. 2a.

considered the basis for separating *ʿibādāt* from other subjects to be the intrinsic beauty and superiority of the act of devotion itself.[1]

Naṣīr al-Dīn al-Ṭūsī (d. 672/1274) followed a more philosophical approach and proposed a tripartite classification. He argued that the religious laws concern individuals either as individual bearers of responsibility or as members of the family, or as people in society. The first category is the section on *ʿibādāt*, the second is the rules included in the section on *munākaḥāt* and other parts of *muʿāmalāt*, and the third is *siyāsāt* (penal law).[2]

Al-Fāḍil al-Miqdād (d. 826/1423) proposed two other modes of division in the classification of the legal subjects. Both approaches were inspired by *al-Qawāʿid*[3] of al-Shahīd al-Awwal. One method is based on the belief that in the course of their moral development, human beings must acquire the traits beneficial to human life and character, and reject those which are destructive. Some of these beneficial traits may bring about instant results, others more distant results, depending on the nature of these traits. Acts of devotion belong to the latter category; rules relating to marriage, transactions, food and drink (*al-aṭʿima wa 'l-ashriba*) and the like belong to the former. The precepts of penal law aim to combat those destructive traits which inhibit the progress of human beings. This method, thus, divides the subjects of *fiqh* into three categories.

The other mode of classification proposed by Miqdād divides *fiqh* into six sections. This approach is on the basis that religions have been laid down for the protection of the five basic elements of human life, viz: faith, life, property, lineage and reason. Acts of devotion are the pillar of faith; the criminal law which gives the right of retaliation to the offended person is to create a guarantee for life; regulations concerning transactions regulate financial relations and protect property; marriage regulations, related laws and some penal precepts are for the reproduction of the human race; precepts related to the prohibition of alcohol and the punishment of drinkers of alcohol and the like protect human reason. Moreover, legal precepts are laid down in order to protect the totality of the Islamic system and guarantee its correct application.[4]

---

[1] Kāshif al-Ghiṭā', *Sharḥ al-Qawāʿid*, fol. 2a.

[2] Naṣīr al-Dīn al-Ṭūsī, p. 41.

[3] Shahīd I, *Qawāʿid*, pp. 4-6.

[4] Miqdād, *Tanqīḥ*, fol. 41; also Jawād al-ʿĀmilī, IV, p. 2. The origin of the second approach can be found in al-Ghazālī's *al-Mustaṣfā* and al-Shāṭibī's *al-Muwāfaqāt*, I, p. 38. See also Abu 'l-ʿAbbās al-Ḥarrānī,

Muḥsin al-Fayḍ followed a new approach in his works on law and Tradition such as *al-Wāfī*, *Muʿtaṣam al-Shīʿa* and *Mafātīḥ al-sharāʾiʿ*. He merged some chapters of *fiqh* and changed the locations of some legal headings, mostly for the purpose of ordering it according to the human life-cycle. For instance, he put the chapters on death and the deceased, *aḥkām al-amwāt* (which in previous texts were in the *k. al-ṭahāra*, traditionally the first chapter of *fiqh*), at the end, followed by the chapter on inheritance. In this way, he tried to create a new codification for law and Tradition. He divided *fiqh* into two sections: one on acts of devotion and the social duties (*al-ʿibādāt waʾl-siyāsāt*) and the other on ordinary affairs and transactions (*al-ʿādāt waʾl-muʿāmalāt*).[1]

Another method, which is inspired by modern western approaches to the classification of legal subjects, divides topics of *fiqh* into the following categories:

I *ʿibādāt*

II Property. This may be of two kinds:

A. Public property, which does not belong to a person but is allocated for use in the general interests of the community.

B. Private property. The regulations of this section are discussed in two independent parts:

1. The lawful means of ownership
2. The rules concerning the disposal of property

III Personal behaviour and practices, i.e. ordinary affairs which do not concern religious devotions or financial matters. These are of two kinds:

A. Family law

B. The rules for social relations and behaviour of individuals in the society

IV Political subjects in general.[2]

* * *

---

p. 455; Zarqāʾ, I, pp. 64-7; Zuḥaylī, pp. 359-60; Maḥmaṣānī, p. 25; Khallāf, p. 57.

[1] See Fayḍ, *Mafātīḥ*, I, p. 14; idem, *Wāfī*, I, p. 16. See also Nāʿīnī, I, p. 33. As one can guess from the titles of the sections, al-Fayḍ was inspired to some extent in his proposal by the method of arrangement of al-Ghazālī's *Iḥyāʾ ʿulūm al-dīn*, which was summarized and refined by al-Fayḍ in a book named *al-Maḥajja al-bayḍāʾ fī iḥyāʾ al-Iḥyāʾ*.

[2] Muḥammad Bāqir al-Ṣadr, *Fatāwā*, I, pp. 132-4.

The chapters of Shīʿī law, which are called 'books' (*kutub*, sing. *kitāb*),[1] are concerned with various legal subjects. Together they provide a catalogue of the personal and social duties of a Shīʿī Muslim.

The arrangement of these chapters varies in different texts, but generally the chapters on devotions are located at the beginning,[2] those on transactions in the middle and those on inheritance and the penal code, at the end.[3] In some Sunnī legal works, the reasons for this arrangement are given at the start of some of the chapters.[4]

Sunni[5] and Shīʿī[6] authors have stated that the reason why they place some chapters before others is that not only are these intrinsically more important but that religion also endows them with an importance above others.

Qāḍī ʿAbd al-ʿAzīz b. al-Barrāj holds that the arrangement of the chapters is related to the generality of the subjects they treat. According to him, acts of devotion which have to be practised by all Muslims at all times and anywhere, have priority over transactions, executive rules, etc., which are restricted by certain conditions. Amongst the acts of devotion, prayer, which is a daily duty for every Muslim and is, in fact, the most regular Islamic duty, together with its requisite ritual purity (*ṭahāra*), come before the other acts of devotion.[7] Ibn Ḥamza, another Shīʿī jurist of the 6th/12th century, adopting the same view, evaluated the degree of the applicability of each of these acts to devotion, and included a discussion of this in the preface of his work *al-Wasīla*.[8] Abu 'l-Fatḥ Muḥammad b. ʿAlī b. ʿUthmān al-Karājakī (d. 449/1057-8) arranged the chapters of *fiqh* in his legal work called *Bustān* like the branches of a tree. He tried to connect the branches to each other so as to create a natural arrangement

---

[1] See for the use in this context of this term *Fuṣūl*, fols. 84b-85a, 87b-88a; Shahīd II, *Rawḍa*, I, p. 26.

[2] As was noted before, al-Ḥalabī inserted all obligations in the section on devotions, including parts of the sections on *īqāʿāt* and *aḥkām*. Al-Shahīd al-Awwal followed al-Ḥalabī in some of his legal works (see especially Nā'īnī, I, p. 33).

[3] In al-Fayḍ's works the penal code comes before the section on transactions. See for instance his *Mafātīḥ*, I, p. 14.

[4] See as an example Ṭaḥṭāwī, II, p. 2.

[5] Muḥammad al-Āmulī, *Nafā'is*, p. 146; *Fuṣūl*, fol. 89a-b.

[6] See for example Muḥaqqiq, *Sharā'iʿ*, I, p. 19; ʿAllāma, *Tabṣira*, p. 1; *Risāla fi 'l-ṭahāra wa 'l-ṣalāt*, fol. 34a.

[7] Ibn al-Barrāj, *Sharḥ Jumal*, p. 54; idem, *Muhadhdhab*, fol. 124. See also Shaykh, *Iqtiṣād*, p. 239; *Fuṣūl*, fol. 89.

[8] Ibn Ḥamza, *Wasīla*, p. 662.

of the topics. In his pattern, the first chapter of each section was a smaller branch growing from trunk of the tree itself. Each later chapter in a section was a smaller branch growing from the main one. We do not know any further details of his pattern which was described by one of his contemporaries as a novel plan.[1]

The different approaches adopted by the scholars with regard to the codification of legal subjects resulted in a variety of arrangements of the chapters in their books. There was also much disagreement about the subdivisions of sections.[2] For instance the number of acts of devotion is five according to Shaykh al-Ṭā'ifa[3] and Ibn Zuhra,[4] six according to Sallār,[5] ten according to al-Ḥalabī,[6] Ibn Ḥamza[7] and al-Muḥaqqiq[8] and forty-five according to Yaḥyā b. Saʿīd.[9]

On the other hand, some authors, especially later ones, merged different chapters and reduced the number of general titles as mush as possible. Thus there is considerable variation between legal texts in respect to their arrangement and the number of chapters. For instance, *al-Nihāya* by Shaykh al-Ṭā'ifa has twenty-two chapters, his *al-Mabsūṭ* seventy one, *Sharā'iʿ al-Islām* by al-Muḥaqqiq fifty-two, *Qawāʿid al-aḥkām* by al-ʿAllāma thirty-one, his *Tabṣirat al-mutaʿallimīn* eighteen, *al-Lumʿa al-Dimashqiyya* by al-Shahīd al-Awwal fifty-two, his *al-Durūs al-Sharʿiyya* forty-eight, *Mafātīḥ al-sharā'iʿ* by al-Fayḍ twelve, and his *al-Wāfī* (which is a collection of traditions) ten.

* * *

What follows is a very brief description of the contents of Shīʿī law, according to the classification and arrangment of al-Muḥaqqiq's *Sharā'iʿ al-Islām*:

A. ACTS OF DEVOTION (*ʿibādāt*):

1. *K. al-ṭahāra* = ritual purity. The chapter includes some laws relating to non-Muslims and the deceased.

---

[1] Nūrī, III, p. 498; AB, III, p. 105.

[2] See Kalbāsī, fol. 21.

[3] Shaykh, *Iqtiṣād*, p. 239.

[4] Ibn Zuhra, p. 549

[5] Sallār, p. 28.

[6] Ḥalabī, *Kāfī*, fol. 2b.

[7] Ibn Ḥamza, loc. cit.

[8] Muḥaqqiq, *Sharā'iʿ*, I, p. 19.

[9] Yaḥyā b. Saʿīd, *Nuzha*, pp. 6-7.

2. *K. al-ṣalāt* = prayer. This chapter includes in some works scientific discussions of the two topics of the times of prayer (*awqāt al-ṣalāt*) and the direction of prayer (*qibla*); there is also discussion on the social status of the Shīʿī jurist (*faqīh*) and the nature of Islamic government in the part devoted to Friday prayer.

3. *K. al-zakāt* = alms, the best known fiscal obligation of Muslims.

4. *K. al-khums*, the one fifth tax which according to Shīʿī law covers all kinds of revenue and not only the booty of war and treasure trove as Sunnī law maintains. A discussion about the authority of Shīʿī jurists is included. Some laws relating to non-Muslim residents of Muslim territory are to be found here, since one of the cases where *khums* is levied is land sold to a non-Muslim by a Muslim. The chapter is followed by a discussion of *anfāl*, i.e. the property of the Islamic state including all natural wealth and wastelands.

5. *K. al-ṣawm* = fasting.

6. *K. al-iʿtikāf* = seclusion, which is regarded as a desirable act of devotion in Islamic law, and should be performed in the congregational mosque of the town.

7. *K. al-ḥajj* = pilgrimage to Mecca during the last month of the Islamic lunar calendar, with its special laws and conditions.

8. *K. al-ʿumra* = a simpler kind of pilgrimage to Mecca which can be performed at any time of the year.

9. *K. al-jihād* = 'holy war', offensive and defensive, and in the second case against either external or internal enemies. This chapter includes discussion of the different categories of land within Muslim territory, on the relation between the Islamic state and non-Muslim governments, on the status of non-Muslims in Muslim territory, and the like.

10. *K. al-amr bi 'l-maʿrūf wa 'l-nahy ʿan al-munkar* = ordering what is good and forbidding what is evil; rules and regulations of these Islamic social obligations.

B. CONTRACTS (*ʿuqūd*)

1. *K. al-tijāra* = transactions; discussion about valid and invalid ways of carrying out transactions, unlawful business, right of cancellation of business agreements, conditions connected with contracts and similar topics. It also includes discussion on ownership and the fiscal system as applied to the various categories of land in Muslim territory, the legal status of working for unjust rulers and their disposals of the properties of the Muslims' treasury, and, in the legal works of the last century up to now, a study of the authority of the Shīʿī jurist (*wilāyat al-faqīh*).

Legal discussion about subjects such as music and interest on loans is to be found in the same chapter.

2. *K al-rahn* = mortgage.

3. *K. al-mufallas* = bankruptcy, the responsibilities of the Islamic state when somebody becomes bankrupt and his assets do not balance his liabilities.

4. *K. al-ḥajr* = interdiction, cases where the owner is legally forbidden from disposing of his own property, as is the case with minors and the insane.

5. *K. al-ḍamān* = suretyship for claims, transference of the liability with regard to a claim. The suretyship for persons (*al-kafāla bi 'l-nafs*) is also discussed in the same chapter.

6. *K. al-ṣulḥ* = conciliation, the mutual agreement of two persons on a certain matter, the details of which are not clear; for example, the mutual agreement between the creditor and the debtor on a specified sum where the amount of the debt is not precisely known.

7. *K. al-sharika* = partnership.

8. *K. al-Muḍāraba* = sleeping partnership, i.e. one party invests the capital and the other provides the labour.

9. *K.al-muzāraʿa wa 'l-musāqāt* = share cropping, i.e. the landlord entrusts his land to a cultivator (*muzāraʿa*) or the owner of an orchard gives it to someone to look after the trees (*musāqāt*), in return for a share of the produce.

10. *K. al-wadīʿa* = deposit, the safe-keeping of someone else's property.

11. *K. al-ʿāriya* = lending an object gratuitously to someone to make use of it.

12. *K. al-ijāra* = hire and lease, the sale of usufruct or the hire of service.

13. *K. al-wikāla* = procuration, power of disposal on another.

14. *K. al-wuqūf wa'l-ṣadaqāt* = endowments and charity.

15. *K. al-suknā wa 'l-taḥbīs* = temporary donation of usufruct.

16. *K. al-hibāt* = donation of objects.

17. *K. al-sabq wa 'l-rimāya* = horse and camel racing and marksmanship contests; the only two cases where betting is regarded as legal, for the actual participants only.

18. *K. al-waṣāyā* = legacies.

19. *K. al-nikāḥ* = marriage.

C. UNILATERAL OBLIGATIONS (*Īqāʿāt*)

1. *K. al-ṭalāq* = divorce

2. *K. al-khulʿ wa 'l-mubāra'a*, two kinds of divorce by which the wife redeems herself from the marriage for a consideration.

3. *K. al-ẓihār*, that is a husband's statement to his wife, saying she is like his mother (this was a saying occasionally used in Arab communities). This declaration requires a religious expiation (*kaffāra*).

4. *K. al-īlā'* = a husband's oath to abstain from marital intercourse for a period of more than four months, in which case he must either give up his oath or divorce his wife.

5. *K. al-liʿān*, husband's affirmation, through a cursing oath and before a court of law, that the wife has been unfaithful, and a similar affirmation by his wife that the husband is lying. After such a counter-affirmation and cursing the marriage is irrevocably dissolved.

6. *K. al-ʿitq* = the manumission of slaves.

7. *K. al-tadbīr wa 'l-mukātaba wa 'l-istīlād*, these are three ways for slaves to acquire their freedom. *Tadbīr* is a manumission which takes effect from the time of the owner's death. *Mukātaba* is a contract between the owner and the slave by which the latter acquires his fredom against a future payment. The third concept, *istīlād*, refers to cases where a female slave gives birth to a child for her owner, in which case she becomes free on her owner's death.

8. *K. al-iqrār* = acknowledgement of debt, family relationship and the like. It is conclusive legal evidence for the creation of an obligation on the part of the person who makes it.

9. *K. al-juʿāla*, the undertaking by a person to pay a certain sum in return for the performance of some specific task, no matter who actually performs it. For instance, someone offers a sum as a reward for the return of some property of his which has been lost.

10. *K. al-aymān* = oaths, undertakings stated in the name of God.

11. *K. al-nadhr* = vow, an undertaking towards God to do or not to do something, unconditionally or provided a certain wish comes true.

D. RULES (*aḥkām*)

1. *K. al-ṣayd wa 'l-dhabāḥa* = hunting and slaughtering.

2. *K. al-aṭʿima wa 'l-ashriba* = food and drinks.

3. *K. al-ghaṣb* = usurpation.

4. *K. al-shufʿa* = pre-emption, the co-owner's right to priority to buy the other share of the property, so that he can dissolve the sale of that share and take it into his own possession if it is sold to an outsider without the co-owner's agreement.

5. *K. iḥyā' al-mawāt* = reclamation of wastelands. This chapter

includes a survey of land law, and is normally followed by a study of the common property of the community (*mushtarakāt*), such as water and pasture.

6. *K. al-luqaṭa* = trove property.
7. *K. al-farāʾiḍ* = inheritance.
8. *K. al-qaḍāʾ* = arbitration, legal procedure.
9. *K. al-shahādāt* = witnesses.
10. *K. al-ḥudūd wa ʾl-taʿzīrāt* = penal law.
11. *K. al-qiṣāṣ* = retaliation, the right of the offended person or his hairs against the offender.
12. *K. al-diyāt* = blood-money and other financial compensations.

Chapter Four

THE PERIODS OF SHĪʿĪ LAW

The present legal system of Shīʿī *fiqh* has developed through various ›hases, and has been reformed and elaborated by many eminent scholars, among whom are Shaykh al-Ṭā'ifa Muḥammad b. Ḥasan al-Ṭūsī, .l-Muḥaqqiq Jaʿfar b. Ḥasan al-Ḥillī, al-ʿAllāma Ḥasan b. Yūsuf b. ıl-Muṭahhar al-Ḥillī, al-Shahīd al-Awwal Muḥammad b. Makkī al-ʿĀmilī .nd Ṣāḥib al-Madārik Muḥammad b. ʿAlī al-ʿĀmilī (d. 1009/1600).

In the legal sources, the history of Shīʿī law is usually divided into wo periods,[1] that of the ancient or early scholars (*qudamā'* or *ıutaqaddimūn*) and that of the moderns or later scholars (*muta'akhkhirūn*). n works of the 6th-7th/12th-13th centuries, the contemporaries of the welve Imāms were considered as the 'ancients' and those who came after his era (i.e from 260/874 onwards) as the 'moderns'.[2] At times, the xpression 'ancients' is applied to Shaykh al-Ṭā'ifa and his predecessors[3] nd the expression 'moderns' given to his successors.[4] Sometimes, however, the expression 'moderns' is used by writers to mean scholars con›mporary with themselves.[5] In later sources the term 'ancients' means ıose who lived before al-Muḥaqqiq or al-ʿAllāma, and the term 'moderns' efers to those who lived after them. In the sources of the 13th/19th entury, the expression *muta'akhkhiru 'l-muta'akhkhirīn* (the moderns of ıe moderns) is used to mean, in earlier works, those who came after

[1] This division is other than that of traditionists in which the Shīʿī ·aditionists have been divided into ten sections (*ṭabaqa*). The bases and ·iteria for these two divisions are quite different as well. (See AB, I, p. 137, quoting Ḥasan al-Ṣadr in his *Bughyat al-wuʿāt fī ṭabaqāt ısha'ikh al-ijāzāt*).

[2] ʿAbd al-Jalīl al-Qazwīnī, p. 209; Muḥaqqiq, *Muʿtabar*, p. 7.

[3] Shaykh al-Ṭā'ifa himself is considered to be one of 'the ancients' in ıahīd II, *Rawḍa*, II, p. 73.

[4] See for instance Muḥaqqiq, *Nukat*, p.438; Yaḥyā b. Saʿīd, *Nuzha*, p. 6.

[5] Ibn Idrīs, p. 265; Ḥurr al-ʿĀmilī, *Amal*, II, p. 5.

al-Shahīd al-Awwal[1] and in later works those who came after Ṣāḥib al-Madārik.[2]

This division does not adequately reflect the development of the law, which can more exactly be defined by a division into eight periods.[3] What follows is a brief description of these periods, together with a mention of the most eminent scholars[4] of each period and their main legal works.[5]

1. THE PERIOD OF THE PRESENCE OF THE IMĀMS

It is generally believed that Shīʿī law was undeveloped in this period which began with the Prophet and ended in 260/874. This is based on the assumption that since the Imāms were present and accessible, there was no great urge to develop the practice of independent judgment and that law was limited to the transmission of traditions. This idea is not correct. In order to have a better grasp of the situation, the circumstances of Shīʿism at the time have to be examined.

(1) It can be clearly seen from religious traditions that Shīʿī Imāms had persistently urged their followers to reason and use their minds. In the case of discussions on *Kalām* theology they praised and encouraged Shīʿī theologians of their times.[6] In the case of legal problems, the Imāms stated explicitly that their own duties lay in explaining general rules and principles; whereas inferences in details and minor precepts for actual cases were left to the learned followers of the Imāms.[7] The Imāms some-

---

[1] Khalkhālī, III, p. 174.

[2] Mudarris, III, p. 439.

[3] Compare with Raḍī al-Dīn al-Qazwīnī's classification of the Shīʿī scholars up to the mid-10th/16th century into seven genreations. See his *Tārīkh-i mashāhīr-ī Imāmiyya*.

[4] By these scholars are meant those whose legal opinions have been considered and quoted in the sources of *fiqh*. In these sources, the views of different Shīʿī jurists and even sometimes of Sunnī ones are usually quoted before examining each case. Obviously, only the views of those scholars who influenced the development of law, were quoted and taken note of. The names of these scholars and their famous reference works have been chronologically listed in the preface of *Maqābis al-anwār* by al-Kāẓimī (pp. 4-19).

[5] In the Shīʿī sources of law, there are special abbreviations for the names of the scholars and the legal sources, as well as some particular terms; many of these are explained in al-Khwānsārī's *Rawḍāt*, II, pp. 114-15, and in the preface of al-Kāẓimī's *Maqābis*, pp. 19-22.

[6] See Kashshī, pp. 268, 278, 484-6, 489-90, 538, 542; Kulaynī, I, pp. 169-74; Mufīd, *Taṣḥīḥ al-iʿtiqād*, pp. 171-2; Quhpāʾī, VI, pp. 223-30, 293-307.

[7] '*ʿAlaynā ilqāʾ al-uṣūl ilaykum wa ʿalaykum al-tafrīʿ*' (we must give you the principles and you have to derive branches): Bazanṭī, p. 477; Fayḍ, *al-Ḥaqq al-mubīn*, p. 7; Ḥurr al-ʿĀmilī, XVIII, p. 41.

times also explained when faced by questions from their followers that the correct replies to their questions could be grasped and derived from general Islamic legal principles.[1] On some occasions, the Imāms themselves followed what they advised as the correct method of reasoning and thus instructed their followers on the proper procedure for inference of legal precepts.[2]

(2) The period of the presence of the Imāms is quite distinct from the following periods of Shīʿī history in respect to the variety of *kalām* theological doctrines held by Shīʿī scholars. Many of the Imāms' compan-ons were eminent *kalām* theologians[3] who held significant opinions on theological subjects, some of which have been quoted in the general *kalām* works, among them: Hishām b. al-Ḥakam, Hishām b. Sālim, Zurāra b. Aʿyan, Mu'min al-Ṭāq, Yūnus b. ʿAbd al-Raḥmān (all of the 2nd/8th century), and al-Bazanṭī and Faḍl b. Shādhān (of the 3rd/9th century).[4] Some other *kalām* schools of the time had followers among Shīʿī thologians of the early centuries of Islam.[5]

Differences of opnions on *kalām* theological subjects resulted in the emergence of a variety of tendencies and groups among the companions of the Imāms, causing intensive debates and arguments among then.[6] Many of the most prominent companions of the Imāms had their own separate

---

[1] See for instance Kulaynī, III, p. 33; V, p. 357; Shaykh, *Tahdhīb*, , p. 363; VII, p. 297; idem, *Istibṣār*, I, pp.77-8; VII, p.297; III, p. 78; Ḥurr al-ʿĀmilī, I, p.327; *Jāmiʿ aḥādīth al-Shīʿa*, I, pp.116-18.

[2] See for instance Kulaynī, III, pp. 83-8; Ḥurr al-ʿĀmilī, II, pp. 38-9, 542, 546, 547-8.

[3] See Iqbāl, pp. 75-84.

[4] See for instance Ṣadūq, *Tawḥīd*, pp. 97-104; Mufīd, *Fuṣūl*, pp. 119-1; idem, *Awā'il al-maqālāt*, p. 116, and the whole text for the opinions of awbakhtīs; Kashshī, pp. 268, 275, 284-5, 490, 540-4; Quhpā'ī, VI, . 8; Raḍī al-Dīn al- Qazwīnī, *Ḍiyāfa*, pp. 180-1; Majlisī II, III, p. 288, 300, 303, 305; Bihbahānī, *Taʿlīqāt*, p. 8; Abū ʿAlī, pp. 45, 46; Kāẓimī, *Kashf al-qināʿ*, pp. 198-200; Māmaqānī, *Tanqīḥ*, the introuction, pp. 208-9. See also Ṣafā'i, pp. 36-68. Asad Allāh al-Kāẓimī, nown as Ṣāḥib al-Maqābis (d. 1234/1818-19) collected the different views f the companions of Imāms from early sources in a book entitled *al-anāhij* (see his *Kashf al-qināʿ*, p. 71).

[5] See Mufīd, *Sarawiyya*, p. 221; idem, *Awā'il al-maqālāt*, p. 77; urtaḍā, *Ibṭāl al-ʿamal bi-akhbār al-āḥād*, fol. 142b; Najāshī, p. 289; haykh, *ʿUdda*, pp. 54-5; idem, *Fihrist*, p. 190; Ibn Shahrāshūb, *aʿālim*, p. 126; Quhpā'ī, V, p. 177; Muḥammad al-Ardabīlī, II, p. 234; ajlisī II, III, p. 304; Futūnī, p. 4.

[6] See Ṣadūq, *Tawḥīd*, p. 100; Kashshī, pp. 279-80; Majlisī II, III, p. 244, 307; Kāẓimī, *Kashf al-qināʿ*, pp. 71-84.

groups of followers[1] who sometimes branded each other as 'infidel' (*kāfir*)[2] and many books were produced on these disputations and confrontations.[3] It is interesting to note that, sometimes, members of one tendency or group would disagree even with their 'leader' on most aspects of ideological principles.[4] On the other hand, many Shīʿīs who gathered around the Imāms restricted themselves to the transmission of traditions and refrained from theological debates. They did not look favourably upon the Shīʿī theologians.[5] The theologians who were appreciated and favoured by the Imāms, strongly resented the reproaches directed against them by the traditionists, and the Imāms consoled the accused[6] by saying that they should tolerate and act moderately towards their adversaries since the latters' capacity for understanding subtle points and minute nuances was extremely limited.[7] Some of the traditionists of Qum, too, squabbled with theologians,[8] fabricated traditions in condemnation of the latter and attributed them to the authority of the Imāms,[9] and wrote books in this vein.[10] On the other hand, the Imāms recommended their followers to refer to theologians and read their books.[11] They even encouraged the people of Qum to honour and respect Shīʿī theologians 'in spite of the fact that the

---

[1] Durust b.Abī Manṣūr, p. 161.

[2] See Kulaynī, VII, p. 285; Kashshī, pp. 279-80, 498-9; Ḥurr al-ʿĀmilī, VI, p. 385.

[3] For instance Hishām b. al-Ḥakam's treatise in refutation to Muʾmin al-Ṭāq (Najāshī, p. 338); *Risāla fī maʿnā Hishām wa Yūnus* by ʿAlī b. Ibrāhīm b. Hāshim al-Qummī (ibid., p. 197); *Risāla fi 'l-radd ʿalā ʿAlī b. Ibrāhīm b. Hāshim fī maʿnā Hishām wa Yūnus* by Saʿd b. ʿAbd Allāh al-Ashʿarī (ibid., p. 134).

[4] See for example Shaykh, *Fihrist*, p. 132, the biography of Abū Jaʿfar al-Sakkāk.

[5] See Kashshī, e.g. pp. 279, 487-8, 496, 498-9. See also Ṣadūq, *Tawḥīd*, pp. 458-60; Ibn Ṭāwūs, *Kashf al-maḥajja*, pp. 18-19; Ḥurr al-ʿĀmilī, XI, pp. 457-9.

[6] See Kashshī, pp. 498-9.

[7] Ibid., p. 488.

[8] Ibid., p. 489, also pp. 483, 506; Muḥammad al-Ardabīlī, I, p. 459, II, p. 357; Abū ʿAlī, p. 28.

[9] Kashshī, p. 497. For examples of those traditions see pp. 491-6, 540-4; Barqī, *Rijāl*, p. 35; Bazanṭī, p. 478.

[10] For example *K. Mathālib Hishām wa Yūnus* by Saʿd b. ʿAbd Allāh al-Ashʿarī (Najāshī, p. 134) and *K. al-Ṭaʿn ʿalā Yūnus* by Yaʿqūb b. Yazīd b. Ḥammād al-Kātib al-Anbārī al-Sulamī al-Qummī (ibid., p. 350).

[11] Kashshī, pp. 483-5, 506; Najāshī, pp. 346-8.

traditionists of their town were hostile to them'.[1]

The Shīʿī books on *rijāl* (biographies of the narrators of Tradition), especially that of al-Kashshī, are full of reports on different theological tendencies and opinions found amongst Shīʿīs of the first centuries of Islam. The works display the impact of intensive arguments and controversies, as well as the impact of the support given by the Imāms to the theologians and their concerns for the prosperity and productivity of Shīʿī thought. In his reply to the followers of Yūnus b. ʿAbd al-Raḥmān, who were considered to be 'infidels' by the rest of the followers of the Imāms, Imām ʿAlī al-Riḍā would tell them: 'I see you moving in the path of deliverance.'[2]

Most Shīʿī jurists during the time of the Imāms were among these theologians, as will be mentioned presently.

(3) Certain tendencies could be found in the Shīʿī community of the period of the presence of the Imāms which were opposed to the traditionally predominant doctrine concerning the nature of the Imāms. Some of the companions of the Imāms did not accept that the Imāms possessed divine qualities such as infallibility and impeccability (*ʿiṣma*) but believed that they were pious learned men (*ʿulamāʾ abrār*), who had merely a scholarly authority.[3] This view was supported by some of the Shīʿī theologians of later periods, amongst them Abū Jaʿfar Muḥammad b. Qiba al-Rāzī, a Shīʿī scholar and theologian of the 4th/10th century, who was a leading figure in the Shīʿī community of his time,[4] and whose views were respected and referred to by later Shīʿī scholars.[5] He supported the idea that the Imāms were merely pious scholars, who had a comprehensive knowledge of the Qurʾān and Tradition. He also refuted the idea that the Imāms had knowledge of the unperceivable (*ʿilm al-ghayb*).[6] Yet, in spite of these opinions, his doctrinal stand was appreciated by later Shīʿī scholars.[7] At least some of the traditionists of Qum, who were considered

---

[1] Kashshī, p. 489.

[2] Ibid., p. 499.

[3] See Ṣadūq, *Khiṣāl*, p. 354; Ḥurr al-ʿĀmilī, XI, pp. 429-30; Baḥr al-ʿUlūm, III, pp. 219-20.

[4] ʿAllāma, *Khulāṣa*, p. 143.

[5] Kāẓimī, p. 305.

[6] Ibid., p. 200. Some other opinions of this scholar, which are different from Shīʿī traditional and popular views, are quoted in the works of al-Sharīf al-Murtaḍā (see as an example his *al-Shāfī*, p. 100).

[7] Shaykh, *Fihrist*, p. 132; Ibn Shahrāshūb, *Maʿālim*, p. 85; ʿAllāma, *Khulāṣa*, p. 143. All stating that Ibn Qiba was *ṣaḥīḥ al-madhhab* or *ḥasan al-iʿtiqād*.

as the backbone of the Shīʿī school, also held similar opinions with regard to the Imāms.[1] It seems that the Nawbakhtīs, too, thought likewise to some extent.[2]

Some of the companions of the Imāms even believed that the Imāms, just like the jurists of those times, practised independent judgment (*ra'y*)[3] or analogical reasoning (*qiyās*).[4] This position was also accepted by some of the traditionists of Qum.[5] Abū Muḥammad Layth b. al-Bakhtarī al-Murādī, known as Abū Baṣīr, one of the most competent scholars among the companions of Imām Jaʿfar al-Ṣādiq[6] who, according to many narratives was praised by the Imāms[7] and was one of the four elite of the Shīʿī religion,[8] did not accept the legal opinions of the seventh Imām, Mūsā al-Kāẓim, and thought that the latter had not yet acquired an adequate knowledge of law.[9] A number of other companions of the Imāms are said to have held similar views.[10]

On this basis, some of the companions of the Imāms openly disagreed with them in scientific questions,[11] and sometimes they even argued with them over points of disagreement[12] or asked them to present the reason for the positions they held in legal questions.[13] Such controversies between the companions of the Imāms sometimes culminated in serious quarrels breaking up friendships permanently,[14] while, according to customary

---

[1] Mufīd, *Taṣḥīḥ al-iʿtiqād*, pp. 218-19.

[2] See their views in similar cases in al-Mufīd's *Awā'il al-maqālāt*, for example pp. 78, 79, 80, 84.

[3] Baḥr al-ʿUlūm, III, p. 220. Also Ṣaffār, *Baṣā'ir*, p. 301; Mufīd, *Sarawiyya*, p. 224; idem, *Ikhtiṣāṣ*, p. 274; *Jāmiʿ aḥādīth al-Shīʿa*, I, p. 273.

[4] Kāẓimī, p. 83.

[5] Mufīd, *Taṣḥīḥ al-iʿtiqād*, p. 219.

[6] Kashshī, p. 238; Tustarī, *Qāmūs al-rijāl*, VII, p. 451.

[7] Kashshī, pp. 136-7, 170; Quhpā'ī, V, p. 83; Muḥammad al-Ardabīlī, II, p. 34.

[8] Kashshī, pp. 238-9. The others are Zurāra b. Aʿyan, Muḥammad b. Muslim and Burayd b. Muʿāwiya al-ʿIjlī.

[9] Ibid., p. 173; Quhpā'ī, V, pp. 84-5.

[10] Kashshī, pp. 147, 148, 158.

[11] Kāẓimī, pp. 71-2.

[12] Ibid., p. 72.

[13] See for instance Kulaynī, III, p. 30; Ṣadūq, *Faqīh*, I, pp. 56-7; idem, *ʿIlal*, I, pp. 264-5; Shaykh, *Tahdhīb*, I, pp. 61-2; idem, *Istibṣār*, I, pp. 62-3; Ḥurr al-ʿĀmilī, I, p. 291, II, p. 980.

[14] See Kulaynī, I, pp. 409-11; Nūrī, I, p. 555.

Shīʿī thought, those cases of dispute ought to have been taken to the Imāms for their judgment, a practice usually followed by most faithful believers.[1]

(4) As mentioned already, the inference of legal precepts in Shīʿī law is fundamentally based on logical analysis and reasoning within the framework of Qur'ānic texts and Tradition. Rational argument is accepted on the basis of Aristotelian deduction, which brings certainty according to the principles of that logical system. The kind of analogical reasoning which is entitled *qiyās* in Islamic law was rejected by the Shīʿa from the time it came into Islamic law, in the 2nd/8th century,[2] because it leads only to a probable cause for a precept, not to the certain one. Some cases of *qiyās* in which the real cause of a precept is found are, as mentioned before, accepted in Shīʿī law.

In the first centuries, the traditionists who were opposed to any kind of rational argument held that this mode of arriving at categorical judgments amounted to *qiyās* and was therefore unlawful.[3] Some later scholars called it permissible *qiyās*,[4] while in fact this mode of analysis bears no connection with the Sunnī concept of *qiyās*.[5] It seems that in the religious mentality of the Shīʿa of the first centuries, all kinds of rational argument were considered a kind of *qiyās*.[6] This was perhaps caused by some outward or terminological similarities. Then, traditionists believed that the injunctions found in Shīʿī Tradition which forbade the practice of *qiyās* were also applicable to any other mode of rational analysis.

These traditions also forbid practising independent judgment, which is called *ra'y* in legal terminology. In the legal usage of the early periods, the term *ijtihād* was used[7] in the sense of personal judgments including *ra'y*.[8]

---

[1] See Kashshī, p. 539; Abū Manṣūr al-Ṭabrisī, II, p. 284.

[2] Ibn Ḥazm, *Iḥkām*, VII, p. 177; idem, *Mulakhkhaṣ ibṭāl al-ra'y wa 'l-qiyās*, p. 5.

[3] Karakī, *Ṭarīq istinbāṭ al-aḥkām*, p. 17. Because of the same interpretation, later Akhbārīs accused Uṣūlīs of following the practice of *qiyās* in their legal judgments. See for instance Ḥusayn al-Karakī, chapter 8.

[4] *Al-Masā'il al-Muhannā'iyya*, fol. 92a; Shahīd II, *Rawḍa*, III, p. 65. See also Bihbahānī, *Taḥqīq fi 'l-qiyās*, fol. 85a.

[5] *Al-Masā'il al-Muhannā'iyya*, fol. 92a; Miqdād, *Tanqīḥ*, fol. 3a; Bihbahānī, *Taḥqīq fi 'l-qiyās*, fol. 85b.

[6] See Kashshī, p. 189; Muḥaqqiq, *Maʿārij*, p. 127.

[7] See as examples Abu 'l-Ḥusayn al-Baṣrī, pp. 689, 722, 761-6; Qāḍī Nuʿmān, *Ikhtilāf uṣūl al-Madhāhib*, pp. 203-28; Mufīd, *Fuṣūl*, p. 68; Murtaḍā, *Dharīʿa*, pp. 672-3.

[8] See further the article *idjtihād* in *EI*, III, p. 1026.

This explains why Shīʿīs refrained from the use of the term *ijtihād* until the 6th/12th century.[1] It also explains the objections raised in Shīʿī theological works toward *ijtihad*,[2] and the refutation of its legitimacy in works written by Shīʿī theologians like the Nawbakhtīs,[3] ʿAbd Allāh b. ʿAbd al-Raḥmān al-Zubayrī[4] and Abu 'l-Qāsim ʿAlī b. Aḥmad al-Kūfī.[5] All these were against *ijtihād* in the above sense. Otherwise *ijtihād*, as a rational mode of reasoning, was quite an acceptable phenomenon among many Shīʿīs from the 2nd/8th century onwards, and from late 4th/10th century it emerged as the only method by which legal subjects were approached.[6] these analytical and rational methods of Shīʿī scholars of the early centuries of Islam appeared to amount to *ra'y* and *qiyās* in the eyes of strict traditionists who objected to the rational analytical modes of reasoning in law.[7]

(5) In some traditions, it is reported that some companions of the Imāms practised *qiyās* on occasions when instructions over a particular problem were not explicitly and clearly given in the Qur'ān and Tradition,[8] and that some of them were practising the method of *ra'y*.[9] Some of the most knowledgeable companions of the Imāms whose opinions and judgments are cited in legal sources, have been accused of following the practice of *qiyās*. Among them are Faḍl b. Shādhān al-Naysābūrī, author of *al-Īḍāḥ* (d. 260/873-4) whose opinions on some legal subjects such as divorce and inheritance, and on some questions of *uṣūl al-fiqh* are quoted in the sources,[10] Yūnus b. ʿAbd al-Raḥmān, whose opinions are cited in

---

1 See Muḥammad Bāqir al-Ṣadr, *Durūs*, I, pp. 55-64.

2 See for instance Mufīd, *Awā'il al-maqālāt*, p. 127; idem, *Fuṣūl*, pp. 66-9. Also Nuʿmānī, *Tafsīr*, pp. 95-6; Murtaḍā, *Dharīʿa*, pp. 792-5; idem, *Intiṣār*, p. 98.

3 Iqbāl, pp. 94, 117, 118, 120.

4 Najāshī, p. 163.

5 Ibid., p. 203.

6 This is according to the predominant Uṣūlī school of Shīʿī law. The Akhbārīs rejected the validity of all kinds of rational argument in law, as noted before.

7 Books such as *al-Radd ʿalā man radd āthār al-Rasūl wa iʿtamad ʿalā natā'ij al-ʿuqūl* by Hilāl b. Ibrāhīm b. Abi 'l-Fatḥ al-Madanī (Najāshī, p. 344) are written with the same understanding.

8 Durust b. Abī Manṣūr, p. 165; Barqī, *Maḥāsin*, I, pp. 212-15; Ḥimyarī, p. 157; Kashshī, p. 239; Mufīd, *Ikhtiṣāṣ*, p. 275; Ḥurr al-ʿĀmilī, XVIII, pp. 33, 38; Nūrī, III, pp. 176-7; *Jāmiʿ aḥādīth al-Shīʿa*, I, pp. 274-6.

9 Barqī, *Maḥāsin*, I, pp. 212-15; Kashshī, pp. 156-7.

10 See Kulaynī, VI, pp. 93-6, VII, pp. 88-90, 95-6, 98-9, 105-8, 116-18

some chapters of *fiqh* such as prayer, alms tax, marriage and inheritance,[1] Zurāra b. Aʿyan al-Kūfī,[2] Jamīl b. Darrāj, the most learned companion of the sixth Imām, Jaʿfar al-Ṣādiq,[3] ʿAbd Allāh b. Bukayr, a great Shīʿī jurist of the 2nd/8th century[4] and a number of other famous companions, who were accused of and blamed for their practice of *qiyās*.[5] It is almost certain that the above were supporters of the analytical mode of reasoning and not of the Sunnī concept of *qiyās*. Their judgments, many of which have been collected by Asad Allāh al-Kāẓimī[6] confirm this point.

It is evident from what has been said in the five sections above that in the period of the presence of the Imāms, two legal tendencies existed in the Shīʿī community. One of them adhered to an analytical, rational approach toward legal problems within the framework of the general principles of the Qurʾān and Tradition.[7] The other was a traditionalist approach which relied on transmitting traditions without any further inferential derivation of law.[8]

Many Shīʿī jurists of this period are mentioned in the Shīʿī works on *ʿilm al-rijāl*[9] and other sources.[10] The names of some of them are also mentioned together with their works in Ibn al-Nadīm's *K. al-Fihrist*.[11]

120-1, 142, 145-6, 148-9, 161-2, 168; Ṣadūq, *Faqīh*, IV, p. 197; ibid., *Muqniʿ*, pp. 170, 175-6; Mufīd, *Fuṣūl*, pp. 123-4; Murtaḍā, *Intiṣār*, p. 286; Ibn Shahrāshūb, *Mathālib*, fols. 233b-234a; Shahīd I, *Durūs*, p. 263; idem, *Qawāʿid*, p. 316; Najafī, XVI, p. 90.

[1] See Kulaynī, VII, pp. 83-4, 115-16, 121-5; Ṣadūq, *Muqniʿ*, p. 175; Murtaḍā, *Intiṣār*, pp. 77-8; ʿAllāma, *Mukhtalaf*, I, p. 136; Shahīd I, *Durūs*, p. 57; idem, *Qawāʿid*, p.325; ʿabd Allāh al-Tūnī, fol. 97.

[2] Kashshī, p. 156. See for some of his legal views Kulaynī, VII, pp. 97, 100-1.

[3] Kashshī, p. 375. Some of his legal opinions are quoted in the sources, e.g. Kulaynī, VI, p. 141, VII, p. 256; Shaykh, *Tahdhīb*, X, p. 137; idem, *Istibṣār*, IV, p. 253.

[4] Kashshī, p. 345.

[5] Ṣadūq, *Faqīh*, IV, p. 197; Murtaḍā, *Ibṭāl al-ʿamal bi-akhbār al-āḥād*, fol. 142b; Futūnī, p. 44; Baḥr al-ʿUlūm, III, pp. 215-19; Kāẓimī, p. 83. See also Shaykh, *ʿUdda*, p. 51.

[6] See his *Kashf al-qināʿ*, pp. 82-3, 198, 244 as some examples.

[7] See Kashshī, p. 156.

[8] See also Khumaynī, *Risāla fi ʾl-ijtihād wa ʾl-taqlīd*, pp. 125-8.

[9] For instance Kashshī, pp. 238, 375, 556, also p. 484; Shaykh, *Fihrist*, p. 52; Ibn Dāwūd, p. 272.

[10] As an example Mufīd, *Al-Radd ʿalā aṣḥāb al-ʿadad*, p.128; Shaykh, *Tahdhīb*, VIII, p.97. See also Ḥasan al-Ṣadr, pp. 298-302.

[11] See Ibn al-Nadīm, pp. 275-9.

the opinions of the jurists of this period are quoted in the legal works of later periods.[1]

2. THE FIRST CENTURY OF THE OCCULTATION

In the period of the 'Minor Occultation' (260/874-329/941) and until the latter part of the 4th/10th century, three different legal schools existed in the Shīʿī community.

I. The School of the traditionists (*Ahl al-ḥadīth*)

This was a continuation of the conservative legal tendency of the period of the Presence, and likewise devoted its efforts to collecting, recording and preserving the traditions from the Imāms. The adherents of this school, like their predecessors in the time of the Imāms, were not sympathetic to rational arguments in religious matters, and condemned even those efforts which applied rational argument to religious questions in order to strengthen the Shīʿī point of view.[2] This school resembled in its outlook the Sunnī school of traditionists, where Aḥmad b. Ḥanbal[3] and his followers[4] rejected *kalām* even when used in defence of Islam.[5]

In their legal approach, there were two groups of traditionists who differed among themselves:

(a) Those who only accepted traditions which were related by transmitters whose reliability had been thoroughly examined. Their knowledge of the traditions dealing with legal questions was extensive. They recognized and implemented those principles of *uṣūl al-fiqh* which were contained in the traditions of the Imāms.[6] Like Sunnī traditionists,[7] however, they were chary of writing about legal subjects with words other than exactly

---

[1] See for instance the introduction to al-Muḥaqqiq's *al-Muʿtabar*, p.7, in which he says that he will quote the views of five jurists of that period. Also Ṣāḥib al-Madārik's *Hidāyat al-ṭālibīn*, fol. 4b. Also the Preface to al-Kāẓimī's *Maqābis al-anwār*, p. 23, in which six such scholars are mentioned. See also Shaykh, *Tahdhīb*, VIII, p. 97.

[2] Ṣadūq, *Iʿtiqādāt*, p. 74. See also Mufīd, *Taṣḥīḥ al-iʿtiqād*, pp. 169-70; Shaykh, *Ghayba*, p. 3.

[3] Ibn al-Jawzī, *Manāqib Aḥmad*, p. 205.

[4] Ibn Qudāma, *Taḥrīm al-naẓar fī kutub ahl al-kalām*, p. 17.

[5] Later traditionists followed their predecessors in this case. Al-Ḥurr al-ʿĀmilī, the renowned Akhbārī scholar of the late 11th.17th century, wrote a treatise against studying *ʿilm al-kalām* (AB, XXIV, p. 431).

[6] Shaykh, *ʿUdda*, p. 248; Kāẓimī, *Kashf al-qināʿ*, pp. 207-14; ʿAbd Allāh al-Tūnī, p. 97; Amīn al-Astarābādī, *Jawāb masāʾil al-Shaykh Ḥusayn*, fol. 101b.

[7] See ʿAbd al-Majīd, pp. 288-9.

those mentioned in the traditions.[1] The legal works of this group of traditionists were collections of traditions compiled according to their subject matter, and sometimes with the omission of the chain of transmitters (*isnād*).[2] Traditionists such as:

(i) Muḥammad b. Yaʿqūb al-Kulaynī

(ii) Muḥammad b. al-Ḥasan b. Aḥmad b. al-Walīd (d. 343/954-5)

(iii) Muḥammad b. ʿAlī b. Bābawayh al-Qummī, al-Ṣadūq

fall into this group.[3] The legal choices[4] of al-Kulaynī and al-Ṣadūq have been quoted in the legal sources.[5]

(b) The other group followed traditions without compromise and completely ignored the principles of *uṣūl al-fiqh* and the rules by which a tradition could be examined. They completely ignored the procedures of debate, reasoning and modes of discourse.[6] The extreme tendencies of these Shīʿī traditionists were comparable to the tendency of the Ḥashwiyya in Sunnism which was the most extreme and inflexible Sunnī traditionist school.[7] However, in the works of Shīʿī theologians of the 4th-6th/10th-12th centuries, terms such as *ḥashwiyya*[8] and *muqallida*[9] together with the terms *aṣḥāb al-ḥadīth*[10] and *akhbāriyya*[11] were applied to all

---

[1] Shaykh, *Mabsūṭ*, I, p.2; Amīn al-Astarābādī, op. cit., fol. 101b.

[2] *K. al-Muqniʿ* sy Ṣadūq is an example of this sort of 'legal works'. See especially p. 2 of this book.

[3] Shaykh, *Fihrist*, pp. 135, 156, 157; Tustarī, *Sahw al-Nabī*, p. 9. See also Anṣārī, *Rasāʾil*, p. 87.

[4] Both al-Kulaynī and al-Ṣadūq in the introduction to their two main works, viz. *K. al-Kāfī* and *Man lā yaḥḍuruh al-faqīh* respectively, acknowledged the authenticity of what they transmitted in those books. Thus in the cases of conflict between traditions, the one they accepted and narrated in their works, demonstrates their viewpoints in each specific case.

[5] Muḥaqqiq, *Muʿtabar*, p. 7; Ṣāḥib al-Madārik, *Hidāyat al-ṭalibīn*, fol. 46; Kāẓimī, *Maqābis*, p. 23.

[6] Shaykh, *ʿUdda*, p. 248; Kāẓimī, *Kashf al-qināʿ*, p. 202.

[7] See Mufīd, *Ifṣāḥ*, p. 77; idem, *Awāʾil al-maqālāt*, p. 65; Murtaḍā al-Rāzī, p. 46.

[8] Mufīd, *Ukbariyya*, fol.59a; idem, *Awāʾil al-maqālāt*, p.86; idem, *Jawāb ahl al-Ḥāʾir*, p.114; ʿabd al-Jalīl al-Qazwīnī, pp. 3, 235, 272, 285, 529, see also Muḥaqqiq, *Muʿtabar*, p.6; Fayḍ, *al-Uṣūl al-aṣīla*, p.61.

[9] Mufīd, *Jawāb ahl al-Ḥāʾir*, p. 112; Shaykh, *ʿUdda*, p. 54.

[10] and the like (*aṣḥāb al-akhbār*, *ahl al-ḥadīth*, *ahl al-akhbār etc.*). See Mufīd, *al-Radd ʿalā aṣḥāb al-ʿadad*,p. 124; idem, *Awāʾil al-maqālāt*, pp. 80-1, 87, 88, 89, 92, 101, 108, 118; idem, *Taṣḥīḥ al-iʿtiqād*, pp. 186, 222; idem, *Sarawiyya*, pp. 222, 223; Murtaḍā, *Tabbāniyyāt*, fol. 2; idem, *al-Mawṣiliyya al-thālitha*, fol. 40a; idem, *Ṭarābulusiyyāt*, fol. 110; idem, *al-Radd ʿalā aṣḥāb al-ʿadad*, fol. 130b; Shaykh, *ʿUdda*, p. 248; idem, *Ghayba*, p.3; Ibn Idrīs, pp. 5, 249. See also Shaykh, *Mabsūṭ*, I, p. 2.

[11] ʿAbd al-Jalīl al-Qazwīnī, pp., 3, 236, 272, 282, 285, 458, 529, 568-9;

the adherents of the traditionist tendency, even the former group.

In the sources of *ʻilm al-rijāl* the names of some jurists of this branch of the traditionists have been recorded, such as Abu 'l-Ḥusayn al-Nāshi', ʻAlī b. ʻAbd Allāh b. Wuṣayf (d. 366/976-7) who is said to have discussed law in the same way as *ahl al-ẓāhir*.[1] However, due to the school's refusal and failure to apply reason and rationality and also due to the absence of any ideas and original thought of their own, the decisions of its adherents[2] did not gain any legal validity and were totally ignored in the sources.[3] As noted, their judgments were nothing but references to traditions.

The traditionist school which, in the period of the Presence, was one of the two prevailing tendencies of Shīʻī scholarly circles, gradually gained control over the whole Shīʻī intellectual community, and totally suppressed the rational theological and legal tendencies which were based on reasoning. The school of Qum, which in those days was the most prominent religious centre of the Shīʻīs, was completely dominated by this current and the Qummī scholars were all traditionists[4] objecting to any kind of reasoning and analytical thought in the Shīʻī community. The overwhelming majority of Shīʻī jurists during this period and up to the late 4th/10th century were adherents of this school of thought.[5]

As will be explained later, in the last decades of the 4th/10th and early 5th/11th centuries, the school was swept away by the teaching of al-Shaykh al-Mufīd and his disciple al-Sharīf al-Murtaḍā. Although a small number of its adherents survived, here and there, in later periods[6] none of them gained prominence or influenced Shīʻī thought.

The methodology and beliefs of the adherents of this school have been

---

ʻAllāma, *Nihāyat al-wuṣūl*, fol. 200b. See also Shahrastānī, pp. 169, 178; Sharīf al-Jurjānī, p. 629; Fakhr al-Rāzī, *Maḥṣūl* (quoted in Kāẓimī, p. 203).

[1] Shaykh, *Fihrist*, p. 89.

[2] It should be noted here that there were differences of opinions among the adherents of this tranch of traditionists too, as the traditions of the Imāms were sometimes contradictory, and each of those jurists was deciding legal problems according to those traditions he had received.

[3] Murtaḍā, *al-Radd ʻalā aṣḥāb al-ʻadad*, fol. 130b; idem, *Tabbāniyyāt*, fol. 2; idem, *al-Mawṣiliyya al-thālitha*, fol. 40a.

[4] Murtaḍā, *Ibṭāl al-ʻamal bi-akhbār al-āḥād*, fol. 142b; Futūnī, p. 4. See also Shaykh, *Fihrist*, p. 157.

[5] Shaykh, *ʻUdda*, p. 248; ʻAllāma, *Nihāyat al-wuṣūl*, fol. 200b.

[6] ʻAbd al-Jalīl al-Qazwīnī, p. 568.

described and criticized in the works of al-Mufīd and al-Murtaḍā.[1]

II. 'Qadīmayn'

While the traditionist school was predominant in Shīʿī academic circles in the second half of the 3rd/9th and a greater part of the 4th/10th centuries, two important figures emerged among Shīʿī scholars, each of whom had his own particular approach to law. Both practised rational reasoning in legal thought. Hence, their methods can be considered as a continuation of the exercise of analytical and rational thought in law which existed in the period of the presence of the Imāms. They are regarded[2] as constituting the first school of Shīʿī deductive law, based not merely on collections of traditions but on speculative analysis and rational argument.

Although these two personalities represented two different legal perceptions and approaches, in many cases, they arrived at the same conclusions and issued similar opinions on legal problems. Their legal judgments are, therefore, quoted jointly in the sources as the opinion of the Qadīmayn, the Two Ancient (scholars).[3] They are:

(i) Ibn Abī ʿAqīl, Abū Muḥammad Ḥasan b. ʿAlī b. Abī ʿAqīl al-ʿUmānī al-Ḥadhdhāʾ, of the first half of the 4th/10th century.[4] He is the author of a legal work entitled *al-Mutamassik bi-ḥabl Āl al-Rasūl*, which was one of the most renowned legal sources during the 4th and 5th/10th and 11th centuries.[5]

(ii) Ibn al-Junayd, Abū ʿAlī Muḥammad b. Aḥmad b. al-Junayd al-Kātib al-Iskāfī, of the middle of the 4th/10th century.[6] He is

---

[1] See Mufīd, *Sarawiyya*, pp. 222, 223; idem, *Taṣḥīḥ al-iʿtiqād*, p.222; idem, *ʿUkbariyya*, fol.59a; idem, *Jawāb ahl al-Ḥāʾir*, pp.112, 116; idem, *al-Radd ʿalā aṣḥāb al-ʿadad*, p.24; Murtaḍā, *al-Mawṣiliyya al-thālitha*, fol.40a; idem, *Tabbāniyyāt*, fol.2; idem, *al-Radd ʿalā aṣḥāb al-ʿadad*, fol.130b; idem, *Ibṭāl al-ʿamal bi-akhbār al-āḥād*, fol.142b. See also Shaykh, *Ghayba*, p.3; idem, *Mabsūṭ*, I, p. 2; idem, *ʿUdda*, pp. 54, 248; ʿAbd al-Jalīl al-Qazwīnī, pp. 529, 568.

[2] See Baḥr al-ʿUlūm, II, p. 218.

[3] This name was invented by Ibn Fahd al-Ḥillī (d. 841/1437-8) in early 9th/15th century. See his *al-Muhadhdhab al-bāriʿ*, fol. 3a. See also his *al-Muqtaṣar*, fol. 2a.

[4] In a letter to Jaʿfar b. Muḥammad b. Qūlawayh (d. 369/979-80), Ibn Abī ʿAqīl permitted him to narrate his works (Najāshī, p. 38).

[5] Najāshī, p. 38; AB, XIX, p. 69.

[6] He was in Naysābūr in 340/951-2 and enjoyed the respect of its people (Mufīd, *Ṣāghāniyya*, p. 17). One of his works is a book of answers he gave to the questions of the Buyid Muʿizz al-Dawla, who died in 356/967 (Najāshī, p. 301).

the author of *Tahdhīb al-Shīʿa li-aḥkām al-sharīʿa* and *al-Aḥmadī fī 'l-fiqh al-Muḥammadī*.

These scholars were, thus, nearly contemporaries. Ibn Abī ʿAqīl, who slightly preceded Ibn al-Junayd,[1] was a *kalām* theologian.[2] He may well be considered a precursor of the legal method of the *kalām* theologians of Baghdad who formed the third era in the development of Shīʿī law to be discussed later. Like other *kalām* theologians, he did not consider traditions transmitted by a single or a few transmitters (*akhbār al-āḥād*) as valid. It is evident from his judgments that his legal approach was firmly based on general Qur'ānic principles and widely transmitted traditions. In cases where there was a general principle in the Qur'ān to which an exception was made in traditions, Ibn Abī ʿAqīl would maintain the general validity of the Qur'ānic principle and ignore the traditions, unless the latter had been universally and unquestionably accepted.[3] In view of the proximity of his time to that of the Presence, however, the uncertainty with regard to the reliability of many traditions affecting later discussions was not yet felt to be a serious problem and there was less disagreement concerning the opinions of the Imāms on fundamental legal principles arising from contradictory traditions.[4] Because of this, the traditions which Ibn Abī ʿAqīl attributes to the Imāms in his book have come to be accepted entirely by Shīʿī scholars after him.[5] His legal method also was appreciated by later scholars,[6] and his legal opinions are quoted in most Shīʿī sources.

Ibn al-Junayd was not held in such high esteem and his legal method was criticized by both his contemporaries and by later scholars. He, too, was a *kalām* theologian and produced many works on theology.[7] Among these was one written in defence of Faḍl b. Shādhān,[8] a supporter of reasoning in law and theology. In legal matters, Ibn al-Junayd held the

---

1 Baḥr al-ʿUlūm, II, p. 218.

2 Najāshī, p.38; Shaykh, *Fihrist*, pp.64, 194; Ibn Dāwūd, p.111.

3 Tustarī, *Qāmūs*, III, p. 198. For similar legal appoaches in Sunnī school see ʿAbd al-Majīd, pp. 219-24, 236.

4 See for example Ṣāḥib al-Madārik, p. 219.

5 ʿAllāma, *Mukhtalaf*, II, pp.157, 167; Miqdād, *Tanqīḥ*, fol. 88b. See also ʿAbd al-Majīd, pp. 267-8 for similar cases in Sunnī law.

6 Najāshī, p. 38; Ibn Idrīs, pp. 99, 192, 397, 398.

7 Najāshī, pp. 301-2; Shaykh, *Fihrist*, p. 134.

8 Najāshī, p. 302.

validity of *akhbār al-āḥād* as a source of law[1] and because of this, al-Mufīd ranged him among the traditionists.[2] He relied, however, on rational analysis when it came to comprehending, inferring and extracting legal principles from the sources and contrary to the traditionists who looked at the literal meaning of tradition alone, he appears to have aimed at a general legal interpretation of each tradition through comparison with other similar traditions.[3] In accordance with a commonly accepted practice in later Shīʿī law, he appears to have tried to discover the rationale (*ʿilla*) of a precept.[4] As mentioned, this method which establishes general principles in legal matters without the need to rely on the specific texts in traditions in every case, was held to be a kind of *qiyās* in the early centuries and was rejected by Shīʿī jurists in the same way that they rejected the Sunnī concept of *qiyās*. Like the adherents of rational reasoning in the time of the Presence, among whom was Faḍl b. Shādhān, Ibn al-Junayd was accused of employing *qiyās*[5] and *ra'y*.[6] As a result, the works of Ibn al-Junayd were abandoned,[7] in contrast to the works of Ibn Abī ʿAqīl. Thus, his legal opinions did not receive much attention during the third and fourth stages of Shīʿī law,[8] in which legal thought was affected to a great extent by the school of the traditionists.

In defence of his methodology, Ibn al-Junayd wrote a number of books, the titles of some of which indicate his method in law, notably *Kashf al-tamwīh wa'l-ilbās ʿalā aghmār al-Shīʿa fī amr al-qiyās* and *Iẓhār mā satarah ahl al-ʿinād min al-riwāya ʿan a'immat al-ʿItra fī amr al-ijtihād*.[9]

---

[1] Among prominent Shīʿī theologians, Abū Muḥammad Ḥasan b. Mūsā al-Nawbakhtī (early 4th/10th century) also maintained the same opinion (see Najāshī, p. 50). It is already well-known that mush disagreement existed among the Muʿtazilī theologians of the time, too, about the validity of *akhbār al-āḥād* (see ʿAbd al-Majīd, p. 94).

[2] Mufīd, *Sarawiyya*, p. 223.

[3] Ḥasan al-Ṣadr, p. 302.

[4] Baḥr al-ʿUlūm, III, p. 214; Tustarī, *Qāmūs*, XI, p. 94.

[5] Mufīd, *Ṣāghāniyya*, p. 19; idem, *Sarawiyya*, pp. 222-3; Najāshī, p. 302. Shaykh, *Fihrist*, p. 134; Ibn Shahrāshūb, *Maʿālim*, p. 87; ʿAllāma, *Khulāṣa*, p. 145; Ibn Dāwūd, p. 292; Yaḥyā al-Baḥrānī, p.306; Amīn al-Astarābādī, p. 30; Ḥusayn al-Karakī, chapter eight; Baḥr al-ʿUlūm, III, p. 207; Abū ʿAlī, p. 346.

[6] Mufīd, *Sarawiyya*, p. 223; Murtaḍā, *Intiṣār*, p. 238.

[7] Mufīd, *Ṣāghāniyya*, p. 19; Shaykh, *Fihrist*, p. 134; Ibn Dāwūd, p. 292.

[8] Mufīd, *Ṣāghāniyya*, p. 19; Kāẓimī, pp. 297-8.

[9] Najāshī, p. 301.

He also justified his approach in his book: *al-Masāʾil al-Miṣriyya.*[1]

Al-Mufīd, the prominent Shīʿī scholar at the beginning of the 5th/11th century, who praised Ibn al-Junayd's intelligence[2] came to disagree seriously with his legal method, subjecting it to criticism in a number of his works, including his *al-Masāʾil al-Ṣāghāniyya,*[3] *al-Masāʾil al-Sarawiyya*[4] and in two special treatises, one entiled: *Naqḍ risālat al-Junaydī ilā ahl Miṣr*,[5] a refutation of Ibn al-Junayd's *al-Masāʾil al-Miṣriyya*, and another called *al-Naqḍ ʿalā Ibn al-Junayd fī ijtihād al-raʾy.*[6] Al-Mufīd's students too have cited and rejected some of Ibn al-Junayd's legal opinions in their works.[7]

Ibn al-Junayd's legal method which, on the one hand (and in contrast to al-Mufīd and his followers), accepted *āḥād* traditions as valid and considered them as the principal source of law, and, on the other, gave formal recognition to reason as the means through which precepts could be ascertained, was closer to the more developed Shīʿī legal methodological practices of later periods than to those of his time.[8] It is evidently because of this similarity of methodology that two centuries after him, his legal opinions were quoted for the first time with a degree of reverence, by Ibn Idrīs, the Shīʿī scholar of the late 6th/12th century.[9] From the second half of the 7th/13th century onwards, when rational analysis pentrated more deeply into Shīʿī law, the works of this scholar received much praise and admiration. Al-ʿAllāma regarded him as one of the outstanding experts of jurisprudence,[10] and cited many of his legal judgments in his own works.[11] The jurists of the fifth stage, especially al-Shahīd al-Awwal, al-Fāḍil al-Miqdād and Ibn Fahd, paid careful attention to Ibn al-Junayd's opinions, and narrated his views on many

---

[1] Mufīd, *Sarawiyya*, p. 224.

[2] Idem, *Ṣāghāniyya*, pp. 18-19.

[3] Ibid., pp. 17-22.

[4] Idem, *Sarawiyya*, pp. 222-4.

[5] Ibid., p. 224; Najāshī, p. 312.

[6] Najāshī, p. 315.

[7] See Murtaḍā, *Intiṣār*, pp. 77-8, 80-1, 83, 217, 227, 237-43, 244, 246; idem, *al-Mawṣiliyya al-thāniya*, fol. 34a; Ibn al-Barrāj, *Sharḥ Jumal*, pp. 244, 251.

[8] Tustarī, *Qāmūs*, XI, p. 94.

[9] See Ibn Idrīs, p. 99.

[10] See ʿAllāma, *Īḍāḥ*, pp. 88-9. See also Baḥr al-ʿUlūm, III, pp. 205-6; AB, IV, p. 510, XX, p. 177.

[11] See ʿAllāma, *Khulāṣa*, p. 145; idem, *Īḍāḥ*, p. 89.

legal problems. Al-Shahīd al-Thānī, one of the later scholars of this same stage says of Ibn al-Junayd that the sharpness of his grasp of problems, and his analysis was exceptional among classical Shīʿī jurists.[1]

Ibn Abī ʿAqīl and Ibn al-Junayd thus must be considered as the founders of Shīʿī systematic law, as distinct from the Tradition.[2]

III. The Intermediate School

In this same period, there existed in Shīʿī centres of scholarship a group of jurists who, while holding the validity of many *āḥād* traditions and while not offering an analytical systematic law comparable to that of the Qadīmayn, followed the practice of *ijtihād*,[3] thus differentiating themselves from the conservative and narrow approach of the traditionists. In short, they held an intermediary position between the two tendencies described above.

The school formulated its juridical opinions through the process of extracting specific precepts from the general principles implied in traditions, or through selection or reconciliation when traditions were contradictory. Opinions formed on this basis were not always uniform, and this sometimes caused intense arguments on certain issues among the followers of this school. The case of '*ʿadad*' (i.e. the argument as to whether the number of days of the month of Ramaḍān like the days of other months, conform to the laws of astronomy or have a fixed and unalterable measure) was such a case about which the scholars of this school were in disagreement among themselves, and produced many treatises in defence of their own, or in refutation of the opposing views.[4]

The most important scholars of this tendency, whose views are sometimes mentioned in the legal sources, are:

(i) ʿAlī b. Bābawayh al-Qummī (d. 329/904-1)

(ii) Abu 'l-Faḍl Muḥammad b. Aḥmad al-Ṣābūnī al-Juʿfī, author of *al-Fākhir* (first half of the 4th/10th century)

(iii) Jaʿfar b. Muḥammad b. Qūlawayh al-Qummī (d. 369/979-80)

(iv) Aḥmad b. Muḥammad b. Dāwūd b. ʿAli al-Qummī (d. 368/978-9)

---

[1] Shahīd II, *Masālik*, II, p. 222.

[2] Baḥr al-ʿUlūm, II, p. 218. See also Mufīd, *Sarawiyya*, p. 222.

[3] Muḥaqqiq, *Muʿtabar*, p. 7; Ṣāḥib al-Madārik, *Hidāyat al-ṭālibīn*, fol. 4b.

[4] See especially Ibn Ṭāwūs, *Iqbāl*, p. 6. Also Kāẓimī, p. 139; AB, V, pp. 236-8.

3. THE RATIONALISTS

As has been seen, the school of the traditionists gained control over the Shīʻī centres of learning from the early years of the period of Minor Occultation (260/874) until the second half of the 4th/10th century. In the last decades of that century, however, the emergence of a new school placed the traditionists under pressure and exposed them to severe criticisms which gradually weakened, and finally reduced them to silence.

The founder of this school was the theologian and jurist al-Shaykh al-Mufīd,[1] Abū ʻAbd Allā Muḥammad b. Muḥammad al-Nuʻmān al-Baghdādī Ibn al-Muʻallim (d. 413/1022). He had studied under Aḥmad b. Muḥammad b. al-Junayd al-Iskāfī, Muḥammad b. ʻAlī b. Bābawayh al-Ṣadūq, Jaʻfar b. Muḥammad b. Qūlawayh, Aḥmad b. Muḥammad b. Dāwūd b. ʻAlī al-Qummī and Abu ʼl-Ḥusayn ʻAlī b. Wuṣayf al-Nāshiʼ,[2] and was accordingly, very well acquainted with the three legal schools of the 4th/10th century.

In order to pave the way for the return of rational analysis in Shīʻī doctrine, he attacked and criticized the conservative approach of the traditionists in an attempt to break their position of dominance. In this, he was to be successful. One factor which was instrumental in his success was that the traditionists of Qum, who spearheaded that school, maintained certain special views with regard to the Imāms, and considered the attribution of any supernatural thing to them as a mark of extremism (*ghuluww*) and religious deviation.[3] Some even considered as an extremist (*ghālī*) anyone who believed that the Prophet was immune to inadvertence (*sahw*).[4] In this matter, most later Shīʻī Akhbārīs as well as some Uṣūlī scholars sided with these early traditionists.[5] These views presumably were not popular among the common people who preferred to elevate the spiritual status of their Imāms, and al-Mufīd took advantage of this unpopularity to break the power of his opponents.

In spite of the fact that he had studied with al-Ṣadūq who was 'the

---

1 See especially Amīn al-Astarābādī, p. 30.

2 Mufīd, *Lamḥ al-burhān* (quoted in Ibn Ṭāwūs, *Iqbāl*, p. 5); Shaykh, *Fihrist*, pp. 89-90, 134, 136, 157.

3 See Māmaqānī, the introduction, p. 212, V, pp. 84, 249.

4 See Ṣadūq, I, pp. 234-5; Majlisī I, *Rawḍa*, II, pp. 451-2.

5 Jazāʼirī, III, p. 131, IV, pp. 35-40. Among the ancient Uṣūlī Shīʻī scholars al-Ṭabrisī supported this view. See his *Majmaʻ al-bayān*, I, p. 181 (also IV, p. 317). See also Abū ʻAlī, p. 45.

most outstanding of the Qummiyyūn'[1] and 'the head of the traditionists',[2] al-Mufīd criticized him harshly in some of his works, among them *Taṣḥīḥ al-iʿtiqād*, a commentary on al-Ṣadūq's *al-Iʿtiqādāt*, *al-Masāʾil al-sarawiyya*[3] and *Jawāb ahl al-Ḥāʾir*. The words he used in *Jawāb ahl al- Ḥāʾir* were so harsh[4] that some scholars doubted if it had indeed been written by al-Mufīd,[5] while some suggested that it was written by al-Sharīf al-Mutaḍa[6] or someone else.[7] It is clear, however, that this treatise is by al-Mufīd,[8] since much of its content is similar to statements in his other works, notably in *Taṣḥīḥ al-iʿtiqād*.[9]

These harsh words, and al-Mufīd's other criticism of the opinions of the traditionists,[10] reflect his great concern about the latters' domination over the Shīʿī intellectual community, and his determination to revive the rational approach in law and theology.[11] His pupil, al-Sharīf al-Murtaḍā also played an important part in weakening the school of traditionists. In many of his works, notably *Jabābāt al-masāʾil al-Mawṣiliyya al-thālitha*,[12] *Ibṭāl al-ʿamal bi-akhbār al-āḥād*[13] and *al-Radd ʿalā aṣḥāb al-ʿadad*[14] he was very critical of the traditionists, and even accused all 'Qummiyyūn' of being religious deviationists,[15] with the only exception of al-Ṣadūq, toward whom he adopted a more moderate approach.

The attacks by al-Mufīd, al-Murtaḍā and other Shīʿī theologians in the

---

1 Shaykh, *Fihrist*, p. 157.

2 Baḥrānī, *Ḥadāʾiq*, I, p. 170.

3 See p. 222.

4 See pp. 112, 116, 118, 120. Also Jazāʾirī, IV, pp. 34-5; Baḥrānī, *Kashkūl*, I, pp. 218-19.

5 ʿAlī b. Muḥammad al-ʿĀmilī, *al-Durr al-Manthūr*, I, p. 100. See also Macdermott, p. 41.

6 Jazāʾirī, IV, p. 34; Baḥrānī, *Kashkūl*, pp. 218-19.

7 AB, V, p. 176.

8 Kāẓimī, p. 211; Tustarī, *Sahw al-Nabī*, p. 2. See also Majlisī II, XVII, p. 123, CX, pp. 165-7.

9 See pp. 156, 160, 178, 182-3, 186, 211, 222.

10 For instance *ʿUkbariyya*, fol. 59a. He also devoted a book to his criticisms to the traditionists, entitled *Maqābīs al-anwār fi ʾl-radd ʿalā ahl al-akhbār* (Najāshī, p. 315; AB, XXI, p. 375).

11 Kāẓimī, pp. 205, 211.

12 Fol. 40a.

13 Fol. 142b.

14 Fol. 130b.

15 Murtaḍā, *Ibṭāl al-ʿamal bi-akhbār al-āḥād*, fol. 142b.

first half of the 5th/11th century, resulted in the decline and fall of the school of traditionists.[1] Aspects of this severe controversy are recorded in some of the sources[2] in which the traditionists are referred to as the '*akhbāriyya*', and the 'rationalists' as '*muʿtazila*' or '*kalāmiyya*'.[3] Al-Mufīd and al-Sharīf al-Murtaḍā too, speak of the approach of '*mutakallimūn*' and '*muḥaqqiqūn*' as against that of the 'traditionists'.[4] In later Shīʿī sources, the adherents of this rationalist school are referred to by the term '*uṣūliyya*'.[5] Al-Mufīd was taught law by Jaʿfar b. Muḥammad b. Qūlawayh, one of the jurists of the Intermediate tendency,[6] and was familiar with the other legal schools of his time. However, because of his rational and analytical tendencies he was an admirer of Ibn Abī ʿAqīl,[7] whose legal approach was similar to his own.

The approach of the rationalists, as was described under the discussion of the legal methods of Ibn Abī ʿAqīl, relied firmly on general Qur'ānic principles and on widely transmitted (*mutawātir*) traditions, and excluded those traditions which did not provide certainty (*āḥād*). Instead of the latter, they conformed to those legal views which were accepted and continually practised among Shīʿīs (*ijmāʿāt*).[8] The process of inferring

---

1 ʿAbd al-Jalīl al-Qazwīnī, p. 568.

2 For instance Shahrastānī, p. 178. It is strange that al-Baḥrānī, who belonged to the later Akhbārīs of the sixth stage of Shīʿī law, thought that 'nothing happened between the traditionists and *mujtahids* (rationalist jurists) in the first centuries, although those ages were full of both types of scholars' (*Ḥadā'iq*, I, p. 169).

3 Shahrastānī, pp. 169, 178; Sharīf al-Jurjānī, p. 629; Fakhr al-Rāzī, *Maḥṣūl* (quoted in Kāẓimī, p. 203).

4 Mufīd, *Awā'il al-maqālāt*, p. 98; Murtaḍā, *Tabbāniyyāt*, fol. 2.

5 See for instance ʿAbd al-Jalīl al-Qazwīnī, pp. 3, 178, 179, 190, 231, 235-7, 240, 272, 281, 282, 284, 415-16, 459, 481, 504, 506, 528, 569; ʿAllāma, *Nihāyat al-wuṣūl*, fol. 200b.

6 Najāshī, p. 95.

7 Ibid., p. 38.

8 See works of al-Mufīd and al-Murtaḍā. Also Rāwandī, *Fiqh al-Qur'ān*, I, p. 4. However, there were some differences between the approach of al-Mufīd and al-Murtaḍā. See further Brunschvig, pp. 208-11 They had such a difference in theological matters as well. Al-Rāwandī (d. 573/1178) collected the cases of disagreements between al-Mufīd and al-Sharīf al-Murtaḍā in their works, in an independent treatise. He gathered ninety-five theological cases upon which their opinions differed. Al-Rāwandī thought it would need a large book to gather all the cases on which they had taken different standpoints (Ibn Ṭāwūs, *Kashf al-maḥajja*, p. 20). Likewise, there were many cases of disagreement between al-Sharīf al-Murtaḍā and Abu 'l-Ṣalāḥ al-Ḥalabī. Al-Karājakī collected these cases in a book entitled *Ghāyat al-inṣāf fī masā'il al-khilāf* in which he tried to support al-Murtaḍā's opinions (Nūrī, III, p. 498/AB, XVI, p. 9).

precepts from the appropriate sources was done through rational analysis, the procedures and rules of conduct of which were familiar to the theologians because of the latters' daily involvemtns with hard theological debates. Nevertheless it should be noted that long years of entrenched traditionist influence on Shīʿī scholarship had left deep marks on the overall patterns of Shīʿī thought, and had, over time, become an integral part of these patterns. The different standpoints over certain problems between the theologians of the Period of the Presence and those of later periods, spring from this fact.[1]

The characteristic of the rationalist school, according to the above account, is their refusal to relay on *āḥād* traditions as a source of law. Al-Mufīd,[2] al-Murtaḍā[3] and their students[4] all emphasized this point. The three eminent scholars of the school, each of whom made his own original contribution to it, were:

(i) Al-Mufīd, author of numerous legal treatises and texts such as *al-Muqniʿa*, *al-Iʿlām bi-mā ittafaqat ʿalayh al-Imāmiyya min al-Aḥkām* and *al-ʿAwīṣ fi 'l-aḥkām*

(ii) Al-Sharīf al-Murtaḍā, author of *al-Intiṣār, al-Masā'il al-Nāṣiriyyāt* and many other treatises

(iii) Abu 'l-Ṣalāḥ Taqī al-Dīn b. Najm al-Dīn al-Ḥalabī, author of *al-Kāfī fi 'l-fiqh* and a pupil of al-Mufīd

Other scholars of this school and interpreters of its views, whose original contributions are less conspicuous, are:

(i) Sallār b. ʿAbd al-ʿAzīz al-Daylamī, author of *al-Marāsim al-ʿAllawiyya wa 'l-aḥkām al-Nabawiyya*

(ii) Qāḍī ʿAbd al-ʿAzīz b. al-Barrāj al-Shāmī, author of *al-Muhadhdhab*, *al-Jawāhir* and *Sharḥ Jumal al-ʿilm wa 'l-ʿamal*

(iii) Abu 'l-Ḥasan Muḥammad b. Muḥammad al-Buṣrawī, a student of al-Murtaḍā and author of *al-Mufīd fi 'l-taklīf*

---

[1] These differences were, however, in theological matters. In legal discussions, they followed the same approach. The invalidity of *āḥād* traditions, which was the main characteristic of this school of law, was for instance supported by Faḍl b. Shādhān as well. See Baḥr al-ʿUlūm, II, p. 232; AB, XXIV, p. 287.

[2] See his: *Taṣḥīḥ al-iʿtiqād*, pp. 179, 212, 227-9; *Tadhkira*, p. 193; *Sarawiyya*, pp. 223-5; *Jawāb ahl al-Ḥā'ir*, pp. 112, 116. See also Ibn Idrīs, p. 409; Muḥaqqiq, *Maʿārij*, p. 127.

[3] In most of his works, as example: *al-Mawṣiliyya al-thālitha*, fol. 40a; *Dharīʿa*, pp. 528-55.

[4] For instance al-Ḥalabī, *Taqrīb al-Maʿārif*, fol. 91a; Karājakī, p. 296; Ibn al-Barrāj, *Sharḥ Jumal*, pp. 170, 177, 256. See also Bahā' al-Dīn al-ʿĀmilī, *Wajīza*, p. 6; Kāẓimī, p. 442.

(iv) Abu 'l-Fatḥ Muḥammad b. ʿAlī al-Karājakī

4. THE SCHOOL OF SHAYKH AL-ṬĀ'IFA

The rationalist school based its legal theories on the Qur'ān and on well-known widely transmitted traditions. *Āḥād* traditions on their own were not considered to be a reliable source for law.

Shaykh al-Ṭā'ifa, Muḥammad b. Ḥasan al-Ṭūsī (d. 460/1067), known simply as 'al-Shaykh' in Shīʿī legal works, strove to retain the authority of *āḥād* traditions as a source of law,[1] while preserving the analytical and rational method of law;[2] a method which has remained the characteristic of Shīʿī law up to the present time. The method of Shaykh al-Ṭā'ifa, in effect, combined the method of the rationalists with that of the traditionists. The legal works of Shaykh al-Ṭā'ifa opened up much new ground in Shīʿī law. His *K. al-Mabsūṭ* treated many cases which Shīʿī jurists had not dealt with previously. His *K. al-Khilāf* was the first notable work in the field of comparative law among Shīʿīs. These two books were modelled upon Sunnī works, and through them an important part of Sunnī legal scholarship passed into Shīʿī law facilitating its further development. Shīʿī law at this stage benefited much from the heritage of Sunnī legal thought of the early centuries of Islam. At the same time, non-Shīʿī concepts, which were alien to traditional Shīʿī thought, also crept into Shīʿī law and created some inconsistencies in it. In his two works, Shaykh al-Ṭā'ifa cited the text of some Sunnī legal works literally and then added his judgments on the basis of Shīʿī general principles or Shīʿī traditions in the form of marginal notes. His efforts to adjust non-Shīʿī concepts to his own legal system were not always successful. As a consequence, some confusion and inconsistencies are apparent in his works, which were later refined by al-Muḥaqqiq al-Ḥillī.

More consonant with traditional Shīʿī legal thought, was Shaykh al-Ṭā'ifa's *K. al-Nihāya*, which became the most authoritative Shīʿī text for two centuries. Apart from this, his *al-Jumal wa 'l-ʿuqūd* and some other legal treatises of his have also survived. His two collections of traditions *Tahdhīb al-aḥkām* and *al-Istibṣār*, became important sources of the law. His approach towards contradictory traditions in these two books, and his legal interpretation of them, deeply influenced Shīʿī law.

The school of Shaykh al-Ṭā'ifa maintained its predominance in Shīʿī

---

[1] See the chapter on *akhbār al-āḥād* in his *ʿUdda*, pp. 25-63.

[2] For this second, he was accused by the Akhbārīs of following the practice of *qiyās*. See Ḥusayn al-Karakī, chapter 8.

legal scholarship for three centuries. During this time, it passed through three stages:

(a) The disciples of Shaykh al-Ṭāʾifa

The century after his death was the period of his pupils and imitators. None of the Shīʿī jurists of this period produced any major novel ideas. They merely quoted and explained al-Shaykh's statements and therefore have been called '*muqallida*' (imitators).[1]

Sadīd al-Dīn Maḥmūd al-Ḥimmaṣī in the latter part of the 6th/12th century said that after al-Shaykh, the Shīʿa had no *muftī* (meaning a jurisconsult with independent judgments) and that all Shīʿī jurists after him were merely narrators and expounders of his views.[2]

The most prominent scholars of this period, whose names and works are mentioned in the legal sources, are:

(i) Abū ʿAlī Ḥasan b. Muḥammad b. Ḥasan al-Ṭūsī, son of al-Shaykh (d. after 515/1121), author of *Sharḥ al-Nihāya* and *al-Murshid ilā sabīl al-taʿabbud*

(ii) Niẓām al-Dīn Sulaymān b. Ḥasan al-Ṣahrashtī, a student of al-Shaykh and author of *Iṣbāḥ al-Shīʿa bi-miṣbāḥ al-sharīʿa*

(iii) ʿAlāʾ al-Dīn ʿAlī b. Ḥasan al-Ḥalabī, author of *Ishārat al-sabq ilā maʿrifat al-ḥaqq*

(iv) Abū ʿAlī Faḍl b. Ḥasan Amīn al-Islām al-Ṭabrisī (d. 548/1158), author of *al-Muntakhab min Masāʾil al-khilāf*

(v) ʿImād al-Dīn Muḥammad b. ʿAlī b. Ḥamza al-Ṭūsī (d. after 566/1171), author of *al-Wasīla ilā nayl al-faḍīla*

(vi) Quṭb al-Dīn Saʿīd b. Hibat Allāh al-Rāwandī (d. 573/1178), author of *Fiqh al-Qurʾān*

(vii) Quṭb al-Dīn Muḥammad b. Ḥusayn al-Kaydarī al-Bayhaqī (d. after 576/1181), author of *al-Iṣbāḥ*

(viii) Rashīd al-Dīn Muḥammad b. ʿAlī b. Shahrāshūb al-Sarawī (d. 588/1192), author of *Mutashābih al-Qurʾān wa mukhtalifuh*

(b) The period of criticism

A century after the death of al-Shaykh, in the second half of the 6th/12th century, a number of scholars arose in opposition to the fundamental principles of his school. Rejecting the validity of *āḥād* traditions as a source of law, they revived the rational method of al-Sharīf al-Murtaḍā.

---

[1] See Kāẓimī, p. 442.

[2] Ibn Ṭāwūs, *Kashf al-Maḥajja*, p. 127; Ḥusayn b. ʿAbd al-Ṣamad, *Wuṣūl al-akhyār*, p. 33; Ṣāḥib al-Maʿālim, p. 179; Abu ʾl-Qāsim b. Ḥasan al-Yazdī, I, p. 20; Khwānsārī, VII, p. 161.

The prominent representatives of this new tendency, which did not develop any further after them, are:

1. Sadīd al-Dīn Maḥmūd b. 'Alī al-Ḥimmaṣī al-Rāzī (d. after 583/1187)[1]
2. 'Izz al-Dīn Abu 'l-Makārim Ḥamza b. 'Alī b. Zuhra al-Ḥalabī (d. 585/1189-90), author of *Ghunyat al-nuzū'*[2]
3. Muḥammad b. Manṣūr b. Aḥmad b. Idrīs al-Ḥillī (d. 598/1202), author of *al-Sarā'ir*[3]

To this list some other scholars of the same period could be added, who in their positive legal doctrine followed al-Shaykh, and hence we mentioned them among his disciples, but in theory and under the influence of the works of al-Sharīf al-Murtaḍā, they maintained the invalidity of *āḥād* traditions. Among them were Quṭb al-Dīn al-Rāwandī[4] and Ibn Shahrāshūb.[5]

The most radical proponent of this tendency was Ibn Idrīs. His criticism of the views and the legal approach of al-Shaykh was so strong that it was considered by some later scholars to have exceeded proper bounds.[6]

Although Ibn Idrīs's critical views did not attract many supporters, they did stimulate efforts to take Shī'ī law out of its static mould, and thus furthered its evolution. The main characteristics of Ibn Idrīs's approach were his critical eye and his independent thought, which are observable even in the preface and conclusion of his *al-Sarā'ir*.[7]

During the 7th/13th century, a number of jurists offered some new opinions[8] which are cited in the legal sources. They are:

(i) Muhadhdhab al-Dīn Ḥusayn b. Muḥammad al-Nīlī (early 7th/13th century)

(ii) Mu'īn al-Dīn Sālim b. Badrān al-Miṣrī (alive in 626/1231), author of *Taḥrīr al-farā'iḍ* and *al-Ma'ūna*

---

[1] See his opinions about *āḥād* traditions in Ibn Idrīs, *Sarā'ir*, pp. 409-11, quoting from al-Ḥimmaṣī's *al-Maṣādir*.

[2] See his view about *akhbār al-āḥād* in his *Ghunya*, pp. 537-9.

[3] See his view on *akhbār al-āḥād* in his *al-Sarā'ir*, p. 4.

[4] See his view in that case in his *Fiqh al-Qur'ān*, I, p. 4.

[5] See his opinion in his *Mutashābih al-Qur'ān*, II, pp. 153-4.

[6] See as an example of those judgments Najafī, XIX, p. 37.

[7] See it, pp. 4, 404. It is to be noted that this book is full of useful philological, genealogical and biographical information which demonstrates that Ibn Idrīs was well acquainted with different branches of Islamic scholarship.

[8] See 'Allāma, *Muntahā*, p. 4. These scholars followed al-Shaykh in their general methodology.

(iii) Zayn al-Dīn Muḥammad b. Qāsim al-Barzihī al-Naysābūrī (alive in 661/1263)

(iv) Najīb al-Dīn Muḥammad b. Jaʿfar b. Hibat Allāh b. Nimā (d. 645/1248)

(v) Sadīd al-Dīn Yūsuf b. al-Muṭahhar al-Ḥillī (alive in 665/1267)

(vi) Aḥmad b. Mūsā b. Ṭāwūs al-Ḥillī (d. 673/1274-5), author of *Bushrā al-muḥaqqiqīn*

(vii) Yaḥyā b. Saʿīd al-Ḥillī (d. 689/1290), author of *Jāmiʿ al-sharāʾiʿ* and *Nuzhat al-nāẓir*

(viii) ʿImād al-Dīn Ḥasan b. ʿAlī al-Ṭabarī (alive in 698/1299), author of *al-ʿUmda*, *Nahj al-ʿirfān* and *al-Faṣīḥ al-munhij*

(c) Al-Muḥaqqiq and al-ʿAllāma

The legal heritage of al-Shaykh, though fertile in new perspectives, was, nevertheless, as yet immature and inconsistent, and needed further refinement and organization. Some of the elements which he adopted from Sunnī law remained tied to their original framework, and were not well absorbed and adjusted to the new system. If Shīʿī law was to benefit fully from these elements, the whole system had to be adjusted and reorganized in order to accommodate them.

This task was accomplished by al-Muḥaqqiq, Najm al-Dīn Abu ʾl-Qāsim Jaʿfar b. Ḥasan al-Ḥillī (d. 676/1277) author of *Sharāʾiʿ al-Islām*, *al-Mukhtaṣar al-nāfiʿ*, *al-Muʿtabar*, *Nukat al-Nihāya* and other legal works. He refined the Shaykh al-Ṭāʾifa's legal heritage in detail, collected and rearranged his opinions on various subjects, harmonized his legal doctrine and thus restored its authority which had been discredited by Ibn Idrīs's criticism. He contested these criticisms vigorously and defended al-Shaykh's legal doctrine.

Al-Muḥaqqiq's main contribution to Shīʿī law, therefore, was his reconstruction and refinement of al-Shaykh's legal system, which placed Shīʿī law on a firmer bases enabled its further development. His student al-ʿAllāma, Ḥasan b. Yūsuf b. al-Muṭahhar al-Ḥillī followed this same course. He strove to elaborate and expand the law on the basis of al-Shaykh's legal doctrine and of al-Muḥaqqiq's reorganization. He wrote many books on different branches of law, which all became important works of reference for later jurists. Among them were *Mukhtalaf al-Shīʿa*, *Tadhkirat al-fuqahā*, *Muntahā al-Maṭlab*, *Taḥrīr al-aḥkām al-sharʿiyya*, *Tabṣirat al-mutaʿallimīn*, *Qawāʿid al-aḥkām*, *Irshād al-adhhān*, *Nihāyat al-iḥkām* and *Talkhīṣ al-marām*.

Al-ʿAllāma contributed to the development of Shīʿī law particularly in two areas. He greatly enlarged the section on legal transactions on the basis of relevant general rules mainly taken from Sunnī law. His efforts in this area reflect his thorough knowledge of Sunnī legal principles. His second contribution was the introduction of mathematics, in which he was well versed, into the law. He seems to be the first prominent scholar to use advanced mathematical rules in the relevant legal subjects such as the law of inheritance,[1] the times of prayer (*awqāt al-ṣalāt*) and the direction of prayer (*qibla*). He also made great contributions to the development of Shīʿī law through his criticism of the transmitters of the traditions, his implementation of a novel classification for the Shīʿī traditions according to the degree of authority of their narrators[2] and his refinement of *uṣūl al-fiqh* through his numerous *uṣūl* works.

To sum up, the legal doctrine of Shaykh al-Ṭāʾifa which had become predominant in the Shīʿī community from the middle of the 5th/11th century onwards, reached its highest level of refinement in the latter half of the 8th/14th century as a result of al-Muḥaqqiq's clarification and systemization, and al-ʿAllāma's elaboration and expansion. Its definitive formulation appeared in the works of these two scholars. The pupils and followers of them all worked within this same legal framework. The most renowned of them, whose views have been cited in the legal works, are:

(i) Abū Muḥammad Ḥasan b. Abī Ṭālib al-Yūsufī al-Ābī, Ibn Zaynab, author of *Kashf al-rumūz* (composed in 672/1274)

(ii) ʿAmīd al-Dīn ʿAbd al-Muṭṭalib b. Muḥammad al-Ḥusaynī al-Aʿrajī (d. 754/1353), author of *Kanz al-fawāʾid*

(iii) Fakhr al-Muḥaqqiqīn, Muḥammad b. Ḥasan al-Ḥillī, son of al-ʿAllāma (d. 771/1370), author of *Īḍāḥ al-fawāʾid*

5. THE SCHOOL OF AL-SHAHĪD AL-AWWAL

It was in the second stage of its development that Shīʿī law emerged as an independent and systematic legal structure. The legal works which have survived from the second and the third stages, reflect the traditional style of Shīʿī law which Shaykh al-Ṭāʾifa followed in his *al-Nihāya*. But

---

[1] He had been preceded in the application of advanced mathematical rules in this case by Muʿīn al-Dīn al-Miṣrī in his *Taḥrīr al-farāʾiḍ* (see AB, III, p. 377), followed by Naṣīr al-Dīn al-Ṭūsī in his *al-Farāʾiḍ al-Naṣīriyya* (ibid., XVI, p. 150).

[2] This novel classification was originally initiated by al-ʿAllāma's teacher Jamāl al-Dīn Aḥmad b. Mūsā b. Ṭāwūs, author of *Bushrā al-Muḥaqqiqīn* (Ṭurayḥī, *Jāmiʿ al-maqāl*, chapter 56) and gained popularity through its vast implementation by al-ʿAllāma in his works.

fter this, and with the appearance of his *al-Mabsūṭ* and *al-Khilāf* which ncorporate Sunnī legal methods and concepts, some fundamental changes ppeared in the form and content of Shī'ī law.

With regard to form, the new expositions of the law turned into a mixure of the two legal systems. They usually covered legal topics on the asis of Sunnī legal texts, first citing the views of Sunnī jurists, usually hose quoted in *al-Khilāf*, and then presenting the opinions of Shī'ī cholars. Al-Ābī, a student of al-Muḥaqqiq and author of *Kashf al-rumūz*, vas one of the first Shī'ī authors who did not follow the approach and efrained from quoting the opinion of Sunnīs in his own book. The students of al-'Allāma, notably Fakhr al-Muḥaqqiqīn in his book *Īḍāḥ l-fawā'id*, followed al-Ābī's lead and omitted the analyses and opinions of Sunnī scholars.

With regard to content, the additional subsidiary legal cases first discussed in *al-Mabsūṭ* and later in the works of al-'Allāma in the section on ransactions, were borrowed from Sunnī works and continued to be presented on the basis of the principles of Sunnī law. Hence, a study of the foundations of Sunnī law became crucial to the understanding and study of Shī'ī legal sources.

Al-Shahīd al-Awwal, Shams al-Dīn Muḥammad b. Makkī al-'Āmilī (d. 786/1384) in his *al-Qawā'id wa 'l-fawā'id* reformulated the fundamental rules and principles of Shī'ī law, and in applying them, changed the contents of Shī'ī law and provided it with an independent identity.

On the basis of the same principles, al-Shahīd opened up new grounds for Shī'ī law and introduced discussions of many new subsidiary cases. Thus his legal system was quite distinct from those of his predecessors both in methods and contents. His legal works, such as *al-Qawā'id wa 'l-fawā'id, al-Durūs al-shar'iyya, Ghāyat al-murād, al-Bayān, al-Alfiyya* and *al-Lum'a al-Dimashqiyya* are among the most important works of Shī'ī law.

Scholars after him for about one and a half centuries continued to adhere to his school and, though they offered certain novel opinions, they mostly directed their efforts towards explaining his views. The most renowned among them were:

(i) Ibn al-Khāzin, Zayn al-Dīn, 'Alī b. Ḥasan b. al-Khāzin al-Ḥā'irī (early 9th/15th century)

(ii) Ibn al-Mutawwij, Aḥmad b. 'Abd Allāh al-Baḥrānī (d. 820/1417-18), author of *al-Nihāya fī tafsīr al-Khamsmi'at āya*

(iii) Al-Fāḍil al-Miqdād, Miqdād b. 'Abd Allāh al-Suyūrī al-Ḥillī (d. 826/1423), author of *Kanz al-'irfān* and *al-Tanqīḥ al-rā'i'*

(iv) Ibn Fahd, Aḥmad b. Muḥammad b. Fahd al-Asadī al-Ḥillī (d. 841/1437-8), author of *al-Muhadhdhab al-bāriʿ*, *al-Mūjaz al-ḥāwī* and *al-Muqtaṣar*

(v) Shams al-Dīn Muḥammad b. Shujāʿ al-Qaṭṭān al-Ḥillī (first half of the 9th/15th century), author of *Maʿālim al-dīn fī fiqh Āl Yāsīn*

(vi) Mufliḥ b. Ḥusayn al-Ṣaymarī (d. after 878/1473-4), author of *Ghāyat al-marām*, *Kashf al-iltibās* and *Jawāhir al-kalimāt*

(vii) Ibn Hilāl, ʿAlī b. Muḥammad b. Hilāl al-Jazāʾirī (d. 909-915/1504-10)

(viii) Ibrāhīm b. Sulaymān al-Qaṭīfī (d. after 945/1539), author of *Īḍāḥ al-Nāfiʿ*

(ix) Al-Shahīd al-Thānī, Zayn al-Dīn, b. ʿAlī b. Aḥmad al-ʿĀmilī (d. 966/1559), author of *al-Rawḍa al-bahiyya*, *Masālik al-afhām* and *Rawḍ al-jinān*

6. THE LAW OF THE SAFAVID PERIOD

Shīʿī law during the period of the Safavids (907-1135/1502-1722) may be divided into three schools which although appearing one after another, continued to exist and evolve side by side for a long time.

(a) The school of al-Muḥaqqiq al-Karakī

Al-Muḥaqqiq ʿAlī b. Ḥusayn b. ʿAbd al-ʿĀlī al-Karakī (d. 940/1534) was a leading figure in Shīʿī scholarship in the early Safavid period and made a major contribution to the development of Shīʿī law.

Al-Karakī's law differed in two respects from earlier formulations. Firstly, he was able through stringent legal reasoning to place Shīʿī law on a more stable and solid footing by way of reconstructing and strengthening its principles. He analysed legal problems thoroughly, paying meticulous attention to the discussions and arguments previously advanced about them, and used his power of reason and analysis to arrive at his own judgment. Earlier analyses of legal questions were rather superficial and inadequate. He based his judgments on a thorough investigation both in favour of and against them. His legal doctrine, therefore, was much more solidly argued than had been doctrines by earlier jurists.

Secondly, he paid close attention to certain problems which had arisen as a result of the change of the political situation with the adoption of Shīʿism as the official religion of Iran. These problems included the limits of the legal power of the *faqīh* (jurist); the legitimacy of Friday prayer in the absence of the Imām, the land tax etc., which prior to the rise of the Shīʿī Safavid dynasty had not been in question. Al-Karakī himself discussed these questions in detail in his legal works, such as his

Jāmiʿ al-maqāṣid, *Taʿlīq al-Irshād* and *Fawāʾid al-Sharāʾiʿ* and also wrote separate treatises on some of them.

Most of the Shīʿī jurists who succeeded al-Karakī up to the end of the Safavids, were influenced by his legal approach. The more well-known of these scholars whose names and views are cited in legal sources are:

(i) Ḥusayn b. ʿAbd al-Ṣamad al-ʿĀmilī (d. 984/1576)

(ii) ʿAbd al-ʿĀlī b. ʿAlī b. ʿAbd al-ʿĀlī al-Karakī, his son (d. 993/1585), author of *Sharḥ al-Irshād*

(iii) Bahāʾ al-Dīn Muḥammad b. Ḥusayn al-ʿĀmilī (d. 1030/1631), author of *Mashriq al-shamsayn*, *Jāmiʿ-i ʿAbbāsī*, *al-Ḥabl al-matīn* and *al-Ithnāʿashariyyāt*

(iv) Muḥammad Bāqir b. Shams al-Dīn Muḥammad al-Astarābādī, al-Dāmād (d. 1040/1630-1), author of *Shāriʿ al-najāt*

(v) Sulṭān al-ʿUlamāʾ, Ḥusayn b. Rafīʿ al-Dīn Muḥammad al-Marʿashī (d. 1064/1653-4)

(vi) Ḥusayn b. Jamāl al-Dīn Muḥammad al-Khwānsārī (d. 1098/1687), author of *Mashāriq al-shumūs*

(vii) Jamāl al-Dīn Muḥammad b. Ḥusayn al-Khwānsārī (d. 1125/1713), author of *Ḥāshiya ʿala ʾl-Rawḍa al-bahiyya*

(viii) Al-Fāḍil al-Hindī, Muḥammad b. al-Ḥasan al-Iṣfahānī (d. 1137/1725), author of *Kashf al-lithām* and *al-Manāhij al-sawiyya*

(b) The school of al-Muqaddas al-Ardabīlī

Al-Muḥaqqiq Aḥmad b. Muḥammad al-Ardabīlī, known as al-Muqaddas (d. 993/1585), author of *Majmaʿ al-fāʾida wa ʾl-burhān* and *Zubdat al-bayān*, developed his own special and independent legal method which gave rise to a distinct and significant school. His method was characterized by systematic, independent rational arguments based on his personal juridical analysis which entirely ignored the opinions and views of previous scholars. Although he did not bring about any fundamental changes in the methodology and structure of the law, his extreme precision and exactitude, together with his independent method and juridical boldness made his school quite distinctive.

Some of the best scholars of this period were followers of his approach. The most famous are:

(i) Muḥammad b. ʿAlī al-Mūsawī al-ʿĀmilī, Ṣāḥib al-Madārik (d. 1009/1600), author of *Madārik al-aḥkām* and *Hidāyat al-ṭālibīn*

(ii) Ḥasan b. Zayn al-Dīn al-ʿĀmilī, Ṣāḥib al-Maʿālim (d. 1011/1602), author of *Maʿālim al-dīn* and *Muntaqā al-jumān*

(iii) ʿAbd Allāh b. Ḥusayn al-Tustarī (d. 1021/1621), author of *Jāmiʿ*

al-fawāʾid

(iv) Muḥammad Bāqir b. Muḥammad Muʾmin al-Sabzawārī (d. 1090/1679), author of *Dhakhīrat al-maʿād* and *Kifāyat al-aḥkām*

Muḥsin al-Fayḍ, author of *al-Wāfī*, *Muʿtaṣam al-Shīʿa* and *Mafātīḥ al-sharāʾiʿ*, may also be included in the above list. Although an advocate of the Akhbārī school of this period, he approved of al-Ardabīlī's independent approach and followed it in practice. Like the followers of al-Ardabīlī (especially Ṣāḥib al-Madārik and al-Sabzawārī), he preferred the opinions of al-Ardabīlī in many cases where the latter deviated from those of previous Shīʿī scholars.[1] Muḥammad Bāqir b. Muḥammad Taqī al-Majlisī, author of *Mirʾāt al-ʿuqūl* and *Biḥār al-anwār*, too, was interested in the views of al-Ardabīlī and Ṣāḥib al-Madārik, and cited them frequently in his own works.

(c) Akhbārism

The school of the traditionists had been overcome by the Shīʿī rationalists at the end of the 4th/10th century, though a limited number of its supporters survived here and there. They were not active and were threfore largely ignored by others. It was not until the beginning of the 11th/17th century that their school was revived by Muḥammad Amīn al-Astarābādī (d. 1036/1626-7) in his book *al-Fawāʾid al-Madaniyya*.[2]

A suitable ground for the revival of the traditionist school had gradually been provided from early 10th/16th century onwards.[3] Around the middle of the same century, a tendency calling for more freedom in Shīʿī law began to gain popularity. Al-Shahīd al-Thānī wrote a treatise against following the legal judgments of the previous jurists without examining their bases.[4] His pupil Ḥusayn b. ʿAbd al-Ṣamad al-ʿĀmilī, *shaykh al-Islām* of the Safavid court, followed the same line and wrote a similar treatise on the same subject in which he held that *ijtihād*, i.e. the normal

---

[1] See for instance Najafī, XVI, p. 71. This author (Muḥammad Ḥasan b. Muḥammad Bāqir al-Najafī, author of *Jawāhir al-kalām*) did not favour the independent method of these scholars and their disregard of the opinions of the previous Shīʿī jurists. So he spoke of those three collectively as 'the followers (*atbāʿ*) of al-Muqaddas'.

[2] For the story of this revival and its background, see especially Amīn al-Astarābādī, *Dānishnāma-yi shāhī*; Khwānsārī, I, p. 121.

[3] It has been said that Ibn Abī Jumhūr al-Aḥsāʾī, a Shīʿī theologian with ṣūfī tendencies of early 10th/16th century, was a follower of the traditionist school (see Khwānsārī, VII, p. 33), but there is enough evidence in his works to deny this accusation. See Nūrī, III, p. 361 quoting Ibn Abī Jumhūr's *Kāshifat al-ḥāl*; also AB, XVIII, p. 300.

[4] AB, X, p. 42. MS M169/3 Los Angeles (cat., pp. 667-8).

method of legal reasoning which is based on rational argument, is not the only way to the discovery of legal norms.[1] In most of his other works, he cirticized the legal method of Shīʿī jurists and blamed them for being imitators of the 'ancients'.[2] ʿAbd al-Nabī b. Saʿd al-Jazāʾirī, a slightly later jurist, criticized the legal approach of the Uṣūlī school in his *al-Iqtiṣād fī sharḥ al-Irshād*[3] (written in 1015/1606-7). A *ṣadr* (the chief religious dignitary) of the Safavid court in the first half of the 11th/17th century is quoted as having said that no Shīʿī *mujtahid* remained in Iran or the Arab world in his time.[4] Al-Muqaddas al-Ardabīlī never hesitated, as noted before, to reject the opinions of all previous jurists wherever they excluded traditions on the basis of a rational argument.[5] His students like Muḥammad b. ʿAlī al-ʿĀmilī, author of *Madārik al-aḥkām* followed the same line. ʿAbd Allāh b. Ḥusayn al-Tustarī in early 11th/17th century made a great contribution to the rivival of the *ḥadīth* literature.[6] Ḥasan b. Zayn al-Dīn al-ʿĀmilī also made, at the same time, his contribution to the field through his works *Muntaqā al-jumān* and *al-Taḥrīr al-Ṭawūsī*. Many other works appeared in the first half of the same century on the *ḥadīth* literature, mostly inspired by the teachings of ʿAbd Allāh al-Tustarī.[7] Subjects such as the validity or invalidity of the traditions as a source of law had again become points of debate among the jurists of early decades of the same century.[8] The value of logic and philosophy in Islamic scholarship had already come under question.[9] Elements such as these contributed enormously to the appearance of a new traditionist

---

[1] Ḥusayn b. ʿAbd al-Ṣamad, *Maqāla fī wujūb al-iftāʾ wa bayān al-ḥaqq ʿalā kull man ʿalim bih*. See also AB, XXI, p. 407.

[2] See his *Risāla fī ḥukm al-ḥuṣr wa 'l-bawārī wa sahm al-Imām*, p. 217; *Tisʿ masāʾil*, p. 256; *Risāla fī taḥqīq baʿḍ al-masāʾil al-fiqhiyya*, pp. 123-4. The MS 1836 of the Majlis Library, Tehran, contains a copy of the first treatise mentioned above alongside some other works on the Uṣūlī-Akhbārī dispute, including Amīn al-Astarābādī's *al-Fawāʾid al-Madaniyya* (see the catalogue of the Majlis Library, IX, p. 493). This shows that Ḥusayn b. ʿAbd al-Ṣamad's works were regarded as in the vanguard of that dispute.

[3] See pp. 18-136 of this work.

[4] Kamaraʾī, *Risāla dar ithbāt-i luzūm-i wujūd-i mujtahid dar zamān-i ghaybat*, pp. 2-3.

[5] See his *Majmaʿ al-fāʾida wa 'l-burhān*, passim.

[6] See Khwānsārī, IV, pp. 235, 240, 243.

[7] Ibid; AB, X, p. 126, XV, p. 73.

[8] See Khwānsārī, IV, p. 238.

[9] Shahīd II, *Risāla fī taqlīd al-mayyit* (quoted in al-Māḥūzī, *al-ʿAshara al-kāmila*, p. 242. See also AB, IV, p. 392).

school and its rapid development and predominance.

The new traditionist school, which was now called by its other old name, Akhbārī, was, like its predecessor, opposed to the rational, analytical approach to the law and adhered strictly to the outward, literal meanings of the traditions. In the above-mentioned work, Amīn al-Astarābādī argued against rational analysis and reasoning as a means of discovering legal norms, and utterly dismissed the principles of *uşūl al-fiqh* which had been evolved in order to define the rational method. This approach basically resembled the more radical wing of the early traditionists which considered all traditions transmitted from the Imāms as authentic.[1]

The focus in Amīn al-Astarābādī's argument was on the invalidity and peccability of the Aristotelian logic which had been the basis for the Shī'ī jurists in their legal reasonings. The main difference between the two Shī'ī legal tendencies of Uşūlī and Akhbārī was the validity or invalidity of reason in connection with religious matters, although many other points of disagreement, mostly of the same type, existed at the same time.[2]

The Akhbārī school found its way to Iraq in the fourth decade of the 11th/17th century and was followed by most of the jurisconsults of Najaf and other Shī'ī centres of learning in Mesopotamia.[3] In Iran, the majority of the jurists of the provinces in the second half of the same century supported this tendency.[4] The religious academy of Işfahān, which was the largest centre of Shī'ī learning, was dominated by the Uşūlīs, although the first Majlisī, Muḥammad Taqī b. Maqşūd 'Alī (d. 1070/1659-60), author of *Rawḍat al-muttaqīn* and *Lawāmi'-i şāḥibqarānī* inclined to Akhbārism,[5] and his son Muḥammad Bāqir, al-Majlisī II supported a method between Akhbārism and Uşūlism.[6] Zayn al-Dīn 'Alī b. Sulaymān b. Darwīsh b. Ḥātim al-Qadamī al-Baḥrānī (d. 1064/1653-4) took Akhbārism

---

[1] See Bihbahānī, *Fawā'id*, pp. 436-8; Khwānsārī, I, pp. 127-30.

[2] See Jazā'irī, *Manba'*, pp. 275-8; Samāhījī, pp. 375-9 (also quoted in Khwānsārī, I, pp. 127-20); 'Abd Allāh al-Jazā'irī, pp. 381-2; Shubbar, *Bughya*, the whole work; Dizfūlī, *Fārūq al-ḥaqq*, the whole work (86 points of disagreement are mentioned); Kāshif al-Ghiṭā, *al-Ḥaqq al-mubīn*, pp. 76-89; Riḍā al-Qazwīnī, *al-Farq bayn al-Akhbāriyyīn wa 'l-Uşūliyyīn*, the whole work.

[3] Majlisī I, *Lawāmi'*, I, p. 16; Khwānsārī, I, p. 137.

[4] See Majlisī I, *Rawḍa*, I, p. 21.

[5] Idem, *Lawāmi'*, I, pp. 16, 30; Khwānsārī, I, pp. 136-7, II, p. 119.

[6] Majlisī II, *Sayr wa sulūk*, fol. 53a. See also his *Zād al-ma'ād*, pp. 557-8 (quoted in Baḥrānī, *Ḥadā'iq*, XII, p. 268).

'rom Iran to Bahrain.[1] During this century, the animosity between Akhbarīs and Uṣūlīs had not yet become strong. Sharper opposition between them, however, began to appear from the last decades of the same century.[2]

The Akhbārī tendency gained supremacy in all Shīʿī centres of learning in the following century, and held Shīʿī law in its grasp for several decades until the second half of that century, when it again declined in the face of Uṣūlī resurgence. Bahrain was the stronghold of his school during this period and has remained so up to the present, after the demise of Akhbārism in Iran and Iraq.

There are few Akhbārī jurists who held independent views on legal matters. Two prominent Akhbārī scholars stand out for their moderate approach. They are:

i) Muḥsin al-Fayḍ
ii) Yūsuf b. Aḥmad al-Baḥrānī, Ṣāḥib al-Ḥadā'iq (d. 1186/1772), author of *al-Ḥadā'iq al-nāḍira*.

Some other leading figures of this school were:

i) Khalīl b. Ghāzī al-Qazwīnī (d. 1088/1677), author of two commentaries on al-Kulaynī's *K. al-Kāfī*
ii) Muḥammad b. Ḥasan al-Ḥurr al-ʿĀmilī, author of *Wasā'il al-Shīʿa*
iii) Niʿmat Allāh b. ʿAbd Allāh al-Jazā'irī (d. 1112/1700), author of *Ghāyat al-marām* and *Kashf al-asrār*
iv) Sulaymān b. ʿAbd Allāh al-Baḥrānī al-Māḥūzī (d.1121/1709)
v) ʿAbd Allāh b. Ṣāliḥ al-Samāhījī al-Baḥrānī (d. 1135/1723).

'. THE SCHOOL OF AL-WAḤĪD AL-BIHBAHĀNĪ

As mentioned above, the Akhbārī school which predominated in Shīʿī centres of scholarship from the first half of the 12th/18th century, rejected the traditional methodology of law upon which *ijtihād* had relied, and forbad its study or usage. As a result, this discipline was abandoned and forgotten. There is no mention of any important *mujtahid*s in the history of Shīʿī law during the middle of that century. Only a very few continued to teach a limited number of students in small schools, distant from urban religious and academic centres.

In the second half of this same century, an outstanding Shīʿī jurist

[1] Baḥrānī, *Lu'lu'a*, p. 13; Tunukābunī, p. 227; AB, XV, p. 76. 'he name 'Bahrain' is used here in its old meaning which included the mainland of al-Qaṭīf and al-Aḥsā' inhabited by Shīʿīs.

[2] See Khwānsārī, I, pp. 134-5. Also ʿAlī b. Muḥammad al-ʿĀmilī, *ihām*, fols. 7b-10a.

with a genius for rational argument and analysis, succeeded in dismantling the influence of the Akhbārī school and in establishing a new rational school in Shīʿī law. This scholar was Muḥammad Bāqir b. Muḥammad Akmal al-Bihbahānī, known as al-Waḥīd (d. 1205/1791), who produced many legal works, among them: *al-Fawā'id al-Ḥā'iriyya* and *Sharḥ Mafātīḥ al-sharā'iʿ*.

Conditions for such a change were, to some extent, facilitated by some Akhbārī scholars in the mid-12th/18th century. Scholars such as Ṣadr al-Dīn Muḥammad b. Muḥammad Bāqir al-Hamadānī (d. after 1151/1738-9) in his *Sharḥ al-Wāfiya*, Yūsuf b. Aḥmad al-Baḥrānī (d. 1186/1772) in the introduction to his *al-Ḥadā'iq al-nāḍira*, Mahdī b. Muḥammad Ṣāliḥ al-Futūnī al-ʿĀmilī (d. 1183/1769-70) in the introduction to his *Natā'ij al-akhbār*,[1] Muḥammad b. ʿAlī al-Maqābī al-Baḥrānī (d. after 1169/1756) in the introduction to his *Nukhbat al-uṣūl*,[2] and others[3] accepted some of the Uṣūlīs' arguments, rejected some Akhbārī approaches and followed a more moderate line. Treatises against the Akhbārī doctrine had already begun to appear before the middle of the century.[4]

Through severe continuous mental effort, al-Bihbahānī managed to re-establish the authority of reason and rational argument in law. The legal system of his school was the first to be constructed entirely in accord with the rules and principles of *uṣūl al-fiqh*. He worked hard on the elaboration of his method and on the rehabilitation of *uṣūl al-fiqh*. His legal work which is representative of a logical law, woven into a solid and integrated legal system, cannot be easily compared with preceding systems

Al-Bihbahānī had prominent pupils and followers who carried on his school and spread his legal doctrine. The most renowned of them are:

(i) Muḥammad Mahdī b. Murtaḍā al-Ṭabāṭabā'i, Baḥr al-ʿUlūm (d. 1212/1797), author of *al-Maṣābīḥ*

(ii) Jawād b. Muḥammad al-Ḥusaynī al-ʿĀmilī (d. 1226/1811), author of *Miftāḥ al-karāma*

(iii) Jaʿfar b. Khiḍr al-Najafī, Kāshif al-Ghiṭā'(d. 1228/1813), author of *Kashf al-ghiṭā'*

(iv) ʿAlī b. Muḥammad ʿAlī al-Ṭabāṭabā'ī al-Karbalā'ī, Ṣāḥib al-Riyāḍ

[1] See AB, XXIV, p. 42.

[2] Ibid., XXIV, p. 93.

[3] See for instance ibid., XXI, p. 402.

[4] For instance *Risāla fī wujūb ittibāʿ al-mujtahid li-ẓannih* by Muḥammad Ismāʿīl b. Muḥammad Ḥusayn al-Khwājū'ī al-Iṣfahānī (d. 1173/1759-60), written in 1137/1724-5.

(d. 1231/1815), author of *Riyāḍ al-masāʾil*

(v) Abu ʾl-Qāsim b. Ḥasan al-Gīlānī al-Qummī (d. 1231/1816), author of *Jāmiʿ al-shatāt*, *Ghanāʾim al-ayyām* and *Manāhij al-aḥkām*

(vi) Asad Allāh b. Ismāʿīl al-Tustarī al-Kāẓimī, Ṣāḥib al-Maqābis (d. 1234/1818-19), author of *Maqābis al-anwār*

(vii) Muḥammad b. ʿAlī al-Ṭabāṭabāʾī al-Mujāhid (d. 1242/1827), author of *al-Manāhil*

(viii) Aḥmad b. Muḥammad Mahdī al-Narāqī (d. 1245/1829), author of *Mustanad al-Shīʿa* and *Manāhij al-aḥkām*

(ix) Muḥammad Bāqir b. Muḥammad Naqī al-Mūsawī al-Shaftī, Ḥujjat al-Islām (d. 1260/1844), author of *Maṭāliʿ al-anwār*

(x) Ḥasan b. Jaʿfar al-Najafī Āl Kāshif al-Chiṭāʾ (d. 1262/1846), author of *Anwār al-faqāha*

(xi) Muḥammad Ḥasan b. Muḥammad Bāqir al-Najafī (d. 1266/1850), author of *Jawāhir al-kalām*.

8. THE SCHOOL OF SHAYKH AL-ANṢĀRĪ

The last fundamental change which occurred in Shīʿī law and which led to the founding of a new school, was associated with the reconstruction of the law and its methodology through the scholarly approach of al-Shaykh Murtaḍā b. Muḥammad Amīn al-Anṣārī (d. 1281/1864). This resulted in a radical change in the system of Shīʿī law.

Al-Anṣārī extended the section of *uṣūl al-fiqh* which dealt with the most general principles of law (*al-uṣūl al-ʿamaliyya*) to a remarkable degree, and rebuilt it with subtlety and precision on a firmly rational base. He next used this method to restructure the law, especially the section of transactions. His legal studies and his overall method were so refined and solid they superseded all previous methods. Wherever he has dealt with a certain subject, his discussions have supplanted all previous works on it.

Al-Anṣārī's method is still dominant in Shīʿī academic life. His works like *al-Makāsib* on the law of sale and *al-Rasāʾil* on *uṣūl al-fiqh* are textbooks in Shīʿī academic centres.

The most eminent of his students and followers who further elaborated the Shīʿī legal system on the basis of his methods were:

(i) Ḥabīb Allāh b. Muḥammad ʿAlī al-Rashtī (d. 1312/1894), author of *al-Iltiqāṭāt*

(ii) Muḥammad Ḥasan b. Maḥmūd al-Shīrāzī, al-Mujaddid (d. 1312/1895)

(iii) Riḍā b. Muḥammad Hādī al-Hamadānī (d. 1322/1904), author of *Miṣbāḥ al-faqīh*

(iv) Muḥammad Kāẓim b. Ḥusayn al-Khurāsānī, known as al-Ākhūnd

(d. 1329/1911), author of *Ḥāshiya ʿala ʾl-Makāsib*

(v) Muḥammad Kāẓim b. ʿAbd al-ʿAẓīm al-Ṭabāṭabāʾī al-Yazdī (d. 1337/1919), author of *al-ʿUrwa al-wuthqā* and *Ḥāshiya ʿala ʾl-Makāsib*

(vi) Muḥammad Taqī b. Muḥibb ʿAlī al-Shīrāzī (d. 1338/1920), author of *Ḥāshiya ʿala ʾl-Makāsib*

(vii) Muḥammad Ḥusayn b. ʿAbd al-Raḥīm al-Nāʾīnī (d. 1355/1936)

(viii) ʿAbd al-Karīm b. Muḥammad Jaʿfar al-Yazdī al-Ḥāʾirī (d. 1355/1937), author of *K. al-Ṣalāt* and the founder of the religious and academic centre in Qum (Iran)

(ix) Ḍiyāʾ al-Dīn b. Muḥammad al-ʿArāqī (d. 1361/1942), author of *Sharḥ Tabṣirat al-mutaʿallimīn*

(x) Muḥammad Ḥusayn b. Muḥammad Ḥasan al-Iṣfahānī al-Kumpānī (d. 1361/1942), author of *Ḥāshiyat al-Makāsib*

(xi) Abu ʾl-Ḥasan b. Muḥammad al-Mūsawī al-Iṣfahānī (d. 1365/1946), author of *Wasīlat al-najāt*

(xii) Ḥusayn b. ʿAlī al-Ṭabāṭabāʾī al-Burūjirdī (d. 1380/1961)

(xiii) Muḥsin b. Mahdī al-Ṭabāṭabāʾī al-Ḥakīm (d. 1390/1971), author of *Nahj al-faqāha* and *Mustamsak al-ʿUrwa al-wuthqā*.

The contemporary scholars of the Shīʿa, the most prominent of them being Āyat Allāh Abu ʾl-Qāsim al-Khuʾī and Āyat Allāh Rūḥ Allāh al-Khumaynī, are followers of al-Anṣārī's school. Their legal opinions are to be found in their works such as *Mabānī Takmilat al-Minhāj* by al-Khuʾī and *K. al-Makāsib al-muḥarrama*, *K. al-Bayʿ*, *Taḥrīr al-Wasīla* and *K. al-Ṭahāra* by al-Khumaynī, and in books composed and published by their students on the basis of their lessons.

Part Two
Main Works on Shīʻī Law

Since law has always been, together with theology, the most widely discussed subject in Shīʿī scholarship, a complete bibliographical study of Shīʿī law would require several volumes. As is usually the case with the Shīʿī intellectual heritage, most Shīʿī works written on this subject are lost. Many others have survived in manuscripts stored in inaccessible private collections. However, among those books that have survived, only a few are commonly referred to in traditional legal discussion which pays little attention to works written by less important and unoriginal authors. The names of, and information currently available about, most of these lost, unavailable or less common works can be obtained from Āghā Buzurg al-Ṭihrānī's *al-Dharīʿa ilā taṣānīf al-Shīʿa*.

What follows is a selected bibliography of some available works on Shīʿī law, arranged in two sections. In the first section (chapter 5), lists are given of some general legal works by the most important Shīʿī jurists. This section is arranged in chronological order according to the author's date of death. In the second section (chapter 6), a list of some extant monographs is given according to the most usual order of Shīʿī legal works as described in chapter three.

There are five more points to be explained about this selected bibliography:

(1) Only purely legal works are mentioned in these lists. Scientific works about topics such as the times of prayer (*awqāt al-ṣalāt*), determining the direction of Mecca (*qibla*), the quantity of water beyond which there cannot be contamination (the *kurr*), figures for weights and measures mentioned in the legal sources (*al-awzān wa 'l-maqādīr*), wills (*waṣāyā*), the division of inheritance (*farā'iḍ*), and the like, are not mentioned, nor are works on supererogation, religious supplication (*duʿā'*) and the moral aspects of acts of devotion, which are, in fact, works of religious ethics rather than law; nor are those works related to the concept of *ijtihād* which should more properly be regarded as a jurisprudential rather than a legal topic. Some examples of the collections of legal opinions (*fatwā*s) compiled to be used by the ordinary people (*rasā'il ʿamaliyya*) are listed in a separate section.

(2) Only works which are published, or those preserved in manuscripts belonging to accessible collections, are mentioned, as noted above.

(3) The manuscripts mentioned for each work are listed in chronological[1]

---

[1] Chronological order is maintained for several manuscripts in the same library, and where several libraries have manuscripts, the libraries are arranged in the chronological order of the earliest manuscript in each library.

order. In the case of widely used books of which many manuscripts are available, only the important or older copies are listed.

(4) All dates in this part are according to the lunar *hijrī* calendar, and the language of all works listed is Arabic, except where stated otherwise.

(5) The authors are fully identified in the first main entry of their works, except those mentioned in Part One.

Chapter Five

SOME COMPREHENSIVE WORKS

A

SYSTEMATIC LEGAL WORKS

AL-ṢADŪQ:

- *Imlā' fī waṣf dīn al-Imāmiyya*, chapter 93 of his *al-Amālī* (see Sezgin, I, p. 545)
  Edition: Qum, 1377 (together with his *al-Muqni'*)

- *Al-Hidāya*
  Editions: Tehran, 1276 (in the collection of *al-Jawāmi' al-fiqhiyya*); Qum, 1377 (together with his *al-Muqni'*)
  Selected MSS: Burūjiridī (AB, XXV, p. 175); Los Angeles 1243/3 (cat., p. 718); Fayḍiyya 1702/2 (cat., III, p. 119); Gawharshād 1601, 722/2 (cat., p. 432-3); Sipahsālār 5553/5 (cat., V, p. 755); Ilāhiyyāt, microfilm 93 (cat., I, p. 230); Mar'ashī 2219/2 (cat., VI, p. 208); Ḥuqūq 216/2j (cat., p. 206); Majlis 1272 (cat., IV, pp. 101-2); India Office 4632 (Sezgin, I, p. 548); Berlin Qu.1779 (ibid.)

- *Al-Muqni'*
  Editions: Tehran, 1276 (in the above-mentioned collection); Qum, 1377
  Selected MSS: Raḍawī 2620 (cat., II, p. 126); Ḥuqūq 216/1j (cat., p. 468); Majlis 1272, 5852/2 (cat., IV, p. 97, XVII, p. 263); Mar'ashī 2219/1 (cat., VI, p. 208); Dār al-Kutub 20034 (cat., III, p. 102)

- *K. fi 'l-fiqh = Arkān shara'i' al-Islām?*
  MS: Mar'ashī 3694/12 (cat., X, p. 95)

AL-MUFĪD:

- *Al-Ishrāf fī 'āmmat farā'iḍ ahl al-Islām*
  MSS: Mar'ashī 243/4, 78/4 (cat., I, pp. 90, 267); Majlis 8/13 Khu'ī (cat., VII, p. 14); Kāshānī (cat., p. 67)

- *Al-Muqni'a*
  Edition: Tabrīz, 1274
  Selected MSS: Raḍawī 2618, 2619 (cat., II, p. 125); Malik 5883 (cat., I, p. 727); Fayḍiyya 1272 (cat., I, p. 269); Āstāna 6004 (cat., p. 193); Sipahsālār 2665 (cat., I, p. 534); Raḍawiyya 28 (cat., pp. 36-7); Dānishgāh 6696 (cat., XVI, p. 335); Adabiyyāt 24/3 Kirmān (cat., p. 25); Majlis 1272, 3288, 3359 (cat., IV, p. 96, X, pp. 911-12, 1185); Mar'ashī 236, 815, 2219/3 (cat., I, p. 261, III, p. 14, VI, p. 208)

AL-MURTAḌĀ:

- *Al-Intiṣār*
  Editions: Tehran, 1276 (in the collection of *al-Jawāmiʿ al-fiqhiyya*), 1315; Najaf, 1392
  Selected MSS: Marʿashī 981, 3598, 3649 (cat., III, p. 174, IX, p. 378, X, p. 46); Raḍawī 2234, 2699 (cat., II, p. 8; V, p. 367); Dānishgāh 3244, 5377 (cat., XI, p. 2203, XV, p. 4226); Wazīrī 656 (cat., II, p. 564); Maʿhad 1305 (cat., p. 113); Princeton 1279/2 New Series; Ilāhiyyāt 77d (cat., I, p. 464); Los Angeles M1195 (cat. p. 156)
  Abridgement: by Niẓām al-Dīn al-Ṣahrashtī, MS: Raḍawī 2849 (cat., V., p. 490)

- *Al-Masāʾil al-Nāṣiriyyāt*
  Edition: Tehran, 1276 (in the collection of *al-Jawāmiʿ al-fiqhiyya*)
  Selected MSS: Raḍawī 2645, 2646 (cat., II, p. 134); Fayḍiyya 1806 (cat., I, p. 242); Dānishgāh 6914/14, 6930 (cat., XVI, pp. 398, 404); Majlis 4326/2, 5187/6 (cat., XII, p. 20, XVI, p. 8); Sipahsālār 2533/3 (cat., V,p.562); Ḥuqūq 216/4j (cat., pp. 459-60); Marʿashī 2219/5 (cat., VI, p. 209); Wazīrī 2226 (cat., IV, p. 1208); Gulpāyigānī 1043/2 (cat., II, p. 223); Kāshān, Raḍawī 73/1 (cat., VII, p.39)

AL-ḤALABĪ:

Al-Kāfī fi ʾl-fiqh
Edition: Qum, 1404
MSS: Millī 863/2 Arabic (cat., VIII, pp. 367-8); Majlis 113, 67/3 Khuʾī, 3544, 4325/1 (cat., IV, p. 84, VII, pp. 226-8, X, p. 1506, XII, p. 19); Ilāhiyyāt 452/1d (cat., I, p. 302); Malik 2647 (cat., I, p. 582); Raḍawī 2540, 7857 (cat., II, p. 103; Bīnish, p. 949); Marʿashī 441/1, 3894 (cat., II, p. 42, X, p. 276); Gulpāyigānī (cat., III, pp. 80-1); Burūjiridī (cat., p. 29); Ḥakīm 96/1 (*Nash*., V, p. 425); Miftāḥ 208/1 (cat., p. 228)

AL-SALLĀR:

Al-Marāsim al-ʿAlawiyya wa ʾl-aḥkām al-Nabawiyya
Editions: Tehran, 1276 (in the collection of *al-Jawāmiʿ al-fiqhiyya*); Beirut, 1400
Selected MSS: Dānishgāh 701 (cat., V, p. 2014); Dār al-Kutub (Fuʾād Sayyid, I, p. 337); Mashhad, Ilāhiyyāt 792/2 (cat., I, p. 284); Raḍawī 2658 (cat., p. 138)
Abridgement: by al-Muḥaqqiq, MS: Ḥakīm (AB, XX, pp. 207-8)

IBN AL-BARRĀJ:

- *Jawāhir al-fiqh*
  Edition: Tehran, 1276 (in the collection of *al-Jawāmiʿ al-fiqhiyya*)
  MSS: Ḥakīm 396, 504 (cat., I, p. 169); Raḍawī 6526 (cat., V, p.401); Majlis 8854; Gulpāyigānī 244/1 (cat., I, p.211)

- *Al-Muhadhdhab*
  MSS: Raḍawī 2598, 7858, 8031 (cat., II, pp.119-20; Bīnish, p.1052); Gulpāyigānī 1887 (cat., II, pp. 96-7); Marʿashī 441/2 (cat., II, p.43); Majlis 3226/3 (cat., X, p.809); Dānishgāh 920/1 (cat., V, pp.2077-8)

AL-SHAYKH:

- *Al-Jumal wa ʾl-ʿuqūd*
  Editions: Tehran, n.d. (facsimile from a manuscript dated 789); Mashhad, 1389

Selected MSS: Mashhad, Ilāhiyyāt 792/1 (cat., I, p.284); Majlis 4953/10, 6342/6, 3082 (cat., X, p.637, XIV, pp.229-30; *Waḥīd*, V, p. 299; cat. of microfilms of Dānishgāh, I, p. 777); Princeton 1886/10 New Series, 3992/4 Yahuda (cat., p. 148); Amīr al-Mu'minīn 512/1 (*Nash*., V, p. 412); Iṣfahān, Dānishgāh 16929 (cat., p.924); Gawharshād 1129/3 (cat., p. 251); Dār al-Kutub 19338b, 19908 (cat., I, pp.221-2)

- *Al-Khilāf = Masā'il al-khilāf*
  Editions: Tehran, 1370, 1377; Qum, 1376, 1404
  Selected MSS: Mahdawī 433 (cat. p.170); Majlis 3093, 8785 (cat., X, p.645; Ḥujjatī, p. 664); Los Angeles M163 (cat., p.219); Tabrīz, Qāḍī (*Nash*., VII, p. 522); Kāshān, Āthār-i Millī 199 (*Nash*., IV, p. 357); Dānishgāh 6283 (cat., XVI, p. 234)
  Abridgement: by Abū ʻAlī Faḍl b. Ḥasan al-Ṭabrisī (d. 548), MSS: Ḥakīm 198 (*Nawādir*, pp. 56-7); Malik 1308 (cat., I, p.744); Majlis 5143 (cat., XV, p.213)

- *Al-Mabsūṭ*
  Editions: Tehran, 1270, 1387-93
  Selected MSS: Marʻashī 276, 398, 2562, 2613 (cat., I, pp.304, 414, VII,pp. 147, 193-4); Malik 1120 (cat., I, p.632); Ḥakīm 518 (*Nawādir*, pp.52-4); British Library Or. 3585 (Riew, pp. 211-12); Los Angeles M1199 (cat., p.338); Raḍawī 2601, 2602 (cat., II, pp.120-1); Sinā 426 (cat., I, p. 254); Ḥaydariyya 586 (cat., p.30); Bankipore 1401 (cat. Arabic, I, p.102)

- *Al-Nihāya fī mujarrad al-fiqh wa 'l-fatāwā*
  Editions: Tehran, 1276 (in the collection of *al-Jawāmiʻ al-fiqhiyya*), 1383-4; Beirut, 1390
  Selected MSS: Marʻashī 241, 1840, 3126 (cat., I, p.265, V, p.226, VII, p.358); Mahdawī 487 (cat., p. 546); Dānishgāh 5467, 6237 (cat., XVI, pp.17, 348) and microfilms 2095, 1713 (cat., I, p. 396); Jaʻfariyya (cat., V, p. 437; AB, XXIV, p. 404); Āṣafiyya 10 Shīʻī law (cat., II, p.253); Malik 3970 (cat., I, p.784); Princeton, Yahuda 2382, 134 (cat., p.137); Tabrīz, Millī (*Nash*., IV, p. 315); Majlis 2728 (cat., IX, pp.58-61)
  Translations: (1) Persian, anonymous (belonging to 5th-6th century), edited Tehran, 1373-4, 1383-4, MSS: Ḥuqūq 328j (cat., pp. 57-8); Majlis 838 (cat., III, pp.69-70); Dānishgāh 292/2, 1228 (cat., III, p.156, VI, pp.2449-50); Millī 1901f (cat., IV, pp.355-6); (2) Perisan, the chapter on holy war, by Muḥammad ʻAlī al-Sirkānī (d. after 1033), MS: Wazīrī (cat. of microfilms of Dānishgāh, I, pp. 702-3)
  Commentaries: (1) on the first chapter, by al-Muḥaqqiq, as the first chapter of his *al-Masā'il al-Miṣriyya* - see below; (2) *Nukat al-Nihāya*, by the same author - see below

IBN ABI 'L-MAJD:

Ishārat al-sabq ilā maʻrifat al-ḥaqq
Edition: Tehran, 1276 (in the collection of *al-Jawāmiʻ al-fiqhiyya*)
MSS: Ḥakīm 396 (cat., I, p.53); Majlis 1272/2 (cat., IV, p.64); Dānishgāh 920/9 (cat., V, pp. 1776-7); Mashhad, Ilāhiyyāt, microfilm 93 (cat., I, p.230)

AL-ṢAHRASHTĪ:

Iṣbāḥ al-Shīʻa bi-miṣbāḥ al-sharīʻa
MSS: Dānishgāh 7141 (cat., XVI, p.464); Marʻashī 3457/1 (cat., IX, pp.255-6); Kāshān, ʻĀṭifī (*Nash*., XI-XII, p. 954)

IBN ḤAMZA:

Al-Wasīla ilā nayl al-faḍīla
Editions: Tehran, 1276 (in the collection of *al-Jawāmiʿ al-fiqhiyya*); Najaf [1400?]
MSS: Dānishgāh 700, 6930/6 (cat., V, pp.2102-3, XVI, p.404); Marʿashī 291, 2219/3 (cat., I, p.336, VI, p.209); Millī, Arabic 197, 1799, 1945 (cat., VIII, p.171, X, pp.380, 623-4); Amīr al-Muʾminīn (cat., V, p.416); Jaʿfariyya (*Nash.*, V, p.437); Sinā 124 (cat., I, p.64); Ḥakīm 33/1 (*Nash.*, V, p. 422); Raḍawī 8070 (Bīnish, p.1071); Nawwāb 232 law (cat., p.481)

IBN ZUHRA:

Ghunyat al-nuzūʿ
Edition: Tehran, 1276 (in the collection of *al-Jawāmiʿ al-fiqhiyya*)
Selected MSS: Majlis, 2 MSS (AB, II, pp. 441-2; Maḥfūẓ I, p. 34; cat. of microfilms of Dānishgāh, I, 1.729); Gawharshād 697 (cat., p.356); Dānishgāh 6868, 6930/5 (cat., XVI, pp.380, 404); Marʿashī 447, 432/1, 2219/10 (cat., II, pp.35, 59, VI, p.210); Sipahsālār 2668 (cat., I, p.487)

IBN IDRĪS:

Al-Sarāʾir al-ḥāwī li-taḥrīr al-fatāwī
Edition: Tehran, 1270
Selected MSS: Raḍawī 5713 (cat., V, pp.451-2); Majlis 4554 (cat., XII, pp. 237-8); Marʿashī 2603 (cat., VII, p.186); Dānishgāh 6651 (cat., XVI, p.326); Āstāna 6336 (cat., p. 127)

AL-MUḤAQQIQ:

- *Al-Mukhtaṣar al-nāfiʿ*
Editions: India, 1267; Tehran, 1326; Cairo, 1376; Najaf, 1384
Selected MSS: Millī 1788 Arabic (cat., X, p.371); Marʿashī 506, 527, 1654, 1679 (cat., II, pp.112, 132, V, pp.52,73); Raḍawī 8196 (Bīnish, p.995); Ilāhiyyāt 836d (cat., II, p.84); Dānishgāh 1617/1 (cat., VIII, p.206); Fayḍiyya 1378,1996 (cat., I, pp. 235-6); Ann Arbor 99 (*Nash.*, X, p. 186); Leiden 967/1 Warn. (cat., IV, p.116); Princeton 153 New Series; British Library Or.4028 (Rieu, p.212); Aṣafiyya 178 Shīʿī law (cat., IV, p. 477)
Translations: (1) Persian, anonymous (belonging to late 7th/13th century), edited Tehran, 1385, MS: Dānishgāh 2407 (cat., IX, p.1027); (2) Persian, anonymous (belonging to 8th-9th centuries), MSS: Dihkhudā 252 (cat., p.390); Mashhad, Ilāhiyyāt 190 (cat., I, p. 43); (3) Persian, by Muḥammad Bāqir b. M. Taqī, MSS: Raḍawī 2716 (cat., V, p.384); Bibliothèque Nationale 2234 (cat. IV, p. 189); (4) Persian, by ʿAlāʾ al-Dīn b. Muḥammad al-Qummī (early 11th/17th century), MS: Gawharshād 1525 (cat., p. 91); (5) Persian, by Muḥammad Ṣāliḥ b. Sulṭān ʿAlī al-Farāhānī, MS: Iṣfahān, ʿUmūmī 3061 (cat., I, p.66); (6) Persian, anonymous, MS: Tehran, Parwāna (cat. of microfilms of Dānishgāh, II, p.209)
Abridgement: *al-Muqtaṣar*, by Ibn Dāwūd al-Ḥillī, MS: Majlis 404 Ṭabāṭabāʾī
Commentaries: (1) *al-Muʿtabar*, by the author - see below; (2) *Kashf al-rumūz*, by al-Ābī - see below; (3) *Taḥṣīl al-manāfiʿ*, by Ibn Dāwūd al-Ḥillī, MS: Rawḍātī (Maḥfūẓ I, p.16); (4) anonymous (written before 790/1388); MS: Marʿashī 2245 (cat., VI, pp.230-1); (5) *al-Tanqīḥ al-rāʾiʿ*, by al-Miqdād - see below; (6) *al-Muhadhdhab al-bāriʿ*, by Ibn Fahd - see below; (7) by al-Karakī, MSS: Adabiyyāt 66/1d (cat.,

p.200); Raḍawī 2384, 2387, 6195 (cat., II, pp.52-4, V, p.413); Iṣfahān, 'Umūmī 3090 (cat., I, p.235); Bengal 623 (cat., I, p.308); Masjid-i A'ẓam 979; Dānishgāh 6963/3 (cat., XVI, p.412); Princeton 234 New Series; Ilāhiyyāt 225/4d (cat., I, p.262); Majlis 5240/2 (cat., XVI, p.251); Ḥuqūq 62/2d, 111b (cat., pp.326, 443); Kāshān, Raḍawī (cat., p.34); Fayḍiyya 1672 (cat., I, p. 93); Leiden 967/3 Warn. (cat., IV, pp.116-17); Wazīrī 2290/6 (cat., IV, p.1235); Rasht 43/1 (cat., p. 1193); Mashhad, Shānachī (*Nash.*, V, p.595); (8) *Īḍāḥ al-Nāfi'*, by al-Qaṭīfī, MS: Malik 2604/2 (Dānishpāzhūh,p.4): (9) by al-Shahīd al-Thānī, MSS: Dānishgāh 1095 (cat., V, p.1869); Majlis 5340/1 (cat., XVI, p.251); (10) by 'Abd al-'Ālī al-Karakī, MS: Ḥakīm 211; (11) *Ghāyat al-marām*, by Ṣāḥib al-Madārik - see below; (12) *Ghurar al-majāmi'*, by Nūr al-Dīn 'Alī b.'Alī b. Ḥusayn al-Mūsawī al-'Āmilī (d. 1061-8), MS: Iṣfahān, Dānishgāh 16890 (cat., p. 908; *Nash.*, V, p.300); (13) *al-Ḍiyā' al-lāmi'*, by Fakhr al-Dīn b. Muḥammad 'Alī al-Ṭurayḥī al-Najafī (d. 1085), MSS: Mar'ashī 1613 (cat., V, pp. 15-16); Millī 225/9f (cat., I, pp.222-3); Kāshānī 94 (cat., p.193); (14) *Jāmi' al-jawāmi'*, anonymous (belonging to late 12th-early 13th centuries), MS: Mar'ashī 2123 (cat., VI, p. 135); (15) by Muḥammad 'Alī b. Mu'min (d. after 1201), MS: Farhād Mu'tamid 147 (cat., p.189); (16) by 'Abd al-Ṣamad al-Hamadānī (d. 1216), MS: Rasht 98/2 (cat., pp. 1203-4); (17) *Riyāḍ al-masā'il*, by Ṣāḥib al-Riyāḍ - see below; (18) *Ḥadīqat al-Mu'minīn*, by the same author - see below; (19) *Majma' al-masā'il*, by 'Alī b. Muḥammad al-Baraghānī (mid-13th century), MS: Rawḍātī (Mu'allim, V, pp.1708-9); (20) by Masīḥ b. Muḥammad Sa'īd al-Ṭihrānī (d. 1263), MS: Masjid-i Jāmi' 161 (cat., p.327); (21) by Muḥammad b. Ḥusayn al-Raḍawī (d. 1266), MS: Raḍawī 6741 (cat., V, p.459); (22) *Mashāriq al-anwār*, by Awrang Zīb b. Muḥammad Taqī al-Qājār (d. after 1269), MS: Mar'ashī (AB, XXI, p.33); (23) *al-Manāfi'*, by Muḥammad b. Muḥammad 'Alī al-Kāshānī (d. 1269), MS: Khāliṣī (cat., pp.77, 124-5); (24) *Jawāli' al-lawāmi'*, by Muḥammad Taqī b. 'Abd al-Riḍā al-Mūsawī al-Khishtī (d. around 1275), MS: Tustariyya 800 (cat., p. 806); (25) by Muḥammad Kāẓim b. 'Alī Naqī al-Rashtī al-Langarūdī (d. after 1281), MS: Fayḍiyya 1117 (cat., I, p.158); (26) *al-Baḥr al-lāmi'*, by Muḥammad Ibrāhīm b. Muḥammad Mahdī al-Qishlāqī (d. 1288), MSS: Mar'ashī 3491 (cat., IX, pp.288-9); Fayḍiyya 837, 893, 894 (cat., I, pp.30-1); (27) *al-Burhān al-qāṭi'*, by 'Alī b. Riḍā Āl Baḥr al-'Ulūm (d.1298), edited Tehran, 1291-2, MS: Dānishgāh 750 (cat., V, p.1791); (28) *al-Anwār al-Raḍawiyya*, by Muḥammad Riḍā b. Ismā'īl al-Mūsawī al-Shīrāzī (d. around 1302), edited Tehran, 1287; (29) by Jamāl al-Dīn b. 'Alī al-Mūsawī (13th century), MS: Mar'ashī 2929/2 (cat., VIII, p.120); (30) *Muntaqad al-manāfi'*, by Ḥabīb Allāh b. 'Alīmadad al-Kāshānī (d. 1340), edited Tehran, 1394; (31) *Jāmi' al-madārik*, by Aḥmad b. Yūsuf al-Khwānsārī - see below; (32-6) five anonymous or unidentified commentaries: (a) MS: Majlis 5059/1 (cat., XV, pp.20-1); (b) Persian, MS: Malik 2632 (cat., II, p.204); (c) MS: Āstāna 6386 (cat., p.135); (d) MS: Majlis 9067; (e) MS: Āstāna 6331 (cat., p.135)

- *Al-Mu'tabar*
  Edition: Tehran, 1318
  MSS: Majlis 1322, 3294 (cat., IV, p. 94, X, pp. 915-16); Raḍawī 2834 (cat., V, p.508); Mar'ashī 1029, 1367, 1584 (cat., IV, pp.35-6, 140-1, 390); Mahdawī 809 (cat., p.171); Farhād Mu'tamid 188 (cat., p.243); Dānishgāh 6411 (cat., XVI, p.261); Wazīrī 1607 (cat., III, p.1001); Ustādī (cat., p.58)

- *Nukat al-Nihāya*
  Edition: Tehran, 1276 (in the collection of *al-Jawāmi' al-fiqhiyya*)
  MSS: Dānishgāh 6746 (cat., XVI, p.352); Raḍawī 2665, 2666 (cat., II, p. 140); Malik 2102 (cat., I, pp.776-7)

- *Sharā'i' al-Islām*
  Editions: Najaf, 1389 and many others (see Mushār, cols. 537-8)
  Selected MSS: Majlis 466 Ṭabāṭabā'ī; 9556, 7717; Yazd, 'Ulūmī (*Nash*., IV, p.440); Bankipore 920-1 (cat., Arabic, I, p.91); Mar'ashī 202,3190, 3787 (cat., I, p.232, VII, p.411, X, p.172); Sinā 868 (cat., II, p.79); Mashhad, Ilāhiyyāt 258 (cat., I, pp.154-5); Burūjirdī (cat., p.20); Ḥakīm 431 (*Nawādir*, pp.45-7); 'Amāra, Shakkāra (Maḥfūẓ II, p.207); Nawwāb 40 law (cat., p.450); Gawharshād 1029 (cat., p.312)
  Translations: (1) *Jāmi'-i Raḍawī*, Persian, by 'Abd al-Ghanī b. Abū Ṭālib al-Kishmīrī (mid-12th century), edited Locknow, 1307, MSS: Dacca Du 373 (cat., I, pp.269-70); Āṣafiyya 1186; Bankipore 1260 (cat. Persian, I, p.201); (2) Persian, by Abu 'l-Qāsim b. Aḥmad al-Yazdī (mid-13th century), edited Tehran, 1387-94, MSS: Dānishgāh 6603 (cat., XVI, p.306); Ḥuqūq 85b (cat., pp.53-4); (3) *Najāt al-mu'minīn*, Persian, by Muḥammad Kāẓim, MS: Gawharshād 8/2 (cat., p.190); (4) Persian, the chapter on endowment, by Muḥammad Ḥasan al-Adīb al-Kirmānī, MS: Adabiyyāt 62 Ḥikmat (cat., p.8); (5) *Jāmi'-i Ja'farī*, Urdu, by 'Ābid Ḥusayn b. Bakhshish Ḥusayn al-Anṣārī (d. 1330), edited Locknow, 1333; (6) *Rawā'i' al-aḥkām*, Hindī, by Muḥammad Ṣādiq al-Kishmīrī, edited Locknow, 1315-17; (7) Persian, anonymous, MS: Los Angeles M350 (cat., p.18); (8) *Droit musulman, Recuil de lois concernant les Musulmans schyites*, French, by A. Querry, edited Paris, 1871-2 AD
  Commentaries: (1) by Najm al-Dīn Ja'far al-Zihdazī (early 8th century), MS: Majlis 5508 (cat., XVI, p.409); (2) *Ghāyat al-marām*, by Mufliḥ al-Ṣaymarī - see below; (3) *Fawā'id al-Sharā'i'*, by al-Karakī - see below; (4) by Ḥusayn b. Mufliḥ al-Ṣaymarī (d. 933), MS: Dānishgāh 2621/4 (cat., IX, p.1496); (5) by al-Shahīd al-Thānī - see below; (6) *Masālik al-afhām*, by the same author - see below; (7) *Madārik al-aḥkām*, by Ṣāḥib al-Madārik, see below; (8) by al-Dāmād, MS: Sipahsālār 7297/2 (cat., IV, p.203); (9) *Sharḥ khuṭbat al-Shara'i'*, by Muḥammad Taqī b. Abu 'l-Ḥasan al-Ḥusaynī al-Astarābādī (mid-11th century), MS: Raḍawī 2487 (cat., II, p. 86); (10) by Muḥammad b. Ḥasan al-Shīrwānī (d. 1098), MS: Dānishgāh 7095 (cat., XVI, p.455); (11) *Safīna-yi tawfīq*, Persian, by 'Abd al-Ṣamad b. 'Āshūr al-Tabrīzī (late 11th century), MS: Masjid-i A'ẓam 498; (12) *Mu'tamad al-anām*, by Muḥammad Ṣādiq b. Muḥammad (late 11th century), MSS: Gawharshād 438 (cat., p.401); Mar'ashī 2811 (cat., VIII, p.13); (13) by 'Alī b. Muḥammad al-'Āmilī (d. 1103), MSS: India Office 1789 (cat., II, p.306); Sipahsālār 2600/4 (cat., IV, p.204); Ṣāḥib al-Dharī'a (AB, VI, p.108); (14) by Muḥammad Ṣāliḥ al-Astarābādī (early 12th century), MS: Mahdawī 592/15 (cat., p.126); (15) *Fawā'id al-marām*, anonymous (written before 1107), MS: Najaf, Madrasat al-Sayyid (AB, XVI, pp.358-9); (16) by Jawād b. 'Alī b. 'Abd al-'Ālī al-Maysī (d. after 1117), MS: Dānishgāh 5252 (cat., XV, pp.418-19); (17) *Ma'ārij al-aḥkām*, by Ḥusayn b. Muḥammad Ibrāhīm al-Ḥusaynī al-Qazwīnī (d. 1208), MSS: Qazwīn, Ḥajj Sayyid Jawādī (*Nash*., VI, p.351); Fayḍiyya 99, 389 (cat., I, pp. 257-9); Raḍawī 7254 (cat., V, p.507); Sulaymān Khān 7 (cat., p.21); Nawwāb 250 law (cat., p. 477); Khāliṣī (cat., p.116); Iṣfahān, Dānishgāh 16650 (cat., p. 916); Mar'ashī 1916, 2410, 2434 (cat., V, pp.287-8, VII, pp.10, 28); Dānishgāh 997-9, 6600/10 (cat., V, pp. 2052-4, XVI, p.306); Majlis 1144 Ṭabāṭabā'ī; Sipahsālār 2697

(cat., V, p.594); Malik 3526 (cat., I, p.692); Wazīrī 1781/9 (cat., III, p.1053); (18) *Baḥr al-ḥaqāʾiq*, by ʿAbd al-Ṣamad al-Hamadānī, MS: Majlis 5916 (cat., XVII, pp.303-5); (19) *Manāhij al-aḥkām*, by ʿAbd al-ʿĀlī b. Umīd ʿAlī al-Rashtī (d. after 1225), MS: Marʿashī 2008 (cat., VI, p.11); (20) by Muḥammad Taqī b. Aḥmad al-Ḥusaynī al-Ṭāliqānī (d. after 1226), MS: Amīr al-Muʾminīn 1698 (AB, XV, p.55); (21) *Waḍāʾiʿ al-aḥkām*, by Zayn al-ʿĀbidīn b. Ḥusayn al-Ṭabāṭabāʾī, MS: Ḥuqūq 142b (cat., p.502); (22) *Muʿtamad al-aḥkām*, by Khalaf b. Ḥasan b. Muḥammad ʿAlī al-Ḥāʾirī (d. after 1232), MS: Burūjirdī (AB, XXI, p.212); (23) *Īḍāḥ al-kalām*, by Ḥusayn b. Muḥammad ʿAlī al-Aʿsam al-Najafī (d. 1237), MSS: Ḥakīm 1152 (cat., I, p.81); Dānishgāh 6892 (cat., XVI, p.390); Raḍawī 2242 (cat., II, p.11); (24) *Kashf al-ẓalām*, by Muḥsin b. Murtaḍā al-Aʿsam al-Najafī (d. 1238), MSS: Gharb 1100/2, 1107, 1222 (cat., pp. 175, 289); Gawharshād 1438, 1448 (cat., p.377); Marʿashī (*Nash.*, VI, p.384); (25) *Miṣbāḥ al-ijtihād*, by Muḥammad Ibrāhīm b. Bahrām Khalaj al-Kharaqānī (d. after 1243), MS: ʿAbd al-ʿAẓīm 347-8 (cat., p.477); (26) *al-Dharāʾiʿ*, by ʿAbd al-Ḥusayn b. Muḥammad ʿAlī al-Aʿsam al-Najafī (d. 1247), MS: Raḍawī 7659 (Bīnish, p.772); (27) *Khaṣāʾiṣ al-aʿlām*, by ʿAbd al-Raḥmān b. Muḥammad Ṣāliḥ al-Qazwīnī (d. 1250), MS: Majlis 1808/1 (cat., IX, p.406); (28) by ʿAlī b. Jaʿfar al-Najfī Āl Kāshif al-Ghiṭāʾ (d. 1253), MS: Gharb 1101 (cat., p.100); (29) *Maṭāliʿ al-anwār*, by al-Shaftī - see below, chapter 6; (30) *Kashf al-qināʿ ʿan al-aḥkām*, by Muḥammad Kāẓim al-Hamadānī (d. after 1252), MS: Bāqiriyya (AB, XVIII, pp.52-3);(31) by Muṣṭafā b. Muḥammad al-Khuʾī (d. after 1252), MS: Wazīrī 2310 (cat. IV, p.1244); (32) *al-Marghūb*, by Muḥammad Mahdī b. ʿAlī al-Gīlānī (d. after 1254), MSS: Gawharshād 1233 (cat., p.390); Marʿashī 2116 (cat., VI, pp.128-9); Millī 1894 Arabic (cat., X, p.546); Malik 2737 (cat., I, p.662); (33) *Shawāriʿ al-Sharāʾiʿ*, by Ḥasan b. Muḥammad ʿAlī al-Yazdī al-Mudarris (d. after 1256), MSS: Dānishgāh 1388, 6870 (cat., VIII, p. 72, XVI, p.386); Wazīrī 2083/1 (cat., IV, p.1154); (34) *Dhakhīrat al-baḍāʾiʿ*, by Niʿmat Allāh b. ʿAbd Allāh (written before 1255), MS: Malik 2084 (cat., I, p.323); (35) by Abu ʾl-Ḥasan b. Muḥammad Hādī al-Ḥusaynī al-Tunukābunī (d. after 1255), MS: Burūjirdī (cat., pp. 8, 15); (36) *al-Nūr al-sāṭiʿ*, anonymous (written before 1256), MS: Ḥusayniyya Kāshif al-Ghiṭāʾ (AB, XIII, p.331, XXIV, p.369); (37) *al-Fawāʾid*, by Ibrāhīm al-Lāhījī (d. after 1256), MS: Marʿashī (ibid., XVI, p.355); (38) by Dāwūd b. Asad Allāh al-Burūjirdī (late 13th century), MS: Marʿashī 1478 (cat., IV, p.269); (39) *Dalāʾil al-aḥkām*, by Ibrāhīm b. Muḥammad Bāqir al-Mūsawī al-Qazwīnī (d. 1262), MSS: Majlis 4429-30 (cat., XII, pp. 118-19); Bengal 620 (cat., I, p.306); Matḥaf 3629 (cat., I, p.237); Raḍawī 7652-4 (Bīnish, pp.754-5); Malik, 3025 (cat., I, p.312); Wazīrī 575 (cat., II, p.486); Ḥuqūq 189-90j (cat., pp.338-9); Masjid-i Aʿẓam 11789-90 ; Ḥakīm, 9 MSS; Karbalāʾ, Ṭuʿma, 4 MSS (Ṭuʿma II, pp. 102-5); Zanjānī 80 (cat., p.226); (40) *Kashf al-ibhām*, by Muḥammad ʿAlī b. Maqṣūd ʿAlī al-Māzandarānī al-Kāẓimī (d. 1264-6), MS: Ṣāḥib al-Dharīʿa (AB, XVII, pp.6-7); (41) *Manhaj al-ijtihād*, by Muḥammad Taqī b. Muḥammad al-Barghānī (d. 1263), MSS: Dānishgāh 1829, 2791 (cat., VIII, p.426, X, p.1642); Gulpāyigānī 203, 207 (cat., I, pp. 181,183); Marʿashī 1233, 2406, 2720-1 (cat., VII, pp.7-8, 246, 285-6); Fayḍiyya 81, 83, 96, 102 (cat., I, pp. 281-2); Ḥujjatiyya 513 (cat., p.92); Masjid-i Aʿẓam 15346; Khayrāt Khān 64-5 (cat., p.1771); Raḍawī 1597, 6664, 7054, 7252 (cat., II, p.119, V, pp.521-2; Bīnish, p.1084); Malik 2744 (cat., I, p.755); Amīr al-Muʾminīn (AB, XIII, pp.317-18); Tabrīz, Qāḍī (*Nash.*, VII, p.523); Rawḍātī (Muʿallim, V, pp.1712-13); (42) Persian, by the same author, MSS:

Mar'ashī 2332 (cat., VI, pp.311-12, 397); Gharb 4503 (cat., p.49); (43) by Muḥammad Ṭāhir al-Rānakū'i al-Ḥā'irī (d. after 1265), MS: Mar'ashī 2323 (cat., VI, pp. 302-3); (44) *Jawāhir al-kalām*, by Ṣāḥib al-Jawāhir - see below; (45) by Muḥammad b. Ḥusayn al-Raḍawī, MS: Raḍawī 6493 (cat., V, p. 458); (46) *Ḥāwī al-marām*, by Muḥammad Bāqir al-Gulpāyigānī (d. after 1268), MSS: Ḥuqūq 117j (cat., p.327); Gulpāyigānī 6-7 (cat., I, pp.70-4); (47) *Nafaḥāt al-ilhām*, by 'Abd al-Ḥusayn al-Qazwīnī (d. after 1270), MS: Mar'ashī 1517 (cat., IV, p.318); (48) by 'Alī al-Khwānsārī al-Hamadānī (d. after 1270), MS: Gharb 4721 (cat., p.146); (49) by Muḥammad Bāqir b. Ja'far al-Marāghī (d. after 1274), MS: Mar'ashī 3502 (cat., IX, pp. 201-2); (50) by Hādī b. Muḥammad Ṣāliḥ al-Kirmānshāhī (d. after 1280), MS: Majlis 5418 (cat., XVI, p.327); (51) *Madārik al-aḥkām*, by Mahdī al-Qumsha'ī al-Iṣfahānī (d. 1281), MS: Ṣāḥib al-Dharī'a (AB, XIII, p.330); (52) *Jāmi' al-jawāmi'*, by Ḥasan b. Muḥsin al-A'rajī al-Kāẓimī (mid-13th century), MS: Khāliṣī (cat., p.85); (53) by Muḥammad 'Alī b. Muḥammad Bāqir al-Shaftī (d. 1282), MS: Mar'ashī 1995/3 (cat., V, p.367); (54) by 'Alī b. 'Abd al-Ghaffār (d. after 1288), MS: Mar'ashī 3393/2 (cat., IX, p.180); (55) *al-Durra al-Ḥā'iriyya*, by 'Alī Naqī b. Ḥasan al-Ṭabāṭabā'ī (d. 1289), edited Iran, n.d., MS: Majlis 5426 (cat., XVI, p.331); (56) by Asad Allāh b. Muḥammad Bāqir al-Mūsawī al-Shaftī (d. 1290), MS: Gulpāyigānī 126 (cat., I, p.126); (57) by Mūsā b. Faḍl Allāh al-Ḥusaynī al-Hamadānī (d. after 1295), MS: Raḍawiyya 36 (cat., I, pp. 22-3); (58) by Muḥammad b. Muḥammad Ḥasan al-Raḍawī al-Ṭūsī (d. after 1291), MS: Raḍawī 7259 (cat., V, p.384); (59) by Ja'far al-Ḥusaynī al-Sabzawārī (d. around 1292), MS: Bāqiriyya (AB, XIII, p.318); (60) by Muḥammad b. 'Āshūr al-Kirmānshāhī (late 13th century), MS: Mar'ashī 3110 (cat., VIII, pp. 333-4); (61) by 'Alī b. Khalīl al-Ṭihrānī (d. 1296), MS: Malik 1449 (cat., I, p.412); (62) *Mawāhib al-afhām*, by Muḥammad Mahdī b. Ḥasan al-Qazwīnī (d. 1300), MS: Ḥakīm; (63) *Makhāzin al-aḥkām*, by Muḥammad Bāqir b. Zayn al-'Ābidīn al-Yazdī (d. around 1300), MS: Ḥakīm 33 (*Nash.*, V, p.433); (64) by Muḥammad Kāẓim b. 'Alī Naqī al-Langarūdī (late 13th century), MS: Fayḍiyya 1117 (cat., I, p.158); (65) *al-Risāla al-Raḍawiyya*, by Riḍā al-Tabrīzī (late 13th century), MS: Ḥuqūq 53j (cat., pp.355-6); (66) *al-Ḥaqā'iq*, by 'Alī b. Muḥammad Ṣādiq al-Khwātūnābādī (12th-13th century), MS: Gulpāyigānī 76 (cat., I, pp.82-3); (67) by Muḥammad Mahdī al-Kujūrī (d. 1293), MS: Shīrāz, Wiṣāl (*Nash.*, V, p.292); (68) by Jamāl al-Dīn b. 'Alī al-Mūsawī, MS: Mar'ashī 2929/8 (cat., VII, p.122); (69) *Majma' al-aḥkām*, by 'Alī Muḥammad b. 'Alī al-Ḥusaynī, MS: Wazīrī 150 (cat., I, pp.183-7); (70) by Muḥammad Amīn al-Ahārī al-Mishkīnī, MS: Mar'ashī 2307 (cat., VI, p.290); (71) by Muḥammad b. Ḥasan al-Langarūdī, MS: Ḥakīm 2057; (72) by 'Alī al-Duzdarī, MS: Mar'ashī 2574 (cat., VII, p. 162); (73) by 'Abd al-Wahhāb b. Aḥmad al-Maḥallātī, MS: Ilāhiyyāt 615/2d (cat., I, p.341); (74) *Dalā'il al-aḥkām*, by Muḥammad Ḥusayn b. Muḥammad 'Alī al-Ṭabīb al-Ṭihrānī, MS: Malik 1740 (cat., I, p.311); (75) *Kāshif al-ibhām*, by Qāsim b. Muḥammad al-Najafī, MS: Mar'ashī 2873 (cat., VIII, p.81); (76) *al-Mawāhib al-Gharawiyya*, by 'Abd al-Bāqī b. 'Alī al-Mūsawī, MSS: Gulpāyigānī 391-2 (cat., I, p. 325); (77) *Daqā'iq al-afhām*, anonymous, MS: Shīrāzī (AB, VIII, p.234); (78) *Jāmi' al-aḥkām*, by Muḥammad b. Ḥasan al-A'rajī al-Kāẓimī (d. 1303), MS: Khāliṣī (cat., p.55); (79) by 'Abbās b. Muḥammad Ḥusayn al-Jaṣānī (d. 1306), MS: Khāliṣī (cat., pp.83-5); (80) by 'Alī b. Zayn al-'Ābidīn (written before 1307), MS: Majlis 421 Ṭabāṭabā'ī; (81) *Lawāmi' al-nikāt*, a collection of the lectures of al-Anṣārī - see below; (82) *Hidāyat al-anām*, by Muḥammad Ḥusayn

b. Hāshim al-Kāẓimī (d. 1308), edited, Najaf, 1330-1, MSS: Raḍawī 8099-8101 (Bīnish, pp.1074-6); (83) *Kashf al-qināʿ*, by Muḥammad Raḥīm b. Muḥammad al-Burūjirdī (d. 1309), MS: Malik 2695 (cat., I, p.596); (84) by Muḥammad Ḥusayn al-ʿArab al-Dāmād (d. after 1310), MSS:Majlis 9526-34; (85) *Dharāʾiʿ al-anām*, by Aḥmad al-Malāʾirī (written before 1310), MSS: Marʿashī 3295 (cat., IX, pp.77-8); Masjid-i Aʿẓam 1084; (86) by Muḥammad ʿAlī b. Muḥammad Ṣādiq al-Raḍawī (d. 1311), MS: Raḍawī 6524 (cat., V, p.490); (87) *Maʿārif al-aḥkām*, by Mahdī b. Ṣāliḥ al-Ṭabāṭabāʾī al-Ḥakīm (d. 1312), MS: Ḥakīm (AB, XXI, p.189); (88) *Shawāriʿ al-aʿlām*, by Muḥammad Ḥusayn b. Muḥammad ʿAlī al-Shahrastānī (d. 1315), MS: Ḥuqūq 248j (cat., p.394); (89) *Wadāʾiʿ al-nubuwwa*, by Hādī al-Ṭihrānī - see below; (90) by Yūsuf b. Muḥammad Riḍā al-Gīlānī (d. after 1321), MSS: Marʿashī 1235-6 (cat., IV, pp.34-5); (91) *Miṣbāḥ al-faqīh*, by Riḍā al-Hamadānī - see below; (92) *Dharāʾiʿ al-aḥlām*, by Muḥammad Ḥasan al-Māmaqānī - see below; (93) by Ḥasan b. Aḥmad al-Ḥusaynī al-Kāshānī (d. 1342), MS: Raḍawī 7176 (cat., V, p.411); (94) by Mahdī b. Ḥusayn al-Khāliṣī (d. 1343), edited Mashhad, 1342; (95) *Muntahā maqāṣid al-anām*, by ʿAbd Allāh b. Muḥammad Ḥasan al-Māmaqānī (d. 1351), edited Najaf, 1348-9; (96) by Muẓaffar b. Muḥammad ʿAlī al-Ḥusaynī al-Rashtī, MS: Marʿashī 1246/1 (cat., IV, p.44); (97) *Miftāḥ al-kalām*, by Muḥammad Hāshim b. ʿAbd Allāh al-Ṭasūjī al-Khuʾī (d. 1358) edited Tabrīz, 1345; (98) by Muḥammad Ḥusayn b. Hibat Allāh al-Raḍawī al-Kāshānī (d. 1385), MS: Kāshān, Raḍawī (cat., p. 36); (99-114) sixteen anonymous or unidentified commentaries: (a) Persion, MSS: Adabiyyāt 44b (cat., p.335); Majlis (*Waḥīd*, IV, p.646); (b) MS: Fayḍiyya 670 (cat., I, p.150); (c) MS: Wazīrī 3767/2 (cat., V, p.1788); (d) MS: Millī 1197/2 Arabic (cat., IX, p. 186); (e) MS: Majlis 81/10 Khuʾī (cat., VII, p.90); (f) MS: Raḍawī 555/1 law (cat., V, p.366); (g) MS: Nawwāb 170/2 jurisprudence (cat., p.470); (h) MS: Fayḍiyya 141/3 (cat., III, p.5); (i) MS: Tustariyya 610 (cat., p.803); (j) MS: Masjid-i Aʿẓam 259; (k) Sipahsālār 6683/1 (cat., IV, p. 204); (l) MS: Gawharshād 521 (cat., p.324); (m) MS: Sulaymān Khān 52 (cat., p.13); (n) MSS: Gawharshād 472, 487 (cat., p.324); (o) MS: Ustādī (cat., p.23); (p) MS: Nawwāb 201 law (cat., p.461)

AL-ĀBĪ:

Kashf al-rumūz
MSS: Marʿashī 205, 1263 (cat., I, p.235, IV, p.68); Gawharshād 1300 (cat., p.377); Raḍawī 2533 (cat., II, p. 101); Sipahsālār 2268 (cat., I, p.481); Dānishgāh 721 (cat., V, pp.1984-7)

YAḤYĀ B. SAʿĪD

Jāmiʿ al-sharāʾiʿ
MSS: Tustariyya (AB, V, p.61); Majlis 4775, 4325/2 (cat., XII, p.19, XIII, pp.172-3); Dānishgāh 1476/2, 1005/2 (cat., V, p.1984, VIII, p.128); Ilāhiyyāt 452/2d (cat., I, p.302); Ḥuqūq 216/3j (cat., pp.419-20); Princeton 960/2 New Series; Sipahsālār 2660 (cat., I, p.387, IV, pp.12-13); Masjid-i Aʿẓam 4346

ANONYMOUS (written in 698):

Jāmiʿ al-khilāf wa ʾl-wifāq bayn al-Imāmiyya wa aʾimmat al-Ḥijāz wa ʾl-ʿIrāq
MS: Dānishgāh 6702 (cat., XVI, p.336)

AL-ʿALLĀMA:

- *Irshād al-adhhān*
Editions: Tehran, 1272; Qum, 1403-4 (both together with al-Ardabīlī's *Majmaʿ al-fāʾida wa ʾl-burhān*)
Selected MSS: Raḍawī 2222 (cat., II, p.5); Majlis 4941, 2870/1, 4645/1 (cat., X, pp.218-19, XIII, p.33, XIV, pp.170-1); Marʿashī 2805, 961, 1487, 3363 (cat., III, p.153, IV, p.284, VIII, p.7, IX, p.138; *Nash*., VI, p.356); Dānishgāh 3665, 722, 3560 (cat., V, pp.1771-4, XII, pp.2580, 2675); Topkapi Sarayi 1082 Arabic (cat., II, p.764); Princeton, New Series 318, 826, 1329, 1444; Gulpāyigānī 50 (cat., I, p.63); Malik 2320 (cat., I, p.29); Bengal 630 (cat., I, pp. 311-12); Leningrad 76 (*Nash*., VIII, p.103); Berlin Spr. 652 (cat., IV, p.133); Daca DU 392 (cat., II, p.533); Ambrosiana C.134 (cat., II, p.187); Dār al-Kutub 21262b, 23235b (cat., I, p.34)
Commentaries: (1) by Fakhr al-Muḥaqqiqīn - see below; (2) *Durar al-niqād*, by ʿAbd al-Raḥmān b. Muḥammad al-ʿAtāʾiqī (d. after 779), MS: Dānishgāh 1280 (cat., VII, p.2711); (3) *Ghāyat al-murād*, by al-Shahīd al-Awwal - see below; (4) *Khulāṣat al-tanqīḥ*, by Ibn Fahd al-Aḥsāʾī - see below; (5) *Taʿlīq al-Irshād*, by al-Karakī - see below; (6) by Nūr al-Dīn ʿAlī b. ʿAbd al-ʿĀlī al-Maysī (d. 938), MS: al-Imām al-Ṣādiq (Maḥfūẓ II, p.250); (7) *al-Hādī ila ʾl-rashād*, by al-Qaṭīfī, MSS: Malik 2723 (cat., I, p.801); Raḍawī 2678, 8103 (cat., II, pp.143-4; Bīnish, p. 1074); Rawḍātī (AB, XXV, p.150) (8) a second commentary by the same author, MS: Raḍawī 751/1 law (cat., V, p.468, footnote 2); (9) by al-Shahīd al-Thānī, MSS: Marʿashī 3354 (cat., IX, p.131); Raḍawī 6 law (cat., II, pp.3-4); Ustādī (cat., p.5); (10) *Rawḍ al-jinān*, by the same author - see below; (11) by Ḥusayn b. ʿAbd al-Ṣamad al-ʿĀmilī, MS: Ḥakīm 1102; (12) *Majmaʿ al-bayān*, by ʿAlī b. Ḥusayn al-Ṣāʾigh al-ʿĀmilī (late 10th century), MS: Dānishgāh 4412/2 (cat., XIII, p.3375); (13) *Majmaʿ al-fāʾida wa ʾl-burhān*, by al-Ardabīlī - see below; (14) *Manhaj al-sadād*, by ʿAbd al-ʿĀlī al-Karkaī, MS: Sipahsālār 2486/1 (cat., I, p.440, V, p.681); (15) *al-Iqtiṣād*, by ʿAbd al-Nabī b. Saʿd al-Jazāʾirī (d. 1021), MSS: Majlis 5886 (cat., XVII, p.281); Marʿashī (AB, II, p.268); (16) by Bahāʾ al-Dīn al-ʿĀmilī, MS: Dānishgāh 1983 (cat., VIII, p.592); (17) by Jawād b. ʿAlī al-Karakī (mid-11th century), MS: Marʿashī (AB, VI, p.22); (18) *Burhān al-sadād*, by Muḥammad b. Aḥmad b. Khātūn al-ʿĀmilī (d. after 1039), MS: Rawḍātī (cat., I, pp. 372 ff); (19) *Thamarat al-jinān*, by Muḥammad b. Maḥmūd al-Ṭabasī (d. after 1058), MSS: Ilāhiyyāt 11j, 96b (cat., I, pp.502-3); Mashhad, Ilāhiyyāt 106 (cat., I, pp.61-2); (20) *Dhakhīrat al-maʿād*, by al-Sabzawārī - see below; (21) by al-Māḥūzī, MS: Najaf, Jazāʾirī (*Nash*., VII, p.716); (22) by al-Fāḍil al-Hindī, MS: Gulpāyigānī 1613 (cat., II, p.107); (23) *Mustaqṣā al-ijtihād*, by Ḥusayn b. Muḥammad Ibrāhīm al-Qazwīnī, MSS: Burūjirdī (cat., p.38); Ḥuqūq 119 b (cat., pp.462-3); (24) *Tanqīḥ al-bayān*, by Naṣr Allāh b. Ḥasan al-Ḥusaynī al-Astarābādī (d. after 1236), MSS: Sipahsālār 2483-5 (cat., I, p.438, III, pp.517-8); Majlis 4332/2 (cat., XII, pp.23-4); (25) *Manhaj al-sadād*, by Aḥmad b. ʿAlī Mukhtār al-Gulpāyigānī (mid-13th century), MSS: Gulpāyigānī 190, 276 (cat., I, pp.172, 241); Marʿashī 2467, 2728 (cat., VII, pp.60, 290-1); (26) *Kanz -al-fawāʾid*, by Muʾmin al-Ardabīlī (mid-13th century), MSS: Nūrbakhsh 125 (cat., I, pp.150-1); Rawḍātī (cat., I, pp.244 ff); (27) *Ṭarīq al-rashād*, by Muḥammad Kāẓim b. Muḥammad Riḍā al-Ṭabarī (mid-13th century), MSS: Fayḍiyya 318, 506, 1096 (cat., I, p.181); (28) *Nahj al-sadād*, by Muḥammad Riḍā b. Muḥammad Jaʿfar al-Tabrīzī (d. after 1258), MS: Marʿashī 1252 (cat., IV, pp.54-5); (29) by Muḥammad Hādī b. Muḥammad Bāqir al-Sharīf al-Khuʾī (d. after 1258), MS: Masjid-i Aʿzam 428; (30) *Ghanīmat al-maʿād*, by Muḥammad Ṣāliḥ b.

Muḥammad al-Baraghānī (d.1275), MSS: Millī 1939 Arabic (cat., X, p. 419); Majlis 4438 (cat., XII, p.122); Sipahsālār 8196 (cat., V, p.353); Nawwāb 214 law (cat., p.463); Khayrāt Khān 71 (cat., p.1753); Maʿhad 1165 (cat., p.102); Marʿashī 2449 (cat., VII, p.47); Wazīrī 357 (cat., I, p.331); Najaf, Madrasat al-Sayyid (AB., XVI, p.71); (31) *Maslak al-rāshidīn*, by the same author, MSS: Raḍawī 2831 (Cat., V, p.504); Marʿashī 2436, 2668 (cat., VII, pp.30,247); Majlis 8464; Ḥujjatiyya 514 (cat., p.84); Fayḍiyya 951 (cat., I, p.136); (32) by ʿAlī Akbar b. Ibrāhīm al-Khwānsārī (d. 1271), MSS: Gulpāyigānī 160-2 (cat., I, pp.146, 148-50); (33) *Manhaj al-rashād*, by Muḥammad Jaʿfar b. Muḥammad Ibrāhīm al-Kalbāsī (d. 1292), MS: Rawḍātī (cat., pp.227 ff); (34) *Muʿtaḍid al-Shīʿa*, anonymous (written in 1277), MS: Malik 1875 (cat., I, p.697); (35) by Muḥammad Mahdī b. Muḥammad Ibrāhīm al-Kalbāsī (d. 1278), MS: Maʿhad 1470 (cat., p.123); (36) by al-Anṣārī - see below; (37) by Muḥammad Ḥasan b. Muḥammad Ṣāliḥ al-Baraghānī (d. after 1288), MS: Marʿashī 3404/1 (cat., IX, p.187); (38) by ʿAbd al-Ḥusayn b. ʿAlī al-Baraghānī (d. around 1290), MS: Marʿashī (AB., XIII, p.77); (39) by Muḥammad Bāqir b. Murtaḍā al-Ṭabāṭabāʾī al-Yazdī (d. 1298), MS: Marʿashī 765/5 (cat., II, p.375); (40) *al-Durar al-manẓūma*, by Muḥammad b. Muḥammad Ṭāhir al-Tunukābūnī (13th century), MS: Majlis 1915/8 (cat., IX, pp.571-2); (41) Persian, by ʿAbd al-Salām al-Anṣārī, MS: Dānishgāh 4408 (cat., XIII, p.3368); (42) by Muḥammad ʿAlī b. Zayn al-ʿĀbidīn al-Nūrī, MS: Wazīrī 3768/2 (cat., V, p.1789); (43) *Dhakhīrat al-maʿād*, by ʿAlī b. ʿAlī Riḍā al-Yazdī al-Mudarris (d. 1316), MS: Majlis 4649 (cat., XIII, pp.34-8); (44-8) five anonymous or unidentified commentaries: (a) MS: Dānishgāh 1643/3 (cat., VIII, p.220); (b) MS: Sipahsālār 2487 (cat., I, p.436); (c) MS: Fayḍiyya 1090 (cat., I, p.136); (d) Persian, MS: Majlis 5743 (cat., XVII, pp.183-4); (e) Persian, MS: Zanjān (cat., pp.111-12)

- *Mukhtalaf al-Shīʿa*
  Editions: Tehran, 1323-4, Qum, 1403
  Selected MSS: Dānishgāh 707, 5599, 5888 (cat., V, pp.2006-8, XVI, pp.335, 389); Majlis 1317 (cat., IV, p.91); Marʿashī 1052, 1545, 1229 (cat., III, p.241, IV, pp.30, 347); Raḍawī 7923, 2563-4 (cat., II, pp. 109-10); al-Imām al-Ṣādiq (Maḥfūẓ II, p.250); Ḥakīm (*Nawādir*, pp.54-5); Najaf, Madrasat al-Khalīlī (AB, XX, p.219); Wazīrī 1596 (cat., III, p.997); Gharb 4591 (cat., p.183); India Office 1790 (cat., II, pp.306-7); Bengal 636 (cat., I, p.314); Bodleian, Arabic d.108
  Commentaries: (1) by al-Karakī, MSS: Raḍawī 2363 (cat., II, p.47); Majlis 679 Ṭabāṭabāʾī; Wazīrī 2095 (cat., IV, p.1163); (2) anonymous (written before 917), MS: Marʿashī 2564/7 (cat., VII, p.153); (3) by al-Dāmād, edited Tehran, 1401 (in the collection of *Ithnāʿashar risāla li ʾl-Dāmād*), MSS: Raḍawī 5194 (cat., V, p. 413); Dānishgāh, microfilm 3450 (cat., II, p.146); (4) by Rafīʿ al-Dīn Muḥammad b. Ḥaydar al-Ḥusaynī al-Ṭabāṭabāʾī al-Nāʾīnī (d. 1082), MSS: Raḍawī 6647 (cat., V, p.414); Marʿashī 2875 (cat., VIII, p.82); (5) anonymous (belonging to 11th century), MS: Ustādī (cat., p.16)

- *Muntahā al-maṭlab*
  Edition: Tabrīz, 1316/33
  Selected MSS: Ḥakīm (*Nawādir*, pp.60-1); Gawharshād 554 (cat., p.416); Khāliṣī (cat., p.125); Raḍawī 2850 (cat., II, p.250); Fayḍiyya 777 (cat., I, p.272); Malik 1012 (cat., I, p.745); Bibliothèque Nationale 6658 (cat., II, p.330); Āstāna 5990 (cat., p.177); Wazīrī 523 (cat., II, p.455); Zanjān (cat., p.165)
  Commentary: by Muḥammad Mahdī b. Hidāyat Allāh al-Ḥusaynī al-Mashhadī (d. 1218); MS: Majlis 1804/5 (cat., IX, p.321)

Nihāyat al-iḥkām
MSS: Dānishgāh 662 (cat., XVI, p.328); Kāshān, Āthār-i Millī 433 (*Nash.*, IV, p.358); Raḍawī 2659, 2661 (Bīnish, p.1063); Ḥakīm 40 (*Nawādir*, pp.61-3); Majlis 8794, 5487 (cat., XVI, p.385); Malik 1928, 2967 (cat., I, pp.779-80); Gharb 400, 477 (cat., p.202); Nawwāb 85 law (cat., p.480); Princeton 1256 New Series; Wazīrī 531 (cat., II, p.461); Nūrbakhsh 374 (cat., II, p.95); Hamadān, Madrasa-yi Dāmghānī (*Nash.*, V, p.384)

Qawā'id al-aḥkām
Editions: Tehran, 1272 (together with al-Karakī's *Jāmi' al-Maqāṣid*), 1315, 1329, 1387-9 (together with Fakhr al-Muḥaqqiqīn's *Īḍāḥ al-fawā'id*)
Selected MSS: Dānishgāh 1273, 704/1, 705, 1407 (cat., V, pp. 1970-8, VII, p.2769, VIII, p.84); British Library Or.7511 (Riew, p.23); Khāliṣī (cat., pp. 89-90); Fayḍiyya 34, 143 (cat., I, pp.204-7); Mar'ashī 1310, 1729 (cat., IV, p.98, V, pp.116-17); Gawharshād 387 (cat., pp.330-1); Raḍawī 3516 (cat., II, pp.95-6); Majlis 5643/1, 603 Ṭabāṭabā'ī (cat., XVII, pp. 97-8); Ilāhiyyāt 175j (cat., I, p.630); Tustariyya 790 (cat., p. 808); Nawwāb 94 law (cat., p.464); Gharb 927 (cat., p.170); Sulaymān Khān 54 (cat., p.16); Ḥujjatiyya 379 (cat., pp.75-6); Princeton 529 New Series; Leiden 460 Warn. (cat., IV, p.162); Los Angeles M 1316 (cat., pp.321-2); Topkapi Sarayi 1090 Arabic (cat., II, p.764)
Translations: (1) Persian, by Muḥammad b. Muḥammad b. 'Abd Allāh (written before 858), MS: Khayrāt Khān 39 (cat., p. 1726); (2) Persian, by Ḥasan Isfandiyārī, edited Tehran, 1382
Commentaries: (1) by al-'Allāma, MS: Dānishgāh 3514/23 (cat., XII, pp.2527-8); (2) *Taḥrīr al-taḥrīr*, by Ḍiyā' al-Dīn 'Abd Allāh b. Muḥammad al-A'rajī al-Ḥillī (d. after 740), MSS: Dānishgāh 704/2, 1192/2 (cat., V, pp.1864-5, VI, p.2154); (3) *Kanz al-fawā'id*, by al-Sayyid 'Amīd al-Dīn - see below; (4) *Īḍāḥ al-maqāṣid*, by Fakhr al-Muḥaqqiqīn - see below; (5) *Jāmi' al-fawā'id fī sharḥ khuṭbat al-Qawā'id*, by the same author, MSS: Tustariyya 790 (cat., p.808); Dānishgāh 1193/1 (cat., VI, p.2198); Majlis 2748/1, 5219/1 (cat., IX, p.118, XVI, p.51); Raḍawī 2529/1, 6307 (cat., II, p.99, IV, p.60); Princeton 529 New Series; India Office 1800/1 (cat., II, p.310); Sipahsālār 224 (cat., I, pp.380-1); Dār al-Kutub 19895b (cat., I, p.204); Amīr al-Mu'minīn 55 (AB, XIII, p.224); (6) *al-Masā'il al-Maẓāhiriyya*, by the same author - see below; (7) *Ma'nā qawl al-'Allāma fī 'l-Qawā'id ''alā ishkāl'*, by the same author, MSS: Dānishgāh 6340/2, 6369/1 (cat., XVI, pp.246,253); (8) marginal glosses by the same author, MS: Mar'ashī 1310 (cat., IV, p.98); (9) anonymous (belonging to 8th century), MS: Majlis 5136 (cat., XV, p.125); (10) *Wasīlat al-qāṣid*, by Ibn al-Mutawwij, MSS: Raḍawī 2782, 5727 (cat., V, pp. 528-9); Dānishgāh 2144/35 (cat., IX, p.828); (11) by Jamāl al-Dīn Aḥmad b. al-Najjār (d. 823-35), edited Tehran, 1315, MSS: Sinā 780 (cat., II, p.59); Dānishgāh 1193 (cat., VI, p.2194); Wazīrī 1323 (cat., III, p.928); Gharb 4584 (cat., p.113); 'Abd al-'Aẓīm 194 (cat., p.463); (12) *Sadīd al-afhām*, by Fakhr al-Dīn Aḥmad b. Muḥammad al-Sabī'ī (d. after 854) - see below; (13) *Sharḥ al-mas'ala al-nahbiyya min Qawā'id al-aḥkām*, by Raḍī al-Dīn 'Abd al-Malik b. Isḥāq b. Fatḥān al-Qummī (d. 851-77), edited Qum, 1393 (in my treatise *Khānidān-i Fatḥān*), MS: Majlis 1231 Ṭabāṭabā'ī; (14) by 'Alī b. Hilāl al-Jazā'irī (d. after 909), MS: Mar'ashī 1706 (cat., V, p.99); (15) *Jāmi' al-maqāṣid*, by al-Karakī - see below (16) a second commentary by the same author, MSS: Dānishgāh 1193 (cat., VI, p.2198); Mar'ashī 944 (cat., III, p.131; Wazīrī 434 (cat., I, p.386); Millī 1825 Arabic (cat., X, pp.409-10); (17) *Kashf al-fawā'id*, by al-Qaṭīfī, MS: Majlis 81/2+5

Khu'ī (cat., VII, pp.165, 232-6); (18) *Fawā'id al-Qawāʿid*, by al-Shahīd al-Thānī - see below; (19) by Nūr al-Dīn ʿAlī b. Aḥmad b. Abī Jāmiʿ al-ʿĀmilī (late 10th century), MS: Gharb 75 (cat., p.150); (20) *Jāmiʿ al-fawā'id*, by ʿAbd Allāh b. Ḥusayn al-Tustarī - see below; (21) *Ḥall ʿibāra muʿḍala min al-Qawāʿid ('law kān al-ikhlāl . . .')*, by Bahā' al-Dīn al-ʿĀmilī, MSS: Dānishgāh 8918/13 (cat., V, p.1866); Majlis 1145/2 Khu'ī, 1805/58 (cat.. VII, pp.161-2, IX, p.360); Raḍawī 2358 (cat., II, p.45); ʿAbd al-ʿAẓīm 200/3 (cat., p.443); Princeton 524 New Series (fols. 21b-26b); Marʿashī 2802/2 (cat., VIII, p.4); (22) *Sharḥ mas'ala min masā'il mīrāth al-Qawāʿid*, anonymous (written before 1040), MS: Masjid-i Aʿẓam 3085/8; (23) *Dalā'il al-aḥkām*, by al-Dāmād, edited Tehran, 1401 (in the collection of *Ithnāʿashar risāla li 'l-Dāmād*), MSS: Ḥakīm 1590; Yazd, ʿUlūmī 613/9 (cat. of microfilms of Dānishgāh I, p.702); (24) anonymous (written before 1070), MS: Dānishgāh 7252 (cat., XVI, p.499); (25) Persian and Arabic, by Muḥammad b. Ḥasan al-Shīrwānī (d. 1098), on some sentences of *Qawāʿid*, MSS: Raḍawī (AB, XIV, p.38); Dānishgāh 7008/15-16+18+25, 7091/9-10 (cat., XVI, pp.426-7, 480); Fayḍiyya 1665 (cat., III, pp. 113-14); (26) by ʿAlī b. Muḥammad al-ʿĀmilī, MS: Majlis 5/3 Khu'ī (cat., VII, p.164); (27) by Muḥammad Hādī b. Muḥammad Ṣāliḥ al-Māzandarānī (d. around 1134), MSS: Dānishgāh 1841 (cat., VIII, p.338); Gulpāyigānī 2113 (cat., III, p.165); (28) *Kashf al-lithām*, by al-Fāḍil al-Hindī - see below; (29) *Muntakhab al-fawā'id*, Persian,by Ibrāhīm b. Aḥmad Salāma al-Najafī (d. after 1223), MS: Dānishgāh 5794 (cat., XVI, pp.92-3); (30) *Miftāḥ al-karāma*, by Jawād al-ʿĀmilī - see below; (31) by Kāshif al-Ghiṭā' - see below; (32) by Ṣāḥib al-Maqābis, MS: Khāliṣī (cat., p.126); (33) *Takmilat al-Qawāʿid*, by Muḥammad ʿAlī b. Muḥammad Bāqir al-Hazārjarībī (d. 1246), MS: Raḍawī 6487 (cat., V, p.388); (34) *Shawāriʿ al-anām*, by Muḥammad Jaʿfar b. Sayf al-Dīn al-Astarābādī (d. 1263), MSS: Marʿashī 3073-4, 3885 (cat., VIII, pp.299-300, X, p.270); Fayḍiyya 290 (cat., I, p.155); Sipahsālār 2224/1 (cat., V, pp.145, 257); Ḥakīm 45, (*Nash.*, V, p.423); (35) by Masīḥ b. Muḥammad Saʿīd al-Ṭihrānī (d. 1263), MS: Masjid-i Jāmiʿ 122 (cat., p.326); (36) by ʿAbd al-Ḥusayn b. ʿAlī al-Baraghānī (d. after 1266), MS: Marʿashī (AB, XIV, p.19); (37) *Manāhij al-aḥkām*, by Muḥammad b. Ḥusayn al-Raḍawī, MSS: Raḍawī 6713, 6741 (cat., V, p.459); (38) *Niẓām al-farā'id*, by ʿAlī b. Gul Muḥammad al-Qārpūzābādī al-Zanjānī (d. 1290), edited Tehran, 1332, MSS: Ilāhiyyāt 12b (cat., I, p.682); Fayḍiyya 1280 (cat., I, p.288); Marʿashī 2378 (cat., VI, p.361); (39) by Fakhr al-Dīn Mahdī b. ʿAbd al-Ṣāḥib al-Narāqī (d. 1325), MSS: Dānishgāh 4847-51 (cat., XIV, pp.3866-7); (40) *Jawāmiʿ al-kalām*, by Muḥammad Raḥīm al-Burūjirdī, MSS: Raḍawī 3837-48 (cat., V, pp.298-401); Malik 2151, 2354-5, 2363-77, 2616, 2634-5 (cat., I, pp.207-12); (41) by Muḥammad Ḥasan al-Muẓaffar (d. 1374), edited Najaf, 1378; (42-48) seven anonymous or unidentified commentaries: (a) MS: Berlin Mo.371 (cat., IV, p.240); (b) MS: Dānishgāh 6912 (cat., XVI, p.397); (c) MS: Fayḍiyya 680 (cat., I, p.155); (d) MS: Majlis 81/5 Khu'ī (cat., VII, p.100); (e) MS: Gharb 10431 (cat., p.151); (f) MS: Dār al-Kutub 20308b (cat., I, p.264); (g) MS: Tustariyya 916 (cat., p.804)

- *Tabṣirat al-mutaʿallimīn*
  Editions: Qum, 1398 and many others (see Mushār, cols. 157-8)
  Selected MSS: Nawwāb 15 law (cat., p.451); Raḍawī 2281, 2280, 6432 (cat., II, pp.21-2, V, p.347); Majlis 4953/9, 8834/1 (cat., XIV, p.229); Amīr al-Mu'minīn 512/2 (*Nash.*, V, p.412); Marʿashī 2074/2 (cat., VI, p.87)

Translation: (1) Persian, anonymous (written before 994), MSS: Sinā 1463/2 (cat., II, p.276); Dānishgāh 5466 (cat., XVI, p.17); Tabrīz, Thiqat al-Islām (*Nash.*, V, p.271); (2) Persian, by Muḥyī b. Muḥammad al-Kirmānī (early 10th century), MS: Dānishgāh, microfilm 3020 from a MS in Shīrāz (cat., II, p.28); (3) Persian, anonymous, MS: Maʿārif 1229 (cat., p.83); (4) Persian, by Z. Dhu 'l-Majdayn, edited Tehran, 1368-9; (5) Urdu, by Fayḍ Ḥusayn, edited India (AB, XIV, p.186)
In verse: by Shaykh Ḥusayn, MS: Wazīrī 2476 (cat., IV, p.1309)
Commentaries: (1) *Ṣirāṭ al-yaqīn*, by Aḥmad b. Zayn al-Dīn al-Aḥsā'ī (d. 1241), edited Tabrīz, 1273-6 (in the collection of *Jawāmiʿ al-kalim*); (2) *al-Takmila li 'l-Tabṣira = al-Tadhkira fī sharḥ al-Tabṣira* (AB., IV, pp.23-4) by Muḥammad Jaʿfar b. Muḥammad ʿAlī al-Kirmānshāhī (d. 1254), MSS: Ilāhiyyāt 126-7 Āl Āqā (cat., I, pp. 754, 756-9); Ḥakīm; Marʿashī 3722 (cat., X, p.121); (3) *Qurrat al-ʿayn al-nāẓira*, by Muḥammad Ismāʿīl b. Muḥammad Ibrāhīm al-Fadā'ī al-Kazzāzī (d. 1263), MS: Masjid-i Aʿẓam 9877; (4) by Muḥammad Jaʿfar al-Astarābādī, MS: Marʿashī 3078 (cat., VIII, p.302); (5) *al-Murshid*, by Muḥammad Ḥusayn b. ʿAlī Akbar al-Khwānsārī (d. after 1263), MS: Gulpāyigānī 122 (cat., I, p.116); (6) *al-Mawāhib al-saniyya*, by ʿAlī b. Muḥammad Jaʿfar al-Astarābādī (d. 1315), MS: Marʿashī 3097 (cat., VII, p.319); (7) *al-Āya al-mubṣira*, by ʿAbbās b. Ismāʿīl al-Qazwīnī (d. after 1311), MS: Gulpāyigānī 306/2 (cat., I, p.265); (8) *al-Lamaʿāt al-nayyira*, by al-Khurāsānī - see below; (9) by Ḥusayn b. Muḥammad Ḥasan al-Hamadānī (d. after 1330), MS; Marʿashī 3843 (cat., X, p.228); (10) by Mūsā b. Jaʿfar al-Kirmānshāhī (d. 1340), MS: Kāshānī 75 (cat., p.168); (11) *al-Takmila*, by Ismāʿīl b. ʿAlī Naqī al-Urūmī, edited Tabrīz, 1337-8; (12) by Ḍiyā' al-Dīn al-ʿArāqī - see below; (13) by Muḥsin b. ʿAbd al-Karīm al-Amīn al-ʿĀmilī (d. 1371), edited Damascus, 1343, 1379; (14) *Kifāyat al-muḥaṣṣilīn*, by Muḥammad ʿAlī b. Muḥammad Ṭāhir al-Tabrīzī al-Mudarris (d. 1373), edited Tabrīz, 1353; (15) *Fiqh al-Ṣādiq*, by Muḥammad Ṣādiq al-Ḥusaynī al-Rūḥānī, edited Qum, 1373

- *Tadhkirat al-fuqahā'*
Edition: Tehran, 1272 and others
Selected MSS: Marʿashī 3745 (cat., X, p.141); Ḥuqūq 4j, 24j (cat., p.289); Ḥakīm 318 (cat., I, p.111); Sinā 1117 (cat., II, p.123); Fayḍiyya 441 (cat., I, pp.42-3); Mashhad, Ilāhiyyāt 66 (cat., I, p.39); Dār al-Kutub 20018 (cat., I, p.149); Tabrīz, Qāḍī (*Nash.*, VII, p. 513); India Office 1791 (cat., II, p.307); Būhār 180 Arabic (cat., p.204); Topkapi Sarayi 1143 Arabic (cat., II, pp.747-8)

- *Taḥrīr al-aḥkām al-sharʿiyya*
Edition: Tehran, 1314
Selected MSS: Adabiyyāt 497 Kirmān (cat., p. 78); ʿAbd al-ʿAẓīm 45 (cat., p.63); Majlis 5218, 4007, 233 Ṭabāṭabā'ī (cat., XI, p.10, XVI, p.50); Mashhad, Ilāhiyyāt 53 (cat., I, pp. 28-9); Dānishgāh 1127, 1004 (cat., V, pp.1808-9, 1813); Marʿashī 2613, 3751, 385 (cat., I, p.402, VII, p.205, X, p.144); Malik 1429 (cat., I, pp.109-10); Gulpāyigānī 130, 261-2 (cat., I, pp.132, 227-8); Millī 925 Arabic (cat., VIII, p.425); Kāshān, Āthār-i Millī (*Nash.*, IV, p.355)
Commentaries: (1) anonymous (belonging to 9th century), MS: Shīrāzī (AB, XIII, p.141); (2) by al-Karakī, MS: Majlis 81/4 Khu'ī (cat., VII, p.82); (3) by Ḥusayn b. ʿAbd al-Ṣamad al-ʿĀmilī, MS: Millī 1943/12 Arabic (cat., X, p.621); (4) anonymous, MS: Majlis 81/8 (Cat., VII, p.81)

- *Talkhīṣ al-marām fī maʿrifat al-aḥkām*
MSS: Marʿashī 472 (cat., II, p.77); Majlis 5314, 4253, 4818 (cat., XI,

pp.268-9, XIII, p.229, XVI, pp.228-9); Raḍawī 2275, 2274 (cat., II, p.20)
Commentaris: (1) *Kashf al-ḥaqā'iq*, by Muḥammad b. Bahrām (written before 954), MS: Raḍawī 2532 (cat., II, p.101); (2) *Khazā'in al-aḥkām*, by ʿAlī b. Khalīl al-Ṭihrānī, MSS: Raḍawī 7632-3 (Bīnish, p.741)

IBN DĀWŪD - Taqī al-Dīn Ḥasan b. ʿAlī b. Dāwūd al-Ḥillī (d. after 707):

Al-Tuḥfa al-Saʿidiyya
MS: Matḥaf 896 (cat., I, p.232)

AL-SAYYID ʿAMĪD AL-DĪN:

Kanz al-fawā'id
MSS: Majlis 180-1 Khu'ī, 4387-8 (cat., VII, pp.337-9, XII, pp.94-5); Ḥakīm 107 (*Nash.*, V, p.425); Masjid-i Aʿẓam 9695; Sinā 537 (cat., I, p.343); Dānishgāh 1857, 766 (cat., V, pp.1989-90, VIII, p.450); Gharb 2529 (cat., p.177); Raḍawī 2529 (cat., II, p.99); Būhār 181 Arabic (cat., p.205); Gawharshād 194 (cat., p.380); Sipahsālār 2264 (cat., I, p.466)

FAKHR AL-MUḤAQQIQĪN:

- *Ḥāshiyat al-Irshād*, marginal glosses cn al-ʿAllāma's *Irshād al-adhhān*, compiled by Ẓahīr al-Dīn ʿAlī b. Yūsuf al-Nīlī (d. after 777)
  MSS: Dānishgāh 768, 6929 (cat., V, pp. 1856-8, XVI, p.403); Raḍawī 2377 (cat., II, pp. 50-1, V, p.405); Ḥakīm 105 (*Nawādir*, pp. 48-50); Majlis 1296, 4452 (cat., IV, p.71, XII, p.133); Sipahsālār 237 Mushīr (cat., IV, pp. 140-1); Marʿashī 2474 (cat., VII, pp.65-6)
- *Īḍāḥ al-fawā'id*, a commentary on al-ʿAllāma's *Qawāʿid al-aḥkām*
  Edition: Qum, 1387-9
  Selected MSS: Dānishgāh 706, 5237, 708 (cat., V, p.1785, XV,p.4172); Majlis 95 Ṭabāṭabā'ī, 27 Khu'ī (cat., VII, pp.24-6); Marʿashī 231, 561, 2606, 305, 283, 265 (cat., I, pp.256, 296, 310, 349, II, p.162, VII, pp.188-9); Ḥuqūq 3j (cat., p.258); Nawwāb 204 law (cat., p.450); Raḍawī 2229-30, 7459 (cat., II, p.8; Bīnish, p.612); Iṣfahān, ʿUmūmī 2947 (cat., I, p.184); Sulaymān Khān 90 (cat., p.6); Malik 1241 (cat., I, p.77)

AL-SHAHĪD AL-AWWAL:

- *Al-Bayān*, uncompleted, only the first five chapters on acts of devotion
  Editions: Tehran, 1319, 1322
  Selected MSS: Majlis 2750/1 (cat., IX, p.124); Marʿashī 67/2, 1677 (cat., I, pp. 78-80, V, p.72); Nawwāb 8 law (cat., p.451); Iṣfahān, ʿUmūmī 3055 (cat., I, p.194); Dānishgāh 1800 (cat., VIII, p.372); Tustariyya 841/1 (cat., p.876)
- *Dhikrā al-Shīʿa*, uncompleted, only the chapters on ritual purity and prayer
  Edition: Tehran, 1271
  Selected MSS: Dānishgāh 1906 (cat., VIII, p.521); Zanjān (cat., p.108); Millī 1842 Arabic (cat., X, p.421); Sulaymān Khān 36 (cat., p.12); Ilāhiyyāt 245b (cat., I, p.551); Malik 5340 (cat., I, p.324)
- *Al-Durūs al-sharʿiyya*
  Edition: Tehran, 1269
  Selected MSS: Nawwāb 27 law (cat., p.457); Sinā 807 (cat., II, p.65) Ilāhiyyāt 136j, 13j (cat., I, pp. 549-50); Dānishgāh 6599 (cat., XVI, p.305); Ḥakīm 1230; Marʿashī 1880, 2172, 495, 876 (cat., II, p.104,

III, p.65, V, p.258, VI, p.174); Raḍawī 2401 (cat., II, p.58); Majlis 8825; Los Angeles, M729 (cat., p.222)
Completion: by Jaʿfar b. Aḥmad al-Ḥulaywas al-Ḥusaynī (d. after 836), MS: Marʿashī 3156/1 (cat., VIII, p.388)
Commentaries: (1) by Ḥasan b. al-Ḥusam (mid-9th century), MS: Gharb 4568 (cat., p.123); (2) *Mashāriq al-shumūs*, by Ḥusayn al-Khwānsārī - see below; (3) *Takmilat Mashāriq al-shumūs*, by Raḍī al-Dīn Muḥammad b. Ḥusayn al-Khwānsārī (early 12th century), edited Tehran, 1311, MSS: Fayḍiyya 744/2 (cat., I, p.146, III, p.19); Mashhad, Adabiyyāt 147 Fayyāḍ (cat., p.227); (4) *Inārat al-ṭurūs*, by Bahā' al-Dīn Muḥammad b. Muḥammad Bāqir al-Mukhtārī al-Nā'īnī (d. around 1140), MS: Marʿashī 3382/3 (cat., IX, p.159); (5) by Ṣāḥib al-Riyāḍ, MS: Dānishgāh 7712/1 (cat., XVI, p.982); (6) *Mishkāt al-anwār al-Ḥusayniyya*, by Muḥammad Ibrāhīm b. ʿAlī al-Ḥā'irī al-Qazwīnī (d. after 1229), MSS: Marʿashī 2872 (cat., VIII, p.80); Fayḍiyya 1431 (cat., I, p.247)

- *Ghāyat al-murād*
Editions: Tehran, 1271, 1302
Selected MSS: Nawwāb 262/1 law (cat., p.472); Raḍawī 2497 (cat., II, p.89); Hamadān, Hamrāh (*Nash*., III, p.1693); Farhād Muʿtamid 131 (cat., p.201); Marʿashī 1407, 594 (cat., II, p.186, IV, p.183); Sipahsālār 2467 (cat., I, p.441); Zanjānī 51 (cat., p.207); Dānishgāh 6739 (cat., XVI, p.349); Jaʿfariyya (*Nash*., V, p.435); Majlis 22 Ṭabāṭabā'ī, 3788 (cat., X, p.1774); Ustādī (cat., p.28); Ilāhiyyāt 24j (cat., I, p.615)

- *Al-Lumʿa al-Dimashqiyya*
Edition: Tehran, 1381
Selected MSS: Raḍawī 337 law, 2811, 6207-8 (cat., II, pp.105-6, V, p.486); Marʿashī 2247/1, 959 (cat., III, p.151, VI, p.231; *Nash*., VI, p.388); Dānishgāh 6298 (cat., XVI, pp.236-7); Malik 1054 (cat., I, p.620)
In verse: (1) *al-Tuḥfa al-Qawāmiyya*, by Qawām al-Dīn Muḥammad b. Muḥammad Mahdī al-Sayfī al-Qazwīnī (early 12th century), edited Tehran, 1365-6 (in the margin of al-Shahīd al-Thānī's *al-Rawḍa al-bahiyya*); MSS: Sipahsālār 6156 (cat., III, p.375); Nawwāb 181 law (cat., p.452); Ḥakīm 1523 (cat., I, p.103); Dānishgāh 756 (cat., V, p.1821); Malik 2565 (cat., I, p.122); Gulpāyigānī 278 (cat., I, p. 242); Burūjirdī (AB, XXII, p.369) [Muḥammad Jaʿfar al-Astarābādī wrote a commentary on this poem entitled *Yanābīʿ al-ḥikma fī sharḥ naẓm al-Lumʿa*, MSS: Marʿashī 1541/3, 2011, 3150, 3859 (cat., IV, p.344, VI, p.14, VIII, p.388, X, p.246); Ḥuqūq 114j (cat., p.507); Tehran, Mīnuwī 1 (*Nash*., VI, p.690)]; (2) *al-Hidāya al-Mahdiyya*, by ʿAbd al-Karīm al-Jurjānī (d. after 1304), MS: Ilāhiyyāt 182j (cat., I, p.694); (3) *Lu'lu' al-aḥkām*, by ʿAlī b. Muḥammad Jaʿfar al-Astarābādī [he later wrote a commentary on this poem entitled *Kanz al-durar al-aytām*, MS: Marʿashī 3096 (cat., VIII, p.319)]
Commentaries: (1) *al-Rawḍa al-bahiyya*, by al-Shahīd al-Thānī - see below; (2) *al-Sharīʿa al-Nabawiyya*, anonymous (written before 1250), MS: Dānishgāh 1721 (cat., VII, p.2752); (3) by Muḥammad Riḍā b. Muḥammad Mahdī Āl Baḥr al-ʿUlūm (d. 1253), MS: Ḥuqūq 21b (cat., p.384); (4) *Tawḍīḥ al-mushkilāt*, by Muḥammad Shafīʿ b. Muḥammad Ḥusayn (mid-13th century), MS: Marʿashī 2408 (cat., VII, pp.9-10); (5) by Muḥammad b. Maʿṣūm al-Raḍawī al-Qaṣīr (d. 1255), MSS: Raḍawī 7155 (cat., V, p.460); Malik 816 (cat., I, p.118); (6) *al-Tuḥfa al-Gharawiyya*, by Khiḍr b. Shallāl al-ʿAfkāwī (d. 1255), MSS: Marʿashī 2206 (cat., VI, p.199); Dār al-Kutub (see its general catalogue, *Fihris al-kutub al-ʿArabiyya*, I, p.569); Majlis 39-45 Khu'ī

(cat., VII, pp.36-42); (7) *Kashf al-niqāb*, by Masīḥ b. Muḥammad Saʿīd al-Ṭihrānī, MSS: Nawwāb 44 law (cat., p.461); Masjidi-i Jāmiʿ 122,160-1 (cat., I, p.335); (8) by Muḥammad b. Ḥusayn al-Raḍawī MS: Raḍawī 6713 (cat., V, p.461); (9) *al-Anwār al-Gharawiyya = al-Mishkāt al-Gharawiyya*, by Muḥammad Jawād b. Taqī al-Najafī Mullā Kitāb (d. after 1267), MSS: Maʿhad 1293-4 (cat., p.112); Dānishgāh 1305 (cat., VII, p.2786); Marʿashī 1518 (cat., IV, pp.318-19); Raḍawī 7760-9 (Bīnish, p. 883); Ustādī (cat., p.25); (10) by Muḥammad Mahdī al-Kalbāsī, MS: Raḍawī 7759 (Bīnish, p.883); (11) by Muḥammad ʿAlī al-Shaftī (d. 1282), MS: Marʿashī 1995/4 (cat., V, p.367); (12) *al-Durra al-Ḥā'iriyya*, by ʿAlī Naqī b. Ḥasan al-Ṭabāṭabā'ī (d. 1289), MS: Majlis 4302 (cat., XI, pp.315-16); (13) *Munyat al-albāb*, anonymous (belonging to 13th century), MS: Majlis 4455 (cat., XII, p.135); (14) *al-Ghurra al-Gharawiyya*, by Mullā ʿAlī (written in 1303), MS: Burūjirdī (AB, XVI, p.34); (15) by Muḥammad ʿAlī al-Raḍawī, MS: Raḍawī 6524 (cat., V, p.490); (16-17) two anonymous or unidentified commentaries: (a) MS: Majlis 3936/18 (cat., X, p.2054); (b) MS: Ustādī (cat., pp.15-16)

IBN AL-MUTAWWIJ:

- *Kifāyat al-ṭālibīn*
  MSS: Raḍawī 2805, 7217 (cat., II, p.102, V, pp.482-4); Marʿashī (AB, XVIII, p.93)
- *Majmaʿ al-gharā'ib*
  MS: Raḍawī 2495 (cat., II, pp.88-9)

AL-MIQDĀD

Al-Tanqīḥ al-rā'iʿ
Edition: Qum, 1404
Selected MSS: Raḍawī 2271-3, 6645, 7528 (cat., II, p.19, V, 389); Malik 1302, 2458 (cat., I, p.176): Marʿashī 3566, 3567, 1725, 2701, 3173 (cat., V, p.113, VII, p.272, VIII, p.399, IX, pp.354-5); Sinā 1390 (cat., II, p.243); Ilāhiyyāt 95, 49 (cat., I, p.759); Dānishgāh 6857, 4886 (cat., XIV, p.3937, XVI, p.383); Majlis 55 Khu'ī, 499 Ṭabāṭabā'ī, 5509 (cat., VII, pp.5405, XVI, p.409); Nawwāb 10 law (cat., p.453); Ḥakīm 81, 516 (cat., I, pp.137-8; *Nawādir*, pp.35-6); Gawharshād 269, 1866 (cat., pp. 244-5); Farhād Muʿtamid 38 (cat., p.169); Ustādī (cat., p.10); Bankipore 836 (cat. Arabic, I, p.83); Princeton 545 New Series; Shīrāz, Dānishgāh
Commentary: by al-Dāmād, MS: Gawharshād 1866 in the margin (cat., p.245)

IBN FAHD:

- *Al-Muhadhdhab al-bāriʿ*
  MSS: Dānishgāh 6736, 2372, 711, 7238 (cat., V, p.2078, IX, p.969, XVI, pp.347-8, 496); Marʿashī 275, 3553, 2190, 2972 (cat., I, p.304, IV, pp.185-6, VII, p.152, IX, pp.344-5); Raḍawī 8034, 2599, 8033 (cat., II, p.120; Bīnish, p.1052); Malik 1182(cat., I, p.759); Fayḍiyya 214, 369 (cat., I, pp. 285-6); Zanjānī 142, 66 (cat., pp.212, 249); Vatican 1717 Arabic (cat., II, p.105); Nawwāb law 169, 60 (cat., p.480); Najaf, Madrasat al-Sayyid (AB, XXIII, p.293); Matḥaf 1633 (cat., p.260); Zanjān (cat., p.167); Majlis 5510, 4397, 233 Khu'ī (cat., VII, p.238, XII, p.101, XVI, p.410); Princeton 2088 New Series; Nūrbakhsh 164/2 (cat., I, p.176); Gharb 1340 (cat., p.200); Wazīrī 91/2 (cat., I, p.113); Ilāhiyyāt 193b (cat., I, p.680); Ḥujjatiyya 511 (cat., p.94); Gulpāyigānī 401 (cat., II, pp.185-6); Masjid-i Aʿẓam

7416, 9176, 9711; Rawḍātī (cat., I, pp. 267 ff); Yazd, ʿUlūmī (*Nash.*, IV, p.450); Tabrīz, Qāḍī (ibid., VII, p.523); Shīrāz, Dānishgāh

- *Al-Muḥarrar*
MSS: Raḍawī 7919 (Bīnish, p.993); Los Angeles M93/6 (cat., p.661)

- *Al-Mūjaz*
MSS: Majlis 2759/2 (cat., IX, pp.124-5); Princeton 3992/1 Yahuda (cat., p.138); Wazīrī 949/2 (cat., II, p.779); Gawharshād 947 (cat., p.420); Gulpāyigānī 682/1 (cat., II, p.201); Dānishgāh 1476/11, 5396/2 (cat., VIII, p.128, XV, p.4237); India Office 1808 (cat., II, pp.312-13); Raḍawī 8028 (Bīnish, p.1051)
Commentary: *Kashf al-iltibās*, by Mufliḥ al-Ṣaymarī - see below

- *Al-Muqtaṣar*
MSS: Los Angeles M930/1 (cat., p.700); Marʿashī 2524 (cat., VII, p.110); Ḥuqūq 62/1d (cat., p.477); Raḍawī 2848, 8002, 2648 (cat., II, p.135, V, p.514; Bīnish, p.1032); Dānishgāh 1158/1 (cat., V, pp.2067-8); Malik 2840 (cat., I, p.725)

IBN FAHD AL-AḤSĀʾĪ - Shihāb al-Dīn Aḥmad b. Muḥammad b. Fahd (d. 840):

Khulāṣat al-Tanqīḥ, a commentary on al-ʿAllāma's *Irshād al-adhhān*
MSS: Ḥakīm 302 (*Nash.*, V, p.424); Dānishgāh 2621/4 (cat., IX, p.1496)

AL-QAṬṬĀN:

Maʿālim al-dīn fī fiqh Āl Yāsīn
MSS: Dānishgāh 1821, 1157 (cat., V, pp.2056-7, VII, p.417); Marʿashī 399 (cat., I, p.414); Malik 781 (cat., I, p.696); Rasht 227M (cat., p.1175)
Commentary: *Dhakhāʾir al-mujtahidīn*, by Abu ʾl-Majd Riḍā b. Muḥammad Ḥusayn al-Iṣfahānī (d. 1362), MS: Rawḍātī (see AB, X, pp. 7, 18)

IBN ṬAYY - Abu ʾl-Qāsim ʿAlī b. ʿAlī b. Muḥammad al-Faqʿānī al-ʿAmilī (d. 855):
Al-Masāʾil al-fiqhiyya = Masāʾil Ibn Ṭayy
MSS: Majlis 4566/12 (cat., XII, pp.263-4); Dānishgāh 1227, 5396/10 (cat., VI, pp. 2457-60, XV, p.4238); ʿAbd al-ʿAẓīm 235/1 (cat., p. 445)

MUFLIḤ AL-ṢAYMARĪ:

- *Ghāyat al-marām*, a commentary on al-Muḥaqqiq's *Sharāʾiʿ al-Islām*
MSS: Gulpāyigānī 155 (cat., I, p.143); Dānishgāh 780, 7748 (cat., V, pp.1952-4, XVI, p.688); Mashhad, Shānachī (*Nash.*, V, p.599); Gawharshād 153, 58 (cat., p.355); Raḍawī 2790, 6518 (cat., V, p. 468); Ḥakīm 109 (*Nash.*, V, p.425); Majlis 4224 (cat., XI, p.243); Majid-i Aʿẓam 375.

- *Kashf al-iltibās*, a commentary on Ibn Fahd's *al-Mūjaz*
MSS: Marʿashī 2830, 3693, 939, 1811 (cat., III, p.127, V, p.195, VIII, p.36, X, p.91); Tabrīz, Qāḍī (*Nash.*, VII, p.519); Majlis 3973, 5946 (cat., X, p.2112, XVII, p.332); Malik 1224, 2733 (cat., I, p.591); India Office 1089 (cat., I, p.313); Dānishgāh 6788 (cat., XVI, p.360)

AL-KARAKĪ:

- *Fawāʾid al-Sharāʾiʿ*, a commentary on al-Muḥaqqiq's *Sharāʾiʿ al-Islām*

MSS: Dānishgāh 703, 7012, 7050, 1708, 7175 (cat., V, p.1934, XVI, pp.428, 439, 456, 474); Sipahsālār 2600 (cat., I, p.393); Ḥujjatiyya 592 (cat., p.50); Nawwāb law 21, 26 (cat., p.455); Ḥakīm 1640, 1642, 540; Marʿashī 1280/1, 2509, 3352, 1155 (cat., III, p.327, IV, p.80, VII, p.95, IX, p.129); Majlis 667 Ṭabāṭabāʾī, 615 Ṭabāṭabāʾī, 5356, 8783, 3534 (cat., X, pp.1492-3, XVI, p.266); Tustariyya (AB, VI, p.107); Gulpāyigānī 47, 2237 (cat., I, p.57, III, p.204); Āstāna 5788 (cat., p.107); Millī, Arabic 1516, 1381 (cat., IX, p.380, X, p.12); Gawharshād 965, 551 (cat., p.269); ʿAbd al-ʿAẓīm 87 (cat., p.75); Malik 2075, 2700 (cat., I, p.229); Los Angeles M87 (cat., p.199); Princeton 695 New Series; India Office 1788 (cat., II, p.306); Dār al-Kutub 19909, 29938 (cat., I, pp.248, 266); Masjid-i Aʿẓam 1290; Fayḍiyya 1418, 1964 (cat., I, p.82); Wazīrī 1902, 2420 (cat., III, p.1090, IV, p.1288); Gharb, 4 MSS (cat., p.100); Raḍawī, 7 MSS (cat., II, pp.45-6, 50; Bīnish, pp.713, 730)

- *Jāmiʿ al-maqāṣid*, an uncompleted commentary on al-ʿAllāma's *Qawāʾid al-aḥkām*, from the beginning to the chapter on marriage
  Edition: Tehran, 1272
  Selected MSS: Majlis 4310 (cat., XII, p.4); Nawwāb law 211, 16 (cat., p.454); Millī 1156 Arabic (cat., IX, p.145); Zanjānī 23/1 (cat., p.198); Gawharshād 1337, 1865 (cat., p.249); Sipahsālār 2538 (cat., I, p.385); Burūjirdī (cat., p.13); Manchester 783 (cat., p.1146); India Office 1803 (cat., I, p.311); Harvard (*Nash*., IX, p.351); Dār al-Kutub 19895b, 20306b (cat., I, p.311); Los Angeles M100 (cat., p.186)
  Commentaries: (1) by Luṭf Allāh b. ʿAbd al-Karīm al-Maysī al-ʿĀmilī (d. 1033), MSS: Zanjānī 23/1 (cat., p.198); Millī 1156 Arabic (cat., IX, p.145); (2) by ʿA. Ṭ. (ʿAbd al-Muṭṭalib?), written after 1081, MS: Dānishgāh 2347 (cat., IX, p.959)

- *Taʿlīq al-Irshād*, a commentary on al-ʿAllāma's *Irshād al-adhhān*
  MSS: Gawharshād 772 (cat., p.256); Majlis 7782, 5638, 5357, 80 Khuʾī (cat., VII, p.79, XVI, p.267, XVII, pp.9405); Ilāhiyyāt 210 Āl Āqā (cat., I, p.762); Raḍawī 2376, and 6 other MSS (cat., II, pp.50-2; Bīnish, pp. 698, 700); Dānishgāh 4166, 6893, 785, 7185, 7684 (cat., V, pp.1858-9, XIII, pp.3134-5, XVI, pp.390, 478, 670); Bengal 633, 634 (cat., I, pp.312-13); Gulpāyigānī 41 (cat., I, p.48); Iṣfahān, ʿUmūmī 3073 (cat., I, p.218); Nujūmī (cat., p.265); Sipahsālār 2600/1, 2488/1 (cat., I, pp.396-7, IV, pp.141-2); Tustariyya 159/1 (cat., p.837); al-Imām al-Ṣādiq (AB, VI, p.16); Khayrāt Khān 53/1, 85/1 (cat., pp.1735-6, 1790); ʿAbd al-ʿAẓīm 130/2 (cat., p.439); Marʿashī 79 (cat., I, p.97); Fayḍiyya 1146 (cat., I, p.72); Wazīrī 1291 (cat., III, p.918); Ustādī (cat., p.13); Rasht 43/1 (cat., p.1193); Miftāḥ 228 (cat., p.141); Ḥakīm 1686; Tarbiyat 36 (cat., p.36); Dār al-Kutub 20038b, 20307b (cat., I, pp.243, 265)

AL-SHAHĪD AL-THĀNĪ:

- *Fawāʾid al-Qawāʿid*, a commentary on al-ʿAllāma's *Qawāʿid al-aḥkām*
  MSS: Wazīrī 1585 (cat., III, p.993); Majlis 1307 (cat., IV, pp.78-90); Zanjān (cat., p.104); Khāliṣī (cat., p.95); Iṣfahān, Dānishgāh 16917/2 (cat., p.923); Tabrīz, Qāḍī (*Nash*., VII, p.517); Qazwīn, Hājj Sayyid Jawādī (ibid., V, p.343)

- *Ḥāshiyat al-Sharāʾiʿ*, a commentary on al-Muḥaqqiq's *Sharāʾiʿ al-Islām*
  MSS: Majlis 5354/1, 4360 (cat., XII, p.73, XVI, p.264); Bankipore 847 (cat. Arabic, I, p.84); Tabrīz, Millī 3349 (cat., I, p.404); Nawwāb, 25 law (cat., p.455); Shīrāzī (AB, VI, pp.106-7)

Masālik al-afhām, another commentary on al-Muḥaqqiq's *Sharā'i' al-Islām*
Editions: Tehran, 1273 and others (see Mushār, cols. 838-9)
Selected MSS: Mar'ashī 1328, 1205, 1621 (cat., IV, pp.6, 111-12, V, pp.25-6); Majlis 4646 (cat., XIII, pp.34-5); Dānishgāh 762, 1121 (cat., V, pp.2037-9); Wazīrī 24 (cat., I, p.40); 'Abd al-'Aẓīm 197 (cat., p.476); Nawwāb 64 law (cat., p.476)
Commentaries: (1) by al-Sabzawārī, MS: Mar'ashī 1264 (cat.,IV, pp.69-70); (2) by Ḥaydar 'Alī b. Muḥammad al-Shīrwānī (early 12th century), MS: Khāliṣī (cat., p.60); (3) by al-Bihbahānī, MS: Gawharshād 190 (cat., pp.280-1); (4) *al-Fadhālik*, by al-Kirmānshāhī - see below

Rawḍ al-jinān, an uncompleted commentary on al-'Allāma's *Irshād al-adhhān*, only the chapters on ritual purity and prayer
Editions: Tehran, 1303, 1307
Selected MSS: Raḍawī 2770 (cat., V, p.449); Sinā 502 (cat., I, p. 293); Nawwāb 28 law (cat., p.457)

Al-Rawḍa al-bahiyya, a commentary on al-Shahīd al-Awwal's *Al-Lum'a al-Dimashqiyya*
Editions: Najaf, 1386-90 and others (see Mushār, cols. 496-8)
Selected MSS: Dānishgāh 709 (cat., V, pp. 1908-16); Āṣafiyya 11 Shī'ī law (cat., II, pp. 239-40); Mathaf 262, 276 (cat., I, pp.240-2); Majlis 4886 (cat., XVIV, pp.2809); Āstāna 5956 (cat., p.123).
Commentaries: (1) *Kashf al-rumūz al-khafiyya*, by Muḥammad b. Ḥasan al-'Āmilī (d. 1030), MS: Raḍawī 2354-6, 6517, 7142 (cat., II, p.44, V, p.407; Bīnish, pp.712,730); Majlis 3362/2 (cat., X, p.1188); Wazīrī 4 (cat., I, pp.4-5); (2) by Aḥmad b. Muḥammad al-Tūnī (d. after 1097), edited Tabrīz, 1291 and others (all in the margin of *al-Rawḍa al-bahiyya*), selected MSS: Majlis 3362/1 (cat., X, p.1187); Khayrāt Khān 57 (cat., p. 1738); Āstāna 6036 (cat., p.107); Tabrīz, Qāḍī (*Nash.*, VII, p.513); (3) by 'Abd al-Ḥusayn b. Abi 'l-Ḥasan al-'Āṣī (d. after 1081), MS: Khāliṣī (cat., p.83); (4) by Muḥammad b. Qāsim al-Iṣfahānī al-Dīlmāj (d. afer 1084), partly edited (Mushār, col. 282), MSS: Fayḍiyya (cat., I, p.81); Ilāhiyyāt 283 Āl Āqā (cat., I, p.763); (5) by Ibrāhīm b. Ḥusayn al-Mar'ashī Khalīfa Sulṭān (d. 1098), edited Tabrīz, 1291 and others (all in the margin of *al-Rawḍa al-bahiyya*), MSS: Mar'ashī 3060/1 (cat., VIII, p.281); Dānishgāh 4107/2 (cat., XIII, p.3085); Majlis 3362/3 (cat., X, pp.1188-9); (6) by Fakhr al-Dīn Muḥammad al-Mūsawī (late 11th century ?), MS: Mar'ashī 2016/1 (cat., VI, p.17); (7) by Abū Ṭālib b. Mīrza Beg al-Mūsawī al-Findiriskī (11th century ?), MS: Dānishgāh 874/1 (cat., III, p.134, V, pp.1863-4); (8) *al-Zahrāt al-dhawiyya*, by 'Alī b. Muḥammad al-'Āmilī, edited Tabrīz, 1291 and others (all in the margin of *al-Rawḍa al-bahiyya*), MSS: Āstāna 6202/1 (cat., p.185); Gharb 1085/1, 4511 (cat., pp.135-6, 287); Ilāhiyyāt 91/1d (cat., I, p.233); Āṣafiyya 90-1 Shī'ī law (cat., I, pp. 241-2); Dānishgāh 6643 (cat., XVI, p.324); Gulpāyigānī 277 (cat., I, p.241); (9) *al-Radd 'alā i'tirāḍāt Khalīfa Sulṭān 'ala 'l-Rawḍa al-bahiyya*, by the same author, MSS: Majlis 1295 (cat., IV, pp.70-1); Ilāhiyyāt 91/2d (cat., I, p.233); Āstāna 6202/1 (cat., p.185); Dānishgāh 7725/2 (cat., XVI, p.684); Raḍawī 144 law (cat., II, p.45); (10) by Ja'far b. 'Abd Allāh al-Ḥuwayzī al-Qāḍī (d. 1115), MSS: Majlis 89 Khu'ī (cat., VII, pp.89-90); Sipahsālār 2558 (cat., I, p.396); Malik 2243 (cat., I, p.226); Dānishgāh 7039 (cat. XVI, p.435); Gulpāyigānī 1107 (cat., II, p.56); Wazīrī 1193, 1548 (cat., III, pp.889-90, 987); (11) by Muḥammad Ibrāhīm b. Muḥammad Ma'ṣūm al-Ḥusaynī al-Qazwīnī (d. 1149), MS: Gharb 188/28-9 (cat., p.224); (12) anonymous (written

before 1119), MS: Malik 6357 (cat., I, p.225); (13) by Jamāl al-Dīn al-Khwānsārī - see below; (14) *al-Manāhij al-sawiyya*, by al-Fāḍil al-Hindī - see below; (15) *Ta'līq 'alā mabḥath al-zawāl min al-Rawḍa al-bahiyya*, by Aḥmad b. Ibrāhīm al-Baḥrānī - see below, chapter 6; (16) *Al-'Ayn fī ta'āruḍ ḥaqqay al-mutabāya'ayn*, by al-Mukhtārī - see below, chapter 6; (17) by Muḥammad b. Muḥammad Ṣāliḥ al-Ḥusaynī al-Khwātūnābādī (d. 1148), MSS: Raḍawī 6495 (cat., V, p.409); Adabiyyāt 153 Kirmān (cat., p. 84); (18) by Muḥammad Rafī' b. Faraj al-Gīlānī (d. after 1150), MS: Malik 1066 (cat., I, p. 228); (19) *Ishārāt al-fiqh*, by Ṣadr al-Dīn Muḥammad b. Muḥammad Naṣīr al-Ṭabāṭabā'ī al-Yazdī (d. 1154), MS: Wazīrī 320/2 (cat., I, p.303); (20) *al-Ibāna al-marḍiyya*, by Muḥammad Ṣāliḥ b. Muḥammad Sa'īd al-Khalkhālī (d. 1175), edited Tehran, 1313, MSS: Mar'ashī 2786 (cat., VII, pp.349-50); Dānishgāh 5830 (cat., XVI, p.100); (21) *Sharḥ 'ibāra mushkilla fī mabḥath ṣalāt al-mayyit*, by Ḥusayn b. Abi 'l-Qāsim al-Khwānsārī (d. 1191), edited Iṣfahān, 1377 (together with Muḥammad Bāqir al-Khwāsārī's *al-Nahriyya*); (22) *Sharḥ 'ibāra mushkila fī mabḥath ṣalāt al-khawf*, by the same author, MS: Sinā 1135/5 (cat., I, p.129); (23) by Muḥammad Ṣādiq (12th century), MS: Gharb 77 (cat., p.131); (24) *al-Mufradāt al-fāriqa*, by 'Abd al-Qādir b. Ṣadr al-Dīn al-Ḥusaynī al-Māzandarānī, MS: Dānishgāh 2865/2 (cat., X, p.1712); (25) by Ḥusayn al-Qazwīnī, MS: Millī 1945/2 Arabic (cat., X, p.624); (26) by al-Kirmānshāhī, MSS: Raḍawī 179 law, 7141 (cat., II, p.54, V, p.410); Gawharshād 1972 (cat., p.267); Khayrāt Khān 56 (cat., pp.1738-9); Mashhad, Ilāhiyyāt 1080, 1099 (cat., II, pp.230, 240); Los Angeles M92 (cat., p.198); (27) by Ismā'īl b. Khudādād al-Hazārjarībī al-Astarābādī (d. after 1226), MSS: Dānishgāh 7291, 7747 (cat., XVI, pp.506, 688); (28) by 'Abd Allāh b. Muḥammad Taqī al-Hazārjarībī al-Tīlakī (d. after 1233), MS: Masjid-i A'ẓam 314; (29) by Muḥammad Mahdī b. Muḥammad Ja'far al-Mūsawī (d. after 1237), MS: Fayḍiyya 186 (cat., I, p.114); (30) by Muḥammad Ja'far b. Ṣafar al-Hamadānī (d. 1238), MS: Gharb 77 (cat., p.131); (31) by Mūsā b. Ja'far Āl Kāshif al-Ghiṭā' (d.1243), MSS: Khayrāt Khān 21/2, 61/1 (cat., pp.1779-80, 1784); (32) by Muḥammad Riḍā Āl Baḥr al-'Ulūm, MS: Ḥuqūq 21b (cat., p.384); (33) *Makhzan al-asrār al-fiqhiyya*, by Muḥammad 'Ali al-Hazārjarībī, MSS: Gulpāyigānī 185, 404, 457 (cat., I, p.168, II, pp.163-4); Wazīrī 641 (cat., II, p.544); Dānishgāh 6628 (cat., XVI, p.320); Raḍawī 7924 (Bīnish, p.997); Khayrāt Khān 97/1 (cat., p.1791); Mar'ashī 2469 (cat., VII, pp.61-2); Los Angeles M944 (cat., p.349); (34) by 'Alī Āl Kāshif al-Ghiṭā' - see below, chapter 6; (35) by 'Abd Allāh b. Muḥammad Ja'far al-Kirmānshāhī (d. after 1253), MS: Ilāhiyyāt 819/7 d (cat., II, p.21); (36) *Faṣl al-khiṭāb al-Ibrāhīmiyya*, by Ibrāhīm b. Muḥammad Ḥusayn al-Madanī al-Shīrāzī (d. around 1255), MS: Tarbiyat 62 (cat., p.57); (37) *Risāla-yi sahla dar sharḥ-i qibla*, Persian, by 'Alī Akbar b. 'Alī b. Muḥammad Ismā'īl (d. after 1255), MS: Dānishgāh 3703 (cat., XII, p.2707); (38) by Muḥammad al-Nā'īnī (d. after 1259), MS: Sipahsālār 6028 (cat., IV, p.202); (39) *Majma' al-ārā'*, by Muḥammad J'far al-Astarābādī, MSS: Mar'ashī 3082/2 3850 (cat., VIII, p.307, X, p.236); Los Angeles M103/4 (cat., p.664); (40) by Masīḥ b. Muḥammad Sa'īd al-Ṭihrānī, MS: Nawwāb 44 law (cat., p.461); (41) by Muḥammad Riḍā b. 'Alī Sharīf al-Gūgadī al-Gulpāyigānī (d. after 1264), MS: Dānishgāh 1953 (cat., VIII, p.568); (42) *Lama'āt*, Persian, by Muḥammad b. Muqīm al-Bārfurūshī al-Māzandarānī (d. after 1264), MS: Fayḍiyya 1559 (cat., II, p.89); (43) *al-Lawāmi'*, by the same author, MSS: Mar'ashī 2401, 2717 (cat., VII, pp. 3, 283); (44) by Muḥammad Bāqir al-Gulpāyigānī (d. after 1267), MS: Gulpāyigānī 234 (cat., I, p.201); (45) *Minhāj al-umma*, by Naṣīr al-Dīn b. Muḥammad al-Narāqī (d. 1273), MSS: Nawwāb 57-9 (cat., p.479); (46) by Muḥammad Ja'far b. Muḥammad Ṣafī al-Ābāda'ī (d. 1280), MS: Burūjirdī (AB, XVI, p.292); (47) by Muḥammad Ibrāhīm al-Qishlāqī, MS: Fayḍiyya 108 (cat., I, p.114); (48) *al-Ḥadīqa al-Najafiyya*, by Muḥammad Taqī b. Ḥusayn 'Alī al-Harawī al-Iṣfahānī (d. 1299), MSS: Gawharshād 1602 (cat., p.288); Ilāhiyyāt 769d, 603d (cat., I, p.541); Mar'ashī 2018 (cat., VI, pp.19-20); Najaf, Ḥusayniyyat Kāshif al-Ghiṭā' (AB, VI, p.390); Tabrīz, Qāḍī (ibid.); (49) *Ṣafā' al-rawḍa*, by Muḥammad Ṣāliḥ b. Ḥasan al-Mūsawī al-Dāmād (d. 1301), MSS: Mar'ashī 3140 (cat., VIII, p.369-70); Raḍawī 6851 (cat., V, p.457); (50) by Ḥasan b. Aḥmad al-Ḥusaynī al-Gīlānī (d. after 1306), MS: Fayḍiyya 323 (cat., I, p.116); (51) *al-Ta'līqa al-anīqa*, by Muḥammad 'Abbās b. 'Alī Akbar al-Mūsawī al-Tustarī al-Laknawī (d. 1306), edited Locknow, 1339 (cat. of Āṣafiyya, IV, p.477); (52) *Ḥadīqat al-Rawḍa = Minhāj al-najāḥ*, by Muḥammad 'Alī b. Aḥmad al-Qarāchadāghī (d. 1310), edited Tabrīz, 1291 and others (all in the margin of *al-Rawḍa al-bayiyya*); (53) by Jawād b. 'Abd al-Ḥusayn al-Najafī (d. 1311), MS: Majlis 4331 (cat., XII, p.22); (54) by Muḥammad 'Alī al-Raḍawī, MS: Raḍawī 6587 (cat., V, p.410); (55) by Muḥammad Ṭāhir b. Ismā'īl al-Mūsawī al-Dizfūlī (d. after 1311), MS: Tustariyya (AB, XIII, pp.293-4); (56) *al-Maqāṣid al-'aliyya*, by 'Alī b. Muḥammad al-A'rajī (d. after 1322), MSS: Khāliṣī (cat., pp.120-2); (57) *Minhāj al-najāt*, by 'Alī b. 'Abd Allāh al-'Alyārī (d. 1327), edited Tabrīz, 1309, 1340; (58) *Minhāj al-milla*, by the same author, MS: Mar'ashī (AB, XXIII, p.176); (59) by Muḥammad 'Alī b. Muḥammad Naṣīr al-Gīlānī al-Mudarris (d.1334), partly edited Tehran, 1323, MS: Mar'ashī 2078/1 (cat., VI, p.91); (60) by Muḥammad Ḥusayn b. Muḥammad Qāsim al-Qumsha'ī (d. 1336), MSS: Tustariyya 819-20 (cat., p.800); (61) Ḥasan b. Aḥmad al-Ḥusaynī al-Kāshānī (d. 1342), MS: Raḍawī 7140 (cat., V, p.411); (62) *al-Ḥāshiya al-raḍiyya*, by Amjad Ḥusayn b. Munawwar 'Alī Allāhābādī (d. after 1343), edited India, 1343; (63) *Sirāj al-umma*, by Muḥammad Ḥasan b. Ṣafar 'Alī al-Bārfurūshī (d. 1345), edited Tehran, 1324-6; (64) by Murtaḍā al-Ḥusaynī al-Sidihī al-Iṣfahānī, MS: Mar'ashī (cat. of microfilms of Dānishgāh, II, p.174); (65) by Muḥammad Ja'far b. Muḥammad Ṭāhir, MSS: Majlis 271 Ṭabāṭabā'ī; (66) by 'Abd al-Ghanī, MS: Tustariyya (AB, XIV, p.38); (67-75) nine anonymous or unidentified commentaries: (a) MS: Dānishgāh 6996/1 (cat., XVI, p.423); (b) MS: Malik 2545 (cat., I, p.225); (c) MS: Raḍawī 180 law (cat., II, pp.54-5); (d) MS: Fayḍiyya 60 (cat., I, p.81); (e) MS: Raḍawiyya 49/2 (cat., p.48); (f) MS: Dānishgāh 2526/2 (cat., IX, p.1326); (g) Fayḍiyya 307 (cat., I, p.81); (h) MS: Mar'ashī 2078/2 (cat., VI, p.92); (i) MS: Majlis 88/2 Khu'ī (cat., VII, p.88)

AL-ARDABĪLĪ:

Majma' al-fā'ida wa 'l-burhān, a commentary on al-'Allāma's *Irshād al-adhhān*
Editions: Tehran, 1274; Qum, 1403-
Selected MSS: Mar'ashī 1852(cat., V, pp.237-8); Majlis 3377-8 (cat., X, pp.1226-8); Dānishgāh 6717 (cat., XVI, p.344); Malik 2195 (cat., I, p.642); Raḍawī, 3 MSS (cat., II, pp.124-5); Millī, 4 MSS (cat., VII, pp. 49, 147, 472); Gulpāyigānī, 3 MSS (cat., II, pp.159-160); Kāshān, Bihniyā (*Rāhnamāy-i kitāb*, XXI, p.695)
Commentaries: (1) by al-Bihbahānī, MSS: Majlis 4451 (cat., XII, p.133); Dānishgāh 770/3 (cat., V, pp.1866-9); Wazīri 23/1 (cat., I, p.36); Khayrāt Khān 61/2 (cat., p.1785); Ilāhiyyāt 153 Āl Āqā (cat., I, p.766); Tustariyya 672/2 (cat., p.873); (2) anonymous; Majlis

135 Khu'ī (cat., VII, p.145); (3) anonymous, MS: Dānishgāh 742 in margin (cat., V, pp.2001-2)

ṢĀḤIB AL-MADĀRIK:

- *Hidāyat al-ṭālibīn = Ghāyat al-marām*, a commentary on al-Muḥaqqiq's *al-Mukhtaṣar al-nāfiʿ*
  MSS: Dānishgāh 1471, 6598 (cat., VIII, p.122, XVI, p.304); Ḥakīm 106 (*Nash*., V, p.425); Jaʿfariyya (ibid., V, p.436); Fayḍiyya 101 (cat., I, pp. 192-3); Ilāhiyyāt 54/2b (cat., I, p.128); Raḍawī 7586 (cat., V, p.461); Majlis 3370, 4641, 5310 (cat., X, pp.1213-15, XIII, p.31, XVI, p.226); Marʿashī 546 (cat., II, p.148); Wazīrī 1691 (cat., III, p. 1022); Malik 2897 (cat., I, p.442); Masjid-i Jāmiʿ 144 (cat., p.332); Congress 38 Arabic (cat., pp.30-1)
  Commentary: by al-Bihbahānī, MS: Rawḍātī (AB, XX, p.72)

- *Madārik al-aḥkām*, a commentary on the section on acts of devotion of al-Muḥaqqiq's *Sharāʾiʿ al-Islām*
  Editions: Tehran, 1268, 1274, 1298, 1322
  Selected MSS: Raḍawī 7931 (cat., V, p.496); Majlis 4202, 3374, 193 Khu'ī (cat., VII, p.339, X, p.1224, XI, pp.219-20); Nawwāb 61-2 law, 97 law (cat., p.475); Gharb 4510 (cat., p.184); Khāliṣī (cat., pp. 106-7); Adabiyyāt 43 Kirmān (cat., p.105); Matḥaf 2900, 3886 (cat., I, p.253); Būhār 183 Arabic (cat., p.207); Berlin Ldg.523 (cat., IV, p.66); Harvard (*Nash*., IX, p.380)
  Commentaries: (1) by Rafīʿ al-Dīn al-Nā'īnī, MS: Marʿashī 3309 (cat., IX, pp. 90-1); (2) by Ibrāhīm b. Ḥusayn al-Marʿashī Khalīfa Sulṭān, MS: Marʿashī 3060/2 (cat., VIII, pp.281-2); (3) by Muḥammad Ibrāhīm b. Muḥammad Maʿṣūm al-Ḥusaynī al-Qazwīnī, MS: Gharb 233 (cat., p.116); (4) by Muḥammad Ismāʿīl b. Ḥusayn al-Khwājū'ī (d. 1173), MSS: Miftāḥ 205, 1036 (cat., p.144); (5) *Tadāruk al-Madārik*, by Ṣāḥib al-Ḥadā'iq, MSS: Najlis 47/2 Khu'ī (cat., VII, pp.43-4); Gulpāyigānī 1870/8 (cat., III, p.91); (6) by al-Bihbahānī, edited Tehran, 1268, 1322 (both together with *Madārik al-aḥkām*), MSS: Sipahsālār 2653 (cat., IV, p.267); Malik 2587 (cat., I, p.246); Dānishgāh 6809 (cat., XVI, p.365); Raḍawī 7587 (Bīnish, p.727); Gulpāyigānī 1029 (cat., II, p.60); Masjid-i Aʿẓam 11756; (7) *al-Fadhālik*, by al-Kirmānshāhī - see below; (8) by Muḥammad Jaʿfar al-Hamadānī, MS: Marʿashī 2538 (cat., VII, pp.122-3); (9) *Kashf al-Madārik*, by Muḥammad Rafīʿ al-Gīlānī al-Iṣfahānī (d. after 1238), edited Tehran, 1269 (in the margin of Baḥr al-ʿUlūm's *al-Durra*), 1322 (together with *Madārik al-aḥkām*), MSS: Dānishgāh 3698/1 (cat., XII, p.2703); Masjidi-i Aʿẓam 134; (10) by Ḍiyā' al-Dīn Muḥammad al-Ḥusaynī al-Marʿashī, MS: Marʿashī 1762 (cat., V, p.145); (11) by Muḥammad Jaʿfar al-Astarābādī, MS: Marʿashī 3854 (cat., X, p.242); (12) anonymous, MS: Tustariyya 192/2 (cat., p.840)

ṢĀḤIB AL-MAʿĀLIM:

Maʿālim al-dīn, uncompleted, only a part of the chapter on ritual purity
Edition: Tabrīz, 1322
Selected MSS: Ilāhiyyāt 54/1b (cat., I, p.128); Millī 436/2 Arabic (cat., VII, pp. 370-1); Masjid-i Aʿẓam 415

NŪR ALLĀH B. SHARĪF AL-ḤUSAYNĪ AL-TUSTARĪ (d. 1019):

Nihāyat al-iqdām
MS: Bankipore 1096 (cat. Arabic, I, p.108)

ABD ALLĀH B. ḤUSAYN AL-TUSTARĪ:

Jāmiʿ al-fawāʾid, a commentary on al-ʿAllāma's *Qawāʿid al-aḥkām*
MSS: Malik 3968 (cat., I, p.195); Dānishgāh 6828 (cat., XVI, p.371); Tarbiyat 112 (cat., p.32); Adabiyyāt 23 Kirmān (cat., p.82); Raḍawī 6736 (cat., V, pp.392-3)

AHĀʾ AL-DĪN AL-ʿĀMILĪ:

Al-Ḥabl al-matīn, uncompleted, only the chapters on ritual purity, prayer and inheritance
Edition: Tehran, 1321
Selected MSS: Princeton 110 New Series; Dānishgāh 1797, 3119, 6812, 1935/5 (cat., VII, pp.368, 552, XI, p.2073, XVI, p.366); Zanjānī 3 (cat., p.190); Malik 2174, 2702 (cat., I, pp.253-4); Millī 781 Arabic (cat., VIII, p.285); Bibliothèque Nationale 776 (cat., I, p.169, II, pp.129-30); Majlis 1297 (cat., IV, p.72); Raḍawī 7182, 2855, 2832, 2833-5 (cat., V, p.416); Masjid-i Aʿẓam 393

- *Mashriq al-shamsayn*, uncompleted, only the chapter on ritual purity
Edition: Tehran, 1321 (together with the author's *al-Ḥabl al-matīn*)
Selected MSS: Raḍawī 2626, 2649, 2832 (cat., II, pp.128, 135); Malik 1009 (cat., I, p.677); Majlis 1320 (cat., IV, pp.92-3); Marʿashī 80, 222 (cat., I, pp.98, 249; Ilāhiyyāt 160j (cat., I, p.662); Millī 79/1 Arabic (cat., VII, pp. 76-7); Sinā 125 (cat., I, p.65); Gulpāyiganī 979/3 (cat., II, p.216); Baku M140/2 (*Nash*., IX, p.239)

UʿIZZ AL-DĪN AL-MŪSAWĪ - Muḥammad b. Abi ʾl-Ḥasan al-Mashhadī (d. after 1044):
Dhakīrat al-jazāʾ
MS: Dānishgāh 4984/1 (cat., XV, p.4077)
Commentary: *Dhakhāʾir al-ʿuqbā*, MS: Dānishgāh 4984/2 (cat., XV, p.4077)

ANONYMOUS (written before 1060):

Sharḥ Qaṭrat al-baḥrayn
MS: Marʿashī 1842 (cat., V, p.228)

ḤASAN ʿALĪ B. ʿABD ALLĀH AL-TUSTARĪ (d. 1075):

Al-Tibyān
MS: Maʿhad 1355 (cat., p.116)

AL-SABZAWĀRĪ:

- *Dhakhīrat al-maʿād*, a commentary on al-ʿAllāma's *Irshād al-adhhān*
Edition: Tehran, 1273-4
Selected MSS: Majlis 4197, 5056 (cat., XI, pp.211-12, XV, p.18); Gharb (cat., p.126); Ḥakīm 1997; Raḍawī 2740-1, 5708 (cat., V, pp.422-3); Gulpāyiganī 1564 (cat., II, p.81); Fayḍiyya 92 (cat., I, p.111); Āstāna 5911 (cat., p.120)
Commentaries: (1) by Muḥammad Saʿīd, MS: Raḍawī 2740 in margin (cat., V, p.423); (2) *Taḥqīq fī ʾl-qiyās*, by al-Bihbahānī (as a part of his commentary on *Dhakhīrat al-maʿād*), MSS: Marʿashī 458/3 (cat., II, p.61); Dānishgāh 2026/3, 3902/2 (cat., VIII, p.644, XII, p.2891); Tustariyya (AB, I, p.70)

- *Kifāyat al-aḥkām*
Edition: Tehran, 1269
Selected MSS: Majlis 4595, 4647/2 (cat., XII, p.295, XIII, p.36);

Ilāhiyyāt 183 Āl Āqā (cat., I, p.794); Dānishgāh 1991 (cat., VIII, p.600); Gharb 394, 1129 (cat., p.176); Malik 1893 (cat., I, p.603); Wazīrī 26, 97/1, 518 (cat., I, pp.41, 126, II, p.451)
Translation: *Hidāyat al-aʿlām*, Persian, by Muḥammad ʿAlī b. Muḥammad Ḥasan al-Naḥwī al-Ardakānī (d. after 1240), MS: Majlis 32 Ṭabāṭabāʾī (cat. of microfilms of Dānishgāh, II, p.12)
Commentaries: (1) by Jaʿfar b. ʿAbd Allāh al-Ḥuwayzī al-Qāḍī, MSS: Raḍawī 6475 (cat., V, p.412); Ḥakīm 299; Mashhad, Shānachī (*Nash.*, V, p.598); (2) *Rawāshiḥ al-ʿināya al-Rabbāniyya*, by Ḥusayn b. Muḥammad al-Baḥrānī Āl ʿUṣfūr (d. 1216), MSS: Marʿashī 2702-3 (cat., VII, pp.272-4); (3) *Nibrās al-hidāya*, by Muḥammad Mahdī al-Ḥusaynī al-Mashhadī, MSS: Raḍawī 5726, 6202, 8418-19 (cat., V, pp. 523-4; Bīnish, p.1055); Majlis 5985 (cat., XVII, p.360); Wazīrī 239 (cat., I, p.239); (4) by Muḥsin al-Aʿrajī, MS: Khāliṣī (cat., p.61); (5) *Nihāyat al-muqtaṣid*, by Muḥammad Jaʿfar al-Hamadānī, MS: Gharb 731 (cat., p.202); (6) by Muḥammad b. Muḥammad Maʿṣūm al-Mashhadī (d. 1255), MSS: Marʿashī 2468, 3233 (cat., VII, p.61, IX, p.30); Majlis 4468 (cat., XII, p.142); (7) *Shawāriʿ al-hidāya*, by Muḥammad Ibrāhīm al-Kalbāsī, MSS: Majlis 3551 (cat., X, pp.1511-12); Marʿashī 1917, 1924 (cat., V, pp.288, 294); Gulpāyigānī 189 (cat., I, p.172); Fayḍiyya 233 (cat., I, p.170); Wazīrī 1488 (cat., III, p. 973); Miftāḥ 75 (cat., p.189)

AL-FAYḌ:

- *Mafātīḥ al-sharāʾiʿ*
  Edition: Beirut, 1389 (Vol.1 on ritual purity and prayer)
  Selected MSS: Cambridge C.18/9 Browne (cat., p.22); Ilāhiyyāt 66b (cat., I, p.667); Dānishgāh, 4 MSS (cat., V, p.2064, IX, p.869, XVI, p.326); Majlis, 3 MSS (cat., IV, pp.94-5, X, pp.382-2, XI, p.282); Sipahsālār 2603 (cat., I, p.528); Ḥuqūq 341j (cat., p.475); Gulpāyigānī, 8 MSS (cat., II, pp.175-6, III, pp. 22, 171); Fayḍiyya, 17 MSS (cat., I, pp.264-6); Malik, 7 MSS (cat., I, pp.705-6); Millī, 5 MSS (cat., VII, p.242, VIII, p.33, IX, pp.152-3, 185); Gharb, 7 MSS (cat., pp.194-5); Wazīrī, 9 MSS (cat., II, pp.471, 538, III, pp. 1018, 1025, 1060); Raḍawī, 24 MSS (cat., II, pp.122-3, V, pp.510-12; Bīnish, pp.1024-6)
  Commentaries: (1) by Muḥammad b. Muḥammad Muḥsin al-Kāshānī ʿAlam al-Hudā (early 12th century), MSS: Sipahsālār 2601 (cat., I, p.398, IV, p.278); Tabrīz, Qāḍī (*Nash.*, VII, p.523); (2) by Nūr al-Dīn Muḥammad Hādī b. Murtaḍā al-Kāshānī (early 12th century), MSS: Dānishgāh 714-15 (cat., V, pp.1940-2); Bankipore 946-9 (cat. Arabic, I, p.93); Ilāhiyyāt 31b (cat., I, p.591); Malik 1421 (cat., I, p.446); Wazīrī 970 (cat., II, p.797); Nūrbakhsh 152 (cat., I, p.170); Raḍawī 247-8 law, 2784 (cat., II, pp.76-7, V, p.461); Sipahsālār 6134 (cat., V, p.236); Fayḍiyya 76 (cat., I, p.159); Majlis 5279 temporary; (3) by Muḥammad Yūsuf b. Muḥammad ʿAlī al-Lāhījī (d. after 1096), MS: Tustariyya (AB, VI, p.214); (4) by Abu ʾl-Ḥasan b. Muḥammad Ṭāhir al-Sharīf al-Futūnī al-ʿĀmilī (d. 1138), MS: Los Angeles M1106 (cat., p.271); (5) *Fatḥ al-Mafātīh*, by Muḥammad Muḥsin b. Muḥammad al-Kāshānī (d. after 1148), MS: Majlis 5476/2 (cat., XVI, p.376); (6) *al-Dhukhr al-lāmiʿ = al-Maṣābīḥ al-lawāmiʿ*, by ʿAbd Allāh b. Nūr al-Dīn al-Jazāʾirī (d.1173), MSS: Marʿashī 3550 (cat., IX, pp.342-3); Raḍawī 7017 (cat., V, p.421); (7) by Muḥammad Ṣāliḥ b. Muḥammad Muʾmin al-Astarābādī (d. after 1184), MSS: Dānishgāh 7664 (cat., XVI, p.667); Majlis 5306 (cat., XVI, p.222); Marʿashī (AB, XIV, p.76); (8) by al-Bihbahānī, MSS: Raḍawī 2391 (cat., II, p.55); Majlis 347 Ṭabāṭabāʾī; Mashhad, Ilāhiyyāt 1578 (cat., II, p.713);

Khāliṣī (cat., p.62); Zanjān (cat., p.105); (9) by the same author, on the introduction to *Mafātīḥ*, MSS: Fayḍiyya 1520/5, 1554/8 (cat., III, pp.97, 100); Princeton 1929 New Series (fols. 251a-260b); (10) *Maṣābīḥ al-ẓalām*, by the same author - see below; (11) *Fattāḥ al-majāmi'*, by al-Kirmānshāhī - see below; (12) *al-Anwār al-lawāmi'*, by Ḥusayn Āl 'Uṣfūr, MSS: Raḍawī 6502-4 (cat., V, p.369); Mar'ashī 1630 (cat.,V, pp.33-4); Majlis 4425 (cat., XII, p.114); (13) by Muḥammad Riḍā al-Astarābādī (d. after 1219), MSS: Gawharshād 1235 (cat., p.334); Raḍawī 7253 (cat., V, p.463); (14) by Abu 'l-Qāsim b. 'Abbās (d. after 1227), MS: Raḍawī 2813 (cat., V, p.464); (15) by Ṣāḥib al-Riyāḍ, MS: Ḥuqūq 11b (cat., p.387); Sipahsālār 277 Mushīr (cat., V, p.236); Princeton 179 New Series; Los Angeles M1317 (cat., p.270); (16) *Maṣābīḥ al-ẓalām*, by 'Abd Allāh Shubbar, MSS: Tustariyya 256, 325, 834 (cat., p.804, 810); Mar'ashī 1079 (cat., III, pp.259-60); Raḍawī 7948 (Bīnish, p.1011); Millī, Arabic 1035/2, 1905 (cat., IX, p.37, X, pp. 565-6); (17) *al-Miṣbāḥ al-sāṭi'*, by the same author (an abridgement of his perious commentary), MSS: Dānishgāh 717 (cat., V, pp.2045-6); Ilāhiyyāt 6 Āl Āqā (cat., I, pp.800-1); Gawharshād 742 (cat., p.396); Ḥujjatiyya 73 (cat., p.85); Bengal 654 (cat., I, p.323); Tabrīz, Qāḍī (*Nash.*, VII, p.522); (18) *Nihāyat al-marām*, by al-Mujāhid, MS: Ḥuqūq 266j (cat., pp.496-7); (19) *al-Maṣābīḥ*, by Muḥammad Ja'far al-Kirmānshāhī, MSS: Ilāhiyyāt 124 Āl Āqā (cat., I, p.800); Kāshān, Raḍawī 187 (cat., p.43); Ḥuqūq 107j (cat., pp. 467-8); Mar'ashī (AB, XXI, p.91); (20) *al-Maṣābīḥ*, by Mahdī b. 'Alī al-Ṭabāṭabā'ī (d. 1260), MS: Ḥuqūq 243j (cat., p.467); (21) *Mubtaghā al-afhām*, by 'Abd al-Wahhāb b. Muḥammad Ṣāliḥ al-Baraghānī al-Qazwīnī (d. after 1266), MS: Mar'ashī 3202 (cat., IX, p.4); (22-4) three anonymous or unidentified commentaries (a) MS: Mar'ashī 2157 (cat., VI, pp.162-3); (b) MS: Dānishgāh 6709 (cat., XVI, p.337); (c) MS: Shīrāz, Aḥmadiyya 264 (*Nash.*, V, p.214)

Mu'taṣam al-Shī'a, uncompleted
MSS: Mar'ashī 217, 3478 (cat., I, p.246, IX, p.275); Raḍawī 6469 (cat., V, p.509); Baghdādī (cat., p.178); Kāshān, Raḍawī 191 (cat., p.43)

Al-Nukhba
Editions: Tehran, 1303, 1324, 2328, 1330
Selected MSS: Wazīrī 965 (cat., II, p.794); Ḥuqūq 11d (cat., I, p. 493); Dānishgāh 1007 (cat., V, pp.2083-5); Ilāhiyyāt 187 Āl Āqā (cat., I, p.806); Millī, Arabic 1386/2, 1393, 1463 (cat., IX, pp.395, 411, 491)
Commentary: *al-Tuḥfa al-saniyya*, by 'Abd Allāh al-Jazā'irī, edited Tehran, 1370 (Vol. 1), MSS: Gulpāyigānī 1687 (cat., III, p.17); Mar'ashī 2213 (cat., VI, p.204); Fayḍiyya 227 (cat., I, p.40); Masjid-i A'ẓam 181/1; Raḍawī 2269 (Bīnish, p.434); Majlis 4437, 4735, 5184 (cat., XII, p.122, XIII, p.116, XVI, pp.1-2); Dānishgāh 751, 1008 (cat., V, p.1820); Gharb 909 (cat., p.71)

USAYN AL-KHWĀNSĀRĪ:

Mashāriq al-shumūs, an uncompleted commentary on al-Shahīd al-Awwal's *al-Durūs al-shar'iyya*, only the chapter on ritual purity
Edition: Tehran, 1311
Selected MSS: Dānishgāh 6778 (cat., XVI, pp.358-9); Sipahsālār 2308 (cat., I, p.448); Majlis (4428/1 (cat., XII, p.117)

L-ḤURR AL-'ĀMILĪ:

Bidāyat al-hidāya

Editions: Tehran, 1270, 1318, 1325; Locknow, 1311
Selected MSS: Malik 2043, 2861 (cat., I, p.88); Ḥakīm 1670m (cat., I, pp.88-9); Marʿashī 429, 701, 716 (cat., II, pp.33, 295, 312); Raḍawī 6609 (Bīnish, p.617); Gulpāyigānī 1227/1, 1369/2 (cat., II, pp. 237, 249); Ḥujjatiyya 178 (cat., p 38); Millī, Arabic 1276/2, 1400 (cat., IX, pp.266, 415-16); Princeton 151/1 New Series
Abridgement: *Nihāyat al-bidāya*, by al-Mukhtārī, MS: Dānishgāh 1859/5 (cat., VIII, p.460)
Translations: (1) *Nūr-i sāṭiʿ*, Persian, by Muḥammad Murād al-Kishmīrī (d. after 1098), MSS: Gawharshād 943 (cat., p.195); Wazīrī 990, 1141 (cat., II, p.809, III, p.871); Raḍawī 2854 (cat., V, p.528); Sipahsālār 2529 (cat., I, p.553); (2) *Kashf al-dirāya*, by Muḥammad Jaʿfar b. Sulaymān al-Farāhī (d. afte 1114), MSS: Raḍawī 2810 (cat., V, p.481); Āstāna 6264 (cat., pp.155-6); Gawharshād 936 (cat., p.163); Marʿashī (AB, XVIII, pp.34, 68); (3) by ʿAbd Allāh b. ʿAlībābā, MS: Gawharshād 1137/1 (cat., p.87)
Commentaries: (1) *Muntakhab al-hidāya*, by Muḥammad Ṭāhir b. ʿAbd Allāh al-Qārī al-Harawī (d. after 1105), MS: Raḍawī 4280, 6471 (cat., V, pp.518-19); (2) anonymous (written before 1153), MS: Wazīrī 1819/1 (cat., III, p.1064); (3) *Mashāriq al-muhtadīn*, by Muḥammad Bāqir b. Muḥammad Taqī al-Sharīf al-Raḍawī al-Qummī (d. after 1181), MS: Rawḍātī (AB, XXI, pp.36-7); (4) *al-Sawāniḥ al-naẓariyya*, by Ḥusayn Āl ʿUṣfūr, MSS: Ilāhiyyāt 137 Āl Āqā (cat., I, p.777); Dānishgāh 2924 (cat., XVI, p.402); (5) *Anwār al-dirāya*, by ʿAbd al-Ḥusayn b. Aḥmad al-Aṣbaghī al-Baḥrānī, MS: Wazīrī 3114/2 (cat., V, p.1537); (6) *Maṣābīḥ al-hidāya*, by Muḥammad Ḥasan b. Muḥammad Maʿṣūm al-Qazwīnī (d. 1240), MSS: Millī 1840 Arabic (cat., X, p.420); Miftāḥ 207 (cat., pp.291-2); Dānishgāh 7362 (cat., XVI, p.521); Ilāhiyyāt 45 Āl Āqā (cat., I, pp, 799-800); Marʿashī 1650, 2126 (cat., V, pp.49-50, VI, p.137); (7) *Majārī al-marām*, by Muḥammad Bāqir al-Gulpāyigānī, MS: Fayḍiyya 1282 (cat., I, p.226)

- *Hidāyat al-umma*
Selected MSS: Gawharshād 300 (cat., p.433); Malik 616-17 and 6 other MSS (cat., I, pp.802-4); Sipahsālār 6186 (cat., V, p.756); Dānishgāh 6761 (cat., XVI, p.355); Ḥakīm 143 Rashtī (cat., p.159); Raḍawī, 8 MSS (Bīnish, p.1077)
Translation: *Hidāyat al-aḥkām*, Persian, by Muḥammad Ḥasan b. Muḥammad Ṣāliḥ al-Harawī, MS: Majlis 2054 (cat., VI, pp.42-3)

AL-FĀḌIL AL-HINDĪ:

- *Kashf al-lithām*, a commentary on al-ʿAllāma's *Qawāʿid al-aḥkām*
Edition: Tehran, 1271-4
Selected MSS: Marʿashī 3767 (cat., X, p.156); Majlis 3489 (cat., X, pp. 1448-9); Fayḍiyya 559 and 5 other MSS (cat., I, p.218); Gulpāyigānī 2325 and 4 other MSS (cat., II, p.151, III, p.229); Gharb 487 (cat., p.175)

- *Al-Manāhij al-sawiyya*, a commentary on al-Shahīd al-Thānī's *al-Rawḍa al-bahiyya*
MSS: Dānishgāh 1159, 2365 (cat., V, pp.2068-9, IX, p.966); Millī 603 Arabic (cat., VIII, p.88); Sipahsālār 2560 (cat., I, p.449); Majlis 222 Khuʾī, 1327 (cat., IV, pp.97-8, VII, p.373); Malik, 3 MSS (cat., I, p.739); Marʿashī 2965-7 (cat., VIII, pp. 148-9); Masjid-i Aʿẓam 370, 4327, 11713; Raḍawī 8005 (cat., p.1037); Gharb 1347 (cat., p.197); Miftāḥ 62 (cat., p.299)

SHĀRIḤ AL-WĀFIYA - Ṣadr al-Dīn Muḥammad b. Muḥammad Bāqir al-Raḍawī al-Qummī (mid-12th century):

Istiqṣā' al-naẓar
MS: Mar'ashī 2704 (cat., VII, p.274)

AL-MAQĀBĪ - Muḥammad b. 'Alī b. 'Abd al-Nabī al-Baḥrānī (d. after 1169):

Majma' al-aḥkām
MSS: Gulpāyigānī 1681 (cat., III, p.14); Ḥakīm 9 (*Nash*, V, p.422)

'ABD AL-RASHĪD B. NŪR AL-DĪN AL-TUSTARĪ (12th century):

Al-Masā'il al-akhbāriyya
MS: Majlis 5944/2 (cat., XVII, pp.328-9)

ṢĀḤIB AL-ḤADĀ'IQ:

Al-Ḥadā'iq al-nāḍira
Editions: Tabrīz, 1315-18; Najaf, 1377-
Selected MSS: Majlis 5196 (cat., XVI, p.26); Dānishgāh 6595 (cat., XVI, p.304); Raḍawī 2730-1, 7592-610 (Bīnish, p.734); Gawharshād 106 (cat., p.287); Nawwāb 102 law (cat., p.456)
Completion: *'Uyūn al-ḥaqā'iq al-nāẓira*, by Ḥusayn Āl 'Uṣfūr, edited Tehran, 1318; Najaf, 1342
Commentaries: (1) *Sharḥ muqaddamat al-Ḥadā'iq*, by Muḥsin al-A'rajī, MS: Bengal 656 (cat., I, p.324); (2) by Ibrāhīm b. Muḥammad al-Mūsawī al-Dizfūlī, MS: Ṣāḥib al-Dharī'a (AB, VI, p.81)

AL-BIHBAHĀNĪ:

Maṣābīḥ al-ẓalām, a commentary on al-Fayḍ's *Mafātīḥ al-sharā'i'*
MSS: Ilāhiyyāt 4-5 Āl Āqā (cat., I, p.784); Dānishgāh 718, 1588, 7713 (cat., V, pp.1942-3, VIII, p.193, XVI, p.683); Malik 2197, 2617, 2741 (cat., I, p.445); Āstāna 7348 (cat., p.136); Fayḍiyya 56, 77 (cat., I, p.251); Majlis 4449-50, 4822/1, 5578, 62 Ṭabāṭabā'ī, 82 Ṭabāṭabā'ī (cat., XII, pp.131-2, XIII, p.233, XVII, p.40); Millī 622 Arabic (cat., VIII, p.102); Mar'ashī 1108 (cat., III, p.280); Gulpāyigānī 281-3, 1680, 1696, 1724 (cat., I, pp.245-6, III, pp. 13-14, 19, 30); Tarbiyat 237 (cat., p.54); Dihkhudā 209 (cat., p.423); Ḥakīm 25-6 (*Nash*., V, p.422); Iṣfahān, Adabiyyāt (ibid., V, p.300); Raḍawī, 5 MSS (Bīnish, p. 887); Gharb, 2 MSS (cat., p.189); Gawharshād 1986 (cat., p.334); Amīr al-Mu'minīn (AB, XIV, p.75); Masjid-i A'ẓam 7408, 9147; Saryazdī 122 (cat., p.423); Ustādī, 2 MSS (cat., p.36); Los Angeles M939 (cat., p.270)

MAHDĪ AL-NARĀQĪ - Mahdī b. Abī Dharr al-Kāshānī (d.1209):

- *Lawāmi' al-aḥkām*
MSS: Gharb 1106 (cat., p.178); Khāliṣī (cat., p.94)

- *Mu'tamad al-Shī'a*
MSS: Mar'ashī 3137 (cat., VIII, p.366); Fayḍiyya 1108 (cat., I, p.262); Khāliṣī (cat., p.117)

BAḤR AL-'ULŪM:

- *Al-Durra*, in verse
Editions: Najaf, 1377 and others (see Mushār, col. 360)
Selected MSS: Raḍawī 2404, 6196, 7648-9 (Bīnish, p.750); Mar'ashī

2792/10 (cat., VII, p.358); Wazīrī 937/1 (cat., II, p.765); Dānishgāh 1623/1, 4555/1 (cat., VIII, p.208, XIII, p.3495); Sipahsālār 6156/1, 7147/2 (cat., IV, p.423)
Commentaries: (1) *al-Fīrūzajāt al-Ṭūsiyya*, by Muḥammad b. Ḥasan al-Ṭūsī al-Mashhadī (d. 1257), MSS: Malik 2592, 2990 (cat., I, p. 557); Raḍawī 6476 (cat., V, p.456); Marʿashī 2804 (cat., VIII, pp. 6-7); Wazīrī 937/2 (cat., II, p.765); Khāliṣī (cat., pp.87-8); Masjid-i Aʿẓam 3027; (2) *al-Ghurra*, by Muḥammad ʿAlī b. Muḥammad Ḥusayn al-Ardakānī (mid-13th century), MS: Dānishgāh 6971 (cat., XVI, p.416); (3) *Khazāʾin al-aḥkām*, by Āqā b. ʿĀbid b. Ramaḍān al-Darbandī (d. 1285), edited Tabrīz, 1274, Tehran, 1284, MSS: Sulaymān Khān 64, 126 (cat., pp.10-11); Fayḍiyya 1581, 1140 (cat., I, p.104); (4) *al-Mawāhib al-saniyya*, by Maḥmūd b. ʿAlī Naqī al-Ṭabāṭabāʾī al-Burūjirdī (d. 1300), edited Tehran, 1280-8, 1375; (5) *al-Ghurra al-Ḥanafiyya*, by Abu ʾl-Ḥasan b. Muḥammad Ibrāhīm al-Shahshahānī al-Iṣfahānī (d. after 1266), MS: Gulpāyigānī 75 (cat., I, p.82); (6) by Abū Turāb b. Muḥammad Ḥusayn al-Qazwīnī (d. 1292-1300), MS: Ṣāḥib al-Dharīʿa (AB, XIII, p.236); (7) by Jamāl al-Dīn b. ʿAlī al-Mūsawī, MS: Marʿashī 2928/1 (cat., VIII, p.120); (8) *Fuṣūṣ fīrūzajāt khafiyya*, by ʿAlī b. Muḥammad Jaʿfar al-Astarābādī, MS: Marʿashī 3091 (cat., VIII, p.315); (9) *al-ʿInāya al-Ilāhiyya*, by ʿInāyat Allāh b. Malik Muḥammad al-Lārījānī (d. after 1326), MSS: Millī 1883-6 Arabic (cat., X, pp.526-9); (10) anonymous, MS: Malik 2908 (cat., I, p.402)

- *Al-Maṣābīḥ = Maṣābīḥ al-aḥkām*
  MSS: Dānishgāh 797, 6797, 7728 (cat., V, pp.2044-5, XVI, pp.362, 685); Sipahsālār 294 (cat., V, p.576); Raḍawī 6534, 7945-6 (cat., V, p.505; Bīnish, p.1010); Fayḍiyya 218, 880, 1288 (cat., I, pp. 248-9); Gulpāyigānī 1010/2 and 2 other MSS (cat., II pp.169, 220); Būhār 190 Arabic (cat., p.215); Ustādī (cat., p.36); Zanjān (cat., p.162)

AL-SHAHRASTĀNĪ - Muḥammad Mahdī b. Abi ʾl-Qāsim al-Mūsawī (d.1216)

Al-Maṣābīḥ
MS: Dānishgāh 6838 (cat., XVI, p.377)

AL-KIRMĀNSHĀHĪ - Muḥammad ʿAlī b. Muḥammad Bāqir (d. 1216):

- *Al-Fadhālik*
  MSS: Gawharshād 1756 (cat., p.357); Marʿashī (AB, XVI, p.130)
- *Fattāḥ al-majāmiʿ*, a commentary on al-Fayḍ's *Mafātīḥ al-sharāʾiʿ*
  MSS: Majlis 4321, 5474/1 (cat., XII, p.15, XVI, p.374); Ilāhiyyāt 828/4d, 125 Āl Āqā (cat., I, p.787, II, p.23); Marʿashī 3489 (cat., IX, p.287); Wazīrī 2001 (cat., IV, p.1123); Gawharshād 1453/2 (cat., 0.356); Kāshān, Raḍawī 174/3 (cat., p.39)

ḤUSAYN B. MUḤAMMAD AL-BAḤRĀNĪ ĀL ʿUṢFŪR (d. 1216):

Sadād al-ʿibād wa rashād al-ʿibād, uncompleted
Edition: Bombay, 1339
MSS: Raḍawī 7701 (Bīnish, p.842); Tabrīz, Qāḍī (*Nash*., VII, p.515)

JAWĀD AL-ʿĀMILĪ:

Miftāḥ al-karāma, a commentary on al-ʿAllāma's *Qawāʿid al-aḥkām*, especially detailed on the differences of opinions between Shīʿī jurists
Edition: Cairo-Damascus-Tehran, 1323-78
Selected MSS: Marʿashī 1435 (cat., IV, pp.220-1); Āstāna (cat.,

pp.171-2, 205); Malik (cat., I, pp.714-16); Masjid-i Aʿẓam 279

MUḤSIN B. ḤASAN AL-AʿRAJĪ AL-KĀẒIMĪ (d. 1227):

- *Al-Jāmiʿ al-kabīr*
  MS: Los Angeles M1091/9 (cat., p.711)
- *Wasā'il al-Shīʿa*
  Edition: Tabrīz, 1321 (vol. 1 on ritual purity)
  MSS: Raḍawiyya 66 (cat., pp.40, 65); Berlin Pet.576/2 (cat., IV, p.253); Khāliṣī (cat., pp.128-39)

KĀSHIF AL-GHIṬĀ' - Jaʿfar b. Khiḍr al-Najafī (d. 1228):

Kashf al-ghiṭā'
Edition: Tehran, 1271
Selected MSS: Dānishgāh 5932/11, 7708 (cat., XVI, pp. 161, 681); Wazīrī 132 (cat., I, p.170)
Translation: Persian, by Muḥammad Bāqir b. Muḥammad al-Lāhījī al-Nawwāb (d. after 1228), MSS: Masjid-i Aʿẓam 369, 2975
Commentary: by Ḥasan Āl Kāshif al-Ghiṭā', MS: Dānishgāh 2022 (cat., VIII, p.641)

ṢĀḤIB AL-RIYĀḌ:

- *Ḥadīqat al-mu'minīn*, a commentary on al-Muḥaqqiq's *al-Mukhtaṣar al-nāfiʿ*
  Selected MSS: Dānishgāh 724, 1512, 7737 (cat., V, pp.1939-40, VIII, p.149, XVI, p.686); Ḥuqūq 224j, 318j (cat., pp.385-6); Adabiyyāt 195 Kirmān (cat., p.94); Sipahsālār 2301, 2492-4 (cat., I, p.462-2); Malik 2791, 3386 (cat., I, p.442); Raḍawī 2475-7, 7745 (cat., II, pp. 82-3; Bīnish, p.873); Gawharshād, 4 MSS (cat., p.332); Fayḍiyya 278, 602, 1055, 1172, 1198/1; Ḥujjatiyya 269-70 (cat., p.66); Gulpāyigānī 216, 610 (cat., I, p.188, II, p.64); Masjid-i Aʿẓam 101, 353, 6056; Wazīrī 1903 (cat., III, p.1090); Gharb 246 (cat., p.153); Zanjān (cat., p.115)
- *Riyāḍ al-masā'il*, another commentary on al-Muḥaqqiq's *al-Mukhtaṣar al-nāfiʿ*
  Editions: Tehran, 1316-17 and others (see Mushār, cols. 501-2)
  Selected MSS: Malik 1822 (cat., I, p.351); Ḥuqūq 264j (cat., pp. '360-1); Millī 543 Arabic (cat., VIII, p.39); Marʿashī 2296 (cat., VI, p.,281); Dār al-Kutub 20023b (cat., I, p.446); Berlin Pet.609 (cat., IV, p.158); Harvard (*Nash.*, IX, p.354)
  Commentaries: (1) *al-Miṣbāḥ al-munīr*, anonymous, MS: Marʿashī (AB, XXI, p.120); (2) by ʿAbd al-Karīm al-Īrawānī al-Qazwīnī (d. after 1260), MS: Tabrīz, Qāḍī (*Nash.*, VII, p.514); (3) *Awthaq al-wasā'il*, by Luṭf ʿAlī b. Aḥmad al-Tabrīzī (d. 1262), MS: Ḥujjatiyya 457 (cat., p.38); (4) by Muḥammad Jaʿfar al-Astarābādī, MSS: Marʿashī 3082/1, 3889/2 (cat., VIII, p.306, X,p.272); (5) *Anwār al-riyāḍ*, by Muḥammad b. ʿAbd al-Ṣamad al-Shahshahānī (d. 1287), MSS: Majlis 3088-92 (cat., X, pp.642-5); Ḥuqūq 74b (cat., p.257); Marʿashī 1860, 2621, 3019, 3168-9 (cat., V, pp.244-5, VII, p.198, VIII, pp.206, 396-7); Fayḍiyya 1245, 1527, 2223, 1083-4 (cat., I, pp. 68-9); Gulpāyigānī 58, 142, 179, 399 (cat., I, pp.69, 132, 164, 329); Ḥujjatiyya 509, 133 (cat., p.37); Masjid-i Aʿẓam 286, 66 temporary, 135 temporary, 3040, 9148; Gawharshād 1403, 1405 (cat., p. 221); (6) *Anwār al-riyāḍ*, anonymous (written in 1269), MS: Fayḍiyya 800/1 (cat., I, p.32, III, p.24); (7) by Muḥammad Jawād b. Aḥmad al-Narāqī (d. 1278), MS: Fayḍiyya 470 (cat., I, p.124);

(8) *Miftāḥ al-Riyāḍ*, by Ismāʿīl b Najaf al-Ḥusaynī al-Marandī (d. after 1293), MS: Ḥujjatiyya 463 (cat., p.89); (9) by Muḥammad Taqī al-Harawī MSS: Ḥuqūq 112j (cat., pp.319-21); Marʿashī 3721 (cat., X, pp.120-1); (10) by ʿAlī Akbar al-Qazwīnī, MS: Millī 1783/9 Arabic (cat., X, p.368); (11) *Zahr al-riyāḍ*, by Muḥammad Ṣāliḥ b. Muḥammad Ḥasan al-Ṭihrānī al-Dāmād, MSS: Dānishgāh 758, 761 (cat., V, p.1922); Marʿashī 1429 (cat., IV, pp.212-13); (12) by Maḥmūd b. Muḥammad al-Khuʾī, edited Tabrīz, 1312; (13) *Wathīqat al-wasāʾil*, by Aḥmad b. ʿAlī al-Ḥusaynī al-Rashtī (d. after 1320), edited Iran, 1320; (14) *Ṭarāʾiq al-Riyāḍ*, by Ghulām Ḥusayn b. ʿAlī Aṣghar al-Darbandī (d. 1323), MS: Marʿashī 2718 (cat., VII, p.284); (15) by Fakhr al-Dīn al-Narāqī, MS: Fayḍiyya 870 (cat., I, p.125); (16) by Maḥmūd b. ʿAlī al-Marʿashī (d. 1338), MS: Marʿashī 2623 (cat., VII, p.199); (17) *Īḍāḥ al-Riyāḍ*, by Ḥabīb Allāh al-Kāshānī, MS: Marʿashī 3147 (cat., VIII, pp. 378-9); (18) by Muḥsin b. Mahdī al-Ṭabāṭabāʾī al-Ḥakīm (d. 1391), MS: Ḥakīm 2279m; (19-21) three anonymous or unidentified commentaries: (a) MS: Raḍawī 8268 (Bīnish, p.719); (b) written before 1268, MS: Raḍawī 2473 (ibid. p. 882); (c) MS: Fayḍiyya 800/2 (cat., III, p.24)

AL-QUMMĪ:

- *Ghanāʾim al-ayyām*
  Editions: Tehran, 1301, 1319
  Selected MSS: Āstāna 8345, 6143 (cat., p.147); Malik 2289 (cat., I, p.528); Ilāhiyyāt 144 Āl Āqā (cat., I, p.787)

- *Manāhij al-aḥkām*
  Edition: Tehran, 1271 (the chapter on prayer)
  Selected MSS: Fayḍiyya 141/5, 1104/2 (cat., III, pp. 5, 55); Raḍawī 63 (cat., p.37); Millī 250 Arabic (cat., VII, pp.218-19); Ustādī (cat., p.37)

ṢĀḤIB AL-MAQĀBIS:

Maqābis al-anwār
Edition: Trabrīz, 1322
Selected MSS: Raḍawī 2845 (Bīnish, p.1029); Dānishgāh 7303 (cat., XVI, p.508); Fayḍiyya 17/2 (cat., III, p.1); Gulpāyigānī 467 (cat., II, p.177)

AL-MUJĀHID:

- *Jāmiʿ al-aqwāl*
  MS: Raḍawī 7543 (Bīnish, p.678)

- *Al-Manāhil*
  Editions: partly edited Tehran, 1274, 1315
  Selected MSS: Ḥuqūq 325j (cat., p.482); Malik 2951 (cat., I, pp. 740-1); Dānishgāh 782-3, 1741, 7719 (cat., V, pp.2069-70, XVI, p.683); Sipahsālār 2614-18 (cat., I, pp. 537-8); Millī, Arabic 751/2, 1688 (cat., VIII, p.208, X, p.270); Raḍawī, 9 MSS (cat., V, pp.505, 516-17; Bīnish, p.1038); Wazīrī 140, 1795 (cat., I, p.178, III, p.1056); Fayḍiyya 1295 (cat., I, p.248); Ḥujjatiyya 103 (cat., p.85); Masjid-i Aʿẓam 2964, 2994; Gharb, 4 MSS (cat., p.188); Ustādī (cat. p.38); Tabrīz, Qāḍī (*Nash.*, VII, p.523)

AḤMAD AL-NARĀQĪ:

- *Hidāyat al-Shīʿa*
  MSS: Marʿashī 125 (cat., I, pp.147-8); Khāliṣī, 2 MSS (cat., pp.127-8); Qum, Rūḥānī (*Āshnāʾī*, I, p.446)

- *Mustanad al-Shīʿa*
Editions: Tehran, 1273-4, 1325-6
Selected MSS: Sipahsālār 2330-1 (cat., I, p.522); Ḥuqūq 79b (cat., p.463); Gharb 1965 (cat., p.186); Malik, 3 MSS (cat., I, pp.672-3)

MUḤAMMAD IBRĀHĪM B. MUḤAMMAD ḤASAN AL-KALBĀSĪ (d. 1262):

Minhāj al-hidāya
Edition: Tehran, 1263
Selected MSS: Dānishgāh 769, 3929 (cat., V, p.2071-2, XII, pp. 2916-17): Raḍawī 2635, 8020, 8240 (cat., II, p.130; Bīnish, pp. 1047-8); Marʿashī 2376 (cat., VI, p.359); Malik 1341; Fayḍiyya, 6 MSS (cat., I, pp.280-1); Berlin Min.248 (cat., IV, p.158)
Commentary: *Miʿrāj al-sharīʿa*, by Muḥammad Mahdī al-Kalbāsī, MSS: Majlis 3556-9 (cat., X, pp.1520-2); Dānishgāh 1215 (cat., VI, p.2355); Raḍawī 7987-92 (cat., V, p.509); Marʿashī 2307 (cat., VI, p.45); ʿAbd al-ʿAẓīm 4 (cat., p.81)

ḤASAN B. JAʿFAR ĀL KĀSHIF AL-GHIṬĀʾ:

Anwār al-faqāha
MSS: Majlis 22, 23/1 Khuʾī, 4469-70 (cat., VII, p.20, XII, pp.142-3); Āstāna 6368 (cat., pp. 79-80); Fayḍiyya 141/6 (cat., III, p.5); Ḥujjatiyya 336 (cat., p.38); Mashhad, Ilāhiyyāt 892 (cat., II, p.58); Raḍawī 7451 (Bīnish, p.609); Gawharshād 441 (cat., p.221); Mahdawī 810/1, 810/3 (cat., p.128); Bāqiriyya (AB, I, p.443)

ṢĀḤIB AL-JAWĀHIR:

- *Jawāhir al-kalām*, a commentary on al-Muḥaqqiq's *Sharāʾiʿ al-Islām*. It has become the most popular reference work in Shīʿī legal studies.
Editions: Najaf-Qum-Tehran, 1377-1401 (in 43 vols.) and 5 others (see Mushār, cols. 261-3)
Selected MSS: Ḥakīm 72-87 (cat., I, pp.170-7); Gharb 1108-26 (cat., pp.78-80); Ṭabāṭabāʾī 730-9 (cat., V., pp.1849-53); Majlis 4657 (cat., XIII, pp.43-4); Gawharshād 1229 (cat., p.255)
Commentaries: (1) *al-Inṣāf*, by Muḥammad Ṭāhā b. Mahdī Najaf al-Tabrīzī (d. 1223), edited Tehran, 1324; (2) *Baḥr al-jawāhir*, Persian, by ʿAlī b. Muḥammad Bāqir al-Burūjinī (early 14th century), MSS: Wazīrī 250 (cat., I, p.254); Masjid-i Aʿẓam 1322

- *Najāt al-ʿibād*, a collection of *fatwā*s - see below
Commentaries: (1) *Wasīlat al-maʿād*, by Ismāʿīl b. Aḥmad al-ʿAqīlī al-Nūrī (d. 1321), edited Tehran, 1324; (2) *Adillat al-rashād*, by Muḥammad Ḥusayn al-Qumshaʾī, MSS: Tustariyya 476-91, 829 (cat., p.788); (3) *Subul al-rashād*, by Abū Turāb b. Abi ʾl-Qāsim al-Mūsawī al-Khwānsārī (d. 1346), edited Najaf, 1332, MSS: Tustariyya 468/1, 538/2 (cat., pp.801, 863, 865); (4) by Abu ʾl-Majd al-Iṣfahānī, MS: Rawḍātī (see AB, XIV, pp.101-2)

HĀDĪ AL-ṬIHRĀNĪ - Muḥammad Hādī b. Muḥammad Amīn (d. 1321):

Wadāʾiʿ al-nubuwwa
Edition: two parts of the book are edited, the chapter on sale (Najaf, 1320) and the chapter on prayer (Tehran, 1342)
Selected MSS: Majlis 1950/2, 2717/2, 2720-1, 2753, 2762 (cat., IX, pp.15-18, 38, 138-9, 165, 661-2); Raḍawī, 6 MSS (Bīnish, p.871); Gharb 8149 (cat., p.205); Masjid-i Aʿẓam 1069/1, 1175, 1952/1; Tustariyya (AB, XV, p.188); Ustādī (cat., p.26)

RIḌĀ AL-HAMADĀNĪ :

Miṣbāḥ al-faqīh, an uncompleted commentary on al-Muḥaqqiq's *Sharāʾiʿ al-Islām*; only the first 5 chapters on acts of devotion and the chapter on mortgage
Edition: Najaf, 1347; Tehran, 1353/1364
MSS: Ḥuqūq 141j (cat., p.468); Dānishgāh 3719 (cat., XII, p.2720); Majlis 5049-50, 5054-5 (cat., XV, pp.13-14, 16-17)

MUḤAMMAD ḤASAN B. ʿABD ALLĀH AL-MĀMAQĀNĪ (d. 1323):

Dharāʾiʿ al-aḥlām, a commentary on al-Muḥaqqiq's *Sharāʾiʿ al-Islām*
Edition: Tabrīz, 1319-21
MSS: Millī 1163 Arabic (cat., IX, p.150); Gulpāyigānī 522 (cat., II, p.81)

AL-KHURĀSĀNĪ :

- *Takmilat al-Tabṣira*
  Edition: Tehran, 1328
  MS: Nūrbakhsh 485/1 (cat., II, p.163)
- *Al-Lamaʿāt al-nayyira*, an uncompleted commentary on the previous work; only the chapter on ritual purity and a part of the chapter on prayer
  Editon: Baghdad, 1331

AL-YAZDĪ :

Al-ʿUrwa al-Wuthqā
Editions: Vol.1, Tehran, 1382 and others: Vols. 2-3, Tehran,1378

ḌIYĀʾ AL-DĪN AL-ʿARĀQĪ :

Sharḥ Tabṣirat al-mutaʿallimīn
Edition: Najaf, 1345 (chapter on sale), Qum, 1397-
MS: Marʿashī 3102 (cat., VIII, p.326)

ABU ʾL-ḤASAN AL-IṢFAHĀNĪ :

Wasīlat al-najāt
Editions: Najaf, 1359 and others

AL-ḤAKĪM:

Mustamsak al-ʿUrwa al-wuthqā, a commentary on al-Yazdī's *al-ʿUrwa al-wuthqā*
Editions: Najaf, 1391 (14 vols.) and 3 others

MUḤAMMAD TAQĪ B. MUḤAMMAD AL-ĀMULĪ (d. 1391):

Miṣbāḥ al-hudā, an uncompleted commentary on al-Yazdī's *al-ʿUrwa al-wuthqā*
Edition: Tehran, 1377-

AḤMAD B. YŪSUF AL-MŪSAWĪ AL-KHWĀNSĀRĪ :

Jāmiʿ al-madārik, a commentary on al-Muḥaqqiq's *al-Mukhtaṣar al-nāfiʿ*
Edition: Tehran

AL-KHUMAYNĪ :

Taḥrīr al-Wasīla
Editions: Najaf, 1387, 1391

B

COLLECTIONS OF *FATWĀS*

ʿIMĀD AL-ṬABARĪ:

Muʿtaqad al-Imāmiyya, Persian
Edition: Tehran, 1381
MSS: Rawḍātī (cat., I, pp. 33ff); Gharb 10836/2 (cat., p.450)

ANONYMOUS (belonging to 6th/7th century):

Kitāb-i fiqh, Persian
MS: Majlis 260 Khuʾī (cat., VII, pp.430-3)

ʿABD AL-RAḤĪM B. MAʿRŪF (9th century):

Nayl al-marām, Persian
MSS: Dānishgāh 764 (cat., V, pp.2099-100); Sipahsālār 6175 (cat., V, p.741); Marʿashī 2891, 2712 (cat., VII, p.281, VIII, p.93); Los Angeles M349 (cat., p.92); Fayḍiyya 846 (cat., II, p.109); Gulpāyigānī 208 (cat., I, p.184); Wazīrī 1587 (cat., III, p.995)

AL-JURJĀNĪ - Ḍiyāʾ al-Dīn ʿAlī b. Sadīd al-Dīn Dāwūd (early 10th century):

- *Risāla dar fiqh*, Persian
  Selected MSS: Wazīri 1123/2 (cat., III, p.865); Dānishgāh 3190/3 (cat., XI, p.2147); Fayḍiyya 1617/2 (cat., III, p.109); Saryazdī 4/5 (cat., p.425)
- *Wājibāt-i namāz*, Parsian
  Selected MSS: Karāchī (cat., I, pp. 26-7); Gharb 10836/11 (cat., p.451)

AL-KARAKĪ:

- *Risāla yi aḥkām*, a Persian translation of al-Karakī's collection of *fatwā*s
  MS: Wazīrī 3808/3 (cat., V, p.1804)
- *Uṣūl al-dīn wa furūʿuh*
  MS: Dānishgāh 2888/6 (cat., X, p.1733)

ḤUSAYN B. ʿABD AL-ḤAQQ AL-ARDABĪLĪ (d. 950):

Zubda = Fiqh-i shāhī, Persian
Edition: Locknow, 1311
MSS: Dānishgāh 771, 723/1, 899/3, 936, 5744 (cat., V, pp.1766-71, XVI, pp.80-1); Princeton 2858 Yahuda (*Nash*., X, p.25); Wazīrī 795, 33 (cat., I, p.44, II, p.670); Malik 2170 (cat., II, p.581); Majlis 37, 126 Khuʾī, 4639, 5834 (cat., II, p.17, VII, p.135, X, p.1727, XIII, pp.29-30, XVII, pp.246-50); Nawwāb 206 law (cat., p.449); Bengal 1477 (cat., II, p.269); Gharb 1400 (cat., p.26)

AL-ARDABĪLĪ:

Risāla dar ṣalāt wa ṣawm, Persian
MSS: Raḍawī 2759 (cat., V, p.439); Dānishgāh 878/9 (cat., V, pp. 1885-6); Gawharshād 998/2 (cat., p.121)

ʿABD ALLĀH AL-TUSTARĪ:

Wājibāt-i namāz, Persian
MSS: Gawharshād 1623 (cat., p.122); Dānishgāh 2711/8, 3224 (cat., X, p.1589, XI, p.2185); Raḍawī 2436, 2441 (cat., II, pp.70-1)

BAHĀʾ AL-DĪN AL-ʿĀMILĪ:

Jāmiʿ-i ʿAbbāsī, Persian, on acts of devotion
Editions: Bombay, 1319 and others
Selected MSS: Sipahsālār 2531 (cat., I, p.15); Bodleian Pers.1784 (cat., III, pp.1031-2); Vatican Pers.15 (cat. Persian, p.41); Leiden 1283 Schult. (cat., IV, p.178)
Translation: Arabic, anonymous, MS: Khāliṣī (cat., p.56)
Completion: (1) by Niẓām al-Dīn Muḥammad b. Ḥusayn al-Sāwijī (d. 1038), edited repeatedly; (2) by Zayn al-ʿĀbidīn al-Ḥusaynī (mid-11th century), on pilgrimage (*mazār*) and inheritance, MSS: Fayḍiyya 847/17 (cat., III, p.30); Āstāna 6054 (cat., p.192); Majlis 45 (cat., I, p.13)
Commentaries: (1) by ʿAlāʾ Burhān al-Tabrīzī (d. after 1054),MS: Āṣafiyya 176 Shīʿī law (cat., IV, p.481); (2) by Muḥammad b. ʿAlī b. Khwātūn al-ʿĀmilī (d. 1057), MSS: Malik 1434, 5878 (cat., II, p.499); Tabrīz, Millī 3076 (cat. of microfilms of Dānishgāh, II, p.75)

AL-DĀMĀD:

Shariʿ al-najāt, Persian, on acts of devotion
Edition: Tehran, 1401 (in the collection of *ithnāʿashar risāla li . . . ʾl-Dāmād*)
Selected MSS: Fayḍiyya 1425/2 (cat., III, p.90); Majlis 4553/5 (cat., XII, pp.236-7); Dānishgāh 7074 (cat., XVI, p.445)

AL-MAJLISĪ I:

Ḥadīqat al-muttaqīn, Persian, on acts of devotion
Selected MSS: Gulpāyigānī 717 (cat., II, p.64); Sipahsālār 1863 (cat., I, p.405); Ḥujjatiyya 400 (cat., p.11); Ustadī (cat., p.46); Cambridge C.16/9 Browne (cat., p.21)

RAFĪʿ AL-DĪN AL-NĀʾĪNĪ: Muḥammad b. Ḥaydar al-Ḥusaynī al-Ṭabāṭabāʾī (d. 1082):

Risāla-yi ʿamaliyya, Persian, on acts of devotion
MS: Dānishgāh 1707/2 (cat., VIII, p.254)

AL-SABZAWĀFĪ:

- *Khilāfiyya*, Persian, on acts of devotion
  Selected MSS: Marʿashī 66, 528/1 (cat., I, pp.76-7, II, p.133); Fayḍiyya 330 (cat., III, p.200); Raḍawī 2393 (cat., II, p.56); Bāqiriyya (AB, XVI, p.280)
- *Risāla dar maʿrifat-i aḥkām-i sharʿiyya*, Persian
  MSS: Raḍawī 7055/8 (cat., V, p.489); Gulpāyigānī 1190 (cat., II, p.88); Wazīrī 1191 (cat., III, p.889)
- *Masāʾil-i mutafarriqa*, Persian, on acts of devotion
  MS: Raḍawī 7055/3 (cat., V, p.489)
- *Risāla-yi ʿamaliyya*, Persian
  MS: Raḍawī 2425 (cat., II, p.66)

AL-FAYḌ:

Minhāj al-najāt, on dogmatics and acts of devotion
MS: Millī 1922/1 Arabic (cat., X, p.591)

AL-MAJLISĪ II:

His numerous Persian treatises on various topics, mostly on acts of devotion
Selected MSS: Marʿashī 15, 187, 1602, 1683, 3034, 3050 (cat., I, pp. 27, 205-17, V, pp.5, 78, VIII, pp.225, 269); Gulpāyigānī 1223, 1305, 1449 (cat., II, pp.63, 236, 260); Fayḍiyya 1747 (cat., III, p.128); Millī 1854f (cat., IV, pp.313-17)

AL-SAMĀHĪJĪ:

- *Mā yajib ʿala ʾl-mukallaf ʿamaluh wa lā yasaʿuh jahluh*
  MS: Tustariyya (AB, XIX, p.35)
- *Nukhbat al-wājibāt*
  MSS: Marʿashī (AB, XXIV, p.100); Tustariyya 633/2 (cat., p.870)

AL-BIHBAHĀNĪ:

- *Ādāb al-tijāra*, on transactions, two versions: Arabic and Persian
  Edition: Arabic version, Tehran, 1290 and others; Persian version, Tabrīz, 1321 and others
- *Al-Tuḥfa al-Ḥusayniyya*, on prayer and fasting
  MSS: Dānishgāh 1615 (cat., VIII, p.205); Sipahsālār 6464/2 (cat., III, p.359); Fayḍiyya 1485 (cat., I, p.40)
  Translation: Persian, MS: Ḥujjatiyya 597/1 (cat., p.115)

MAHDĪ AL-NARĀQĪ:

- *Anīs al-tujjār*, Persian, on transactions
  Editions: Tehran, 1317, 1329, 1349
  MSS: Sipahsālār 2546 (cat., I, pp.368-9); Ḥuqūq 185j (cat., p.20); Raḍawī 6184 (Bīnish, p.609); Wazīrī 1017 (cat., III, p.823)
- *Al-Tuḥfa al-Raḍawiyya*, Persian
  MSS: Wazīrī 1937 (cat., III, p.1100)

ʿABD AL-ṢAMAD AL-HAMADĀNĪ:

Al-Tuḥfa al-shahīdiyya, Persian
MS: Millī 3029/6f (cat., VI, p.810)

MUḤAMMAD ḤUSAYN B. ʿABD AL-BĀQĪ AL-HUṢAYNĪ AL-KHWĀTŪNĀBĀDĪ (d. 1233):

Maṣābīḥ al-qulūb, Persian, on acts of devotion
MSS: Marʿashī 420 (cat., II, p.24); Gulpāyigānī 1066, 1557 (cat., II, p.170); Ustādī (cat., p.55)

ḤUSAYN ĀL ʿUṢFŪR:

Al-Fatāwā al-Ḥusayniyya
MS: Marʿashī 2350 (cat., VI, p.325)

KĀSHIF AL-GHIṬĀʾ:

Bughyat al-ṭālib, on dogmatics and prayer
Selected MSS: Majlis 4588 (cat., XII, pp.286-7); Marʿashī 602/1,

1539 (cat., II, p.195, IV, p.339); Tarbiyat 252 (cat., p.28); Los Angeles M93/3 (cat., p.661); Harvard (*Nash.*, IX, p.348)
Completion: by Ḥasan Āl Kāshif al-Ghiṭāʼ, on fasting and seclusion, MS: Marʻashī 602/5 (cat., II, p.196)
Translation: *Tuḥfat al-rāghib*, Persian, by Ṣāḥib al-Maqābis, MSS: Malik 2590 (cat., II, p.58); Raḍawī 2284 (Bīnish, p.634)

ṢĀḤIB AL-RIYĀḌ:

- *Zahr al-riyāḍ*, Persian, compiled by Abū ʻAlī Muḥammad b. Ismāʻīl al-Ḥāʼirī al-Māzandarānī (d. 1216) on the basis of *Riyāḍ al-masāʼil*
  Selected MSS: Dānishgāh 5703, 7163 (cat., XVI, pp.71, 471); Wazīri 1376, 1454 (cat., III, pp.942, 954); Burūjirdī (AB, XII, p.71); Nujūmī (cat., p.274)
- *Mukhtaṣasr-i Risāla-yi ʻamaliyya*, Persian, on acts of devotion, by Ibrāhīm b. Ḥusayn al-Ḥusaynī
  MS: Marʻashī 1956 (cat., V, p. 329)

AL-QUMMĪ:

- *Muʻīn al-khawāṣṣ*, on acts of devotion
  Selected MSS: Marʻashī 18, 720 (cat., I, p.30, II, p.315); Gulpāyigānī 1391/1 (cat., II, p.254); Sipahsālār (cat., I, pp.426, 524); Tustariyya (AB, XXI, p. 284); Dānishgāh 3608 (cat., XII, p.2613); Gawharshād 1747 (cat., p.403)
- *Murshid al-ʻawāmm*, Persian, on acts of devotion
  Selected MSS: Raḍawī 2612-13, 7614, 7938 (Bīnish, p.1002); Gulpāyigānī 694, 726 (cat., II, pp.165, 206); Fayḍiyya (cat., II, p.98); Ḥuqūq 211j (cat., p.191); Majlis 189, 2902, 4086, 5991 (cat., I, p.57, X, p.292, XII, pp. 8405; XVII, pp.364-5); Millī 2152f, 2196f (cat., V, pp. 206, 281-2)

AL-MUJĀHID:

Iṣlāḥ al-ʻamal
Selected MSS: Marʻashī 635/4, 1082 (cat., II, p.236, III, pp.261-2)
Translation: Persian, by Ḥasan b. Muḥammad ʻAlī al-Ḥāʼirī al-Yazdī, MSS: Fayḍiyya, 906 and 5 other MSS (cat., II, pp.28-9); Ḥujjatiyya 403 (cat., p.7); Ilāhiyyāt 821d (cat., II, p.4); Dānishgāh 7230 (cat., XVI, p.494)
Abridgements: (1) *Miṣbāḥ al-ṭarīq*, Persian, by Ḥasan b. Muḥammad ʻAlī al-Yazdī, MSS: Dānishgāh 7160 (cat., XVI, p.469); Fayḍiyya, 3 MSS (cat., II, p.100); Masjid-i Aʻẓam 4465; (2) *Tuḥfat al-muqallidīn*, Persian, by Ḥusayn b. Muḥammad al-Wāʻiẓ al-Tustarī (d. after 1240), MS: Ḥujjatiyya 703/6 (cat., p. 122); (3) by Karīm b. Ḥasan al-Īrawānī, MS: Marʻashī 2591 (cat., VII, p.179)

ʻABD ALLĀH SHUBBAR - ʻAbd Allāh b. Muḥammad Riḍā al-Ḥusaynī al-Kāẓimī (d. 1242):

- *Risāla fi ʼl-ṭahāra wa ʼl-ṣalāt*
  MS: Raḍawī 2747 (cat., V, p.442)
- *Zubdat al-dalīl = al-Wajīza*
  MSS: Marʻashī 3397 (cat., IX, pp.182-3); Rasht 2r (cat., p.1132)

AḤMAD AL-NARĀQĪ:

Wasīlat al-najāt, Persian, on acts of devotion
MSS: Sipahsālār 1924 (cat., I, p.554); Marʻashī 2918 (cat., VIII,

p.111); Fayḍiyya 767 (cat., II, p.110)

ṢĀHIB AL-FUṢŪL = Muḥammad Ḥusayn b. Muḥammad Raḥīm al-Iṣfahānī (d. 1254):

Risāla-yi ʿamaliyya, Persian
MS: Gawharshād, 1717 (cat., p.122)

KHIḌR B. SHALLĀL AL-ʿAFKĀWĪ AL-NAJAFĪ (d. 1255):

Jannat al-khuld, on dogmatics and acts of devotion
MSS: Dānishgāh 7147 (cat., XVI, p.465); Millī 18 Arabic (cat., VII, p.20); Raḍawī 2351 (Bīnish, p.684); Ḥakīm 1650m (cat., I, p.163)

AL-SHAFTĪ:

- *Tuḥfat al-abrār*, Persian, on prayer
  Selected MSS: Wazīrī 129 (cat., I, p.168); Fayḍiyya 769 and 2 other MSS (cat., II, p.20; Ustādī (cat., p.44)
  Abridgements: (1) by Muḥammad Taqī al-Harawī; [he later wrote a commentary on this abridgement, entitled *Kashf al-astār*, MS: Mashhad, Adabiyyāt 119 Fayyāḍ (cat., p.135)]; (2) *al-Wajīza*, Persian, by Muḥammad Jaʿfar al-Ābāda'ī, edited Iran, n.d., selected MSS: Marʿashī 528/3 (cat., II, p.134); Ḥujjatiyya 273 (cat., p.30); Sipahsālār 2371 (cat., I, p.508); Masjid-i Aʿẓam 9205; (3) *Hidāyat al-akhyār*, Persian, by the same author, MS: Marʿashī 528/4 (cat., II, p.134)
- *Jawāhir al-masā'il*, Persian, on prayer, compiled by Muḥammad Mahdī b. Muḥammad Bāqir al-Maḥallātī on the basis of al-Shaftī's *Maṭāliʿ al-anwār*
  MS: Marʿashī 2541 (cat., VII, pp.124-5)
- *Manāsik-i ḥajj*, Persian
  MS: Gawharshād 1765 (cat., p.107)

MUḤAMMAD IBRĀHĪM AL-KALBĀSĪ:

Irshād al-mustarshidīn, Persian
Selected MSS: Marʿashī 528/2 (cat., II, p.133); Gulpāyigānī 926, 1053 (cat., II, p.9); Fayḍiyya, 2 MSS (cat., II, p.12); Wazīrī 241 (cat., I, p.240)

ṢĀḤIB AL-JAWĀHIR:

Najāt al-ʿibād
Edition: Tehran, 1291 and others
Selected MSS: Dānishgāh 1830 (cat., VIII, p.428); Malik 2929 (cat., I, p. 765); Marʿashī 2397 (cat., VI, p.378)
Translations: (1) Persian, by ʿAlī b. Ibrāhīm al-Ḥusaynī al-Sāwijī, MS: Gulpāyigānī 570 (cat., II, p.86); (2) Persian, by Abū Ṭālib b. ʿAbd al-Muṭṭalib al-Ḥusaynī al-Hamadānī (d. 1266), edited Tehran, 1293

AL-ANṢĀRĪ:

- *Ṣirāṭ al-najāt*, Persian, compiled by Muḥammad ʿAlī al-Yazdī
  Edition: Tehran, 1319 and others
  Selected MSS: Ḥujjatiyya 619 (cat., p.19); Gulpāyigānī 1588 (cat., II, p.86)
  Translation: Arabic, MS: Amīr al-Mu'minīn (AB, XV, pp.38-9)
- *Risāla-yi ʿamaliyya*, Persian, complied by ʿAlī b. Muḥammad al-Tustarī

MS: Gawharshād 1099 (cat., p.123)

ḤASAN B. 'ALĪ AL-ḤUSAYNĪ (d. after 1268):

Hidāyat al-ṭālibīn, Persian, on prayer
MS: Mar'ashī 740 (cat., II, p.341)

MUḤAMMAD B. MAHDĪ AL-ASHRAFĪ AL-MĀZANDARĀNĪ (d. 1315):

Sha'ā'ir al-Islām = Su'āl wa jawāb, Persian
Edition: Tehran, 1312

AL-YAZDĪ:

Al-'Urwa al-wuthqā - see above, section A. It is the most popular Arabic collection of *fatwā*s among later Shī'ī jurists up to the present time, on which most of them wrote marginal glosses when their opinions differed from those stated in this work.
Translation: *al-Ghāya al-quṣwā*, Persian, by 'Abbās b. Muḥammad Riḍā al-Qummī (d. 1359), edited Baghdad and Tabrīz, 1330-6

ABU 'L-ḤASAN AL-IṢFAHĀNĪ:

Wasīlat al-najāt - see above, section A

AL-BURŪJIRDĪ - Ḥusayn b. 'Alī al-Ṭabāṭabā'ī (d. 1380):

Tawḍīḥ al-masā'il, Persian, now the most popular Persian collection of *fatwā*s, on which most contemporary Shī'ī jurists have written marginal glooses. Many different versions of this work have appeared, reflecting the slightly varying opinions of different jurists.
Editions: Tehran, 1337 and others

AL-ḤAKĪM:

Minhāj al-ṣāliḥīn
Editions: Najaf, 1372 and others

AL-KHUMAYNĪ:

Taḥrīr al-Wasīla - see above, section A.

C

MISCELLANEOUS WORKS

AL-MUFĪD:

- *Al-'Awīṣ fi 'l-fiqh*
MSS: Mar'ashī 243/12, 255/17, 78/11, 3694/2 (cat., I, pp.93, 269, 285, X, p.92); Dānishgāh 6963/8, 1045/1, 7177/9 (cat., V, pp.1947-8, XVI, pp.413, 475); Princeton 1399/2 New Series; Wazīrī (*Nash*., IV, p.397); Gawharshād 1090/1 (cat., p.353); Majlis 8/20 Khu'ī (cat., VII, p.196); Gulpāyigānī 2248/2 (cat., III, p.208); Khāliṣī (cat., p.281)
Abridgement: anonymous, MS: Majlis 4900 (cat., XIV, p.96)
Translation: Persian, by Abu 'l-Qāsim b. Muḥammad Kāẓim al-Ḥusaynī al-Mūsawī, MS: Dānishgāh 4419/1 (cat., XIII, p.3391)

- *Al-I'lām fī mā ittafaqat 'alayh al-Imāmiyya min al-aḥkām mimmā ittafaqat al-'Āmma 'alā khilāfihim fīh*
  Edition: Najaf, 1372
  MSS: Dānishgāh 1476/3 (cat., VIII, p.128); Ṣāḥib al-Dharī'a (cat. of microfilms of Dānishgāh, I, p.676)

- *Al-Masā'il al-Naysābūriyya*
  MS: Mar'ashī (AB, V, p.240)

- *Al-masā'il allatī sa'alahā al-shaykh Abū Ja'far al-Ṭūsī*
  MS: Majlis 5643/3 (cat., XVII, p.97)

AL-MURTAḌĀ:

- *Jawābāt al-masā'il al-Mawṣiliyya*
  MSS: Raḍawī 1448/4-5 (cat., II, p.38); Majlis 2819/2-3 (cat., X, pp. 126-31); Khāliṣī (cat., p.288); Ḥakīm 438 (cat., I, p.32); Ṣāḥib al-Dharī'a (cat. of microfilms of Dānishgāh, I, p.574)

- *Jawābāt masā'il ahl Mayyāfāriqīn*
  MSS: Raḍawī 1448/6 (cat., II, p.38); Dānishgāh 2144 (cat., IX, p.815); Millī 1943/6 Arabic (cat., X, p.618); Majlis 2819/4 (cat., X, pp.131-3); Khāliṣī (cat., p.288); Ḥakīm 438 (cat., I, p.32); Ṣāḥib al-Dharī 'a (cat. of microfilms of Dānishgāh, I, p.574)
  Translation: Persian, by M.H.B. Kūhsurkhī, edited Mashhad, 1389 (in *Nāma-yi Āstāni-i Quds,* XXXI, pp.36-57)

- *Jawābāt masā'il al-sharīf Abi 'l-Ḥusayn al-Muḥassan b. Muḥammad b. al-Nāṣir al-Ḥasanī al-Rassī = al-Masā'il al-Rassiyyāt*
  MSS: Raḍawī 2646 (cat., II, p.134); Sipahsālār 2533/2 (cat., V, p.562); Khāliṣī (cat., p.288); Majlis 5187/5 (cat., XVI, p.7); Dānishgāh 6914/10 (cat., XVI, p.398); Ṣāḥib al-Dharī 'a (cat. of microfilms of Dānishgāh, I, p.574); Ḥakīm (*Nash*., V, p.427)

- *Jawābāt al-masā'il al-Rāziyyāt*
  MSS: Dānishgāh 2319/4 (cat., IX, p.949); Raḍawī 2429 (cat., II, p.67); Khāliṣī ((cat., p.288); Ṣāḥib al-Dharī 'a (cat. of microfilms of Dānishgāh, I, p.574); Ḥakīm 438 (cat., I, p.31); Mar'ashī 3694/5 (cat., X, p.93)

- *Jawābāt al-masā'il al-Tabbāniyyāt*
  MSS: Raḍawī 1448/1 (cat., II, p.37); Khāliṣī (cat., p.288); Ṣāḥib al-Dharī 'a (cat. of microfilms of Dānishgāh, I, p.574); Ḥakīm 436 (cat., I, p.30)

- *Jawābāt al-masā'il al-Ṭarābulusiyyāt*
  MSS: Sipahsālār 2533/8 (cat., V, p.560); Majlis 5187/8 + 13 (cat., XVI, pp. 8-11); Dānishgāh 6166, 6914/22 (cat., XVI, pp.311, 398-9); Khāliṣī (cat., p.289); Ṣāḥib al-Dharī 'a (cat. of microfilms of Dānishgāh, I, p.574); Ḥakīm 438 (cat., I, pp.31-2)

- *Mutafarridāt al-Imāmiyya*
  MS: Dānishgāh 1080/5 (cat., III, pp.612-13)
  Translation: Persian, by Muḥammad Ṣādiq al-Sirkānī, MS: Wazīrī (cat. of microfilms of Dānishgāh, I, p.703)

- *Shatāt al-fawā'id wa 'l-masā'il*, including:
  (a) *al-Masā'il al-Nīliyyāt*
  (b) *al-Masā'il al-Ramliyyāt*
  (c) *al-Masā'il al-Wāsiṭiyyāt*
  and some others of his scattered writings
  MSS: Berlin Pet.40 (cat., IV, pp.347-8); Princeton 2751 Yahuda (cat., 137); Majlis 5187/11 (cat., XVI, p.10); Sipahsālār 2524/1 (cat., V,

pp.557-9); Raḍawī 1448 (cat., II, p.66); Ṣāḥib al-Dharī'a (AB, XX, p.222); Ḥakīm 432 (cat., I, p.33); Kāshān, 'Āṭifī (*Nash.*, XI-XII, pp. 953-4)

- Two other collections of al-Sharīf al-Murtaḍā's answers to various legal and theological questions
  MS: Dānishgāh 1080/6-7 (cat., II, p.613)

ABŪ YA'LĀ - Muḥammad b. Ḥasan b. Ḥamza al-Ja'firī (d. 463):

Masā'il mutafarriqa
MS: Majlis 8/28 Khu'ī (cat., VII, p.352)

AL-SHAYKH:

Al-Masā'il al-Ḥā'iriyyāt
MSS: Amīr al-Mu'minīn (Ḥujjatī, p.663); Mar'ashī 1519/3 (cat., IV, p. 320)

AL-RĀWANDĪ:

Masā'il, Persian
Edition: Tehran, 1374 (in *Farhang-i Iran zamīn*, III, pp.263-7)

IBN SHAHRĀSHŪB:

Mutashābih al-Qur'ān wa mukhtalifuh
Edition: Tehran, 1369
MS: Majlis 5440 (cat., XVII, p.325)

IBN IDRĪS:

Masā'il fī ab'āḍ al-fiqh wa jawābātuhā
MS: Ḥakīm 570 (cat., I, p.28)

AL-MUḤAQQIQ:

- *Al-'Izziyya*
  MSS: Ustādī (cat., p.69); Majlis 1307 (cat., IV, p.92); Dānishgāh 1474/1 (cat., VIII, p.124); Khāliṣī (cat., p.289); Burūjirdī (cat., p.37); Raḍawī 205 (Bīnish, p.915)
- *Al-Masā'il al-Baghdādiyya*
  MSS: Raḍawī 2655 (cat., II, p.137); Majlis 2761/13 (cat., IX, pp. 162-3); Khāliṣī (cat., p.289); Masjid-i A'ẓam 4377
- *Al-Masā'il al-Kamāliyya*
  MS: Malik 1626/11 (Dānishpazhūh, pp.3-4)
- *Al-Masā'il al-Khwāriyyāt = al-Masā'il al-Ṭabariyya*
  MSS: Dānishgāh 5923/1, 2319/5 (cat., IX, p.494, XVI, p.154); Millī 1943/10 Arabic (cat., X, p.620)
- *Al-Masā'il al-Miṣriyya*
  MSS: Raḍawī 2654 (cat., II, p.137); Majlis 1307, 2761/12 (cat., IV, p.92, IX, pp.161-2); Dānishgāh 5923/2, 1474/2 (cat., VIII, p.124, XVI, p.154); Khāliṣī (cat., p.289); Masjid-i A'ẓam 4377
- *Al-Muṣṭalaḥāt al-fiqhiyya*
  MS: Dānishgāh 7387/101 (cat., XVI, p.534)

YAḤYĀ B. SA'ĪD:

Nuzhat al-nāẓir (also attributed to Muhadhdhab al-Dīn Ḥusayn b.

Muḥammad al-Nīlī, a scholar of the same period, see Afandī, V, p.338; Āghā Buzurg, XXIV, pp.125-6)
Edition: Tehran, 1318; Najaf, 1386
Selected MSS: Bengal 624 (cat., I, p.308); Kāshān, Raḍawī 237 (cat., p.44); Majlis 8148, 2766 (cat., IX, p.175); Princeton 2321 Yahuda (cat., p.137); Marʿashī 683, 1129, 1771, 2796/3 (cat., II, p.277, III, p.302, V, p.151, VII, p.362); Gulpāyigānī 1043/3 (cat., II, p.222); Dānishgāh 7128 (cat., XVI, p.461); Wazīrī 110/5 (cat., I, p.146)

AL-ʿALLĀMA:

- *Ajwibat al-masāʾil al-Muhannāʾiyya*
Edition: Qum, 1401
Selected MSS: Dānishgāh 1022/1, 1474/4, 2144/3, 2477/6, 2396/1, 6710/59 (cat., V, pp.2021-5, VIII, p.126, IX, pp.820, 1245, XV, p.4237, XVI, p.342); Raḍawī 2822, 2330-2, 2727, 2799 (cat., II, p. 36, V, pp.396-8); Majlis 4566, 5192 (cat., XII, pp.259-60, XVI, pp. 18-20); Gulpāyigānī 1751 (cat., III, p.45); Malik 2510 (cat., I, p.667); Ḥuqūq 10/2d (cat., p.459); Ilāhiyyāt 246/4d (cat., I, p.266); Marʿashī 1409 (cat., IV, pp.187-9); Nawwāb 213 law (cat., p.475); India Office 1797 (cat., II, p.309); Princeton 960/1 New Series

- *Ajwibat masāʾil Ibn Zuhra*
MSS: Dānishgāh 1474/3, 3514/17 (cat., VIII, p.125, XII, p.26526); Ḥakīm 548 (cat., I, p.28); Ḥuqūq 178/1j (cat., p.460)

- *Ajwibat al-masāʾil al-fiqhiyya*
MSS: Majlis 5643/2 (cat., XVII, p.97); Dānishgāh 2621/5 (cat., IX, p.1497)

IBN DĀWŪD:

ʿIqd al-jawāhir fi ʾl-ashbāh wa ʾl-naẓāʾir
MS: Marʿashī 67/1 (cat., I, pp.77-80)

FAKHR AL-MUḤAQQIQĪN:

- *Al-Masāʾil al-Āmuliyyāt*
MSS: Dānishgāh 1012/2, 2144/2 (cat., V, pp.2015-17, IX, p.820)

- *Masāʾil baʿḍ al-ajilla*
MSS: Dānishgāh 1474/5 (cat., VIII, p.127); Marʿashī 457/1 (cat., II, p.59)

- *Masāʾil baʿḍ al-fuḍalāʾ*
MS: Ilāhiyyāt 106/5d (cat., I, p.235)

- *Al-Masāʾil al-fiqhiyya*
MSS: Dānishgāh 1804, 5396/3, 5237 (cat., VIII, p.380, XV, pp.4172, 4237); Ḥakīm 548 (cat., I, p.28)

- *Al-Masāʾil al-Maẓāhiriyya*, compiled by Zayn al-Dīn ʿAlī b. Ḥasan b. Maẓāhir al-Ḥillī (d. after 786)
MS: Dānishgāh 1192/1 (cat., VI, p.2341)

- *Al-Masāʾil al-Nāṣiriyyāt*
MS: Malik 649 (cat., I, p.667)

IBN NAJM AL-DĪN - Ḥasan b. Ayyūb al-Aṭrāwī al-ʿĀmilī (mid-8th century):

Masāʾil Ibn Najm
MS: Tehran, Riḍā Zanjānī (AB, XX, pp.333-4)

AL-SHAHĪD AL-AWWAL:

- *Ajwibat al-masāʼil al-fiqhiyya*, compiled by his son
  MSS: Raḍawī 2369-70, 2351 (cat., II, p.39)
- *Ajwibat masāʼil al-Miqdād b. ʻAbd Allāh al-Suyūrī*
  MSS: Raḍawī 421, 7210 (cat., II, p.130, V, p.355)
- *Ajwibat masāʼil Muḥammad b. Mujāhid*
  MS: Ḥakīm 742 (cat., I, p.29)
- *Arbaʻ masāʼil fiqhiyya*
  MS: Dānishgāh 2711 (cat., X, p.1591)

IBN FAHD:

- *Ajwibat al-masāʼil al-fiqhiyya*
  MS: Bāqiriyya (AB, XII, p.242)
- *Al-Masāʼil al-baḥriyya*
  MSS: Raḍawī 2632 (cat., II, p.130); Majlis 4566/15 (cat., XII, p.265)
- *Al-Masāʼil al-Shāmiyya = Masāʼil saʼalahā al-shaykh Ẓahīr al-Dīn b. al-Ḥusām al-ʻĀmilī*
  MSS: Majlis 4566/14 (cat., XII, p.265); Dānishgāh 6963/7 (cat., XVI, p.413)
- *Al-Lawāmiʻ*
  MSS: Raḍawī 2633, 2637, 6537 (cat., II, pp.130-1, V, p.487); Majlis 4566/16 (cat., XII, pp.265); Zanjānī 23/3 (cat., p.198)

MUFLIḤ AL-ṢAYMARĪ:

Al-Tanbīh ʻalā gharāʼib man lā yaḥḍuruh al-faqīh
MS: Majlis 2761/11 (cat., IX, p.161)

AL-KARAKĪ:

- *Ajwibat al-masāʼil al-fiqhiyya*, compiled by Faḍl Allāh al-Ḥusaynī al-Astarābādī
  MSS: Dānishgāh 2144/43 (cat., IX, p.829); Majlis 4566/17, 5340/3 (cat., XII, p.266, XVI, p.252); Sipahsālār 6041/3 (cat., IV, p.110); Ustādī (cat., p.68); Raḍawī 677 (Bīnish, p.847)
  Translation: by Muḥammad Ṣādiq al-Sirkānī, MS: Wazīrī (cat. of microfilms of Dānishgāh, I, p.702)
- *Ajwibat al-masāʼil al-fiqhiyya*
  MSS: Raḍawī 2333-4 (cat., II, pp.36-7); Dānishgāh 6963/4-5 (cat., XVI, p.412); Tustariyya (AB, XII, p.247)
- *Ajwibat al-masāʼil al-Ṣaymariyya*
  MS: Shīrāzī (AB, II, p.89, V, p.204)
- *Ajwibat masāʼil waradat fī Muḥarram sana 929 ʻan al-sāda al-ʻulamāʼ*
  MS: Dānishgāh 872/1 (cat., V, p.1807)
- *Ajwibat masāʼil mawlānā Yūsuf al-Māzandarānī*
  MS: Sipahsālār 6041/2 (cat., V, p.120)
- *Ajwibat al-masāʼil al-fiqhiyya*, compiled by ʻAlī b. Abi ʼl-Fatḥ al-Mazraʻī al-ʻĀmilī
  Edition; Sidon, 1348-9 (in al-Amīn al-ʻĀmilī's *Maʻādin al-jawāhir*, I, pp. 345-51)
- *Ajwibat al-masāʼil al-fiqhiyya*, answers to different legal questions:

(i) MS: Malik 1302 (cat., I, p.176); (ii) MS: Ḥakīm 1697 (cat., I, p.166); (iii) MS: Gulpāyigānī 827 (cat., II, p.8); (iv) MS: Sipahsālār 2333 (cat., I, p.409, V, p.561); (v) MS: same library 1176/1 (cat., III, pp.285-6); (vi) Dānishgāh 6963/6 (cat., XVI, p.413); (vii) MS: same library 7177/7 (ibid., XVI, p.475); (viii) MS: same library 7387/98 (cat., XVI, p.534)

- *Fatāwā*
  MS: Āstāna 5844/2 (cat., p.219)

- *Al-Masmūʻa*, Persian, his answers to legal questions compiled by Shams al-Dīn Muḥammad Mitqālbāf
  MS: Najaf, Madrasat al-Sayyid (AB, XXI, p.25)

AL-SHAHĪD AL-THĀNĪ:

- *Ajwibat masāʼil Ḥusayn b. Rabīʻa al-Madanī*
  MS: Majlis 5192/6 (cat., XVI, p.21)

- *Ajwibat masāʼil Ibn Farrūj*
  MS: Majlis 5192/5 (cat., XVI, p.21)

- *Ajwibat al-masāʼil al-Māziḥiyya*
  MS: Ḥuqūq 228/5j (cat., p.231); Raḍawī 160 law (cat., II, p.48); Marʻashī 1259/3 (cat., IV, p.60)

- *Ajwibat al-masāʼil al-Najafiyya*
  MS: Raḍawī 7245/1 (cat., V, pp.496-7)

- *Ajwibat al-masāʼil al-Shāmiyya*
  MS: Raḍawī 7245/2 (cat., V, p.497)

- *Ajwibat masāʼil Shukr b. Ḥamdān*
  MS: Dānishgāh 3414/22 (cat., XII, p.2527)

- *Ajwibat masāʼil al-sayyid Sharaf al-Dīn al-Samākī*
  MSS: Dānishgāh 2099/5 (cat., VIII, p.727); Ḥuqūq 288/4j (cat., p.231); Raḍawī 159 law (cat., II, p.48); ʻAbd al-ʻAẓīm 235 (cat., p.445); Bengal (cat., I, p.320); Ḥakīm (AB, XX, pp.6-7)

- *Fawāʼid mutafarriqa*
  MS: Raḍawī 2897 (cat., V, p.469)

- *Majmūʻat al-ifādāt = al-Rasāʼil*, a collection of 12 treatises of which 8 are legal (see below, chapter 6)
  Edition: Tehran, 1313
  Selected MSS: Majlis 265, 4471/8, 5354/3 (cat., XII, p.146, XVI, p.265); Ḥuqūq 228j (cat., pp.232, 285, 311, 328, 330, 401, 492); Raḍawī 2364-8 (cat., II, pp.47-8, 141-2); Dānishgāh 2099, 3205/8, 6255/1, 7203 (cat., VII, pp.272-8, XI, p.2163, XVI, pp.228, 486); Zanjān (cat., pp.140-1); Dār al-Kutub 19179b, 3326j (cat., I, pp.278, 381, 388, 391); Los Angeles M120, M169 (cat., p.667); Tustariyya 140 (cat., pp 835-6); Baku M140/41 (*Nash.*, IX, p.242): Ḥakīm 1656m; ʻAbd al-ʻAẓīm 235 (cat., p.445); Marʻashī 1777, 2362, 444/7 (cat., II, p.49, V, pp.157-8, VI, p.346); Gulpāyigānī 1751/5 (cat., III, p.41); Masjid-i Aʻẓam 451/1

- *Masāʼil al-tilmīdh*
  MS: Burūjirdī (AB, XX, p.341)

- *Al-Mukhtār min mawāḍiʻ al-khilāf fī masāʼil kitāb al-Lumʻa al-Dimashqiyya*
  MS: Bengal 640 (cat., I, p.316)

- *Al-Tanbīh ʻalā masāʼil iddaʻā fīhā al-Shaykh al-Ṭūsī al-ijmāʻ maʻa*

annah nafsah khālaf fī ḥukm mā idda'ā al-ijmā' fīh = Risāla fī ijmā'āt Shaykh al-Ṭā'ifa
Editions: Tehran, 1308 (together with al-Shahīd al-Awwal's *al-Alfiyya*); Mashhad, 1392 (in the collection of *al-Dhikrā al-alfiyya li 'l-Shaykh al-Ṭūsī*, pp.789-98)
MSS: Gulpāyigānī 1484 (cat., II, p.45); Dānishgāh 6369/3 (cat., XVI, p.253); Ilāhiyyāt 561/3 (cat., I, pp.328-9); Amīr al-Mu'minīn 358 (*Nash.*, V, p.414)

ḤUSAYN B. 'ABD AL-ṢAMAD B. SHAMS AL-DĪN MUḤAMMAD AL-ḤĀRITHĪ AL-'ĀMILĪ (d. 984):

- *Masa'alatān*
  MSS: Mar'ashī 744/2 (cat., II, p.345); Millī 1943/3 Arabic (cat., X, pp. 616-17); Gulpāyigānī 48/3 (cat., I, p.58); Majlis 1836/12 (cat., IX, pp.489-91)
- *Masā'il fiqhiyya*
  MS: Sipahsālār 2333/1 (cat., I, p.409, V, p.561)
- *Al-Tusā'iyya = Tis' masā'il*
  MSS: Majlis 1805/53, 4900/48, 5960/3 (cat., IX, p.356, XIV, p.74, XVII, pp.344-5); Princeton 538/3 Yahuda (cat., p.149)

ṢĀḤIB AL-MA'ĀLIM:

Ajwibat masā'il Muḥammad b. Juwaybar al-Madanī = al-Masā'il al-Madaniyyāt
MSS: Ḥakīm 903m (cat., I, p.165); Dānishgāh 7312/6 (cat., XVI, p.510); Malik 1049

'ABD ALLĀH AL-TUSTARĪ:

Al-Rasā'il, a collection of around 20 treatises on various legal topics (see below, chapter 6)
MSS: Raḍawī 7055 (Bīnish, p.982); Najaf, Sharī'at (AB, V, pp. 243, 245, 302, XI, pp.47, 64, 149, 155, 156, 157, XV, p.175, XVI, p.55, XVIII, pp.84, 88, 103, XXIV, p.105, XXV, p.110)

BAHĀ' AL-DĪN AL-'ĀMILĪ:

- *Ajwibat masā'il al-Shaykh Jābir*
  MS: Dānishgāh 2621/6 (cat., IX, p.1497)
- *Ajwibat masā'il al-shaykh Ṣāliḥ b. Ḥasan al-Jazā'irī*
  MSS: Dānishgāh 4316/3, 1130/7, 3598/9, 5873/6 (cat., V, pp.1797-8, XIII, p.3279, XV, p.4241, XVI, p.117); Ḥakīm 18/7 Rashtī (cat., p.39); Majlis 5192/7 (cat., XVI, p.22); Adabiyyāt 120/11 Ḥikmat (cat., p.42); Sinā 1245/6 (cat., II, p.181); Mar'ashī 1691/3 (cat., V, p.86); Sipahsālār 4510/4 (cat., II, p.277); Zanjān (cat., p.89)
  Translation: Persian, by Muḥammad Ṣādiq al-Sirkānī, MS: Wazīrī (cat. of microfilms of Dānishgāh, I, pp. 702, 705)
- *Jawāb-i masā'il-i Shāh 'Abbās*, Persian
  MS: Sipahsālār 8150/3 (cat., III, p.276); Dānishgāh 7013/11 (cat., XVI, p.429); Millī (cat. of microfilms of Dānishgāh, II, p.266)
- *Al-Masā'il al-fiqhiyya*
  MS: Majlis 2761/10 (cat., IX, pp.160-1)

AL-DĀMĀD:

- *Al-I'ḍālāt al-'awīṣāt*
  MS: Fayḍiyya 1415/3 (cat., III, p.90)
- *Al-Ithnā'ashariyya = 'Uyūn al-masā'il al-fiqhiyya*
  MSS: Princeton 232/3 New Series; Dānishgāh 859, 1837/8 (cat., V, pp.1760-1, VIII, p.434); Ḥuqūq 10/3d (cat., pp.230-1); Iṣfahān, Madrasa-yi Ṣadr (*Nash*., V, p.312); Tiflis 699/9 (ibid., VIII, p.260)

MUḤAMMAD TAQĪ B. ABI 'L-ḤASAN AL-ḤUSAYNĪ AL-ASTARĀBĀDĪ (mid-11th century):

Munāqashāt fiqhiyya
MS: Raḍawī 2647 (cat., II, p.135)

SULṬĀN AL-'ULAMĀ':

Al-Masā'il
MS: Mar'ashī 3038/1 (cat., VIII, pp.238-9)

AL-MAJLISĪ I:

Ajwiba-yi masā'il-i fiqhī, Persian, compiled by Kalb 'Alī al-Burūjirdī
MS: Millī 2582/2f (cat., VI, p.112)

RAFĪ' AL-DĪN AL-NĀ'ĪNĪ:

Ajwiba-yi masā'il-i fiqhī, Persian, compiled by Mahdī b. Riḍā al-Ḥusaynī
MS: Raḍawī 2772 (cat., V, p.355)

ḤUSAYN AL-KHWĀNSĀRĪ:

Ajwibat al-masā'il, a collection of answers given by this scholar and his two sons, Raḍī al-Dīn and Jamāl al-Dīn, to various legal and theological questions
MS: Raḍawī 2644 (cat., II, p.133)

AL-SHĪRWĀNĪ - Muḥammad b. Ḥasan, Mullā Mīrzā (d. 1098):

Ajwiba-yi masā'il-i fiqhī, Persian
MS: Fayḍiyya 1665 (cat., III, p.113); Dānishgāh 7008 (cat., XVI, pp.426-7)

AL-MAJLISĪ II:

- *Ajwibat masā'il al-Mawlā Majd al-Dīn al-Tustarī*
  MS: Princeton 388 New Series (fols. 49a-51b)
- *Ayādī Sabā*, Persian, compiled by Muḥammad Ja'far b. Muḥammad Ṭāhir al-Khabūshānī
  MS: Mar'ashī 602/4 (cat., II, p.196)
- *Jawāb-i masā'il-i Khurāsān*, Persian, compiled by Ḥāmid b. Muḥammad Budalā' al-Ḥusaynī
  MS: Dānishgāh 5914/4 (cat., XVI, p.150)
- *Jawāb-i masā'il-i mīrzā sayyid 'Alī*, Persian, compiled by Ḥāmid b. Muḥammad Budalā' al-Ḥusaynī
  MS: Dānishgāh 5914/5 (cat., XVI, p.150)
- *Hidāyat al-ikhwān*, Persian
  MS: Fayḍiyya 1747/1 (cat., III, p.128)

- *Majmūʿa-yi suʾāl wa jawāb*, Persian, compiled by Muḥammad Kāẓim al-Sabzawārī
  MS: Gulpāyigānī 536/4 (cat., II, pp. 198-9)
- *Majmuʿa-yi suʾāl wa jawāb*,Persian, different from above
  MS: Marʿashī 2530 (cat., VII, p.117)
- *Al-Masāʾil al-Hindiyya*
  Edition: Iṣfahān, 1403 (in M. Mahdawī's *Zindigīnāma-yi ʿAllāma-yi Majlisī)*
  MS: Ustādī (cat., p.35)
- *Naẓm al-laʾālī*, Persian, compiled by Muḥammad b. Aḥmad al-Ḥusaynī al-Lāhījānī
  MSS: Millī 2011f (cat., V, pp.11-12); Majlis 6895 (fols. 46a-69a); Gawharshād 614 (cat., p.132); Marʿashī 2535 (cat., VII, p.120)
- *Suʾāl wa jawābi-i fiqhī*, Persian
  MS: Dānishgāh 5914/6 (cat., XVI, p.150)

AḤMAD B. IBRĀHĪM AL-BAḤRĀNĪ (d. 1132):

- *Ajwibat masāʾil al-sayyid Yaḥyā b. al-sayyid Ḥusayn al-Aḥsāʾī*
  MS: Princeton 229/19 Yahuda (cat., p.139)
- *Ajwibat masāʾil al-shaykh ʿAbd al-Imām al-Aḥsāʾī*
  MS: Princeton 229/21 Yahuda (cat., p.139)
- *Ajwibat masāʾil al-shaykh ʿAlī b. Luṭf Allāh al-Baḥrānī*
  MS: Princeton 229/17 Yahuda (cat., p.139)
- *Ajwibat masāʾil al-shaykh Nāṣir b. Muḥammad al-Khaṭṭī al-Jārūdī*
  MS: Princeton 229/16 Yahuda (cat., p.139)

AL-SAMĀHĪJĪ:

- *Ajwibat masāʾil al-sayyid ʿAbd Allāh b. al-sayyid ʿAlawī ʿAtīq al-Ḥusayn*
  MSS: Berlin Pm. 505/8 (cat., III, p.315); Tustariyya 633/9 (cat., p.870); London, Ismāʿīlī Institute 631
- *Ajwibat masāʾil al-shaykh Sulaymān*
  MS: Berlin Pm. 505/15 (cat., III, p.323)
- *Al-Fākiha al-Kāẓimiyya*
  MS: Tustariyya (AB, XVI, p.97)
- *Ḥall al-ʿuqūd*
  MS: Berlin Pm. 505/25 (cat., IV, p.211)
- *Hidāyat al-sāʾil*
  MS: Kāshānī 164 (cat., p.296)
- *Al-Lumʿa al-jaliyya fī taḥqīq al-masāʾil al-Ismāʿīliyya*
  MSS: Berlin Pm. 505/24 (cat., III, p.314); Tustariyya 633/12 (cat., p.871); Burūjirdī (AB, XVIII, p.350)
- *Al-Masāʾil al-Bihbahāniyya*
  MS: Berlin Pm. 505/18 (cat., III, p.491)
- *Al-Masaʾil al-Ḥusayniyya*
  MSS: Raḍawī 6981 (cat., V, p.499); Los Angeles M106/1 (cat., p.664)
- *Al-Masāʾil al-Kāzirūniyya*
  MS: Berlin Pm 505/26 (cat., III, p.315)

- *Al-Masā'il al-Muḥammadiyya*
  MS: Raḍawī 6935 (cat., V, pp.499-500)
- *Al-Masā'il al-Nāṣiriyya*
  MS: Berlin Pm. 505/28 (cat., III, p.315)
- *Al-Nafḥa al-'anbariyya fī jawābāt al-masā'il al-Tustariyya*
  MS: Tustariyya 633/10 (cat., p.870)
- *Al-Risāla al-Fahliyāniyya = Jawābāt masā'il al-sayyid Abī Ṭālib*
  MS: Berlin Pm. 505/5 (cat., IV, p.361)
- *Al-Risāla al-sayfiyya fī jawābāt al-masā'il al-Dashtastāniyya*
  MS: Berlin Pm. 505/23 (cat., III, p.314)
- *Mas'alat al-shaykh 'Abd Allāh b. al-shaykh Faraj*
  MS: Berlin Pm. 505/11 (cat., III, p.323)

AL-FĀḌIL AL-HINDĪ:

Al-Iḥtiyāṭāt al-fiqhiyya
MS: Tustariyya (AB, XI, pp.34-5, XV, p.348)

'ABD ALLĀH B. NŪR AL-DĪN AL-JAZĀ'IRĪ (d. 1173):

- *Al-Anwār al-jaliyya fī ajwibat al-masā'il al-Jabaliyya al-ūlā*
  MSS: Dānishgāh 691/2 (cat., VI, p.2144); Gharb 10076/4 (cat., p.433); Ḥakīm 69 (cat., I, p.76); Tustariyya 284 (cat., p.848)
- *Al-Dhakhīra al-abadiyya fī ajwibat al-masā'il al-Aḥmadiyya*
  MSS: Tustariyya (AB, X, p.12); Ḥusayniyyat Kāshif al-Ghiṭā' 14 (ibid.)
- *Al-Dhakhīra al-bāqiya fī ajwibat al-masā'il al-Jabaliyya al-thāniya*
  MSS: Dānishgāh 691/3 (cat., VI, p.2226); Sipahsālār 4510/5 (cat., IV, p.550); Tustariyya 290/3, 421/2 (cat., pp.849, 860)
- *Al-Maqāṣid al-'aliyya fī jawābāt al-masā'il al-'Alawiyya*
  MSS: Sipahsālār 4510/1 (cat., V, p.631); Tustariyya 290/1 (cat., p.849); Shīrāzī (AB, XXI, p.382)

AL-KHWĀJŪ'Ī - Muḥammad Ismā'īl b. Muḥammad Ḥusayn al-Iṣfahānī (d. 1173):

- *Ajwibat al-masā'il*
  MS: Mar'ashī 1986/4 (cat., V, p.359)
- *Al-Rasā'il*, a collection of around 20 treatises on various legal and theological questions (see below, chapter 6)
  MSS: Los Angeles M95, M120 (cat., pp.562, 666); Mashhad, Adabiyyāt 25 Fayyāḍ (cat., pp.210-14)

ṢĀḤIB AL-ḤADĀ'IQ:

- *Ajwibat al-masā'il al-fiqhiyya*
  MSS: Mar'ashī 3450/3 (cat., IX, p.242); Gulpāyigānī 2248/1 (cat., III, p.208); Los Angeles M106/4 (cat., p.664)
- *Ajwibat al-masā'il al-thalāth*
  MS: Mar'ashī 3450/2 (cat., IX, p.241)
- *Ajwibat al-masā'il*
  MS: Sipahsālār 7351/2 (cat., III, pp.275-6)
- *Al-Anwār al-Ḥīriyya*
  MS: Raḍawī 6992 (cat., V, pp.367-9)

- *Al-Durar al-Najafiyya*
  Editions: Tehran, 1307, 1314
  MSS: ʿAbd al-ʿAẓīm 407 (cat., p.465); Marʿashī 3423 (cat., IX, pp.209-10)

- *Al-La'ālī al-zawāhir*
  MS: Majlis 5852/1 (cat., XVII, pp.262-3)

- *Al-Masā'il al-Bihbahāniyya = Ajwibat masā'il al-sayyid ʿAbd Allāh b. al-sayyid ʿAlawī al-Bilādī*
  MS: Marʿashī 3450/1 (cat., IX, p.241)

AL-BIHBAHĀNĪ:

- *Ajwibat al-masā'il*, Persian, compiled by Muḥammad Ḥasan b. ʿAbd al-Wahhāb al-Khurāsānī
  MS: Dānishgāh 1622 (cat., VIII, p.208)

- *Su'āl wa jawāb*, Persian, compiled by Muḥammad b. ʿAbd Allāh al-Ḥusaynī al-Qummī
  MSS: Ḥuqūq 108/1j (cat., pp.349-50)

AL-KIRMĀNSHĀHĪ:

Maqāmiʿ al-faḍl, Persian
Edition: Tehran, 1275, 1316
Selected MSS: Dānishgāh 6756 (cat., XVI, p.354); Ḥuqūq 108j (cat., pp.203-4); Ilāhiyyāt 30b (cat., I, p.409); Millī 2338f (cat., V, p. 457); Marʿashī 3003, 3165 (cat., VIII, pp.177-8, 394); Masjid-i Aʿẓam 6/3

ṢĀḤIB AL-RIYĀḌ:

Su'āl wa jawāb, Persian
MS: Millī 2911/3f (cat., VI, p.630)

AL-QUMMĪ:

- *Jāmiʿ al-shatāt*, Persian and Arabic
  Editions: a selected version of it has been edited Tehran, 1277, 1303, 1324
  Selected MSS: Dānishgāh 1827/1-3, 1682, 7637/3 (cat., VIII, pp.242, 424, XVI, p.661); Sipahsālār 2350, 2358-63 (cat., I, pp.427-9); Āstāna 6418 (cat., p.99); Mllī 2344/1f, 2911/2f (cat., V, p.462, VI, p.529)
  Translation: Arabic, anonymous (written in 1266), MS: Marʿashī 1746 (cat., V, p.130)
  Rearrangements: (1) by Muḥammad Ḥasan b. Muḥammad Ṣāliḥ al-Ḥusaynī al-Nūrbakhshī, MSS: Tustariyya (AB, V, p.60); Khayrāt Khān 38 (cat., pp.1729-30); Zanjān (cat., p.245); (2) by Muḥammad b. Muḥammad ʿAlī al-Kāshānī al-Turkābādī (d. 1269), MS: Khāliṣī (cat., pp.95-6)

- *Jawāmiʿ al-rasā'il*, a collection of 20 treatises by al-Qummī, compiled by Hidāyat b. Riḍā al-Qummī (see below, chapter 6)
  Selected MSS: Tustariyya 426 (cat., p.861); Fayḍiyya 818 (cat., I, pp.67-8); Marʿashī 960 (cat., III, p.152); Masjid-i Aʿẓam 11766; Raḍawī 7261, 7667 (Bīnish pp.777-8)

- *Al-Rasā'il*, another collection of 20 treatises by al-Qummī. 11 of these are the same as those included in the previous collection (see below, chapter 6).

Edition: Tehran, 1319 (together with his *Ghanā'im al-ayyām*)

IBN ṬAWQ AL-BAḤRĀNĪ - Aḥmad b. Ṣāliḥ (mid-13th century):

- *Ajwibat masā'il al-sayyid Ḥusayn*
  MS: Mar'ashī 2358/13 (cat., VI, p.338)
- *Ajwibat masā'il al-shaykh Muḥammad al-Darāzī*
  MS: Mar'ashī 2358/7 (cat., VI, p.336)

AL-MUJĀHID:

Su'āl wa jawāb, Persian
MS: Mar'ashī 715/2 (cat., II, p.310)

AḤMAD AL-NARĀQĪ:

Rasā'il wa masā'il, Persian and Arabic
MS: Gulpāyigānī 1682 (cat., II, p.84, III, p.15)

'ALĪ B. JA'FAR ĀL KĀSHIF AL-GHIṬĀ' (d. 1254):

Al-Taqrīrāt, his lectures compiled by some of his pupils
MSS: Malik 2992 (cat., I, p.227); Gharb, 3 MSS (cat., p.77)

MUḤAMMAD JA'FAR B. MUḤAMMAD 'ALĪ AL-KIRMĀNSHĀHĪ (d. 1254):

Tuḥfat al-abrār, Persian
MS: Raḍawī 6997 (cat., V, p.377)

MUḤAMMAD MAHDĪ B. MUḤAMMAD SHAFĪ' AL-ASTARĀBĀDĪ (d. 1259):

Najm al-mu'min, Persian
MS: Mashhad, Ilāhiyyāt 1118/1 (cat., II, p.250)

AL-SHAFTĪ:

Su'āl wa jawāb, Persian, compiled by Muḥammad Ibrāhīm b. Abi 'l-Ḥasan al-Mūsawī
Edition: Iṣfahān, 1248 (Vol. 1)
Selected MSS: Sipahsālār 2357, 2361 (cat., I, pp.424-5); Gawharshād 414, 1401 (cat., p.131); Mar'ashī 2542 (cat., VII, p.125); Gulpāyigānī 435, 877 (cat., II, p.102); Ḥujjatiyya 92-3, 211 (cat., p.17); Zanjānī 145 (cat., p.257); Saryazdī 134 (cat., p.422); Ustādī, 2 MSS (cat., p.48); Dānishgāh 7161/2 (cat., XVI, p.470)
Abridgement: anonymous, MS: Sipahsālār 2371 (cat., I, p.509)

ṢĀḤIB AL-JAWĀHIR:

- *Su'āl wa jawāb*
  MS: Fayḍiyya 1082/2 (cat., III, p.53)
- *Al-Taqrīrāt*, his lectures compiled by Muḥammad 'Alī bl-Shaftī
  MS: Mar'ashī 1995/4 (cat., V, p.367)

MAḤMŪD B. MUḤAMMAD 'ALĪ AL-KIRMĀNSHĀHĪ (d. 1271):

Ajwibat al-masā'il al-thalāth, Persian and Arabic
MS: Mar'ashī 1537/3 (cat.,IV, p.338)

MUḤAMMAD MAHDĪ B. MUḤAMMAD IBRĀIM AL-KALBĀSĪ (d. 1278):

Ajwibat al-masā'il al-thalāth
MSS: Millī Arabic 15, 16 (cat., VII, pp.18-19)

AL-ANṢĀRĪ:

Lawāmiʿ al-nikāt, his lectures compiled by Maḥmūd b. Jaʿfar al-Maythamī al-ʿArāqī (d. 1308)
Selected MSS: Dānishgāh 744-9 (cat., V, pp.1943-2000); Raḍawī 6654-6 (cat., V, pp.487-8); Malik 1419, 2734 (cat., I, p.624); Gharb, 3 MSS (cat., pp.178-9); Amīr al-Muʾminīn (AB, XII, p.328, XVIII, p.358)

ANONYMOUS

Majmūʿa-yi suʾāl wa jawāb-i fiqhī, Persian
MS: Majlis 4546/1 (cat., XII, pp.218-19)

AL-ĀSHTIYĀNĪ - Muḥammad Ḥasan b. Jaʿfar (d. 1319):

Suʾāl wa jawāb, Persian, compiled by Muḥammad ʿAlī al-Yūzbāshī
MS: Gawharshād 990 (cat., pp.130-1)

HĀDĪ AL-ṬIHRĀNĪ:

Ajwibat al-masāʾil
MS: Tustariyya 878 (cat., p.789)

ĀL BAḤR AL-ʿULŪM - Muḥammad b. Muḥammad Taqī al-Ṭabāṭabāʾī (d. 1326):

Bulghat al-faqīh, a collection of 16 treatises on various legal topics (see below, chapter 6)
Editions: Tabrīz, 1325; Tehran, 1329; Najaf, 1389

AL-KHURĀSĀNĪ:

- *Ḥaqq al-qaḍāʾ*, his lectures compiled by Maḥmūd b. Muḥsin al-Najafī al-Kāshānī
  MS: Marʿashī 2429 (cat., VII, p.24)
- *ʿIddat masāʾil min abwāb shattā*
  Edition: Baghdad, 1331 (in a collection of his writings entitled *Shadharāt*)

AL-YAZDĪ:

Al-Suʾāl wa ʾl-jawāb, compiled by ʿAlī Akbar al-Khwānsārī
Editon: Najaf, 1340

ṢĀDIQ B. MUḤAMMAD AL-TABRĪZĪ (d. 1351):

Al-Fawāʾid fī sharḥ baʿḍ al-mabāḥith al-mushkila fī ʾl-fiqh
Edition: Tabrīz, 1351

ʿABD ALLĀH B. MUḤAMMAD ḤASAN AL-MĀMAQĀNĪ (d. 1351):

- *Al-Masāʾil al-Baghdādiyya*
  Edition: Najaf, 1336
- *Al-Masāʾil al-Baṣriyya*
  Edition: Najaf, 1342
- *Al-Masāʾil al-Khuʾiyya*
  Edition: Najaf, 1344 (in a collection of his treatises entitled *al-Ithnāʿashariyya*)

- *al-Masā'il al-arba'īn al-'Āmiliyya*
  Edition: Najaf, 1344 (in the above-mentioned collection)

MUḤAMMAD ḤUSAYN ĀL KĀSHIF AL-GHIṬĀ' (d. 1373):

Taḥrīr al-Majalla, a commentary on the Ottoman code, *Majallat al-aḥkām al-'adliyya*
Najaf, 1359-62

ḤUSAYN AL-ḤILLĪ:

Buḥūth fiqhiyya, his lectures compiled by 'Izz al-Dīn Baḥr al-'Ulūm
Edition: Najaf, 1384

Chapter Six

SOME MONOGRAPHS

A

GENERAL

1. SEXUALLY SPECIFIC

AL-MUFĪD:

Aḥkām al-nisā'
MSS: Kāshānī 4 (cat., p. 47); Mar'ashī 243/1, 78/1 (cat., I, pp. 89, 267); Majlis 8/10 Khu'ī (cat., VII, pp.85-7); Ḥakīm 998 (cat., I, p.36)

ABU 'L-QĀSIM B. MUḤAMMAD AL-GULPAYIGĀNĪ (d. after 1092):

Sulaymāniyya, Persian, on laws respecting women
MS: Dānishgāh 3334 (cat., XI, p.2318)

'ALĪ B. ḤUSAYN AL-KARBALĀ'Ī (early 12th century):

'Aqd al-kisā' fī fiqh al-nisā'
MS: Majlis 5695 (cat., XVII, pp.151-2)

MU'IZZ AL-DĪN B. 'ALĪ AKBAR AL-ḤUSAYNĪ (13th century):

Tuḥfat al-nisā', Persian
MS: Gulpāyigānī 1639 (cat., III, p.28)

'ALĪ AKBAR AL-QAZWĪNĪ (13th century):

Risāla fi 'l-khunthā wa aḥkāmih
MS: Millī 1783/7 Arabic (cat., X, pp.367-8)

AḤMAD B. 'INĀYAT ALLĀH AL-ḤUSAYNĪ AL-ZANJĀNĪ (d. 1393):

Farq-i miyān-i mard wa zan dar aḥkām, Persian
Edition: Qum, n.d.

2. ON QUR'ĀNIC LAW

AMĪN AL-ISLĀM AL-ṬABRISĪ:

Ma'din al-'irfān fī fiqh Majma' al-bayān, excerpts from al-Ṭabrisī's commentary on the Qur'ān, *Majma' al-bayān*, compiled by Ibrāhīm b. Ḥasan al-Warrāq (before 968)
MS: Los Angeles M1061/2 (cat., p.708)

AL-RĀWANDĪ:

Fiqh al-Qur'ān
Edition: Qum, 1397-9
Selected MSS: Dānishgāh 5471 (cat., XVI, p.17); Mar'ashī 1570, 1042 (cat., III, p.235, IV, p.379); Majlis 5506 (cat., XVI, p.407)

AL-MIQDĀD:

Kanz al-'irfān
Editions: Tehran, n.d., 1384-5; Najaf, n.d.
Selected MSS: Dānishgāh 5129 (cat., XV, p.4121); Wazīrī 634 (cat., II, p.535); Ilāhiyyāt 74 Āl Āqā (cat., I, p. 794); Sipahsālār 5191 (cat., V, p.451); Masjid-i A'ẓam 9697; Majlis 4439 (cat., XII, p.123); Fayḍiyya 623 (cat., I, p.222); Raḍawī 6149 (cat., IV, p.401)

KAMĀL AL-DĪN ḤASAN B. MUḤAMMAD AL-NAJAFĪ AL-ASTARĀBĀDĪ (late 9th century):

Ma'ārij al-su'ūl wa madārij al-ma'mūl
MSS: Majlis 3868, 288 Ṭabāṭabā'ī (cat., X, pp.1900-1); India Office 1810 (cat., II, pp.313-16); Raḍawī 1553 (cat., II, p.455); Nawwāb 31 Qur'ān commentaries (cat., p.532); Āṣafiyya 457 Qur'ān commentaries (cat., I, p.381)

ABU 'L-FATḤ B. MAKHDŪM AL-SHARĪFĪ AL-ARDABĪLĪ (d. 976):

Tafsīr-i shāhī, Persian
Edition: Tabrīz, 1380
Selected MSS: Raḍawī 1251-3 (Bīnish, p.661); Khāliṣī (cat., p.51); Zanjān (cat., p.99); Ḥuqūq 108b, 85j (cat., pp.60-1); Āṣafiyya 251 Qur'ān commentaries (cat., I, p.405); Dānishgāh 909, 1055 (cat., I, pp.59-61)

AL-ARDABĪLĪ:

Zubdat al-bayān
Editions: Tehran, 1368, 1386
Selected MSS: Dānishgāh 1808 (cat., VIII, p.394); Raḍawī 1208, 1209 (cat., II, p.402); Iṣfahān, 'Umūmī 2677, 2695, 2883, 3062 (cat., I, pp.174-5); 'Abd al-'Aẓīm 285 (cat., p.467); Berlin Ldg. 717/1 (cat., IV, p.254); Princeton, New Series 3, 705.
Commentaries: (1) *al-Mut'a*, by Sayyid Mīrzā Khālid, MS: Sipahsālār 4509/3 (cat., V, p.498); (2) *Mafātīḥ al-aḥkām*, by Muḥammad Sa'īd b. Qāsim al-Ḥusaynī al-Ṭabāṭabā'ī al-Quhpā'ī (d. 1092), MSS: Majlis 4828 (cat., XII, p.198); Nūrbakhsh 200 (cat., I, p.196); Mar'ashī 2140 (cat., VI, pp.150-1); (3) by Muḥammad b. 'Abd al-Fattāḥ al-Tunukābunī al-Sarāb (d. 1124), MSS: Wazīrī 1290 (cat., III, p.918); Mahdawī 592/10 (cat., p.125); (4) *Taḥṣīl al-iṭmīnān*, by Muḥammad Ibrāhīm b. Muḥammad Ma'ṣūm al-Ḥusaynī al-Qazwīnī, MSS: Majlis 5553 (cat., XVI, p.415); Gharb 10198 (cat., pp.70-1); (5) by Muḥammad Rafī' al-Gīlānī, MS: Masjid-i A'ẓam 870/6

MUḤAMMAD B. 'ALĪ AL-ḤUSAYNĪ AL-ASTARĀBĀDĪ (d. 1028):

Āyāt al-aḥkām
Edition: Tehran, [1392?]
Selected MSS: Sipahsālār 2053 (cat., I, p.86, III, p.26); Raḍawī 1436 (cat., II, p.403); Millī 1300 Arabic (cat., IX, p.285)

MUʿIZZ AL-DĪN AL-MŪSAWĪ:

Jawāhir al-ḥaqā'iq
MS: Qazwīn, Ḥājj Sayyid Jawādī (*Nash.*, VI, p.342)

AL-FĀḌIL AL-JAWĀD - Jawād b. Saʿd Allāh al-Kāẓimī (d. after 1044):

Masālik al-afhām
Edition: Tehran, 1387
Selected MSS: Marʿashī 2697 (cat., VII, p. 269); Ḥakīm 129 (*Nash.*, V, p.426); Majlis 3331, 4491 (cat., X, p.1126, XII, p.168); Berlin Pm. 50 (cat., IV, p.157); Dānishgāh 64 (cat., I, p.208); Ilāhiyyāt 98b (cat., I, p.660); Malik 916 (cat., I, p.669); Rawḍātī (cat., I, pp.200 ff)

ANONYMOUS (written in 1036-46):

Imāṭat al-lithām ʿan al-āyāt al-wārida fi 'l-ṣiyām = Rafʿ al-lithām
MS: Sipahsālār 2539 (cat., I, pp.361-4)
Translation: Persian, by the author, MS: Raḍawī 2283 (cat., II, p.23)

MALIK ʿALĪ AL-TŪNĪ (late 11th century):

Āyāt al-aḥkām, Persian
MS: Raḍawī 2430 (cat., II, p.68)

AḤMAD B. ISMĀʿĪL AL-NAJAFĪ AL-JAZĀ'IRĪ (d. 1151):

Qalā'id al-durar
Editions: Tehran, 1327; Najaf, 1383

MUḤAMMAD B. ʿALĪ B. ḤAYDAR AL-MŪSAWĪ AL-ʿĀMILĪ (d. 1139):

- *Īnās sulṭān al-mu'minīn*
  MSS: Majlis 3902 (cat., X, pp.1926-7); Rawḍātī (see AB, II, p.518)
- *Āyāt al-aḥkām*
  MS: Marʿashī 2928/6 (cat., VIII, p.122)

3. ON GENERAL PRINCIPLES OF LAW

AL-SHAHĪD AL-AWWAL:

Al-Qawāʿid wa 'l-fawā'id
Editions: Tehran, 1308; Najaf, 1399
Selected MSS: Marʿashī 2579, 1152, 1659 (cat., III, p.325, V, pp. 55-6, VII, pp.168-9); Fayḍiyya 700 (cat., I, p.208); Ilāhiyyāt 121/2b (cat., I, p.134); Princeton 3962 Yahuda (cat., p.138); Nawwāb 53-4 law (cat., p.464); Dānishgāh 1011 (cat., V, p.1980); Gawharshād 710 (cat., p.371); Majlis 5833 (cat., XVII, p.246); Gharb 620 (cat., p.172); Adabiyyāt 214 Kirmān (cat., p.101)
Abridgements and rearrangements: (1) *Jāmiʿ al-fawā'id fī talkhīṣ al-Qawāʿid*, by al-Miqdād, MS: Raḍawī 2313 (cat., II, pp.31-2); (2) *Naḍd al-qawāʿid al-fiqhiyya*, by the same author, MSS: Raḍawī 2663, 8046-7 (cat., II, p.139); Marʿashī 2508, 461 (cat., II, pp. 67-8, VII, p.95); Dānishgāh, microfilm 2170 (cat., I, p.394); Ḥujjatiyya 504/2 (cat., p.111); (3) *Tamhīd al-qawāʿid*, by al-Shahīd al-Thānī, edited Tehran, 1271, selected MSS: Majlis 1339 (cat., IV, p.106); Raḍawī 2862, 7334 (Bīnish, p.668); Millī 1384/1 Arabic (cat., IX, p. 389); Nawwāb 11 law (cat., p.453); Berlin Pet. 548 (cat., IV, p.248) [ʿAlī b. Muḥammad al-ʿĀmilī wrote a commentary on this work,

MSS: Dānishgāh 1802 (cat., VIII, p.375); Gharb 215/1, 4320 (cat., pp.96, 228).]
Commentaries: (1) by Bahā' al-Dīn al-'Āmilī, edited Tehran, 1308 (in the margin of *al-Qawā'id*), MS: Shīrāzī (AB, VI, p.173); (2) *al-Qalā'id al-saniyya*, by Muḥammad b. 'Alī al-Ḥarfūshī al-'Āmilī (d. 1059), partly edited Tehran, 1308 (in the margin of *al-Qawā'id*), selected MSS: Dānishgāh 1812 (cat., VIII, p.400); Amīr al-Mu'minīn (*Nash.*, V, p.415); Mar'ashī 2705 (cat., VII, p.275); Masjid-i A'ẓam 3053; Rawḍātī, 2 MSS (cat., I, pp.252-60)

IBN ABĪ JUMHŪR - Muḥammad b. 'Alī b. Ibrāhīm al-Aḥsā'ī (d. after 920):

Al-Aqṭāb al-fiqhiyya
MSS: Dānishgāh 3663 (cat., XII, p.2674); Majlis 5469 (cat., XVI, p.370); Mar'ashī 3394 (cat., IX, pp.180-1)

AL-KARAKĪ:

Risāla fī 'l-taqiyya
MSS: Majlis 4566/10 (cat., XII, p.263); Dānishgāh 6963/9 (cat., XVI, p.413); Gulpāyigānī 1751/7 (cat., III, p.41); Princeton 1935/2 New Series

AL-SABZAWĀRĪ:

Risāla fī taḥdīd al-nahār al-shar'ī
MSS: Majlis 2761/3 (cat., IX, p.152); Millī 781 Arabic (cat., VIII, pp.337-8)

KĀSHIF AL-GHIṬĀ':

Al-Qawā'id al-shar'iyya, compiled by Mūsā b. Muḥammad Riḍā Āl Kāshif al-Ghiṭā'
Edition: Tehran, 1316 (together with the author's *al-Ḥaqq al-mubīn*)

IBN ṬAWQ AL-BAḤRĀNĪ:

Risāla fī taḥdīd awwal al-nahār
MS: Mar'ashī 2358/6 (cat., VI, p.336)

AḤMAD AL-NARĀQĪ:

- *'Awā'id al-ayyām*
  Editions: Tehran, 1266, 1321
  Selected MSS: Fayḍiyya 965, 749, 996/1 (cat., I, pp.186-7, III, p.47)
- *Manāhij al-aḥkām*
  Edition: Tehran, 1269
  Selected MSS: Dānishgāh 7640, 7667/2 (cat., XVI, pp.662, 668); Fayḍiyya 160, 288 (cat., I, pp.271-2); Āstāna 5906 (cat., p.176); Gharb, 4 MSS (cat., p.197)

AL-MARĀGHĪ - 'Abd al-Fattāḥ b. 'Alī al-Ḥusaynī, Mīr Fattāḥ (d.1266-74):

Al-'Anāwīn
Editions: Tehran, 1274, 1297
MS: Mahdawī 831 (cat., p.162)

MUḤAMMAD JA'FAR AL-ASTARĀBĀDĪ:

Al-Maqālīd al-Ja'fariyya
MSS: Dānishgāh 2192 (cat., IX, p.876); Mar'ashī 3857-8, 3882-3 (cat.,

X, pp.245-6, 266-7)

AL-ANṢĀRĪ:

- *Risāla fī qāʿidat lā ḍarar*
  Editions: Tabrīz, 1303 (together with his *K. al-Ṭahāra*), 1375 (together with his *al-Makāsib*)
  Commentary: by ʿAbd Allāh al-Māmaqānī, edited Najaf, 1345 (in his *al-Qalāʾid al-thamīna*)
- *Al-Taqiyya*
  Edition: Tabrīz, 1303 (together with his *K. al-Ṭahāra*), 1375 (together with *al-Makāsib*)
  Commentaries: (1) by ʿAbd Allāh al-Māmaqānī, edited Najaf, 1345 (in his *al-Qalāʾid al-thamīna*); (2) by Fattāḥ b. Muḥammad ʿAlī al-Shahīdī al-Tabrīzī (d. 1372), edited Tabrīz, 1375 (together with his *Hidāyat al-ṭālib*)

ʿABD AL-ṢĀḤIB MUḤAMMAD B. AḤMAD AL-NARĀQĪ (d. 1297):

Mashāriq al-aḥkām
Edition: Tehran, 1294
MS: Fayḍiyya 1107 (cat., I, p.245)

ANONYMOUS (written before 1312):

Al-Qawāʿid al-Bāqiriyya
MS: Dānishgāh 3845 (cat., XII, p.2826)

MUḤAMMAD ḤASAN AL-SHĪRĀZĪ, al-Mujaddid:

Al-Qawāʿid al-Ḥusayniyya, his lectures compiled by Ḥasan b. Ismāʿīl al-Qummī al-Ḥāʾirī
MS: Burūjirdī (AB, XVII, p.182)

AL-ĀSHTIYĀNĪ:

Risāla fī qāʿidat nafy al-ʿusr wa 'l-ḥaraj
Edition: Tehran, 1314

HĀDĪ AL-ṬIHRĀNĪ:

Risāla fi 'l-farq bayn al-ḥaqq wa 'l-ḥukm
MSS: Majlis 1950/3, 2753/5 (cat., IX, pp.139-40, 662)

ĀL BAḤR AL-ʿULŪM:

Risāla fi 'l-farq bayn al-ḥaqq wa 'l-ḥukm, included in his *Bulghat al-faqīh* (see above, chapter 5)

MUḤAMMAD ḤUSAYN B. MUḤAMMAD AL-KHWĀNSĀSRĪ (d. 1328):

Nafy al-ḥaraj fī aḥkām al-sharīʿa
MS: Marʿashī 3041/22 (cat., VIII, p.250)

MUḤAMMAD TAQĪ B. ḤASAN AL-MUDARRIS AL-IṢFAHĀNĪ (d. 1333):

Risāla fi 'l-farq bayn al-ḥaqq wa 'l-ḥukm
Edition: Tehran, 1363 (in a collection of his treatises entitled *al-Rasāʾil al-Taqawiyya*)

ḤABĪB ALLĀH AL-KĀSHĀNĪ:

Tashīl al-masālik

Edition: Tehran, 1374

AL-NĀ'ĪNĪ:

Risāla fī qā'idat lā ḍarar
Edition: Najaf, 1357-8 (together with his *Munyat al-ṭālib*)

ḤASAN B. ĀGHĀ BUZURG AL-MŪSAWĪ AL-BUJNŪRDĪ (d. 1395):

Al-Qawā'id al-fiqhiyya
Edition: Najaf, 1389 -

AL-KHUMAYNĪ:

- *Risāla fī qā'idat lā ḍarar*
Edition: Qum, 1383-4 (in a collection of his treatises entitled *al-Rasā'il*)
- *Risāla fi 'l-taqiyya*
Edition: Qum, 1383-4 (in the above-mentioned collection)

B

ON ACTS OF DEVOTION

1. GENERALITIES

FAKHR AL-MUḤAQQIQĪN:

Al-Fakhriyya fī ma'rifat al-niyya
Edition: Tehran, 1315 (in the collection of *Kalimāt al-Muḥaqqiqīn*)
Selected MSS: Majlis 4953/7 (cat., XIV, p.228); Princeton 1886 New Series; Mar'ashī 611/2, 2704, 2247/2 (cat., II, p.207, VI, pp.88, 232); Iṣfahān, Adabiyyāt (*Nash.*, V, p.303); Raḍawī 2432 (cat., II, p.68)

AL-SHAHĪD AL-AWWAL:

Al-Taklīfiyya
MSS: Raḍawī 8289 (Bīnish, p.666); Mar'ashī 1176/2 (cat., III, p.347)

IBN FAHD:

Al-Tuḥfa al-jaliyya fī ma'rifat al-niyya
MSS: Los Angeles M1313/1 (cat., p.724); Malik 2308 (cat., I, p.619); Dānishgāh 879/6, 2312/2, 882/7, 5396/11 (cat., V, pp.1992-3, IX, p.945, XV, p.4238); Gulpāyiganī 21 (cat., I, p.29); Mar'ashī 680/6, 3612/1, 3733/7 (cat., II, p.274, X, pp.11, 130); Raḍawī 2553, 6207, 8221 (cat., II, p.107, V, p.485); Miftāḥ 240/2 (cat., p.230); Wazīrī 2310 (cat., IV, p.1253); Ilāhiyyāt 306/1j (cat., I, p.205); Khāliṣī (cat., p.100); Vatican 720/1 Arabic (cat., I, p.68)

Taḥammul al-'ibāda 'an al-ghayr wa kayfiyyat al-istināba = Risāla ilā ahl al-Jazā'ir
MS: Malik (AB, XI, p.140)

IBN ABĪ JUMHŪR:

Risāla fi 'l-niyya
MS: Mar'ashī 2754/12 (cat., VII, p.312)

AL-QAṬĪFĪ:

Risāla fi 'l-niyya

MS: Raḍawī 2451 (cat., II, p.74)

AL-SHAHĪD AL-THĀNĪ:

Risāla fī 'l-niyya
MS: Fayḍiyya 1743/2 (cat., II, p.127)

ḤUSAYN B. 'ABD AL-ṢAMAD:

Al-'iqd al-Ḥusaynī
Edition: Yazd, n.d.
Selected MSS: Qādiriyya 500 (cat., II, p.319); Sipahsālār 2013 (cat., I, p.485); Leningrad 52 (*Nash*., VIII, p.103); Millī, Arabic 1259/1, 1262/1 (cat., IX, pp.245, 250); Dānishgāh 5387/2 (cat., XV, p.4232); Majlis 1306 (cat., IV, p.78); Wazīrī 320/11 (cat., I, 305)

'ABD AL-'ĀLĪ AL-KARAKĪ:

Risāla fī 'l-bulūgh wa ḥaddih
MS: Sipahsālār 2595/2 (cat., I, p.433)

AL-MUJTAHID - Ḥusayn b. Ḥasan al-Ḥusaynī al-Karakī (d. 1001):

Risāla fī 'l-niyya
MS: Majlis 3988/2 (cat., X, p.2160)

RAḌĪ AL-DĪN B. MUḤAMMAD NABĪ AL-QAZWĪNĪ (d. after 1134):

Risāla fī 'l-niyya
MS: Zanjān (cat., p.130)

AL-BIHBAHĀNĪ:

- *Risāla fī buṭlān 'ibādat al-jāhil*
  Edition: Tabrīz, n.d. (see AB, XI, p.130)
  Selected MSS: Sipahsālār 907/14 (cat., V, p.36); Ḥuqūq 235/3j, 247/2 (cat., p.349); Millī 1868/4 Arabic (cat., X, p.457); Mar'ashī 458/14, 1470/2 (cat., II, p.65, IV, p.263); Gulpāyigānī 1870/15 (cat., III, p.92); Fayḍiyya 1189/10, 1538/5, 1554/6, 1565/14 (cat., III, pp.66, 99, 100, 101); Raḍawī 8154 (Bīnish, p.806); Majlis 58 Ṭabāṭabā'ī; Mashhad, Ilāhiyyāt 1578 (cat., II, p.715); Berlin Pm. 511/5 (cat., III, p.313)
- *Al-Ifāda al-ijmāliyya fī 'l-'ibādāt al-makrūha*
  MS: Majlis 4097/2 (cat., XI, p.94)

ANONYMOUS:

- *Risāla fī 'l-riyā' fī 'l-'ibāda*
  MS: Dānishgāh 1118/2 (cat., V, pp.1899-900)
- *Risāla fī 'l-shakk fī 'l-sharṭiyya wa 'l-juz'iyya*
  MS: Dānishgāh 1118.2 (ibid)

IBN ṬAWQ AL-BAḤRĀNĪ:

Risāla fī qaṣd al-thawāb wa 'l-'iqāb fī 'l-'ibāda
MS: Mar'ashī 2358/4 (cat., VI, pp.334-5)

'ABD AL-RASŪL AL-FĪRŪZKŪHĪ (d. around 1322):

Risāla fī ishtirāṭ al-qurba fī 'l-'ibādāt
Edition: Tehran, 1321

ꟾUNĪR AL-DĪN AL-BURŪJIRDĪ (d. 1342):

Al-Farq bayn al-farīḍa wa 'l-nāfila
MS: Mar'ashī 2907 (cat., VIII, p.103)

ABD ALLĀH AL-MĀMAQĀNĪ:

Makhzan al-la'ālī fī furū' al-'ilm al-ijmālī
Edition: Najaf, 1344 (in his *al-Ithnā'ashariyya*)

ꞁL-BALĀGHĪ - Muḥammad Jawād b. Ḥasan al-Najafī (d. 1352):

'Iqd fī 'l-'ilm al-ijmālī
Edition: Najaf, 1343 (together with his *Ḥāshiyat al-Makāsib*)

ALĪ B. 'ABD AL-ḤUSAYN AL-ĪRAWĀNĪ (d. 1353):

'Iqd al-la'ālī fī furū' al-'ilm al-ijmālī
Edition: Tehran, 1367

ꞁIYĀ' AL-DĪN AL-'ARĀQĪ:

Rawā'i' al-amālī fī furū' al-'ilm al-ijmālī
Editions: Najaf, n.d.: Qum, 1394

L-KHU'Ī:

Al-Durar al-ghawālī fī furū' al-'ilm al-ijmālī, his lectures compiled by Riḍā al-Luṭfī
Edition: Najaf, 1367

. COMPREHENSIVE WORKS

L-MURTAḌĀ:

Jumal al-'ilm wa 'l-'amal, on dogmatics and acts of devotion
Edition: Najaf, 1387
Selected MSS: Mar'ashī 1945/2 (cat., V, p.310); Fayḍiyya 1968/3 (cat., III, p.157); Majlis 5187/14 (cat., XVI, pp.11-12); Dānishgāh 920, 5242 (cat., V, p.1843, XV, p.4174); Kār al-Kutub 19908, 20037 (cat., I, p.221)
Commentary on the legal section: by Ibn al-Barrāj, edited Mashhad, 1394; selected MSS: Dānishgāh 920/3, 1005/1 (cat., V, p.1936); Majlis 67/1 Khu'ī (cat., VII, p.154); Raḍawī 7859 (Bīnish, p.862); Mar'ashī 441/3 (cat., II, p.43); Tustariyya (AB, XIII, p.178)

L-SHAYKH:

Al-Iqtiṣād, on dogmatics and acts of devotion
Edition: Qum, 1400
Selected MSS: Dānishgāh 920/10 (cat., V, p.1783) and microfilm 2969 (cat., I, p.285); Millī 1922/5 Araibic (cat., X, p.593); Amīr al-Mu'minīn (Ḥujjatī, p.622); Ḥakīm 472 (ibid.); Dār al-Kutub 20304 (cat., I, p.96); Mar'ashī 3994/11 (cat., X, p.95); Los Angeles M1339/4 (cat., p.725)

UḤAMMAD B. ḤĀRITH AL-ḤUSAYNI AL-ASTARĀBĀDĪ (d. after 885):

Al-Risāla al-Ḥā'iriyya fī 'l-'ibādāt al-shar'iyya
MS: Farhād Mu'tamid 45 (cat., p.180)

AL-SHAHĪD AL-THĀNĪ:

- *Al-Iqtiṣād wa 'l-irshād*, on dogmatics and acts of devotion
  MSS: Ilāhiyyāt 538d, 561/2d (cat., I, pp.328, 460-1); Gulpāyigānī 1020/3 (cat., II, p.221)
- *Al-Isṭanbuliyya fi 'l-wājibāt al-ʿayniyya*
  MSS: Raḍawī 7244, 6197, 7437 (cat., V, p.428; Bīnish, p.780); Ḥakīm 1757m (cat., I, p.52)
- *Al-Rūmiyya*
  MS: Dānishgāh 1301/4 (cat., VII, p.2719)

ḤUSAYN B. ʿABD AL-ṢAMAD:

Al-Wājibāt al-malikiyya
MS: Gulpāyigānī 8/3 (cat., I, p.18)

BAHĀ' AL-DĪN AL-ʿĀMILĪ:

- *Al-Ithnāʿashariyyāt*, five treatises on acts of devotion
  Edition: the treatise on prayer is edited Tehran, 1309 (together with al-ʿAllāma's *Tabṣirat al-mutaʿallimīn*)
  Selected MSS: Sinā 225/1 (cat., I, p.105); Ḥakīm 9 Rashtī (cat., p.27); Dānishgāh 918/4, 7087/6 (cat., V, pp.1758-9, XVI, p.449); Adabiyyāt 120 Ḥikmat (cat., p.41); Marʿashī 75, 104/3 (cat., I, pp. 87, 125); Raḍawī 2683 (cat., V, p.352); Mīrzā Jaʿfar 148 (cat., p. 40); Nūrbakhsh 590 (cat., II, pp.235-6); Nawwāb 6 law (cat., p.449); Ustādī (cat., p.57); Farhang (cat., pp.40-1); Sipahsālār 2670/2 (cat., III, pp.44-5); Princeton 538/1 Yahuda (cat., p.149); Bodleian Arab.e.175; Tiflis 699/7 (*Nash.*, VIII, p.260); Baku M140 (ibid., IX, p.239)
  Translation: Persian, by Ṣadr al-Dīn Muḥammad b. Muḥibb ʿAlī al-Tabrīzī (d. after 1013), MSS: Marʿashī (AB, IV, p.74); Leningrad A643 (cat. Persian, I, p.241); Dānishgāh 5884/3-4, 7242/2 (cat., XVI, pp.130, 497)
  Commentaries: (1) by the author, on the treatise on prayer, MS: Raḍawī 2728 (cat., V, pp.404-5); (2) anonymous (written in 1012), MS: Dānishgāh 7087/8 (cat., XVI, p.449); (3) anonymous (written before 1030), MS: Marʿashī 2398 (cat., VI, pp.378-9);
  (4) *al-Fawā'id al-ʿaliyya*, by Hārūn b. Khamīs al-Jazā'irī (d. after 1036), MS: Raḍawī 2509 (cat., II, p.93, V, p.353); (5) anonymous (written before 1042), MS: Ilāhiyyāt 184/6 (cat., I, p.724);
  (6) *al-Anwār al-bahiyya*, by Nūr al-Dīn ʿAlī b. Ḥusayn al-Mūsawī al-ʿĀmilī (d. 1068), MSS: Marʿashī 81 (cat., I, p.99); Majlis 4670 (cat., XIII, pp.52-3); (7) *al-Fiṭra al-malakūtiyya*, by ʿAbd al-Ḥasīb b. Aḥmad al-ʿĀmilī (d. after 1058), MS: Raḍawī 2792 (cat., V, p.471); (8) by al-Khwājū'ī, MS: Gawharshād 1702 (cat., p.256); (9) by ʿAbd al-Ḥusayn b. Qāsim al-Ḥillī (d. 1375), MS: Amīr al-Mu'minīn (AB, XIII, p.62); (10) anonymous, MS: Raḍawī 2728 (Bīnish, p.700)

3. ON RITUAL PURITY AND PRAYER

AL-SHAYKH:

ʿAmal al-yawm wa 'l-layla
Edition: Qum, 1401 (in *Andīshahāy-i naw dar ʿulūm-i Islāmī, IV, pp. 17-30)*

ANONYMOUS (belonging to 8th-9th century?):

Risāla fi 'l-ṭahāra wa 'l-ṣalāt
MS: Majlis 81/1 Khu'ī (cat., VII, p.184)

ʿABD AL-ʿALĪ B. MAḤMŪD AL-KHĀDIM AL-JĀPALAQĪ (late 10th century):

Fiqh-i shāhī, Persian
MS: Gawharshād 978/2 (cat., pp.157-8)

BĀYAZĪD AL-THĀNĪ - Abū Muḥammad ʿAlī b. ʿInāyat Allāh al-Basṭāmī (d. after 1011):

Maʿārij al-taḥqīq
MS: Majlis 1321 (cat., IV, pp.93-4)

MĀJID B. HĀSHIM AL-BAḤRĀNĪ (d. 1028):

Al-Yūsufiyya
MS: Marʿashī 2249/1 (cat., VI, pp.233-4)

AL-DĀMĀD:

Risāla fi 'l-ṭahāra wa 'l-ṣalāt
MSS: Majlis 4553/1 (cat., XII, p.234); Raḍawī 2445 (cat., II, p.73)

FAKHR AL-DĪN B. MUḤAMMAD ʿALĪ AL-ṬURAYḤĪ AL-NAJAFĪ (d. 1087):

Al-Fakhriyya
MS: Marʿashī 118 (cat., I, p.142)

NIʿMAT ALLĀH AL-JAZĀ'IRĪ:

Hadiyyat al-mu'minīn = Hadiyyat al-ikhwān
MSS: Malik 2536 (cat., I, p.807); Millī 1919/1 Arabic (cat., X, p. 577); Dānishgāh 1020/2 (cat., V, pp.2103-6); Ustādī (cat., p.43)

AḤMAD AL-JAZĀ'IRĪ (d. 1151):

Tabṣirat al-mubtadi'īn
MS: Miftāḥ 244/3 (cat., p. 230; see also AB, III, p.321, XV, p.183)

ANONYMOUS (written before 1186):

Risāla fi 'l-ṭahāra wa 'l-ṣalāt
MS: Gulpāyigānī 307/1 (cat., I, p.267)

MŪSĀ B. JAʿFAR AL-NAJAFĪ ĀL KĀSHIF AL-GHIṬĀ' (d. 1243):

Munyat al-rāghib, a commentary on Kāshif al-Ghiṭā's *Bughyat al-ṭālib* (see above, chapter 5)
MSS: Raḍawī 8024 (Bīnish, p.1049); Marʿashī 3897 (cat., X, p.278); Sipahsālār 2666-7 (cat., I, p.549); Majlis 610 Ṭabāṭabā'ī; Fayḍiyya 1635 (cat., I, p.282); Gulpāyigānī 77 (cat., I, p.83); Khāliṣī (cat., p.126); Matḥaf 2963 (cat., p.259); Amīr al-Mu'minīn (AB, XIII, p.127); Shīrāzī (AB, XXIII, pp.202-3)

MUḤAMMAD ḤASAN B. MĪRZĀ ĀQĀSĪ AL-QUMMĪ (d. 1304):

Miṣbāḥ al-faqāha
Edition: Najaf, 1372-7

AL-KHUʾĪ:

Al-Tanqīḥ, his lectures compiled by ʿAlī al-Gharawī al-Tabrīzī
Edition: Najfa, 1378 -

4. ON FISCAL OBLIGATIONS

MĪRAK MŪSĀ B. MUḤAMMAD AKBAR AL-ḤUSAYNĪ AL-TŪNĪ (late 11th century):

Risāla dar zakāt wa khums
MS: Raḍawī 6740 (cat., V, p.432)

AL-MAJLISĪ II:

Zakātiyya = Risāla dar zakāt wa khums
Selected MSS: Marʿashī 187/3 (cat., I, p.206); Gulpāyigānī 1223/4 (cat., II, p.236)

KĀSHIF AL-GHIṬĀʾ:

Risāla fī ʾl-ʿibādāt al-māliyya wa mā yalḥaquhā min al-wuqūf wa ʾl-ʿitq . . .
MS: Ḥujjatiyya 700/4 (cat., p.121)

MUḤAMMAD B. ʿABD AL-WAHHĀB AL-KĀẒIMĪ (d. after 1303):

Al-Mishkāt fī masāʾil al-khums wa ʾl-zakāt
MS: Marʿashī 2349 (cat., VI, p.325)

RITUAL PURITY

1. GENERAL

AL-DĀMĀD:

Al-Taʿlīqāt fī ʾl-ṭahāra
MS: Nūrbakhsh 400 (cat., II, pp.110-11)

AL-BIHBANĀNĪ:

- *Risāla fī anna ʾl-aṣl fī ʾl-ashyāʾ al-ṭahāra*
  MS: Gulpāyigānī 1862/13 (cat., III, p.87)
- *Risāla fī kayfiyyat wujūb al-ṭahāra*
  MS: Sipahsālār 2487 (cat., I, pp.421, 436)

MUḤAMMAD TAQĪ B. MUḤAMMAD RAḤĪM AL-IṢFAHĀNĪ (d. 1248):

K. al-Ṭahāra
MS: Ustādī (cat., p.27)

AL-ANṢĀRĪ

- *K. al-Ṭahāra*
  Edition: Tabrīz, 1303
- *Al-Taqrīrāt fī ʾl-ṭahāra*, collections of his lectures compiled by his pupils: (i) by Muḥammad Shafīʿ b. Muḥammad Saʿīd al-Fūmanī al-Gīlānī, MS: Rasht 70-1t (cat., p.1103); (ii) by Yaʿqūb b. Muqīm al-Bārfurūshī, MS: Marʿashī 2106 (cat., VI, pp.120-1); (iii) anonymous, MS: Marʿashī 1796 (cat., V, p.182);

(iv) anonymous, MS: Majlis 100 Ṭabāṭabā'ī

AL-RASHTĪ:

K. al-Ṭahāra
MS: Masjid-i Aʿẓam 367

MUḤAMMAD ṬĀHĀ B. MAHDĪ NAJAF AL-TABRĪZĪ AL-NAJAFĪ (d. 1323):

Risāla fi 'l-ṭahāra
Edition: n.p., 1334

AL-KHU'Ī:

Durūs fī fiqh al-Shīʿa, his lectures compiled by Mahdī al-Khalkhālī
Edition: Najaf - Tehran, 1378 -

AL-KHUMAYNĪ:

K. al-Ṭahāra
Edition: Qum - Najaf, 1382-90

2. ON WATERS

AL-SHAHĪD AL-THĀNĪ:

Risāla fī infiʿāl mā' al-bi'r, included in his *Majmūʿat al-ifādāt* (see above, chapter 5)

NŪR ALLĀH AL-TUSTARĪ:

Al-Baḥr al-ghazīr fī taqdīr al-mā' al-kathīr
MS: Ḥakīm 152/4 (*Nash.*, V, p.427)

BAHĀ' AL-DĪN AL-ʿĀMILĪ:

Al-Kurriyya
Edition: Tehran, 1321 (together with his *al-Ḥabl al-matīn*)
Selected MSS: Majlis 1805, 4900/54 (cat., IX, pp.359-60, XIV, p.77); Dānishgāh 4316/7 (cat., XIII, p.3279); Farhang 38a (cat., pp.40-1); Millī 1404/6 (cat., IX, p.417); Sinā 417/9 (cat., I, p.250); Baku M149/15 (*Nash.*, IX, p.239).

MASʿŪD B. FAḌL ALLĀH AL-ḤUSAYNĪ AL-BIHBAHĀNĪ (d. after 1031):

Al-Tabāʿud bayn al-bi'r wa 'l-bālūʿa
MS: Gulpāyigānī 48/10 (cat., I, pp.61-2)

MURĀD B. ʿALĪ KHĀN AL-TAFRISHĪ:

Al-Kurriyya
MS: Dānishgāh 1803 (cat., VIII, p.380)

AL-MĀHŪZĪ - Sulaymān b. ʿAbd Allāh al-Baḥrānī (d. 1121):

Taḥqīq mas'alat al-tabāʿud bayn al-bi'r wa 'l-bālūʿa
MS: Najaf, Jazā'irī (*Nash.*, VII, p.716)

SHĀRIḤ AL-WĀFIYA:

Risāla fi ʿadam infiʿāl al-mā' al-qalīl
MSS: Gulpāyigānī 1862/11 (cat., III, p.82); Gharb 265 (cat., p.179)

AL-KHWĀJŪ'Ī:

Risāla fī taḥdīd al-kurr
MS: Dānishgāh 7103/1 (cat., XVI, p.455)

ṢĀḤIB AL-ḤADĀ'IQ:

Qāṭiʻat al-qāl wa 'l-qīl fī infiʻāl al-mā' al-qalīl
MS: Majlis 633 Ṭabāṭabā'ī

ANONYMOUS (belonging to late 12th century):

Risāla fī ḥukm mā dūn al-kurr
MS: Gulpāyigānī 1862/4 (cat., III, p.86)

AL-KIRMĀNSHĀHĪ:

Qaṭʻ al-maqāl fī nuṣrat al-qawl bi 'l-infiʻāl
MSS: Majlis 5474/2 (cat., XVI, pp.374-5); Ilāhiyyāt 98 Āl Āqā,828/1d (cat., I, p.714, II, p.22); Gharb 4813 (cat., p.169); Gulpāyigānī 1862/12 (cat., III, p.87)

ṢĀḤIB AL-MAQĀBIS:

Al-Lu'lu' al-masjūr fī maʻnā lafẓ al-ṭahūr
MSS: Majlis 1314 (cat., IV, pp.88-9); Fayḍiyya 17/1 (cat., III, p.1); Ḥakīm 177/2 (*Nash.*, V, p.428); Princeton 737/2 New Series

MUḤAMMAD ḤUSAYN AL-KHWĀNSĀRĪ:

Shāfī al-ʻalīl fī aḥkām al-mā' al-qalīl
MS: Marʻashī 3041/19 (cat., VIII, p.249)

3. ON ABLUTION

MUʻĪN AL-DĪN AL-MIṢRĪ:

Risāla fī kayfiyyat wujūb ghusl al-jināba
MS: Ḥakīm 198

AL-SHAHĪD AL-THĀNĪ:

Risāla fī ḥukm mā idhā aḥdath al-mujnib fī athnā' ghusl al-jināba
included in his *Majmūʻat al-ifādāt* (see above, chapter 5)

AL-KARAKĪ:

Risāla fī wujūb al-ṭahāra li-mass Kitāb Allāh
MS: Khayrāt Khān 53/2 (cat., p.1736)

ʻABD ALLĀH AL-TUSTARĪ:

- *Risāla fī kifāyat al-iṣbaʻ al-wāḥida fi 'l-masḥ*
- *Risāla fī taḥqīq maʻnā al-kaʻbayn*
- *Risāla fī ghusl al-jumʻa*
- *Risāla fi 'l-istibrā'*

All included in his *al-Rasā'il* (see above, chapter 5)

ANONYMOUS:

Risāla fī anna 'l-ghusl min al-jināba wājib nafsī

MS: Marʿashī 1383/1 (cat., IV, p.156)

SHUKR ALLĀH B. AMĀN ALLĀH AL-ḤUSAYNĪ:

Risāla fī kayfiyyat wuḍu' al-jabīra
MS: Wazīrī 990/3 (cat., II, p.809)

AL-MUKHTĀRĪ:

Al-Qawl al-faṣl fi 'l-masḥ wa 'l-ghasl
MSS: Dānishgāh 1859/3 (cat., VIII, p.459); Marʿashī 3382/2 (cat., IX, p.159)

AL-KHWĀJŪ'Ī:

- *Risāla fī ḥukm al-ghusl qabl al-istibrā'*
  MS: Marʿashī 1986/1 (cat., V, p.357)
- *Risāla fī ḥukm al-ḥadath al-aṣghar al-mutakhallil athnā' al-ghusl*
  MS: Marʿashī 1142/5 (cat., III, p.317)
- *Mas'ala fī waẓīfat rajul iḥtāj ila 'l-ghusl fī arḍ bārida*
  MS: Mashhad, Adabiyyāt 25/22 Fayyāḍ (cat., p.214)

SHUBBAR B. MUḤAMMAD AL-MŪSAWĪ AL-NAJAFĪ (d. after 1179):

Risāla fī wujūb ghusl al-jumʿa
MS: Dānishgāh 7200/1 (cat., XVI, p.485)

KĀSHIF AL-GHIṬĀ':

Kashf al-iltibās bayn al-ḥayḍ wa 'l-istiḥāḍa wa 'l-nifās
MSS: Los Angeles M93/1 (cat., p.661); Ḥujjatiyya 700/3 (cat., p.121)

IBN ṬAWQ AL-BAḤRĀNĪ:

Risāla fī wujūb al-tayammum ʿalā man manaʿah al-ziḥām ʿan al-khurūj
MS: Marʿashī 2358/8 (cat., VI, p.336)

ʿALĪ AKBAR AL-QAZWĪNĪ:

Risāla fi 'l-wuḍū'
MS: Millī 1783/8 Arabic (cat., X, p.368)

ʿABD ALLĀH AL-KIRMĀNSHĀHĪ:

Mas'ala fī tajdīd al-ghusl
MS: Ilāhiyyāt 819/6d (cat., II, p.21)

MUḤSIN B. MUḤAMMAD RAFĪʿ AL-RASHTĪ AL-IṢFAHĀNĪ (d. after 1268):

Najāt al-niswān
MS: Marʿashī 2659/5 (cat., VII, p.240)

MUḤAMMAD ʿABBĀS AL-MŪSAWĪ AL-LAKNAWĪ:

Ṣafḥat almās fī kayfiyyat al-irtimās
MS: Marʿashī 1803 (cat., V, p.188)

AL-KHURĀSĀNĪ:

Risāla fi 'l-dimā' al-thalātha
Edition: Baghdad, 1331 (in his *Shadharāt*)

MAHDĪ B. ḤUSAYN AL-KHĀLIṢĪ AL-KĀẒIMĪ (d. 1343):

Risāla fī tadākhul al-aghsāl, as a commentary on the relevant discussion in al-Muḥaqqiq's *Sharāʾiʿ al-Islām*
Edition: Mashhad, 1342

ʿABD ALLĀH AL-MĀMAQĀNĪ:

Kashf al-rayb wa 'l-sūʾ fī ighnāʾ kull ghusl ʿan al-wuḍūʾ
Edition: Najaf, 1344 (in his *al-Ithnāʿashariyya*)

4. ON THE DECEASED

IBN FAHD:

Masʾala fī ṣalāt al-mayyit
MS: Majlis 2750.3 (cat., IX, p.125)

SHAMS AL-DĪN AL-ASTARĀBĀDĪ (mid-10th century):

Risāla fī kayfiyyat waḍʿ al-mayyit baʿd al-ghusl
MS: Marʿashī 2785/2 (cat., VII, p.348)

AL-MUJTAHID:

Risāla fī istiqbāl al-qibla
MS: Majlis 3988/9 (cat., X, p.2166)

AL-FAYḌ:

Aḥkām al-amwāt
MS: Millī 1262/2 (cat., IX, p.251)

AL-SHĪRWĀNĪ:

Risāla dar aḥkām-i amwāt, Persian
MS: Dānishgāh 7008/13 (cat., XVI, p.426)

HĀSHIM B. MURTAḌĀ AL-ḤUSAYNĪ (d. after 1128):

Aḥkām al-amwāt, Persian
MS: Raḍawī 2742 (cat., V, pp.356-7)

AL-MUKHTĀRĪ:

Qubāla qabaliyya fī bayān istiqbāl al-mayyit wa tawjīhih ila 'l-qibla
MS: Dānishgāh 1859/6 (cat., VIII, p.460)

AL-KHWĀJŪʾĪ:

- *Risāla fī jawāz al-takfīn fi 'l-ṣūf wa 'l-wabar wa 'l-shaʿr*
  MS: Mashhad, Adabiyyāt 25/24 Fayyāḍ (cat., p.214)
- *Risāla fī ḥukm al-isrāj ʿind al-mayyit*
  MS: Mashhad, Adabiyyāt 25/9 Fayyāḍ (cat., p.212)

ḤUSAYN AL-QAZWĪNĪ:

Risāla fī ḥukm al-nabsh
MSS: Raḍawī 2595/5 (cat., II, p.118); Zanjānī 76/15 (cat., pp.220-1)

KĀSHIF AL-GHIṬĀʾ:

Aḥkām al-janāʾiz

MS: Gulpāyigānī 1391/2 (cat., II, p.254)

MUḤAMMAD ḤUSAYN AL-KHWĀTŪNĀBĀDĪ:

- *Risāla dar jawāz-i naql-i ajsād bi-mashāhid*, Persian
  MSS: Dānishgāh 5524/1, 5818/2 (cat., XVI, pp.28, 98)
- *Kitābat bar kafan wa naql-i ajsād pas az dafn*, Persian
  MS: Ustādī (cat., p.55)

5. ON IMPURITIES

ANONYMOUS (written before 907):

Ḥukm mulāqī al-najis
MS: Mar'ashī 2564/7 (cat., VII, p.153)

AL-KARAKĪ:

Risāla fī mā tanajjas ba'ḍuh wa ishtabah mawḍi' al-nijāsa
MSS: Dānishgāh 2144/40 (cat., IX, p.828): Shīrāz, Dānishgāh

MUḤAMMAD YŪSUF B. ḤASAN AL-ḤUSAYNĪ AL-ASTARĀBĀDĪ (mid-10th century):

Aḥkām-i nijāsāt, Persian
MS: Mar'ashī 2252/2 (cat., VI, pp.237-8)

AL-SHAHĪD AL-THĀNĪ:

Risāla fī ḥukm mā idhā tuyuqqin al-ṭahāra wa 'l-nijāsa wa shukk fi 'l-sābiq minhumā, included in his *Majmū'at al-ifādāt* (see above, chapter 5)

ZAYN AL-'ĀBIDĪN AL-TABRĪZĪ (10th century):

Risāla fī ḥukm al-'araq min al-mutanajjis
MS: Masjid-i A'ẓam 3085/1

AMĪN AL-ASTARĀBĀDĪ:

Risāla fī ṭahārat al-khamr
MS: Dānishgāh 1257/12 (cat., VII, p.2667)

AḤMAD B. ZAYN AL-'ĀBIDĪN AL-'ĀMILĪ (d. after 1044):

Risāla fī nijāsat al-khamr, in refutation of the previous treatise
MSS: Dānishgāh 3749 (cat., XII, p.2743); Adabiyyāt 251/2 Kirmān (cat., p.40); Sipahsālār 2916/23, 4506/2 (cat., I, p.283)

ṢAFĪ AL-DĪN B. FAKHR AL-DĪN AL-ṬURAYḤĪ AL-NAJAFĪ (d. after 1100):

Al-Yanbū' al-munbajis fi 'l-radd 'alā man qāl inna 'l-munajjis lā yunajjis
MS: Masjid-i A'ẓam 966/2; Burūjirdī (AB, XI, p.201)

AL-MĀḤŪZĪ:

Faṣl al-khiṭāb fī nijāsat Ahl al-Kitāb wa 'l-Nuṣṣāb
MS: Najaf, Jazā'irī (*Nash.*, VII, p.717)

AḤMAD AL-BAḤRĀNĪ:

- *Risāla fī taḥqīq ghusālat al-nijāsa*

MS: Princeton 229/13 Yahuda (cat., p.139)

-*Risāla fī ḥukm mulāqī al-mutanajjis*
MS: Princeton 229/20 Yahuda (cat., p.139)

KHALAF B. ʿABD ʿALĪ AL-BAḤRĀNĪ (da. after 1182):

Risāla fī nijāsat ʿaraq al-junub min al-ḥarām
MS: Ḥakīm 2205m

ḤUSAYN B. ABI 'L-QĀSIM AL-MŪSAWĪ AL-KHWĀNSĀRĪ (d. 1191):

Risāla fī tanajjus mulāqī al-mutanajjis
Edition: Iṣfahān, 1377 (together with Muḥammad Bāqir al-Khwānsārī's *al-Nahriyya*)
MSS: Marʿashī 1519/6 (cat., IV, p.320)

ḤUSAYN AL-QAZWĪNĪ:

- *Risāla fī ḥukm al-hawāmm wa 'l-sawāmm wa 'l-ḥasharāt*
MSS: Raḍawī 2595/2 (cat., II, p.118); Zanjānī 76/2 (cat., pp.220-1)
- *Risāla fī tanjīs al-mutanajjis*
MSS: Raḍawī 2595/3 (cat., II, p.118); Zanjānī 76/3 (cat., pp.220-1)

AL-BIHBAHĀNĪ:

Mas'ala fī ḥukm ʿaṣīray al-tamr wa 'l-zabīb
MSS: Raḍawī 7220 (cat., V, p.442); Gulpāyigānī 1820/21 (cat., III, p.92)

AL-SHAFTĪ:

Risāla fī taṭhīr al-ʿajīn bi-takhbīzih wa ʿadamih
MS: Burūjirdī (AB, XI, p.149)

ASAD ALLĀH B. MUḤAMMAD BĀQIR AL-SHAFTĪ (d. 1290):

Risāla fi 'l-ʿaṣīr al-ʿinabī wa 'l-zabībī wa 'l-tamrī
MS: Rawḍātī (Muʿallim, III, pp.837-8)

AḤMAD B. MUḤAMMAD BĀQIR AL-MŪSAWĪ AL-BIHBAHĀNĪ (d. after 1294):

Tanbīh al-anām fī ṭahārat ʿaraq al-junub min al-ḥarām
MS: Dānishgāh 934 (cat., V, p.1834)

MUḤAMMAD TAQĪ AL-HARAWĪ:

Risāla fī ʿaraq al-junub min al-ḥarām
MS: Dānishgāh 3713/3 (cat., XII, p.2713)

MUḤAMMAD HĀSHIM B. ZAYN AL-ʿĀBIDĪN AL-MŪSAWĪ AL-KHWĀNSĀRĪ (d. 1318):

Ḥall al-ʿasīr fī aḥkām al-ʿaṣīr
Edition: Tehran, 1317 (in his *Maʿdin al-fawā'id*)

MUḤAMMAD RIḌĀ B. ʿALĪ AL-ASTARĀBĀDĪ (d. after 1325):

Risāla fī nijāsat Ahl al-Kitāb
Edition: India, 1324

SHAYKH AL-SHARĪʻA - Fatḥ Allāh b. Muḥammad Jawād al-Namāzī al-Iṣfahānī (d. 1339):

Ifāḍat al-Qadīr fī aḥkām al-ʻaṣīr
MS: Marʻashī 1319 (cat., IV, p.105)

AL-BALĀGHĪ:

Risāla fī tanjīs al-mutanajjis
Edition: Najaf, 1343 (together with his *Ḥāshiyat al-Makāsib*)

ABU 'L-MAJD:

Risāla fī ʻadam tanjīs al-mutanajjis
Edition; n.p. (Iran), 1337 (together with his *Wiqāyat al-adhhān*)

ABŪ ʻABD ALLĀH B. NAṢR ALLĀH AL-ZANJĀNĪ (d. 1360):

Risāla fī ṭahārat Ahl al-Kitāb
Edition: Baghdad, 1345

6. ON VESSELS

AL-MUJTAHID:

Risāla fi 'l-awānī
MS: Dānishgāh 2144/45 (cat., IX, p.832)

ANONYMOUS:

Risāla fī ḥukm istiʻmāl awānī al-dhahab wa 'l-fiḍḍa fi 'l-ṭahāra
MS: Majlis 1804/5 (cat., IX, p.321)

AL-ĀSHTIYĀNĪ:

Risāla fī ḥukm awānī al-dhahab wa 'l-fiḍḍa
Edition: Tehran, 1313 (together with his *Izāḥat al-shukūk*)

ʻABD AL-RASŪL AL-FĪRŪZKŪHĪ:

Risāla fi 'l-awānī
Edition: Tehran, 1321

ABU 'L-MAKĀRIM AL-ZANJĀNĪ:

Risāla fī ḥurmat awānī al-dhahab wa 'l-fiḍḍa
MS: Zanjānī 113 (cat., p.240)

7. COMPLEMENTARY DISCUSSIONS

MULLĀ MU'MIN - Muḥammad b. Ḥasan al-Tabrīzī (early 14th century):

Risāla fī jawāz ḥalq al-liḥya
Edition: Tabrīz, 1300
MS: Princeton 1076 New Series

ḤASAN B. HĀDĪ AL-ṢADR AL-ʻĀMILĪ (d. 1354):

- *Dhikrā dhawī al-nuhā fī ḥurmat ḥalq al-liḥā*
  MS: Dānishgāh 5518/2 (cat., XVI, p.27)
- *Al-Ghāliya li-ahl al-anẓār al-ʻāliya = Risāla dar ḥurmat-i rīshtarāshī*, Persian
  MS: Fayḍiyya 2071/1 (cat., III, p.175)

AL-BALĀGHĪ:

Risāla fī ḥurmat ḥalq al-liḥya
Edition: Qum, 1394

PRAYER

1. GENERAL

AL-SHAHĪD AL-AWWAL:

Al-Alfiyya
Editions: Tehran, 1271, 1308, 1312, 1319; Beirut, 1403
Selected MSS: Princeton 1886/9 New Series; Gawharshād 1129/1 (cat., p.219); Gulpāyigānī 258/1 (cat., I, p.225); Marʿashī 67/6, 680/2 (cat., I, p.80, II, p.273); Mashhad, Ilāhiyyāt 471/2 (cat., I, p.296); Raḍawī 2250, 2246, 2695 (cat., II, pp.12-13, V, p.366); Nawwāb 150/1 law (cat., p.469); Āstāna 5844/1 (cat., p.218); Majlis 4339/5 (cat., XII, p.39)
Translations: (1) Persian, anonymous (written before 928), MS: Raḍawī 36 law (cat., II, p.12); (2) Persian, by ʿAzīz Allāh b. ʿInāyat Allāh al-Ḥusaynī al-Khalkhālī (d. after 953), MS; Millī 1955/1f (cat., IV, p.422); (3) *Zayniyya*, Persian, anonymous (belonging to 10th century); MS: Gawharshād 1666/5 (cat., p.130); (4) Persian, anonymous (written before 1053), MS: Karachī, Anjuman-i Taraqqī-yi Urdū 1:18 (cat., p.24); (5) Persian, by Muḥammad Maʿṣūm b. Muḥammad Riḍā al-Hāshimī al-Ḥusaynī (d. after 1075), MS: Gawharshād 1191/2 (cat., p.86); (6) Persian, by Muḥammad Hādī b. Mīr Lawḥī al-Ḥusaynī (d. after 1096), MS: Dānishgāh 5914/8 (cat., XVI, p.150); (7) *Farāʾiḍ-i yawmiyya*, Persian, by Muḥammad Mahdī b. Muḥammad Bāqir al-Khwānsārī (d. 1324), edited Tehran, 1313 (AB, XVI, p.151); (8-10) three anonymous or unidentified Persian translations: (a) MS: Dānishgāh 7586 (cat., XVI, p.642); (b) MS: Dānishgāh 1593/1 (cat., VIII, p.195); (c) MS: Ilāhiyyāt 551/5d (cat., I, p.395)
In verse: (1) *al-Jumāna al-bahiyya*, by Ḥasan b. Rāshid al-Ḥillī (d. after 825), MS: Marʿashī 67/7 (cat., I, p.80); (2) *al-Durra al-ṣafiyya*, by Nūr al-Dīn ʿAlī b. ʿAbd al-Ṣamad al-ʿĀmilī (d. after 954), MS: Dānishgāh 4316/2 (cat., XIII, p.3279)
Commentaries: (1) anonymous (written before 822), Princeton 3992/3 Yahuda; (2) *al-Anwār al-ʿaliyya*, by Fakhr al-Dīn Aḥmad b. Muḥammad sl-Sabīʿī, MS: Dār al-Kutub 20039b (cat., I, p.85); (3) *al-Najāt*, anonymous (written before 877), MSS: Marʿashī 611/3 (cat., II, p. 208); Burūjirdī (AB, XXIV, p.60); (4) *al-Masālik al-Jāmiʿiyya*, by Ibn Abī Jumhūr, edited Tehran, 1314 (together with al-Shahīd al-Thānī's *al-Maqāṣid al-ʿaliyya*); selected MSS: Majlis 2981 (cat., X, pp.675-7, 1033); Raḍawī 2581 (cat., II, p.115); Marʿashī 2261/1 (cat., VI, p.245); Āstāna 5844/1 (cat., p.218); Masjid-i Aʿẓam 3128; (5) by al-Karakī, edited Tehran, 1312-14 (in the margin of al-Shahīd al-Thānī's *al-Maqāṣid al-ʿaliyya*), selected MSS: Marʿashī 680/1, 1461 (cat., II, p.275, IV, p.258); Raḍawī 2386, 2481-2 (cat., II, pp.53, 84, 86); Dānishgāh 872/4(cat.,V, pp.1859-60); Miftāḥ 981/1 (cat., p.264); Burūjirdī (AB, XIII,p.113); Gulpāyigānī 258/2 (cat., I, p.225); Āstāna 5844/1, 8335/1 (cat., pp.187, 218); Ustādī (cat., p.57); Ilāhiyyāt 225/5d (cat.,I, p.262); Malik 5840 (cat., I, p.216); Millī 1605 Arabic (cat., X, p.142); Bodleian, Pococke 37 (cat., I, p.66, II, p.570); Dār al-Kutub 20038 (cat., II, p.34); Los Angeles M1283/2 (cat., p.722); (6) by al-Qaṭīfī, MS: Majlis 81/8 Khuʾī (cat., VII, pp.156-7); (7) a second commentary by the same author, MS: Majlis 81/13 Khuʾī (cat., VII, pp.147-8); (8) *al-Maqāṣid al-ʿaliyya*, by al-Shahīd al-Thānī, edited Tehran, 1312-14, selected MSS: Ilāhiyyāt 844d (cat., I, p.87); Zanjān (cat., p.164); Raḍawī

2846 (cat., V, p.513); Princeton 1399/4 New Series; Wazīrī 958 (cat., II, p.789); Marʿashī 2773/1 (cat., VII, p.331); (9) another commentary by the same author, MSS: Majlis 81/7 Khuʾī (cat., VII, p.80); Gharb 762 (cat., p.93); Miftāḥ 249 (cat., p.231); (10) a third commentary by the same author, MSS: Marʿashī 53/2 (cat., I, p.63); Raḍawī 2371 (cat., II, p.49); (11) by Niẓām al-Dīn ʿAbd al-Ḥayy b. ʿAbd al-Wahhāb al-Ḥusaynī al-Ashraqī al-Jurjānī (mid-10th century), MS: Gawharshād 821 (cat., pp.314-15); (12) *al-Aʿlām al-jaliyya*, by Ḥusayn b. ʿAlī al-Uwālī al-Hajarī (d. after 950), MSS: Raḍawī 2238 (cat., II, pp.9-10); Zanjān (cat., p.92); (13) by Ḥusayn b. ʿAbd al-Ṣamad al-ʿĀmilī, MSS: Raḍawī 2482-3 (cat., II, pp.84-5); Gharb 4550 (cat., p.138); Sipahsālār 2526 (cat., I, p.445); Fayḍiyya 1600/1 (cat., III, p.105); Marʿashī 1968/2, 2828, 3614 (cat., V, p.339, VIII, p.35, X, p.13); Princeton 1889/2 New Series (14) by ʿAbd al-ʿAlī al-Jāpalaqī, MS: Princeton 283 New Series; (15) Persian, by the same author, MSS: Gawharshād 978/1 (cat., p.314); Raḍawī 2484 (cat., II, p.85); (16) by Ṣāḥib al-Madārik, edited Tehran, 1312-14 (in the margin of al-Shahīd al-Thānī's *al-Maqāṣid al-ʿaliyya*), MSS: Dānishgāh 1096, 1858 (cat., V, pp.1861-2, VIII, p.458); Masjid-i Jāmiʿ 299/1 (cat., p.377); Majlis 5960/2 (cat., XVII, p.344); (17) by Muḥammad b. Naṣṣār al-Ḥuwayzī (9th-10th century), MS: Ḥakīm 22/2 Rashtī (cat., p.42); (18) by ʿAbd Allāh al-Tustarī, MSS: Dānishgāh 6274 (cat., XVI, p.231); Raḍawī 2375, 2780 (cat., II, p.50, V, p.406); Tustariyya 857/1 (cat., p.877); (19) by Muḥammad b. ʿAlī b. Khwātūn al-ʿĀmilī (da. after 1003), MS: Raḍawī 2361 (cat., II, p.46); (20) by ʿAlī b. Tāj al-Dīn al-Anṣārī, MS: Gawharshād 1666/1 (cat., p.314); (21) by Muḥammad b. Niẓām al-Dīn al-Astarābādī (11th century), MSS: Raḍawī 2486 (cat., II, p.86); Wazīrī 3201/5 (cat., V, p.1569); (22) Persian, by Sulṭān Muḥammad al-Kāshānī, MS: Raḍawī 3841 (cat., II, p.85); (23) by al-Dāmād, MS: Raḍawī 2758 (cat., V, p.384); (24) by ʿAlī b. Muḥammad al-ʿĀmilī, MS: Jawādayn (AB, VI, p.24); (25) by Jawād b. ʿAlī b. ʿAbd al-ʿĀlī al-Maysī (d. after 1117), MS: Fayḍiyya 1731 (cat., I, p.73); (26) by Muḥammad Jaʿfar b. Muḥammad Bāqir al-Sabzawārī (d. after 1127), MS: Raḍawī 2777 (cat., V, p.454); (27) *al-Tuḥfa al-Ḥusayniyya*, anonymous, MS: Raḍawī 2287 (cat., II, p.24); (28) by al-Qummī, included in his *Jawāmiʿ al-rasāʾil* (see above, chapter 5); (29) *Mishkāt al-warā*, by Muḥammad Jaʿfar al-Astarābādī, MSS: Marʿashī 3081/2 (cat., VIII, p.305); Dānishgāh 1242/1 (cat., VII, p.2739) [Muḥammad Ḥusayn b. Muḥammad Ismāʿīl al-Basṭāmī wrote a commentary entitled *Maṣābīḥ al-asrār* on this work, MS: Majlis 3319/1 (cat., X, pp.972-3)]: (30) *Qinṭār al-waẓāʾif*, by Muḥammad Yūsuf b. Muḥammad Ṣādiq al-Ḥusaynī al-Gīlānī, MS: Raḍawī 2317 (cat., VI, p.297); (31) by Ḍiyāʾ al-Dīn al-Ḥusaynī, MS: Raḍawī 6439 (Bīnish, p.855); (32) by Aḥmad b. ʿAlī al-Iṣfahānī, MS: Masjid-i Aʿẓam 1792; (33-41) nine anonymous or unidentified commentaries; (a) MS: Raḍawī 7235 (cat., V, p.406); (b) MS: Ḥakīm 391; (c) MS: Gawharshād 1666/4 (cat., p.257); (d) MS: Gharb 4809/3 (cat., p.414); (e) MS: Gawharshād 966 (cat., pp.313-14); (f) MS: Fayḍiyya 1415/4 (cat., III, p.90); (g) MS: Wazīrī 3444 (cat., V, p.1656); (h) MS: Rawḍātī (AB, VI, p.25); (i) Raḍawī 2779 (cat., V, p.454)

IBN FAHD:

- *Risāla fī fiqh al-ṣalāt*
  MS: Burūjirdī (AB, XVI, p.293)

- *Ghāyat al-Ījāz*
  Edition: Tehran, 1300
  MSS: Princeton 3992/5 Yahuda (cat., p.149); Gawharshād 1129/4

(cat., p.354); Majlis 4645/2 (cat., XIII, p.34); Marʿashī 959 (cat., III, p.151); Dānishgāh 2144/36, 1015/7, 5876/2 (cat., V, p.1951, IX, p.828, XVI, p.387); Raḍawī 2500 (cat., II, p.90); Masjid-i Aʿẓam 575/2

- *Al-Hidāya = Wājibāt al-ṣalāt*
  MS: Los Angeles M1313/4 (cat., p.724); Rawḍatī (AB, XXV, pp.164)
- *Miṣbāḥ al-mubtadī*
  MSS: Los Angeles M1313/8 (cat., p.724); Tustariyya 873/1 (cat., pp.878-9); Raḍawī 2652 (cat., II, p.136); Millī, Arabic 1919/10, 800/2 (cat., VIII, p.303, X, p.584); Kāshānī (cat., p.252); Fayḍiyya 1835/2 (cat., III, p.139); Raḍawī 2651-2, 6038 (cat., II, p.136, V, p.506); Dānishgāh 7045 (cat., XVI, p.438); Ilāhiyyāt 583/2d (cat., I, p.336); Wazīrī 2456/2, 3201/3 (cat., V, pp. 1300, 1569); Gulpāyigānī 999/1 (cat., II, p.219); Masjid-i Aʿẓam 1160/5
- *Shadhrat al-naḍīd*
  MSS: Los Angeles M1313/6 (cat., p.724); Majlis 8834/3

IBRĀHĪM B. LAYTH AL-ḤUSAYNĪ (mid-9th ccentury):

Al-Muqaddama al-farʿiyya
MS: Princeton 3992/2 Yahuda (cat., p.149)

AL-TUWALĀNĪ - Shams al-Dīn ʿAlī al-Naḥārīrī al-ʿĀmilī (mid-9th century):

Kifāyat al-muhtadī = al-Tuwalāniyya
MSS: Raḍawī 2283, 2718, 6187 (cat., II, p.22, V, p.390); Ilāhiyyāt 168/3d (cat., I, p.251); Dānishgāh 1163/1 (cat., VI, p.2233); Millī 1190/1 Arabic (cat., IX, p.175); Los Angeles M97/5 (cat., p.663)

IBN ABĪ JUMHŪR:

Al-Risāla al-Barmakiyya
Translation: Persian, MS: Dānishgāh 1015/41 (cat., V, pp.1827-8)

AL-MAYSĪ - Nūr al-Dīn ʿAlī b. ʿAbd al-ʿĀlī (d. 938):

Wājibāt al-ṣalāt
MS: Matḥaf 186 (cat., I, p.239)

AL-KARAKĪ:

- *Al-Alfiyya*
  MSS: Khāliṣī (cat., p.67); Gulpāyigānī 43/2 (cat., I, p.54)
- *Al-Jaʿfariyya*
  Editions: Tehran, 1314, 1318
  Selected MSS: Raḍawī 2319, 2316, 2321, 2325 (cat., II, pp.32-3); Majlis 546 Ṭabāṭabāʾī, 1161 Ṭabāṭabāʾī, 3112/2 (cat., X, pp.674-5); Wazīrī 952/1 (cat., II, p.784); ʿAbd al-ʿAẓīm 122/1 (cat., p.438); Dānishgāh 872/7 (cat., V, pp.1841-2); Mahdawī 500/1 (cat., p.120); Marʿashī 680/1 (cat., II, p.273); Nawwāb 18 law (cat., p.454); Dār al-Kutub 21237 (cat., I, p.400); Bankipore 844 (cat. Arabic, I, p.84)
  Translation: (1) Persian, by Ḥasan b. ʿAbd al-Ghaffār (early 10th century), MS: Majlis 3112/1 (cat., X, p.673); (2) Persian, by Abu ʾl-Maʿālī b. Badr al-Dīn Ḥasan al-Ḥusaynī al-Astarābādī (d. after 935), MSS: Tiflis 699/10 (*Nash.*, VIII, p.260); Ṣāḥib al-Dharīʿa (AB, IV, pp.94, 104); (3) Persian, by ʿAlī b. Ḥasan al-Zawārī, MS: Wazīrī 2284/2 (cat., IV, p.1232); (4) Persian, by Ḥasan b. Ghiyāth

al-Astarābādī, MS: Ilāhiyyāt 304d (cat., I, p.28); (5-7) three anonymous or unidentified Persian translations: (a) MS: Masjid-i Jāmi' 313/4 (cat., p.383); (b) MS: India Office 121 Ashburner (cat., p.78); (c) MS: Bankipore 1247 (cat. Persian, I, p.199)
In verse: *al-'Ābidiyya*, by 'Abd al-Ḥusayn b. 'Abd al-Riḍā al-Kāẓimī (d. after 1120), MS: Burūjirdī (AB, XV, p.204)
Commentaries: (1) by the author, MSS: Dānishgāh 872/7 (cat., V, p.1862); Raḍawī 113/2 law (cat., II, p.34); (2) *al-Maṭālib al-Muẓaffariyya*, by Muḥammad b. Abī Ṭālib al-Mūsawī al-Astarābādī (d. after 940), selected MSS: Āṣafiyya 146 Shī'ī law (cat., II, pp. 245-6); Raḍawī 2622-3, 2478-80,6497 (cat., II, pp.83-4, 126-7, V, pp.506-7); Ḥujjatiyya 121 (cat., p.86); Ḥuqūq 31d, 320j (cat., p.469); Malik 2380, 2797 (cat., I, p.688); Majlis 33, 139 Khu'ī (cat., VII, p.153); Dānishgāh 2694/1, 6659 (cat., X, p.1577, XVI, p.327); Mathaf 2806, 3038 (cat., I, p.256); India Office 1811 (cat., II, p.314); (3) *al-Gharawiyya*, by Sharaf al-Dīn 'Alī al-Ḥusaynī al-Astarābādī (d. after 938), MSS: Raḍawī 2499 (cat., II, p.90); Princeton 1935/1 New Series; Ḥakīm 58 (*Nash.*, V, p.423); (4) *al-Ḥaydariyya*, by Shāh Ṭāhir b. Raḍī al-Dīn al-Ḥusaynī al-Ismā'īlī al-Dakanī (d. 952), MSS: Raḍawī 2621 (cat., V, p.455, 507); Los Angeles M829 (cat., p.216); (5) by al-Maysī, MS: Zanjān (cat., p.113); (6) *Sharḥ khuṭbat al-Ja'fariyya*, by Muḥammad Mahdī al-Raḍawī al-Mashhadī (d. after 954), MS: Ilāhiyyāt 99/1 (cat., I, p.715); (7) by 'Abd al-Ḥayy al-Ashraqī al-Jurjānī, MS: Bengal 634 (cat., I, p.313); (8) *al-Fawā'id al-'aliyya*, by al-Fāḍil al-Jawād, MSS: Gharb 1132 (cat., p.167); Mar'ashī 1712 (cat., V, pp.103-4); Majlis 9391; Shīrāzī (AB, XVI, p.350); Rawḍātī (cat., I, pp. 260 ff); (9) *al-Ashi''a al-badriyya*, by Muḥammad Ismā'īl al-Faḍā'ī al-Kazzāzī, MS: Masjid-i A'ẓam 386, 9872-4; (10) by 'Alī Akbar b. Ibrāhīm al-Khwānsārī (d. 1271), MSS: Gulpāyigānī 89 (cat., I, p.92); (11) anonymous, MS: Gawharshād 560 (cat., p.318)

Al-Najmiyya, on dogmatics and prayer
MSS: Mahdawī 500/2 (cat., p.120); Raḍawī 2746 (cat., V, p.526); Gulpāyigānī 43/4 (cat., I, p.54); Los Angeles M1051 (cat., p.707)
Commentary: *al-Kawākib al-durriyya*, by Ḥusayn b. 'Alī al-Uwālī al-Hajarī, MS: Raḍawī 2543 (cat., II, p.104)

Ma'ānī af'āl al-ṣalāt
MS: Gharb 4712/6 (cat., p.380)

ABBĀS B. MUḤAMMAD RIḌĀ AL-TŪNĪ (d. after 949):

Wajīza fī farḍ al-ṣalāt
MS: Millī 1028 Arabic (cat., IX, p.31)

IUḤAMMAD B. ḤARITH AL-MANṢŪRĪ AL-BAḤRĀNĪ (d. after 952):

Al-Sayfiyya, on dogmatics and prayer
MS: Majlis 4339/2 (cat., XII, p.38)

ⅭAMĀL AL-DĪN ḤUSAYN B. FAḌL ALLĀH AL-DĀMGHĀNĪ (d. after 972):

Wājibāt al-ṣalāt
MS: Āstāna 383/1 (cat., p.232)

ABD AL-'ĀLĪ AL-KARAKĪ:

Al-Niẓāmiyya
Commentary: *Hādī al-muḍillīn wa murshid al-muṣallīn*, by 'Abd al-Hādī b. Rafī' al-Dīn Ḥusayn al-Ḥusaynī al-Dilījānī (d. after 1048), MSS:

Marʿashī 801, 1167, 2153 (cat., III, pp.1, 339, VI, p.160)

ṢĀḤIB AL-MAʿĀLIM:

Al-Ithnāʿashariyya
MSS: Sipahsālār 6062/1 (cat., III, pp.42-3); Dānishgāh 3702/4 (cat., XI, p.2016)
Commentaries: (1) *al-Anwār al-qamariyya*, by Fayḍ Allāh b. ʿAbd Qāhir al-Ḥusaynī al-Tafrīshī (d. 1025), MS: Nujūmī (cat., p.293); (2) by Muḥammad b. Ḥasan al-ʿĀmilī, MSS: Āṣafiyya 96 Shīʿī law (cat., II, pp.243-4); Hamadān, Madrasa-yi Dāmghānī (*Nash.*, V, p.384); (3) by Bahāʾ al-Dīn al-ʿĀmilī, MSS: Raḍawī 2729 (cat., V, p.405); Dānishgāh 918/12 (cat., V, pp.1855-6); Adabiyyāt 14/3d (cat., pp.197-8); Majlis 3718/6, 5960/1 (cat., X, pp.1694-5, XVII, p.344); Masjid-i Jāmiʿ 299/2 (cat., p.377); Sipahsālār 7939/1 (cat., IV, pp. 139-40); (4) *al-Fawāʾid al-Gharawiyya*, by Sharaf al-Dīn ʿAlī b. Ḥujjat Allāh al-Shūlastānī (d. after 1057), MSS: Majlis 4944/1 (cat., XVII, pp.327-8); Raḍawī 2509 (cat., II, p.92); Sipahsālār 6065 (cat., V, p.386)

BAHĀʾ AL-DĪN AL-ʿĀMILĪ:

Risāla mukhtaṣara fī fiqh al-ṣalāt
MS: Bodleian Arab.e.175

MUʿIZZ AL-DĪN AL-MŪSAWĪ:

Tuḥfat al-Riḍā
MS: Raḍawī 6533 (cat., V, pp.379-81)

ANONYMOUS (written before 1057):

Al-Risāla al-maʿnawiyya
MS: Gulpāyigānī 1991/1 (cat., III, pp.129-30)

MUḤAMMAD AL-ḤUSAYNĪ (d. after 1074):

Risāla fi ʾl-ṣalāt
MS: Dānishgāh 2155 (cat., IX, p.850)

ABU ʾL-QĀSIM AL-GULPĀYIGĀNĪ:

Al-Masālik
MSS: Raḍawī 5721 (cat., V, p.500); Millī 294 Arabic (cat., VII, pp. 262-3)

ANONYMOUS (written before 1095):

Risāla fi ʾl-ṣalāt
MS: Dānishgāh 2711/2 (cat., X, p.1588)

AL-MAJLISĪ II:

Ādāb al-ṣalāt, Persian
MS: Marʿashī 187/1 (cat., I, p.205)

AL-MĀḤŪZĪ:

- *Al-Fawāʾid al-sariyya*, a commentary on the treatise on prayer of Bahāʾ al-Dīn al-ʿĀmilī's *al-Ithnāʿashariyya*
  MS: Najaf, Jazāʾirī (AB, XVI, p.342)
- *Wājibāt al-ṣalāt*

MSS: Gharb 2435 (cat., pp.203-4); Najaf, Jazā'irī (AB, XV, pp.56-7)

MUḤAMMAD ṬĀHIR B. RAḌĪ AL-DĪN MUḤAMMAD AL-ḤUSAYNĪ (early 12th century):

Taqwīm al-ṣalāt, Persian
Edition: Tehran, 1364
MSS: Majlis 2049, 4731 (cat., VI, p.47, XIII, pp.111-12); Millī 2933/2f (cat., VI, pp.677-8)

AḤMAD AL-BAḤRĀNĪ:

Al-Masā'il al-khamsa
MS: Majlis 2701/2 (cat., IX, p.4)

ṢĀḤIB AL-ḤADĀ'IQ:

- *Risāla fi 'l-ṣalāt*
  Editions: Najaf, 1356, 1371
  MS: Mar'ashī 3450/4 (cat., IX, p.242)
- *Sharḥ Risālat al-ṣalāt*, a commentary on the previous work
  MSS: Mar'ashī 3450/5 (cat., IX, p.243); Raḍawī 6467 (cat., V, p.434); Nūrbakhsh 437/1 (cat., II, p.132); Zanjān (cat., p.114); Dānishgāh 7667/1 (cat., XVI, p.668)
- *Risāla fi 'l-ṣalāt*, different from above
  MS: Mar'ashī 3450/6 (cat., IX, pp.243-5)

ḤUSAYN ĀL 'UṢFŪR:

Al-Nafḥa al-qudsiyya
MSS: Mar'ashī 2475 (cat., VII, p.66); Ustādī (cat., p.66)

ABŪ ṬĀLIB B. ABI 'L-ḤASAN AL-ḤUSAYNĪ AL-QUMMĪ (mid-13th century):

Irshād al-ṣāliḥīn, Persian
MS: Millī 1942f (cat., IV, p.407)

AL-SHAFTĪ:

Maṭāli' al-anwār, a commentary on the chapter on prayer of al-Muḥaqqiq's *Sharā'i' al-Islām*
Selected MSS: Mar'ashī 2799, 1632, 1900, 1906, 1913, 1929, 2980, 3304 (cat., V, pp.35, 272-3, 277, 285, 297, VII, p.367, VIII, p.157, IX, p.84); Majlis 5788-90 (cat., XVII, pp.221-3); Dānishgāh 1000-2, 4888 (cat., V, pp.2047-52, XIV, pp.3937-8); Sipahsālār 2474-8 (cat., I, pp.459-61); Raḍawī 7971, 7976-80 (Bīnish, pp.1016-17)

ḤUSAYN B. DILDĀR 'ALĪ AL-NAṢĪRĀBĀDĪ (d. after 1250):

Manāhij al-tadqīq wa ma'ārij al-taḥqīq
Edition: India (AB, XXII, p.343)

AL-ANṢĀRĪ:

- *K. al-Ṣalāt*
  Edition: Tehran, 1305
  MS: Ustādī (cat., p.26)
- *K. al-Ṣalāt*, his lectures on prayer compiled by one of his pupils
  MS: Majlis 44 Ṭabāṭabā'ī

AL-ḤĀʾIRĪ - ʿAbd al-Karīm b. Muḥammad Jaʿfar al-Yazdī (d. 1355):

- *K. al-Ṣalāt*
  Edition: Tehran, 1353
- *K. al-Ṣalāt*, his lectures on prayer compiled by Maḥmūd al-Āshtiyānī
  Edition: Tehran, 1387-90

AL-NĀʾĪNĪ:

K. al-Ṣalāt, his lectures on prayer compiled by Muḥammad Taqī al-Āmulī
Edition: Tehran, 1372-3 (3 vols.)

AL-BURŪJIRDĪ:

Nihāyat al-taqrīr, his lectures on prayer complied by Muḥammad al-Muwaḥḥidī al-Lankarānī
Edition: Qum, 1376 (2 vols.)

2. ON TIMES OF PRAYER

BĀYAZĪD AL-THĀNĪ:

Awqāt al-ṣalāt
MS: Dānishgāh 944/11 (cat., V, pp.1784-5)

AL-MAJLISĪ II:

Awqāt-i namāz, Persian
MSS: Marʿashī 187/17, 3050/3 (cat., I, pp.211-12, VIII, p.269)

AL-MĀḤŪZĪ:

Risāla fī awqāt al-ṣalāt
MS: Ḥusayniyyat Kāshif al-Ghiṭāʾ 55 (AB, XI, p.124)

AL-MUKHTĀRĪ:

Ḥisān al-yawāqīt
MS: Marʿashī 3382/5 (cat., IX, p.160)

AḤMAD AL-BAḤRĀNĪ:

Taʿlīq ʿalā mabḥath al-zawāl min al-Rawḍa al-bahiyya
MSS: Dānishgāh 7524/1 (cat., XVI, p.608); Princeton 229/6 Yahuda (cat., p.138)

IBN ṬAWQ AL-BAḤRĀNĪ:

Idrāk al-rakʿa fī ʾl-waqt
MS: Marʿashī 2358/5+11 (cat., VI, pp.335, 337)

ʿALĪ B. MUḤAMMAD ḤUSAYN AL-SHAHRASTĀNĪ (d. 1344):

Risāla fī maʿrifat waqt al-maghrib
Edition: Tehran, 1320

. ON THE DIRECTION OF PRAYER[1]

HĀDHĀN B. JIBRI'ĪL AL-QUMMĪ (d. after 593):

Izāḥat al-ʿilla
Editions: Tehran, 1311, 1390 (both in al-Majlisī II's *Biḥār al-anwār*, first edition, XVIII, part 2, pp.153-6; second edition, LXXXIV, pp.73-85)
Selected MSS: Majlis 4339/11, 5194/2, 2761/16 (cat., IX, p.164, XII, p.42, XVI, p.24); Raḍawī 6045, 7187 (Bīnish, p.587); Gulpāyigānī 2397/5 (cat., III, p.245); Marʿashī 679 (cat., II, p.272); Dānishgāh 882/3 (cat., V, pp.1774-5)

L-MUḤAQQIQ:

Istiḥbāb al-tayāsur li-ahl al-ʿIrāq
Editions: Tehran, 1307 (in al-Shahīd al-Thānī's *Rawḍ al-jinān*, between pp.199-200) and others
Selected MSS: Dānishgāh 882/4, 2888/2, 5923/3 (cat., V, p.1838, X, p.1733, XVI, p.154); Majlis 3988/8, 3280/22 (cat., X, pp.900-1, 2165); Raḍawī 7188 (cat., V, p.430); Ustādī (cat., p.69). It is also included in Ibn Fahd's *al-Muhadhdhab al-bāriʿ*, the chapter on prayer.

L-KARAKĪ:

Risāla fī 'l-qibla (see AB, XVII, p.45)
MSS: Millī 1493/11 Arabic (cat., X, 0.621); Dānishgāh 3597/6 (cat., XV, p.4240)

USAYN B. ʿABD AL-ṢAMAD:

Tuḥfat ahl al-īmān
MSS: Majlis 1836/9 (cat., IX, pp.487-8); Millī 1943/4 Arabic (cat., X, p. 617); Gawharshād 1750/2 (cat., p.368); Gulpāyigānī 48/1 (cat., I, p.58); Raḍawī 7386 (Bīnish, p.633)

Qiblat ʿIrāq al-ʿajam wa Khurāsān
MSS: Marʿashī 744/4 (cat., II, p.346); Fayḍiyya 1679/1 (cat., III, p.117); Gulpāyigānī 48/4 (cat., I, p.58)

NONYMOUS:

Risāla fī maʿrifat al-qibla
MS: Sipahsālār 840/2 (cat., V, p.398)

IAḤMŪD AL-ḤUSAYNĪ AL-SHŪLASTĀNĪ:

Risāla fī maʿrifat al-qibla
MS: Mashhad, Ilāhiyyāt 773/5 (cat., I, pp.416-17)

ALĀ' AL-MULK FĀḌIL KHĀN (10th century):

Risāla fī taḥqīq al-qibla
MS: Sipahsālār 2925/11 (cat., III, pp.380-1)

L-MUJTAHID:

Risāla fī 'l-qibla
Translation: Persian, by Muḥammad Ṣādiq al-Sirkānī, MS: Ustādī (cat., p.68)

---

[1] For Shīʿī scientific works on the subject see AB, XVII, pp.37-46.

BAHĀʾ AL-DĪN AL-ʿĀMILĪ:

Risāla fī taḥqīq jahat al-qibla
Selected MSS: Dānishgāh 821/4, 918/9, 987/3, 1626/2, 4005/6, 4316/5 (cat., V, pp.1853-4, VIII, p.210, XII, p.2993, XIII, p.3279); Sipahsālār 2670/6, 7539/9, 7542/4,8190/12 (cat., I, pp.419-20, III, p.44, IV, p.133); Marʿashī 104/4, 1003/5 (sat., I, p.126, III, p.195); Gulpāyigānī 48/2, 146/2 (cat., I, pp.58, 135); Masjid-i Aʿẓam 476/5; Princeton 151/2 New Series; Raḍawī 6544 (cat., V, p.438)

MUḤAMMAD YAḤYĀ B. SHARĪF AL-SĀWIJĪ (d. after 1075):

Minhāj al-qibla, Persian
MS: Marʿashī 1453 (cat., IV, p.242)

MUḤAMMAD B. MUḤAMMAD ZAMĀN AL-KĀSHĀNĪ (d. after 1172):

Qibla-yi Ithnāʿashariyya, Persian
MSS: Dānishgāh 7060/2 (cat., XVI, p.442); Adabiyyāt, 189J (cat., pp.376-7); Majlis 627, 1966/7 (cat., IX, pp.682-4); Nūrbakhsh 108/4 (cat., I, p.131)

MUḤAMMAD ṢĀLIḤ B. MUḤAMMAD SAʿĪD AL-KHALKHĀLĪ (d. 1175):

Al-Ibāna al-marḍiyya, a commentary on the relevant discussion in al-Shahīd al-Thānī's *al-Rawḍa al-bahiyya*
Edition: Tehran 1313
MS: Marʿashī 2786 (cat., VII, pp.349-50); Dānishgāh 5830 (cat., XVI, p.30)

MUḤAMMAD JAʿFAR AL-ASTARĀBĀDĪ:

Risāla fī ʾl-qibla
MS: Marʿashī 3066/2 (cat., VIII, p.287)

ʿALĪ B. RIḌĀ ĀL BAḤR AL-ʿULŪM:

Risāla fī ʾl-qibla
Edition: Tehran, 1291 (together with his *al-Burhān al-qāṭiʿ*)

ʿALĪ B. ʿABD ALLĀH AL-ʿALYĀRĪ AL-TABRĪZĪ (d. 1327):

Minhāj al-milla fī taʿyīn al-waqt wa ʾl-qibla, as a commentary on the relevant discussions in al-Shahīd al-Thānī's above-mentioned work
MS: Marʿashī (AB, XXIII, p.176)

MUḤAMMAD ʿALĪ B. MUḤAMMAD NAṢĪR AL-MUDARRIS AL-GĪLĀNĪ (d. 1334):

Al-Waqt wa ʾl-qibla, a commentary on the relevant discussions in al-Shahīd al-Thānī's above-mentioned work
Edition: Tehran, 1323
MS: Marʿashī 2078/1 (cat., VI, p.91)

MUḤAMMAD HĀSHIM B. MUḤAMMAD ʿALĪ AL-KHURĀSĀNĪ (d. 1352):

Risāla dar maʿrifat-i qibla, Persian
Editions: Tehran, 1332, 1352, Mashhad, 1350

. ON CLOTHES FOR PRAYER

ŪR ALLĀH AL-TUSTARĪ:

Risāla fī taḥqīq mā lā tatimm al-ṣalāt fīh
MS: Ilāhiyyāt 51/9d (cat., I, p.127)

AHĀ' AL-DĪN AL-'ĀMILĪ:

Al-Ḥarīriyya
Editions: Tehran, 1315 (in the collection of *Kalimāt al-muḥaqqiqīn*), 1318 (in the margin of al-Khurāsānī's *Durar al-fawā'id*)
MS: Dānishgāh 918/3 (cat., V, p.1875)

L-KHWĀJŪ'Ī:

Al-Dhahabiyya
MS: Dānishgāh 791/3 (cat., V, p.1883)

Al-Ḥarīriyya
MS: Mar'ashī 2476/3 (cat., VII, p.68)

Risāla fī 'l-libās al-mashkūk
MS: Majlis 3752/1 (cat., X, p.1736)

IUSAYN AL-QAZWĪNĪ:

Mukhtār al-madhhab fī mā yaṣḥabuh al-insān min al-dhahab
MSS: Raḍawī 2595/1 (cat., II, p.118); Zanjānī 76/1 (cat., pp.220-1)

L-ĀSHTIYĀNĪ:

Izāḥat al-shukūk fī 'l-libās al-mashkūk
Edition: Tehran, 1313

ALĪ B. MUḤAMMAD ḤUSAYN AL-SHAHRASTĀNĪ:

Risāla fī ma'rifat ḥukm al-mashkūk min al-libās
Edition: Tehran, 1320

IUḤAMMAD B. MUḤAMMAD BĀQIR AL-ḤUSAYNĪ AL-FĪRŪZĀBĀDĪ (d. 1345):

Jāmi' al-kalim
Edition: Najaf, 1339

L-BALĀGHĪ:

Risāla fī 'l-libās al-mashkūk
Edition: Najaf, 1352 (together with his *Ḥāshiyat al-makāsib*)

L-ĪRAWĀNĪ - 'Alī b. 'Abd al-Ḥusayn al-Najafī (d. 1353):

Al-Dhahab al-masbūk
Edition: Tehran,1367

L-NĀ'ĪNĪ:

Risāla fī 'l-libās al-mashkūk
Edition: Najaf, 1357-8 (together with his *Munyat al-ṭālib*)

ḌIYĀ' AL-DĪN AL-'ARĀQĪ:

Risāla fī 'l-libās al-mashkūk

Editions: Najaf, n.d., Qum, 1394 (both together with his *Rawāʾiʿ al-amālī*)

ABU ʾL-ḤASAN B. MUḤAMMAD AL-ANGAJĪ AL-TABRĪZĪ (d. 1357):

Izāḥat al-iltibās ʿan ḥukm al-mashkūk min al-libās
Edition: Tabrīz, 1313

MUḤAMMAD JAʿFAR B. MUḤAMMAD ṬĀHIR AL-SHĪRĀZĪ (d. 1395):

Izāḥat al-shukūk ʿan ḥukm al-libās al-mashkūk
Edition: Shīrāz, 1366

AL-KHUʾĪ:

Risāla fi ʾl-libās al-mashkūk
Edition: Najaf, 1361

5. ON PLACE OF PRAYER

ʿALĪ NAQĪ B. MUḤAMMAD HĀSHIM AL-KAMARAʾĪ AL-IṢFAHĀNĪ (d. 1060):

Risāla fi ʾl-ṣalāt fi ʾl-maghṣūb
MS: Majlis 3333/5 (cat., X, p.1130)

ZAYN AL-ʿĀBIDĪN B. MUḤAMMAD YŪSUF AL-ḤUSAYNĪ AL-LĀRĪJĀNĪ (d. after 1168):

Kashf al-maṭlūb fī buṭlān al-ṣalāt fi ʾl-makān al-maghṣūb
MSS: Millī 1081/4 (cat., IX, p.75): Marʿashī 3056 (cat., VIII, p.276)

ḤUSAYN AL-QAZWĪNĪ:

Risāla fī ḥukm al-ʿibāda fi ʾl-makān al-maghṣūb
MSS: Raḍawī 2595/4 (cat., II, p.118); Zanjānī 76/4 (cat., pp.220-1)

MUḤAMMAD ʿALĪ B. MUḤAMMAD BĀQIR AL-SHAFTĪ:

Risāla fi ʾl-ṣalāt fi ʾl-makān al-maghṣūb
MS: Marʿashī 1995/2 (cat., V, p.366)

6. ON CALL FOR PRAYER

MUḤAMMAD ṢĀLIḤ B. ʿABD AL-WĀSIʿ AL-KHWĀTŪNĀBĀDĪ (d. 1126):

Al-Tahlīliyya = Hal al-tahlīl marratān fī ākhir al-iqāma aw marra wāḥida
MS: Dānishgāh 591/4 (cat., V, p.1837)

MUḤAMMAD HĀDĪ B. MUḤAMMAD ṢĀLIḤ AL-MĀZANDARĀNĪ (d. around 1134):

Risāla fi ʾl-adhān wa ʾl-iqāma
MS: Nawwāb 271/2 (cat., p.474)

AL-SARĀB - Muḥammad b. ʿabd al-Fattāḥ al-Tunukābunī (d. 1124):

Risāla fī fuṣūl al-adhān wa ʾl-iqāma
MSS: Dānishgāh 888/3 (cat., V, pp.1960-1); Gulpāyigānī 1862/3 (cat., III, p.85)

MUḤAMMAD MU'MIN B. MUḤAMMAD HĀSHIM AL-ḤUSAYNĪ (mid-12th century):

Risāla fī istiḥbāb al-shahāda bi-wilāyat ʿAlī b. Abī Ṭālib fi 'l-adhān wa 'l-iqāma
MS: Dānishgāh 2603/3 (cat., IX, p.1457)

MUḤAMMAD NAṢĪR B. MUḤAMMAD MAʿṢŪM:

Kanz al-Shīʿa
MS: Marʿashī 2517 (cat., VII, pp.102-3)

AL-KHWĀJŪ'Ī:

Risāla fī kayfiyyat al-adhān wa 'l-tashahhud
MS: Mashhad, Adabiyyāt 25/6 Fayyāḍ (cat., pp.211-12)

KĀSHIF AL-GHIṬĀ':

Risāla fi 'l-manʿ min al-shahāda bi 'l-wilāya fi 'l-adhān
MS: inserted in the next treatise

AL-AKHBĀRĪ - Muḥammad b. ʿAbd al-Nabī al-Naysābūrī (d. 1232):

Risāla dar shahādat bar wilāyat dar adhān, Persian
MS: Majlis 2797/6 (cat., X, pp.72-3)

MUḤAMMAD B. ASGHAR ḤUSAYN AL-AMRŪHAWĪ (d. after 1333):

- *Bāb-i jinān*, Urdu
  MS: Marʿashī 1891/2 (cat., V, p.266)
- *Khayr al-ʿamal*, Urdu
  MS: Marʿashī 1891/3 (cat., V, p.267)

INCIDENTAL DISCUSSIONS

ʿABD ALLĀH AL-TUSTARĪ:

Risāla fī idkhāl al-shahāda bi 'l-wilāya fi 'l-tashahhud, included in his *al-Rasā'il* (see above, chapter 5)

ḤAYDAR ʿALĪ AL-SHĪRWĀNĪ (early 12th century):

Risāla fī wujūb al-ṣalāt ʿala 'l-Nabī
MS: Dānishgāh 4292/1 (cat., XIII, pp.3261-2)

MUḤAMMAD ḤUSAYN AL-KHWĀTŪNĀBĀDĪ:

Risāla dar wujūb-i ṣalawāt, Persian
MS: Ustādī (cat., p.55)

7. ON RECITATION

ʿABD ALLĀH AL-TUSTARĪ:

Risāla fi 'l-jahr wa 'l-ikhfāt fi 'l-awwalatayn, included in his *al-Rasā'il* (see above, chapter 5)

BAHĀ' AL-DĪN AL-ʿĀMILĪ:

Risāla fī istiḥbāb al-sūra fi 'l-ṣalāt
MSS: Raḍawī 242 law (cat., II, p.74); Marʿashī 1003/9 (cat., III, p.196)

MUḤAMMAD ṢĀDIQ B. MUḤAMMAD AMĪN AL-ḤILLĪ AL-SHĪRĀZĪ (d. after 1057):

Risāla fī istiḥbāb al-sūra
MS: Dānishgāh 7126/1 (cat., XVI, p.461)

AL-MĀḤŪZĪ:

- *Risāla fī afḍaliyyat al-tasbīḥ ʿala ʾl-qirāʾa fi ʾl-rakʿatayn al-akhīratyan*
  MSS: Adabiyyāt 275/2 Kirmān (cat., p.42); Miftāḥ 244/5 (cat., p.230); Najaf, Jazāʾirī (*Nash.*, VII, p.716)
- *Risāla fī kayfiyyat al-tasbīḥ fi ʾl-akhīratayn*
  MS: Najaf, Jazāʾirī (*Nash.*, VII, p.716)

MUḤAMMAD JAʿFAR B. MUḤAMMAD BĀQIR AL-SABZAWĀRĪ:

Al-Takbīrāt al-sabʿ
MS: Marʿashī 478/3 (cat., II, p.83)

AḤMAD AL-BAḤRĀNĪ:

Risāla fī jawāz al-ʿudūl ʿan kull sūra ʿada ʾl-Jaḥd wa ʾl-Tawḥīd
MS: Princeton 229/15 Yahuda (cat., p.149)

AL-KHWĀJŪʾĪ:

- *Tadhkirat al-waḍāḍ = Risāla fī istiḥbāb rafʿ al-yadayn fi ʾl-qunūt*
  MS: Princeton 1317 New Series (fols. 23b-44b)
- *Risāla fī afḍaliyyat al-tasbīḥ fi ʾl-akhīratayn*
  MS: Adabiyyāt 25/25 Fayyāḍ (cat., p.214)

ʿALĪ B. MUḤAMMAD AL-MAQĀBĪ AL-BAḤRĀNĪ:

Risāla fi ʾl-jahr wa ʾl-ikhfāt
MS: Raḍawī 5216 (Bīnish, p.796)

MUḤAMMAD B. AḤMAD AL-BAḤRĀNĪ (late 12th century):

Risāla fī wujūb al-jahr bi ʾl-tasbīḥāt fi ʾl-akhīratayn = Risāla fi ʾl-tasbīḥāt al-arbaʿa
MS: Majlis 23/2 Khuʾī (cat., VII, p.45)

IBN ṬAWQ AL-BAḤRĀNĪ:

Risāla fī wujūb al-ikhfāt fī ghayr al-awwalatayn
MS: Marʿashī 2358/16 (cat., VI, p.339)

AL-ĀSHTIYĀNĪ:

Risāla fi ʾl-jamʿ bayn qaṣday al-Qurʾān wa ʾl-duʿāʾ
Edition: Tehran, 1314 (together with his *Risāla fī qāʿidat nafy al-ʿusr wa ʾl-ḥaraj*)

8. ON PROSTRATION

AL-KARAKĪ:

Risāla fī jawāz al-sujūd ʿala ʾl-turba al-Ḥusayniyya al-mashwiyya
MSS: Marʿashī 1280/2 (cat., IV, p.80); Dānishgāh 2888/1 (cat., X, p.1732); Dār al-Kutub 20325 (cat., I, 0.388); Qādiriyya 523 (cat., II, p.323); Shīrāz, Dānishgāh

ABD ALLĀH AL-TUSTARĪ:

Risāla fī kifāyat musammā al-jabha fi 'l-sujūd, included in his *al-Rasā'il* (see above, chapter 5)

AHĀ' AL-DĪN AL-'ĀMILĪ:

Risāla fī sujūd al-tilāwa
MS: Dānishgāh 7087/5 (cat., XVI, p.449)

. ON TERMINATING SALUTE

ĀYAZĪD AL-THĀNĪ:

Al-Tuḥfa al-marḍiyya = al-Salāmiyya
MS: Dānishgāh 944/7 (cat., V, p.1825)

NONYMOUS:

Risāla fi 'l-taslīm fi 'l-ṣalāt
MS: Tustariyya (AB, XI, p.147)

NONYMOUS (written in or before 1058):

Risāla fī wujūb al-taslīm fi 'l-ṣalāt
MS: Mar'ashī 1383/2 (cat., IV, p.157)

IUḤAMMAD ṬĀHIR B. MUḤAMMAD ḤUSAYN AL-QUMMĪ (d. 1098):

Al-Salāmiyya
MSS: Dānishgāh 2215/3 (cat., IX, p.891); Amīr al-Mu'minīn (AB, XII, p.214); Najaf, Madrasat al-Sayyid (ibid., XI, p.199); Qum, Rūḥānī (*Āshnā'ī*, I, p.448)

L-MUKHTĀRĪ:

Risāla fī istiḥbāb al-taslīm 'ala 'l-nabī fi 'l-tashahhud al-akhīr
MS: Mar'ashī 3382/6 (cat., IX, p.161)

BN ṬAWQ AL-BAḤRĀNĪ:

Rawḥ al-nasīm fī aḥkām al-taslīm
MS: Mar'ashī 2358/1 (cat., VI, p.333)

10. ON FRIDAY PRAYER

L-KARAKĪ:

Risāla fī ṣalāt al-jum'a
Edition: Qum, 1395 (in the collection of *Āshnā'ī bā chand nuskha-yi khaṭṭī*, pp.273-83)
MSS: Raḍawī 2423 (cat., II, p.65); Mar'ashī 110/3, 1409/6 (cat., I, p.132, IV, p.187); Zanjānī 23/2 (cat., p.198); Dānishgāh 4412/1 (cat., XIII, p.3374); Gawharshād 1721/3 (cat., p.346); Khāliṣī (cat., p.102)
Translation: Persian, by Muḥammad Ṣādiq al-Sirkānī, MS: Wazīrī (cat. of microfilms of Dānishgāh, I, p.703)

AL-SHAHĪD AL-THĀNĪ:

- *Maqāla fi 'l-ḥath 'alā ṣalāt al-jum'a*
Selected MSS: Dānishgāh 2099/14, 7019/5 (cat., VIII, p.728, XVI, p.431); Majlis 2761/17 (cat., IX, p.164); Sipahsālār 7461/4 (cat., V,

p.289); Baku M140/43 (*Nash.*, IX, p.242)
Translation: Persian, by Muḥammad Ṣādiq al-Sirkānī, MS: Wazīrī (cat. of microfilms of Dānishgāh, I, p.703)

- *Risāla fī wujūb ṣalāt al-jumʿa*, included in his *Majmūʿat al-ifādāt* (see above, chapter 5)
Translation: Persian, by Abu 'l-Qāsim Saḥāb, edited Tehran, 1366
- *Maqāla fī wujūh al-baḥth ʿan ṣalāt al-jumʿa*
MS: Dānishgāh 4412/5 (cat., XIII, p.3375)

ḤUSAYN B. ʿABD AL-ṢAMAD:

Risāla fī wujūb ṣalāt al-jumʿa
MSS: Majlis 1836/11 (cat., IX, p.489); Ḥakīm 451m; Khāliṣī (cat., p.103)

ḤASAN B. ʿALĪ B. ʿABD AL-ʿĀLĪ AL-KARAKĪ (late 10th century):

Al-Bulgha fī iʿtibār idhn al-Imām fī mashrūʿiyyat ṣalāt al-jumʿa
MS: Khāliṣī (cat., p.103)

ʿABD AL-ʿALĪ AL-JĀPALAQĪ:

- *Risāla fī ṣalāt al-jumʿa*
MS: Dānishgāh 972/1 (cat., V, pp.2089-90)
- *Risāla dar namāz-i jumʿa*, Persian
MS: Dānishgāh 972/2 (cat., V, pp.2090-1)

AL-MUJTAHID:

Al-Bulgha fī ʿadam ʿayniyyat ṣalāt al-jumʿa
MS: Gulpāyigānī 146/9 (cat., I, p.136); Khāliṣī (cat., pp. 101-2)

NŪR ALLĀH AL-TUSTARĪ:

Al-Lumʿa fī ṣalāt al-jumʿa
MSS: Ḥakīm 375/5 (*Nash.*, V, p.427); Khāliṣī (cat., p.103)

ʿABD ALLĀH AL-TUSTARĪ:

Risāla dar namāz-i jumʿa, Persian
MS: (a part of it) Raḍawī 7055/4 (cat., V, p.488)

ʿIMĀD AL-DĪN B. YŪSUF (early 11th century):

Risāla fī ṣalāt al-jumʿa
MS: Tehran, Muḥaddith Urmawī (AB, XV, p.77)

BAHĀ' AL-DĪN AL-ʿĀMILĪ:

Risāla fī ṣalāt al-jumʿa
MS: Dār al-Kutub 20324b (cat., I, p.391)

AL-DĀMĀD:

Risāla fī ṣalāt al-jumʿa
Editions: Tehran, 1397 (in the editor's introduction to his *al-Qabasāt*), 1401 (in the collection of *Ithnāʿashar risāla li 'l-Dāmād*)

MURTAḌĀ B. MUḤAMMAD AL-ḤUSAYNĪ AL-SĀRAWĪ (d. after 1049):

Jamʿa min masā'il al-jumʿa
MS: Marʿashī 3032/1 (cat., VIII, p.221)

ANONYMOUS (written in 1054):

Risāla fī wujūb ṣalāt al-jumʿa
MS: Ilāhiyyāt 206/3d (cat., I, p.259)

ANONYMOUS (written in or before 1058):

Risāla fī wujūb waḥdat ṣalāt al-jumʿa
MS: Marʿashī 1383/3+4 (cat., IV, pp.157-8)

ʿABD ALLĀH B. MUḤAMMAD AL-TŪNĪ (d. 1071):

Risāla fī nafy al-wujūb al-ʿaynī ʿan ṣalāt al-jumʿa
MSS: Majlis 128/2 Khuʾī, 3263/4, 4386/2 (cat., VII, pp.177-8, X, pp.874-5, XII, p.93); Dānishgāh 2875/1 (cat., X, p.1719); Millī 1858/1 Arabic (cat., X, p.439); Marʿashī 2526 (cat., VII, pp.112-13); Tustariyya (AB, XV, pp.74-5); Los Angeles M1204/1 (cat., p.715)
Commentary: marginal glosses by Aḥmad b. Muḥammad al-Tūnī (d. after 1071), MS: Millī 1858/1 in margin (cat., X, pp.439-40)

ḤASAN ʿALĪ B. ʿABD ALLĀH AL-TUSTARĪ (d. 1075):

Risāla fī ḥurmat ṣalāt al-jumʿa fī zaman al-ghayba, Persian
MS: Majlis 4943/5 (cat., XIV, p.198); Ḥuqūq 8/1d (cat., p.222)

MUḤAMMAD B. QĀSIM (d. after 1068):

Risāla dar namāz-i jumʿa, Persian
MS: Raḍawī 6198 (cat., p.804)

MUḤAMMAD MUQĪM B. MUḤAMMAD ʿALĪ AL-YAZDĪ (d. 1084):

Al-Ḥujja fī wujūb ṣalāt al-jumʿa
Edition: Yazd, n.d. (together with Ḥusayn b.ʿAbd al-Ṣamad's *al-ʿIqd al-Ḥusaynī*)
MS: Wazīrī 320/5 (cat., I, p.304)

KHALĪL B. GHĀZĪ AL-QAZWĪNĪ (d. 1088):

Risāla fī ḥurmat ṣalāt al-jumʿa
MS: Los Angeles M1224 (cat., p.62)

BAHĀʾ AL-DĪN MUḤAMMAD B. MAḤMŪD B. ḤUSĀM AL-MASHRIQĪ AL-NAJAFĪ (d. after 1086):

Risāla fī ṣalāt al-jumʿa
MS: Raḍawī 6466 (cat., V, p.436)

AL-SABZAWĀRĪ:

- *Risāla fī ṣalāt al-jumʿa*
  MSS: Wazīrī 1980/5 (cat., III, p.1116); Marʿashī 3032/2 (cat., VIII, pp.222-3); Raḍawī 7150 (cat., V, p.435); Los Angeles M119 (cat., p.283)
- *Risāla dar namāz-i jumʿa*, Persian
  MSS: Dānishgāh 4412/8 (cat., XIII, p.3375); Tarbiyyat 34/2 (cat., p.43)

ʿALĪ RIḌĀ B. KAMĀL AL-DĪN ḤUSAYN AL-ARDAKĀNĪ AL-SHĪRĀZĪ, AL-TAJALLĪ (d. 1085):

Risāla dar namāz-i jumʿa, Persian

MSS: Dānishgāh 4659/2 (cat., XIV, p.3603); Majlis 5353 (cat., XVI, p.263)

AL-FAYḌ:

- *Abwāb al-jinān*, Persian
  MSS: Sipahsālār 2013 (cat., I, p.351); Gulpāyigānī 1383/3 (cat., II, p.252); Raḍawī 2422 (cat., II, p.65); Majlis 5341/8 (cat., XVI, p.253)
- *Al-Shihāb al-thāqib*
  Editions: Najaf, 1368; Beirut, 1403
  MSS: Raḍawī 6499 (cat., V, p.464); Majlis 120/11 Khu'ī (cat., VII, p.173); Adabiyyāt 53 Kirmān (cat., p.96); Los Angeles M1204/3 (cat., p.715); Ustādī, 2 MSS (cat., p.64)

MUḤAMMAD TAQĪ B. ʿABD ALLĀH AL-KISHMĪRĪ (d. after 1097):

- *Risāla fī wujūb ṣalāt al-jumʿa*
  MSS: Dānishgāh 790/1, 6846/2 (cat., V, pp.2091-2, XVI, p.381); Majlis 9474 (pp.66-78)
- *Risāla fī ṣalāt al-jumʿa*
  MS: Dānishgāh 790/2 (cat., V, p.2092)

MUḤAMMAD ṬĀHIR AL-QUMMĪ:

- *Jā' al-ḥaqq*, Persian, in refutation of Khalīl al-Qazwīnī
  MSS: Dānishgāh 974/2 (cat., V, pp.1184-5); Majlis 5470/3 (cat., XVI, p.372)
- *Risāla dar namāz-i jumʿa*, Persian, in refutation of Ḥasan ʿAlī al-Tustarī
  MSS: Raḍawī 2422 (cat., II, pp.71-2); Dānishgāh 874/7, 790/3 (cat., V, pp.2092-4); Majlis 5470 (cat., XVI, p.371)

SALMĀN B. KHALĪL AL-QAZWĪNĪ (late 11th century):

Al-ʿUrwa al-wuthqā li-waḍʿ al-ḥayra al-ʿuẓmā ʿan al-ṣalāt al-wusṭā fī 'l-ghayba al-kubrā
MS: Wazīrī 2238/1 (cat., IV, p.1214)

AL-MAJLISĪ II:

Risāla fī ṣalāt al-jumʿa
MSS: Majlis 5341/1 (cat., XVI, p.253); Dār al-Kutub 19179b (cat., I, p.370)

MUḤAMMAD ISMĀʿĪL B. MUḤAMMAD BĀQIR AL-ḤUSAYNĪ AL-KHWĀTŪNĀBĀDĪ (d. 1116):

Risāla fī ṣalāt al-jumʿa
MS: Majlis 3052/1 (cat., X, pp.496-8)

ANONYMOUS (written in 1055-1110):

Risāla dar namāz-i jumʿa, Persian
MS: Los Angeles M395 (cat., p.63)

AL-SARĀB:

- *Risāla dar namāz-i jumʿa*, Persian, in refutation of ʿAlī Riḍā al-Tajallī
  MS: Dānishgāh 4659/1 (cat., XIV, p.3603)

- *Risāla fī ṣalāt al-jumʿa*
MSS: Raḍawī 6465 (cat., V, p.437); Dānishgāh 888/9, 2875/2, 6905/1 (cat., V, pp.2904-7, X, p.1719, XVI, p.392); Wazīrī 1267/2 (cat., III, p.911); Tarbiyat 34/2 (cat., p.45); Gawharshād 867/2 (cat., p.346); Gulpāyigānī 146/8 (cat., I, p.136); Khāliṣī (cat., p.68); Dār al-Kutub 20324 (cat., I, p.391); Mashhad, Shānachī (*Nash.*, V, p.599)

- *Ḥāshiya ʿalā risālat al-Tūnī fī nafy wujūb ṣalāt al-jumʿa*, in refutation of ʿAbd Allāh al-Tūnī
MSS: Millī 1858/2 Arabic (cat., X, p.440); Majlis 128/3 Khu'ī (cat., VII, pp. 179-80); Los Angeles M1204/2 (cat., p.715)

MUḤAMMAD KĀẒIM B. MUḤAMMAD ḤUSAYN AL-TŪYSIRKĀNĪ (d. after 1123):

- *Risāla fī ṣalāt al-jumʿa*, in refutation of all three treatises by al-Sarāb on this subject
MS: Dānishgāh 3552 (cat., XII, p.2572)

- *Risāla fī ṣalāt al-jumʿa*, different from above
MS: Adabiyyāt 275/4 Kirmān (cat., p.43)

AMĪN AL-TŪNĪ (early 12th century):

Risāla fī ṣalāt al-jumʿa, in refutation of al-Sarāb's third treatise on this subject
MSS: Millī 1858/3 Arabic (cat., X, p.441); Dānishgāh 2875/3 (cat., X, p.1720); Majlis 128/4 Khu'ī (cat., VII, pp.180-1)

JAMĀL AL-DĪN AL-KHWĀNSĀRĪ:

Risāla dar namāz-i jumʿa, Persian
Selected MSS: Majlis 4805/1, 5431, 422 Ṭabāṭabā'ī, 1025 Ṭabāṭabā'ī (cat., XIII, pp.202-3, XVI, p.333); Dānishgāh 2099/2, 3394, 4412/3, 4435, 4659/3, 6905/2 (cat., VIII, p.726, XIII, pp.3375, 3394, XIV, p. 3606, XVI, p.393); Mashhad, Ilāhiyyāt (cat., I, p.125); Nawwāb 130/1 law (cat., p.467); Ilāhiyyāt 206/2d (cat., I, p.259); Ustādī (cat., p.18); Ṣāḥib al-Dharīʿa (AB, XV, p.79)

AL-SAMĀHĪJĪ:

- *Al-Qāmiʿa li 'l-bidʿa fī tark ṣalāt al-jumʿa*
MSS: Majlis 165 Khu'ī (cat., VII, pp.207-9); Tustariyya 633/8 (cat., p.870)

- *Hidāyat al-ṣirāṭ fī ḥurmat al-jamʿ bayn al-ẓuhr wa 'l-jumʿa*
MS: Raḍawī 6982 (cat., V, p.530)

AL-FĀḌIL AL-HINDĪ:

Risāla fī ṣalāt al-jumʿa
MSS: Majlis 2761/5 (cat., IX, pp.156-8)

MUḤAMMAD TAQĪ B. MUḤAMMAD ṢĀDIQ AL-MŪSAWĪ AL-QĀ'INĪ (d. after 1127):

- *Risāla fī ṣalāt al-jumʿa*
MS: Raḍawī 6544/1 (cat., V, p.437)

- *Risāla fī ṣalāt al-jumʿa*, in refutation of Muḥammad Rafīʿ al-Gīlānī's critique of the previous treatise (see below)
MS: Raḍawī 6544/5 (cat., V, p.438)

- *Maqāla fī ṣalāt al-jumʻa*, in refutation of the second treatise by al-Gīlānī (see below)
  MS: Raḍawī 6544/7 (cat., V, p.438)
- *Masʼala fī ṣalāt al-jumʻa*, Persian
  MS: Raḍawī 6544/4 (cat., V, p.438)

MUḤAMMAD RAFĪʻ B. FARAJ AL-GĪLĀNĪ (mid-12th century):

- *Risāla fī ṣalāt al-jumʻa*, in refutation of Muḥammad Taqī al-Qāʼinī's first treatise
  MSS: Raḍawī 6544/2 (cat., V, p.438); Majlis 128/5 Khuʼī, 5341/2 (cat., VII, pp.281-2, XVI, p.253); Marʻashī 3032/5 (cat., VIII, p.223)
- *Masʼala fī ṣalāt al-jumʻa*, in refutation of al-Qāʼinī's critique of previous treatise
  MS: Raḍawī 6544/6 (cat., V, p.438)

BADR AL-DĪN B. IBRĀHĪM AL-NAYSĀBŪRĪ (mid-12th century):

Risāla fī ṣalāt al-jumʻa, in refutation of al-Gīlānī's first treatise
MS: Raḍawī 6544/3 (cat., V, p.438)

ANONYMOUS:

Several anonymous treatises on the subject belonging to 11th or early 12th centuries:

- *Ṣalāt al-jumʻa wa aḥkāmuhā fī zaman al-ghayba*
  MS: Ḥuqūq 55d (cat., p.398)
- *Fāʼida fī ḥurmat ṣalāt al-jumʻa fī zaman al-ghayba*
  MS: Marʻashī 3032/4 (cat., VIII, p.222)
- *Ḥurmat ṣalāt al-jumʻa*
  MS: Sipahsālār 6530/7 (cat., V, pp. 289-90)
- *Risāla dar ḥurmat-i namāz-i jumʻa*, Persian
  MS: Dānishgāh 6530/5 (cat., XVI, p.286)
- *Risāla fī ṣalāt al-jumʻa*
  MS: Khāliṣī (cat., p.102)
- *Risāla fī nafy al-wujūb al-ʻaynī ʻan ṣalāt al-jumʻa*
  MS: Khāliṣī (cat., pp.102-3)

ṢADR AL-DĪN MUḤAMMAD AL-ṬABĀṬABĀʼĪ AL-YAZDĪ (d. 1154):

Risāla fī ṣalāt al-jumʻa
MS: Wazīrī 320/9 (cat., I, p.305)

AL-KHWĀJŪʼĪ:

Risāla fī ṣalāt al-jumʻa, a refutation of al-Fayḍ's *al-Shihāb al-thāqib*
MSS: Majlis 3752/2 (cat., X, pp. 1736-7); Dānishgāh 7103/2 (cat., XVI, p.455); Marʻashī 3032/3 (cat., VIII, p.222); Rawḍātī (AB, XXIV, p.269); Tabrīz, Thiqat al-Islām (*Nash*., IV, p.327)

ANONYMOUS

Wajīza fī ṣalāt al-jumʻa
MS: Raḍawī 2743/1 (cat., V, pp.438-9)

NONYMOUS (written in 1191):

Mas'ala fī qirā'at Fātiḥat al-Kitāb fī khuṭbat ṣalāt al-jum'a
MS: Raḍawī 2743/2 (cat., V, p.439)

UḤAMMAD JA'FAR B. 'ALĪ AṢGHAR AL-ARDASTĀNĪ (12th century):

Risāla dar ḥurmat-i namāz-i jum'a, Persian
MS: Gulpāyigānī 711 (cat., II, p.85)

L-BIHBAHĀNĪ:

Risāla fī ṣalāt al-jum'a
MSS: Ilāhiyyāt 385/7d (cat., I, p.291); Majlis 572 Ṭabāṭabā'ī; Gulpāyigānī 1870/20 (cat., III, p.92); Fayḍiyya 1565/4 (cat., III, p.101)

ALĪ B. MUḤAMMAD AL-'UṢFŪRĪ AL-BAḤRĀNĪ (d. after 1206):

Kashf al-rayba an ḥukm ṣalāt al-jum'a fī azminat al-ghayba
MS: Mar'ashī 2753 (cat.,VII, p.307)

UḤAMMAD B. MUḤAMMAD ṢĀLIḤ AL-RŪḤAFZĀ'Ī AL-DAMĀWANDĪ (d. after 1216):

Risāla fī ṣalāt al-jum'a
MSS: Mar'ashī 2286 (cat., VI, pp.271-2); Karbalā', Madrasat Ḥasan Khān (AB, XV, p.80)

UḤSIN AL-A'RAJĪ:

Risāla fī ṣalāt al-jum'a
MS: Khāliṣī (cat., p.135)

ABD AL-NABĪ B. MUḤAMMAD 'ALĪ AL-QAZWĪNĪ (mid-12th century):

Risāla fī ṣalāt al-jum'a
MS: Tehran, Muḥīṭ Ṭabāṭabā'ī (AB, XV, p.75)

ḤMAD B. MUḤAMMAD 'ALĪ AL-KIRMĀNSHĀHĪ (d. 1235):

Kashf al-rayn wa 'l-mayn 'an ḥukm ṣalāt al-jum'a wa 'l-'īdayn
MS: Bankipore 1032 (cat. Arabic, I, p.101)

ASAN B. MUḤAMMAD 'ALĪ AL-MUDARRIS AL-YAZDĪ (d. after 1256):

Lum'a min ḥāl ṣalāt al-jum'a fī zaman al-ghayba
MS: Wazīrī 2083 (cat., IV, p.1154)

UḤAMMAD B. DILDĀR 'ALĪ AL-NAQAWĪ AL-NAṢĪRĀBĀDĪ (d. 1284):

Risāla fī ṣalāt al-jum'a
MS: Mar'ashī 3160/2 (cat., VIII, p.391)

UḤAMMAD B. 'ĀSHŪR AL-KIRMĀNSHĀHĪ:

Ṣalāt al-jum'a = Taḥqīq al-ḥaqq?
MS: Mar'ashī 2575/fol. 30a-b (cat., VII, p.165)

Aḥkām ṣalāt al-jum'a = Jalā' al-shubahāt?
MS: Mar'ashī 2575/fols. 164-185 (cat., VII, p.165)

MUḤAMMAD NAṢĪR B. MUḤAMMAD MAʿṢŪM AL-BĀRFURŪSHĪ (late 13th century):

Mirʾāt al-muṣallīn
MS: Marʿashī 1585 (cat., IV, p.390)

MUḤAMMAD TAQĪ AL-SHĪRĀZĪ:

Risāla fī ṣalāt al-jumʿa, his lectures compiled by Muḥammad Kāẓim al-Shīrāzī
Edition: Tehran, 1323 (together with the author's *Ḥāshiyat al-Makāsib*

AL-BURŪJIRDĪ:

Al-Badr al-zāhir fī ṣalāt al-jumʿa wa ʾl-musāfir, his lectures compiled by Ḥusayn ʿAlī al-Muntaẓirī
Edition: Qum, 1378

11. ON ERRORS IN PRAYER

ANONYMOUS (presumably by either al-ʿAllāma or Fakhr al-Muḥaqqiqīn):

Al-Khalal fi ʾl-ṣalāt
MS: Majlis 4953/13 (cat., XIV, p.231)

AL-SHAHĪD AL-AWWAL:

Khalal al-ṣalāt
Edition: Tehran, 1322 (together with his *al-Bayān*)

IBN FAHD:

- *Bughyat al-rāghibīn - Risāla fī kathīr al-shakk*
  MS: Jawādayn (AB, III, p.132)
- *Al-Khalal fi ʾl-ṣalāt = al-Sahwiyya*
  MS: al-Imām al-Mahdī (Maḥfūẓ II, p.212)

MUFLIḤ AL-ṢAYMARĪ:

Risāla fī sahw al-ṣalāt al-yawmiyya
MS: Majlis 6405 (cat., XVI, p.309)

AL-KARAKĪ:

Khalal al-ṣalāt
Edition: Tehran, 1322 (together with al-Shahīd al-Awwal's *al-Bayān*)
Selected MSS: Raḍawī 2358, 2448, 6980 (cat., II, pp. 53, 73, V, p.418); Gawharshād 1655/3 (cat., p.296); Ḥuqūq 56/3d (cat., p.336 Majlis 6342/8; Ilāhiyyāt 106/4d (cat., I, p.235); Sipahsālār 2913/4, 8180/4 (cat., IV, pp.64, 395); Millī 1190/3 Arabic (cat., IX, p.176); Marʿashī 1003/5, 1466/3, 2261/3 (cat., III, p.199, IV, p.258, VI, p.246); Masjid-i Aʿẓam 445/5; Tustariyya (AB, XII, p. 267, XIV, p.212); Princeton 976/3 New Series

AL-QAṬĪFĪ:

Al-Risāla al-Najafiyya fī sahw al-ṣalāt al-yawmiyya
MSS: Majlis 9398/2, 5405 (cat., XVI, p.309); Raḍawī 1449, 2448 (cat II, p.103); Khāliṣī (cat., p.100); Rawḍātī (AB, XI, pp.227-8)

AL-SHAHĪD AL-THĀNĪ:

Al-Khalal fi ʾl-ṣalāt

MS: Majlis 580/8 Akhawī (*Waḥīd*, V, p.299)

ANONYMOUS:

Risāla fi 'l-sahw alladhī lam yudhkar fi 'l-kutub al-mashhūra
MS: British Library Or.3530/2 (Rieu, p.213)

AL-FAYḌ:

Ḍawābiṭ al-khams
Edition: Tehran, 1300 (in the margin of Ibn Fahd's *Ghāyat al-Ījāz*)
MSS: Millī 1922/2 Arabic (cat., X, p.591); India Office 1835 (cat., II, p.321); Dānishgāh 792/3 (cat., V, p.1944)

MUḤAMMAD ṬĀHIR AL-QUMMĪ:

Risāla dar shakkiyyāt, Persian
MS: Qum, Rūḥānī (*Āshnā'ī*, I, p.448)

AL-SHĪRWĀNĪ:

Risāla dar shakkiyyāt, Persian
MS: Raḍawī 6651 (cat., V, p.433); Fayḍiyya 1665/3 (cat., III, p.113); Iṣfahān, Adabiyyāt (*Nash.*, V, p.304)

AL-MAJLISĪ II:

Aḥkām-i shakk wa sahw dar namāz, Persian
Selected MSS: Fayḍiyya 1747/4 (cat., III, p.128); Mar'ashī 187/2, 1602/2, 1683/1, 3034/5 (cat., I, p.206, V, pp. 5, 78, VIII, p.225); Millī 1854/3f (cat., IV, p.313); Raḍawī 6044, 6702 (Bīnish, p.804)

ḤAYDAR 'ALĪ AL-SHĪRWĀNĪ:

Al-Khalal fi 'l-ṣalāt
MSS: Dānishgāh 4292/2 (cat., XIII, p.3262); India Office 1840 (cat., II, p.323)

MUḤAMMAD ASHRAF B. 'ABD AL-ḤASĪB AL-ḤUSAYNĪ (d. 1145):

Risāla dar khalil-i ṣalāt, Persian
MS: Dānishgāh 5894/6 (cat., XVI, p.137)

ḤASAN B. IBRĀHĪM AL-NAJMĀBĀDĪ (d. around 1284):

Al-Khalal fi 'l-ṣalāt
MS: Tustariyya (AB, VII, p.249)

ḤUSAYN QULĪ B. RAMAḌĀN AL-HAMADĀNĪ (d. 1311):

Khalal al-ṣalāt
MS: Tustariyya (AB, IV, p.372, VII, p.249)

AL-ĀSHTIYĀNĪ:

Al-Khalal fi 'l-ṣalāt, as a commentary on the relevant discussion in al-Muḥaqqiq's *Sharā'i' al-Islām*
MSS: Raḍawī 7741 (Bīnish, p.871); Shīrāzī (AB, VII, p.249)

AL-FISHĀRAKĪ - Muḥammad b. Qāsim al-Ṭabāṭabā'ī (d. 1316-18)

Risāla fī qā'idat lā tu'ād
Edition: Qum, 1393 (in Muḥammad Hādī Ma'rifa's *Ḥadīth lā tu'ād*)

MUḤAMMAD ḤUSAYN AL-KHWĀNSĀRĪ:

Risāla fi 'l-shakk bayn al-rak'atayn al-ūlayayn
MS: Mar'ashī 3041/10 (cat., VIII, p.245)

AL-YAZDĪ:

Risāla fī ḥukm al-ẓann fi 'l-ṣalāt wa bayān kayfiyyat ṣalāt al-iḥtiyāṭ
Edition: Tehran, 1378 (together with his *Ḥāshiyat al-Makāsib*)

MUḤAMMAD TAQĪ AL-SHĪRĀZĪ:

Aḥkām al-Khalal fi 'l-ṣalāt, his lectures compiled by Muḥammad kāẓim al-Shīrāzī
Edition: Tehran, 1323 (together with the author's *Ḥāshiyat al-Makāsib*

AL-KHUMAYNĪ:

K. al-Khalal fi 'l-ṣalāt
Edition: Qum, 1399

12. ON PRAYER OF OMISSION

MUNTAJAB AL-DĪN 'ALĪ B. 'UBAYD ALLĀH AL-RĀZĪ (d. after 585):

Al-'Uṣra fi 'l-muwāsa'a fī qaḍā' al-ṣalawāt
MS: Mar'ashī (AB, XV, p.271)

'ABD ALLĀH AL-TUSTARĪ:

Risāla fī jawāz al-fā'ita fī waqt al-ḥāḍira, included in his *al-Rasā'il* (see above, chapter 5)

ANONYMOUS (belonging to early 13th century):

Risāla fi'l-muwāsa'a wa 'l-muḍāyaqa
MS: Princeton 645/1 New Series

ṢĀḤIB AL-MAQĀBIS:

Manhaj al-taḥqīq fi 'l-tawsa'a wa 'l-taḍyīq
MSS: Majlis 400 Ṭabāṭabā'ī; Raḍawī 1996 (cat., V, p.368)

NAṢR ALLĀH B. ḤASAN AL-ḤUSAYNĪ AL-ASTARĀBĀDĪ (d. after 1255):

Risāla fi 'l-muwāsa'a wa 'l-muḍāyaqa
MSS: Sipahsālār 2527, 2554 (cat., I, p. 437)

AL-ANṢĀRĪ

- *Risāla fi 'l-muwāsa'a wa 'l-muḍāyaqa*
  Editions: Tabrīz, 1303 (together with his *K. al-Ṭahāra*), 1375 (togethe with his *K. al-Makāsib*)
  MS: Dānishgāh 6956/2 (cat., XVI, p.411)
  Commentary' by 'Abd Allāh al-Māmaqānī, edited Najaf, 1345 (in his *al-Qalā'id al-thamīna*)
- *Risāla fi 'l-qaḍā' 'an al-mayyit*
  Editions: Tabrīz, 1303 (together with his *K. al-Ṭahāra*), 1375 together with his *K. al-Makāsib*)
  MS: Dānishgāh 6956/5 (cat., XVI, p.411)

ĀṢIF AL-ḌARĪR - ʻAbd al-Wāḥid b. Muḥammad Ḥasan (13th century):

Risāla fī taqdīm al-fawā'it ʻala 'l-ḥawāḍir
MS: Marʻashī 2278/2 (cat., VI, p.264)

AḤMAD B. MUṢṬAFĀ AL-KHU'AYNĪ, MULLĀ ĀQĀ (d. 1307):

Mujlī al-sharīʻa fī mas'alat al-taḍyīq wa 'l-tawsaʻa
MS: Marʻashī 3676 (cat., X, p.69)

13. ON TRAVELLER'S PRAYER

AL-KARAKĪ:

Fawā'id fī ṣalāt al-musāfir
MSS: Dānishgāh 2144/pp.81-6 (cat., IX, p.806); Princeton 1935/3 New Series

AL-SHAHĪD AL-THĀNĪ:

Natā'ij al-afkār fī ḥukm al-muqīm fi 'l-asfār, included in his *Majmūʻat al-ifādāt* (see above, chapter 5)

BAHĀ' AL-DĪN AL-ʻĀMILĪ:

Risāla fi 'l-takhyīr bayn al-qaṣr wa 'l-itmām fi 'l-amākin al-arbaʻa
MSS: Dānishgāh 918/14 (cat., V, p.1968); Majlis 1805/54, 4900/50 (cat., IX, pp.356-7, XIV, p.75)

ḤAYDAR ʻALĪ AL-SHĪRWĀNĪ:

Ḥadd al-masāfa al-mūjiba li 'l-qaṣr wa 'l-ifṭār
MSS: Dānishgāh 4292/3 (cat., XIII, p.3262); India Office 1841 (cat., II, p.323)

ṢADR AL-DĪN MUḤAMMAD B. MUḤAMMAD B. ʻALĪ al-RAḌAWĪ AL-KĀSHĀNĪ (mid-12th century):

Muntahā al-marām fi 'l-qaṣr wa 'l-itmām
MSS: Raḍawī 5725 (cat., V, p.519); Kāshān, Raḍawī 60 (cat., pp. 37-8)

ṢADR AL-DĪN MUḤAMMAD AL-ṬABĀṬABĀ'Ī AL-YAZDĪ:

ʻUddat al-musāfirīn
MS: Wazīrī 320/10 (cat., I, p.305)

SHUBBAR B. MUḤAMMAD AL-MŪSAWĪ AL-NAJAFĪ:

Risāla fi 'l-qaṣr wa 'l-itmām
MS: Dānishgāh 3978 (cat., XII, p.2973)

ABU 'L-QĀSIM JAʻFAR B. ḤUSAYN AL-MŪSAWĪ AL-KHWĀNSĀRĪ (d. 1158):

Risāla dar aḥkām-i musāfir, Persian
MS: Dānishgāh 2603/4 (cat., IX, p.1458)

MUḤAMMAD B. AḤMAD AL-BAḤRĀNĪ (d. 1186):

Mir'āt al-akhyār fī aḥkām al-asfār
MS: Dānishgāh 725 (cat., V, pp.2008-9)

BAḤR AL-ʿULŪM:

Mablagh al-naẓar fī ḥukm qāṣid al-arbaʿa min masāʾil al-safar
Edition: Cairo, 1324-5 (in Jawād al-ʿĀmilī's *Miftāḥ al-karāma*, III, pp.501-43)

AL-ANṢĀRĪ:

Risāla fī ṣalāt al-musāfir
MS: Dānishgāh 757 (cat., V, p.1864)

ABŪ ṬĀLIB B. ABĪ TURĀB AL-ḤUSAYNĪ AL-QĀʾINĪ (d. 1293-5):

Ṣalāt al-musāfir
Edition: Mashhad, 1318

ḤUSAYN QULĪ AL-HAMADĀNĪ:

Ṣalāt al-musāfir, his lectures compiled by one of his pupils
MS: Tustariyya (AB, IV, p.372, XV, p.83)

AL-RASHTĪ:

Ṣalāt al-musāfir, his lectures compiled by one of his pupils
MS: Gharb 9871 (cat., p.159)

ʿABD ALLĀH B. MUḤAMMAD NAṢĪR AL-MĀZANDARĀNĪ (d. 1330):

Ṣalāt al-musāfir
MS: Zanjānī 114 (cat., p.240)

AL-BURŪJIRDĪ:

Al-Badr al-zāhir fī ṣalāt al-jumʿa wa ʾl-musāfir (see above, monographs on Friday prayer)

ALMS

1. GENERAL

MUḤAMMAD ṬĀHIR AL-QUMMĪ:

Risāla dar zakāt, Persian
MSS: Dānishgāh 4108/6 (cat., XIII, p.3088); Fayḍiyya 1689/4 (cat., III, p.118)

AL-ḤURR AL-ʿĀMILĪ:

Urjūza fi ʾl-zakāt
MSS: Majlis 11/3 Khuʾī (cat., VII, p.9); Gulpāyigānī 327/7 (cat., I, p.282)

ABU ʾL-QĀSIM JAʿFAR B. ḤUSAYN AL-KHWĀNSĀRĪ:

Zakātiyya, Persian
MS: Fayḍiyya 1807 (cat., II, p.67)

MUḤAMMAD B. MUḤAMMAD ZAMĀN AL-KĀSHĀNĪ:

Nūr al-hudā
MSS: Majlis 1966/6 (cat., IX, p.681); Nūrbakhsh, 108/3 (cat., I,

p.131); Mashhad, Ilāhiyyāt 503/1 (cat., I, p.267); Amīr al-Mu'minīn (AB, XXIV, p.386)

AL-QUMMĪ:

Risāla dar zakāt, Persian
MS: Tustariyya (AB, XII, p.40)

AL-AKHBĀRĪ:

Mishkāt al-hudāt
MS: Dānishgāh 3341/3 (cat., XI, p.2330)

AL-ANṢĀRĪ:

- *K. al- Zakāt*
  Edition: Tabrīz, 1303 (together with his *K. al-Ṭahāra)*
  MSS: Fayḍiyya 1002, 1345 (cat., I, pp. 70, 135); Malik 6089 (cat., I, p.550)
- *K. al-Zakāt*, his lectures compiled by Ḥasan ʿAlī al-Ṭihrānī al-Mashhadī
  MS: Gawharshād 5834 (cat., p.241)

AL-RASHTĪ:

- *K. al-Zakāt*
  MSS: Majlis 2838 (cat., X, p.164); Tustariyya 616 (cat., p.800)
- *K. al-Zakāt*, his lectures compiled by one of his pupils
  MS: Gharb 4527 (cat., p.77)

HĀDĪ AL-ṬIHRĀNĪ:

K. al-Zakāt
MSS: Majlis 2755/2 (cat., IX, p.143); Tustariyya 344/1 (cat., pp.853-4)

2. SPECIFIC

AL-KHWĀJŪ'Ī:

Risāla fī istithnā' al-ma'ūna min al-zakāt
MS: Marʿashī 1986/3 (cat., V, p.358)

AL-KIRMĀNSHĀHĪ:

Risāla fi 'l-ma'ūna al-mustathnāt min al-zakāt
MS: Ḥujjatiyya 261/11 (cat., p.103)

AL-QUMMĪ:

Risāla fī istithnā' al-ma'ūna wa ujrat al-ḥaṣṣād min al-zakāt, included in both his *Jawāmiʿ al-rasā'il* and his *al-Rasā'il* (see above, chapter 5)

AḤMAD B. ʿALĪ MUKHTĀR AL-GULPĀYIGĀNĪ (d. after 1264):

Risāla fi 'l-tawkīl fī ikhrāj al-zakāt
MS: Marʿashī 3494/4 (cat., IX, pp.291-2)

ʿABD AL-HĀDĪ B. ISMĀʿĪL AL-ḤUSAYNĪ AL-SHĪRĀZĪ (d. 1382):

Al-Qaṭra fī zakāt al-fiṭra, his lectures compled by ʿAlī al-Muḥammadī
Edition: Najaf, 1380

KHUMS

1. GENERAL

ḤUSAYN AL-KHWĀNSĀRĪ:

Risāla dar khums, Persian
MS: Dānishgāh 1801 (cat., VIII, p.375)

AL-KHWĀJŪ'Ī:

Risāla fī 'l-khums
MSS: Fayḍiyya 1186/8 (cat., III, p.65); Mashhad, Adabiyyāt 26/1 Fayyāḍ (cat., p.211)

AL-AKHBĀRĪ:

Tawfīr al-khums
MS: Dānishgāh 3341/4 (cat., XI, p.233)

AL-ANṢĀRĪ:

K. al-Khums
Edition: Tabrīz, 1303 (together with his *K. al-Ṭahāra*)
MSS: Fayḍiyya 1002, 1345 (cat., I, pp.135, 170); Malik 6089 (cat., I, p.550); Dānishgāh 6956 (cat., XVI, p.411)

MUḤSIN B. ʻABD ALLĀH AL-ARDABĪLĪ (d. 1294):

Risāla dar khums, Persian
MS: Marʻashī (AB, VII, p.255)

FAYYĀḌ B. MUḤAMMAD AL-ZANJĀNĪ (d. 1360):

Dhakhā'ir al-imāma
Edition: Tehran, 1359

AL-BURŪJIRDĪ:

Zubdat al-maqāl, his lectures compiled by ʻAbbās Abū Turābī al-Qazwīnī
Edition: Qum, 1380

MUḤAMMAD HĀDĪ B. JAʻFAR AL-ḤUSAYNĪ AL-MĪLĀNĪ (d. 1395):

K. al-Khums
Edition: Mashhad, 1400

ḤUSAYN ʻALĪ AL-MUNTAẒIRĪ:

K. al-Khums
Edition: Qum, [1402?]

2. SPECIFIC

AL-DĀMĀD:

Ithbāt al-siyāda li-man yantasib ilā Hāshim umman
MS: Millī 2360f (cat., V, p.483)

MAḤMŪD B. FATḤ ALLĀH AL-ḤUSAYNĪ AL-KĀẒIMĪ (d. after 1079):

Risāla fī wujūb al-khums ḥāl istitār al-Imām

MSS: Dānishgāh 1122/5 (cat., V, pp.1876-7); Mar'ashī 2525/3 (cat., VII, p.111)

AL-KIRMĀNSHĀHĪ:

Maṣraf-i radd-i maẓālim, Persian
MS: Sipahsālār 2442/1 (cat., I, p.505)

ANONYMOUS:

Risāla fī irtizāq al-qāḍī wa 'l-faqīh min sahm al-imām
MS: Dānishgāh 1119/2 (cat., V, pp.1889-90)

MUḤAMMAD RAḤĪM AL-BURŪJIRDĪ:

Ithbāt al-siyāda li 'l-muntasabīn ilā Hāshim umman
MSS: Raḍawī 5850-1 (Bīnish, p.783)

MUḤAMMAD ḤUSAYN AL-KHWĀNSĀRĪ:

Risāla fī ta'alluq al-khums bi-majmū' al-arbāḥ
MS: Mar'ashī 3041/1 (cat., VIII, p.241)

'ABD ALLĀH AL-MĀMAQĀNĪ:

Hidāyat al-anām fī ḥukm amwāl al-imām
Edition: Tabrīz, 1321

RĀḤAT ḤUSAYN AL-RAḌAWĪ AL-GŪPĀLPŪRĪ (d. after 1372):

Rāfi' al-ibhām 'an wilāya wa maṣārif sahm al-imām
Edition: Locknow, 1372

FASTING

1. GENERAL

IBRĀHĪM B. 'ALĪ AL-KAF'AMĪ (d. 905):

Manhaj al-salāma
MS: Majlis 2764/2 (cat., IX, p.168)

AL-KARAKĪ:

Risāla dar ṣawm, Persian
MS: Dānishgāh 3597/5 (cat., XV, p.4240)

AL-QAṬĪFĪ:

Risāla fi 'l-ṣawm
MSS: Millī 1919/12 Arabic (cat., X, p.585); Raḍawī 2437 (cat., II, p.70)

ANONYMOUS (written before 963):

Ṣawmiyya, Persian
MS: Raḍawī 2491 (cat., II, p.87)

BAHĀ' AL-DĪN AL-'ĀMILĪ:

Mas'ala fi 'l-ṣawm
MSS: Dānishgāh 918/11 (cat., V, pp.1796-7); Majlis 1805/57, 4900/53 (Cat., IX, pp.358-9, XIV, p.76)

KĀSHIF AL-GHIṬĀʾ:

Risāla fi ʾl-ṣiyām
MSS: Ḥujjatiyya 700/2 (cat., p.121); Los Angeles M93/4 (cat., p.661)

AL-QUMMĪ:

K. al-Ṣawm
MS: Malik (AB, XV, p.99)

AL-AKHBĀRĪ:

Takhlīṣ al-aḥkām fī masāʾil al-ṣiyām
MS: Dānishgāh 3341/5 (cat., XI, p.2330)

ʿALĪ ĀL KĀSHIF AL-GHIṬĀʾ:

Risāla fi ʾl-ṣawm
MS: Burūjirdī (AB, XI, p.206)

MUḤAMMAD TAQĪ AL-NŪRĪ:

Al-Risāla al-ṣawmiyya, Persian
MSS: Burūjirdī (AB, XI, p.205); Dānishgāh 7181/1 (cat., XVI, p.477)

ANONYMOUS (written in 1258):

K. al-Ṣawm
MS: Najaf, Madrasat al-Ṣadr (AB, XV, p.99)

ANONYMOUS:

Risāla-yi ṣawmiyya, Persian
Edition: Hamadān, 1249

AL-ANṢĀRĪ:

K. al-Ṣawm
Edition: Tabrīz, 1303 (together with his *K. al-Ṭahāra*)
MSS: Fayḍiyya 1002, 1345 (cat., I, pp. 70, 135); Malik 6089 (cat., I, p.550)

MUḤAMMAD BĀQIR AL-TABRĪZĪ (late 13th century):

Al-Ṣawmiyya,
MS: Raḍawī 2756 (Bīnish, p.819)

ḤASAN B. IBRĀHĪM AL-NAJMĀBĀDĪ:

K. al-Ṣawm
MS: Tustariyya (AB, XV, p.99)

MUḤAMMAD HĀSHIM AL-KHWĀNSĀRĪ:

Risāla dar ṣawm, Persian
Editions: Iṣfahān, 1310, 1317 (in his *Majmuʿa-yi shish risāla*)

2. ON TIME OF FASTING

AL-MUFĪD:

Al-Radd ʿalā aṣḥāb al-ʿadad
Edition: Qum, 1398 (in ʿAlī b. Muḥammad al-ʿĀmilī's *al-Durr al-manthūr*, II, pp.122-34)
Selected MSS: Marʿashī 243/8, 255/15, 78/8 (cat., I, pp.92, 268, 285); Majlis 8/17 Khuʾī (cat., VII, pp.184-5)

AL-MURTAḌĀ:

Al-Radd ʿalā aṣḥāb al-ʿadad = Risāla fī nuṣrat al-qawl bi ʾl-ruʾya
MSS: Raḍawī 1448/3 (cat., II, p.38); Dānishgāh 1080/4 (cat., III, p.612); Ṣāḥib al-Dharīʿa (AB, X, p.185)

MUḤAMMAD ṢĀLIḤ B. ʿABD AL-WĀSIʿ AL-KHWĀTŪNĀBĀDĪ:

Ḥukm al-ḥākim bi-thubūt al-hilāl
MSS: Majlis 3052/3 (cat., X, p.499); Millī 1919/2 Arabic (cat., X, p.578); Tabrīz, Qāḍī (*Nash.*, VII, p.511); Burūjirdī (AB, XI, p. 230)

AL-SARĀB:

Ruʾyat al-hilāl qabl al-zawāl
MSS: Dānishgāh 88/7, 1859/2, 2865/1, 6905/3, 7204/1 (cat., V, p.1921, VIII, p.459, X, p.1712, XVI, pp.393, 486); Marʿashī 478/4, 1490/12+17 (cat., II, p.83, IV, pp.189,192); Adabiyyād 70/13d (cat., pp. 299-300)

MUḤAMMAD HĀDĪ B. MUḤAMMAD ṢĀLIḤ AL-MĀZANDARĀNĪ:

Risāla fī taʿyīn ghurrat Ramaḍān fī mā idhā ghummat shuhūr al-sana kulluhā
MS: Dānishgāh 7203/8 (cat., XVI, p.486)

MUḤAMMAD JAʿFAR B. MUḤAMMAD BĀQIR AL-SABZAWĀRĪ:

Ruʾyat al-hilāl qabl al-zawāl
MSS: Dānishgāh 1866 (cat., VIII, p.742); Marʿashī 478/1 (cat., II, p.82)

MUḤAMMAD RAḤĪM B. MUḤAMMAD JAʿFAR AL-SABZAWĀRĪ (mid-12th century):

Ḥukm ruʾyat al-hilal qabl al-zawāl
MS: Gawharshād 1467/1 (cat., p.434)

AL-BIHBAHĀNĪ:

Risāla fī ʿadam al-iʿtidād bi ʾl-ruʾya qabl al-zawāl
MSS: Raḍawī 8219 (cat., V, p.442); Gulpāyigānī 1870/10 (cat., III, p.91; Rawḍātī (AB, XX, p.72)

ABU ʾL-QĀSIM B. ḤASAN AL-MŪSAWĪ (13th century):

Ḥukm ruʾyat al-hilāl qabl al-zawāl
MS: Fayḍiyya 1189/17 (cat., III, p.66)

MUḤAMMAD ʿALĪ AL-ZANJĀNĪ:

Rayḥānat al-ṣudūr, Persian

MS: Sipahsālār 2536 (cat., I, p.417)

ʿALĪ B. ʿABD ALLĀH AL-ʿALYĀRĪ:

Minhāj al-najāt = Sharḥ mabḥath ruʾyat al-hilāl min al-Rawḍa al-bahiyya
Edition: Tabrīz, 1309

3. ON OTHER TOPICS

AL-SHAHĪD AL-AWWAL:

Jawāz ibdāʿ al-safar fī shahr Ramaḍān
MSS: Majlis 4566/11 (cat., XII, p.263); Raḍawī 7735 (Bīnish, p.809); Zanjān (cat., p.137)

IBN FAHD:

Masʾala fi ʾl-iḥbāṭ wa ʾl-tafkīr wa ḥukm al-ṣawm idhā irtadd al-ṣāʾim
MS: Majlis 2750.4 (cat., IX, p.126)

ʿABD ALLĀH AL-TUSTARĪ:

Taṭawwuʿ al-ṣawm li-man ʿalayh al-farīḍa, included in his *al-Rasāʾil* (see above, chapter 5)

ḤUSAYN B. ḤAYDAR AL-ḤUSAYNĪ AL-KARAKĪ (mid-11th century):

Ishtirāṭ ṣiḥḥat al-ṣawm al-wājib bi ʾl-ghusl min al-jināba
MS: Majlis 4865 (cat., XIII, pp.302-3)

RAḌĪ AL-DĪN MUḤAMMAD B. ḤASAN AL-QAZWĪNĪ (d. 1096):

Masʾala fī īṣāl al-ghibār al-ghalīẓ ila ʾl-ḥalq fi ʾl-ṣawm
MS: Marʿashī 1409/fols. 121b-126a (cat., IV, p.193)

ʿABD ALLĀH B. ʿALĪ AL-ṢAYMARĪ (11th century):

Mandūb al-ṣiyām
MS: Majlis 2761/9 (cat., IX, p.160)

SHUBBAR B. MUḤAMMAD AL-MŪSAWĪ AL-NAJAFĪ:

Al-Irtimās fi ʾl-ṣawm
MS: Dānishgāh 7200/2 (cat., XVI, p.485)

AL-QUMMĪ:

- *Risāla fī taḥdīd waqt ifṭār al-musāfir*
- *Risāla fī ḥukm man ajnab laylat al-ṣiyām*

Both included in his *Jawāmiʿ al-Rasāʾil* (see above, chapter 5)

ANONYMOUS:

Risāla fī mufṭiriyyat al-dukhān
MS: Gulpāyigānī 763/2 (cat., II, p.208)

MUḤAMMAD TAQĪ AL-NŪRĪ:

Kashf al-awhām fī jawāz shurb al-ghalyān fi ʾl-ṣiyām, Persian
MS: Dānishgāh 7181/2 (cat., XVI, p.477)

ʿABD ALLĀH AL-MĀMAQĀNĪ:

Ḥukm al-musāfara li-man ʿalayh qaḍāʾ Ramaḍān maʿ ḍīq al-waqt
Edition: Najaf, 1344 (in his *al-Ithnāʿashariyya*)

SECLUSION

LUṬF ALLĀH B. ʿABD AL-KARĪM AL-MAYSĪ AL-ʿĀMILĪ:

Al-Iʿtikāfiyya = Māʾ al-ḥayāt wa ṣāfī al-furāt
MS: Raḍawī 2244 (cat., II, p.11); Burūjirdī (see AB, XIX, pp.11-12)

MUḤAMMAD JAʿFAR AL-ASTARĀBĀDĪ:

Al-Kafāf fī masāʾil al-iʿtikāf
MS: Marʿashī 1703/2 (cat., V, p.97)

ḤAJJ

1. GENERAL

FAKHR AL-MUḤAQQIQĪN:

Wājibāt al-ḥajj
MSS: Dānishgāh 1022/3 (cat., V, p.1871); Marʿashī 3307/3 (cat., IX, p.88)

AL-SHAHĪD AL-AWWAL:

Khulāṣat al-iʿtibār fī ʾl-ḥajj wa ʾl-iʿtimār
Edition: Sidon, 1348 (in al-Amīn al-ʿĀmilī's *Maʿādin al-jawāhir*, I, pp.265-70)
MSS: Sinā 417/6 (cat., I, p.250); Tehran, Muḥīṭ Ṭabāṭabāʾī (AB, VII, p.214)

IBN FAHD:

- *Kifāyat al-muḥtāj*
  MS: Los Angeles M1313/3 (cat., p.724)
- *Manāsik al-ḥajj*
  MSS: Los Angeles M1313/2 (cat., p.724); Raḍawī 2372 (cat., II, p.49)

AL-KARAKĪ:

Risāla fī ʾl-ḥajj wa ʾl-ʿumra
MSS: Ilāhiyyāt 142/3d (cat., I, p.246); Millī 1957/7f, 1190/2 Arabic (cat., IV, p.430, IX, p.175); Majlis 4339/9 (cat., XII, p.41); Dānishgāh 7177/2 (cat., XVI, p.475); Raḍawī 2641 (cat., II, pp.132-3)

ANONYMOUS (written before 947):

- *Wājibāt al-ḥajj wa ʾl-ʿumra*
  MS: Marʿashī 3307/4 (cat., IX, p.88)
- *Manāsik al-ḥajj*
  MS: Marʿashī 3307/6 (cat., IX, p.89)

AL-SHAHĪD AL-THĀNĪ:

- *Manāsik al-ḥajj*

MSS: Raḍawī 2630, 6073 (cat., II, p.129, V,p.514); Dānishgāh 2099/10 (cat., VIII, p.727); Marʿashī 2796/5 (cat., VII, p.363); Ilāhiyyāt 206/1d (cat., I, p.259)

- *Manāsik al-ḥajj*, a shorter treatise on this subject
  MSS: Marʿashī 3307/2 (cat., IX, p.87); Sinā 1229/13 (cat., II, p.174); Dānishgāh 7065/1 (cat., XVI, p.443); Majlis 3455/183 (cat., X, pp.1353-4); Shīrāzī (AB, XXIV, p.441); India Office 1812 (cat., II, p.314)

ANONYMOUS (written before 972):

Al-Ḥajj wa ʾl-ʿumra
MS: Sinā 1229/14 (cat., II, p.174)

AL-ARDABĪLĪ:

Manāsik-i ḥajj, Persian
MSS: Raḍawī 2373 (cat., II, p.49); Gawharshād 998/3 (cat., p.107); Dānishgāh 878/6 (cat., VI, pp.1870-1); Ḥujjatiyya 597/2 (cat., p.115); Marʿashī 3008/4-5 (cat., VIII, p.185)

ANONYMOUS (written before 994):

Manāsik al-ḥajj
MS: Raḍawī 2656 (Bīnish, p.1036)

ṢĀḤIB AL-MAʿĀLIM:

Manāsik al-ḥajj
MS: Marʿashī 1691/1 (cat., V, p.85)

ʿABD ALLĀH AL-TUSTARĪ:

Afʿāl al-ḥajj
MS: Dānishgāh 918/15 (cat., V, pp.1779-81)

ANONYMOUS (early 11th century):

Manāsik al-ḥajj
MS: Raḍawī 2657 (Bīnish, p.1036)

SULṬĀN AL-ʿULAMĀʾ:

Afʿāl-i ḥajj, Persian
MS: Majlis 3749/1 (cat., X, pp.1734-5)

AL-MAJLISĪ I:

Manāsik-i ḥajj, Persian
MS: Marʿashī 15 (cat., I, p.27)

AL-SABZAWĀRĪ:

Manāsik-i ḥajj, Persian
MS: Millī 2198f (cat., V, p.283)

AL-MAJLISĪ II:

- *Manāsik-i ḥajj*, Persian
  MSS: Marʿashī 187/31 (cat., I, p.216); Gulpāyigānī 1305 (cat., II, p.63); Millī 1854/8f (cat.,IV, pp.316-17)
- *Wājibāt-i ḥajj wa ʿumra*, Persian

MS: Marʿashī 187/32 (cat., I, p.217)

ANONYMOUS:

Risāla fī farḍ al-ḥajj wa 'l-ʿumra
MS: Dānishgāh 5396/12 (cat., XV, p.4239)

MUḤAMMAD QĀSIM B. MUḤAMMAD RIḌĀ AL-HAZĀRJARĪBĪ (d. after 1113):

Manāsik-i ḥajj, Persian
MS: Marʿashī 3053 (cat., VIII, p.272)

ḤAYDAR ʿALĪ AL-SHĪRWĀNĪ:

Tuḥfat al-sarā'ir
MS: Dānishgāh 1289 (cat., VII, p.2627)

AL-FĀḌIL AL-HINDĪ:

Al-Zuhra fī manāsik al-ḥajj wa 'l-ʿumra
MS: Majlis 2761/8 (cat., IX, pp.159-60)

MUḤAMMAD B. ʿALĪ B. ḤAYDAR AL-MŪSAWĪ AL-ʿĀMILĪ:

Iẓhār mā ʿindī bi Mansak al-Fāḍil al-Hindī
MS: Dānishgāh 3049 (cat., X, p.1993)

BAḤR AL-ʿULŪM:

Al-ʿIjāla al-mūjaza fī furūḍ al-nāsik
MS: Fayḍiyya 218 (cat., I, p.182)

ṢĀḤIB AL-RIYĀḌ:

Manāsik-i ḥajj, Persian, translated from Arabic by Muḥammad ʿAlī b. Muḥammad Sharīf al-Dihdashtī al-Bihbahānī
MS: Millī 2470f (cat., V, p.645)

AL-QUMMĪ:

Risāla dar ḥajj, Persian
MSS: Dānishgāh 853/1 (cat., V, p.1871); Sinā 417/7 (cat., I, p.250); Ḥujjatiyya 596 (cat., p.29)

AḤMAD AL-TABRĪZĪ (early 13th century):

Manāsik al-ḥajj
MS: Raḍawī 2638 (Bīnish, p.1036)

AL-AKHBĀRĪ:

Aḥkām al-ḥajj
MS: Dānishgāh 3341/6 (cat., XI, p.2330)

AL-SHAFTĪ:

Manāsik-i ḥajj, Persian
MSS: Millī 3029/2f (cat., VI, pp.807-8); Fayḍiyya 1918 (cat., II, p.104); Raḍawī 8004 (Bīnish, p.1036)

MAḤMŪD AL-KIRMĀNSHĀHĪ:

Irshād al-sālik, a commentary on Muḥammad ʿalī al-Kirmānshāhī's

Dalīl al-nāsik
MS: Marʿashī 1516 (cat., IV, p.317)

ANONYMOUS (belonging to 13th century):

Manāsik al-ḥajj
MS: Marʿashī 3047/11 (cat., VIII, p.262)

ḤUSAYN B. MUḤAMMAD AL-ḤUSAYNĪ (d. after 1309):

Tuḥfat al-ḥujjāj, Persian
MS: Ḥujjatiyya 473 (cat., p.5)

ABŪ ṬĀLIB B. ABI 'L-QĀSIM AL-MŪSAWĪ AL-ZANJĀNĪ (d. 1329):

K. al-Ḥajj
MS: Marʿashī 3144 (cat., VIII, p.376)

AL-ḤAKĪM:

Dalīl al-nāsik
Edition: Najaf, 1377

AL-SHĀHRŪDĪ - Maḥmūd b. ʿAlī al-Ḥusaynī (d. 1394):

K. al-Ḥajj, his lectures compiled by Muḥammad Ibrāhīm al-Jannātī
Edition: Najaf, 1382 - (5 vols.)

AL-GULPĀYIGĀNĪ - Muḥammad Riḍā b. Muḥammad Bāqir al-Mūsawī:

K. al-Ḥajj, his lectures compiled by Aḥmad al-Ṣābirī
Edition: Qum, [1400?]

2. SPECIFIC

ḤUSAYN B. MUFLIḤ AL-ṢAYMARĪ (d. 933):

Aḥkām al-ṭawāf bi 'l-Bayt al-Ḥarām
MS: Marʿashī 3307/1 (cat., IX, p.87)

ʿABD ALLĀH AL-TUSTARĪ:

Al-Waṣiyya bi 'l-ḥajj al-wājib, included in his *al-Rasā'il* (see above, chapter 5)

AL-KHWĀJŪ'Ī:

Mas'ala fi 'l-ḥajj al-baladī
MS: Mashhad, Adabiyyāt 25/10 Fayyāḍ (cat., pp.211-12)

MUḤAMMAD ḤUSAYN AL-KHWĀNSĀRĪ

- *Risāla fi 'l-ʿaqd ḥāl al-iḥrām*
  MS: Marʿashī 3041/17 (cat., VIII, p.248)
- *Risāla fī ṣayd al-muḥrim*
  MS: Marʿashī 3041/16 (cat., VIII, p.248)

ʿ*UMRA*

ʿAL-KHWĀJŪʾĪ:

Risāla fī aqall mā bayn al-ʿumratayn
MS: Mashhad, Adabiyyāt 25/2 Fayyāḍ (cat., p.211)

IBN ṬAWQ AL-BAḤRĀNĪ:

Aḥkām al-ʿumra
MS: Marʿashī 2358/17 (cat., VI, p.340)

MAZĀR (PILGRIMAGE TO HOLY SHRINES)

ḤAYDAR ʿALĪ AL-SHĪRWĀNĪ:

Ḥurmat al-mashāhid al-musharrafa
MS: Fayḍiyya 1861/2 (cat., III, p.141)

ʿABD ALLĀH AL-MĀMAQĀNĪ:

Izāḥat al-waswasa ʿan taqbīl al-aʿtāb al-muqaddasa
Edition: Najaf, 1345

HOLY WAR

1. GENERAL

KĀSHIF AL-GHIṬĀʾ

Ghāyat al-murād
MSS: Raḍawī 2498 (cat., II, pp.89-90); Millī 1806 Arabic (cat., X, p.386); Malik 3996 (cat., I, p.519); Sipahsālār 8426 (cat., V, p.348)

ṢĀḤIB AL-RIYĀḌ:

Al-Jihādiyya
MS: Raḍawī 6193/1 (cat., V, p.404)

AL-QUMMĪ:

Al-Tuḥfa al-ʿAbbāsiyya, Persian
MSS: Raḍawī 2711 (cat., V, pp.381, 404); Salṭanatī 611 (cat., II, pp.92-3)

MUḤAMMAD ḤUSAYN AL-KHWĀTŪNĀBĀDĪ:

Jihādiyya, Persian
MS: Raḍawī 2348 (Bīnish, p.695)

ANONYMOUS:

Al-Jihādiyya
MS: Raḍawī 6193/2 (cat., V, p.404)

HĀSHIM (early 13th century):

Al-Jihādiyya
MS: Raḍawī 2342 (cat., II, pp.39-40)

AL-AKHBĀRĪ:

K. al-Jihād
MS: Dānishgāh 3341/8 (cat., XI, p.2330)

ABU 'L-ḤASAN B. MUḤAMMAD KĀẒIM (early 13th century):

Āyat al-jihād, Persian
MS: Marʿashī 1480 (cat., IV, pp.271-2)

MUḤAMMAD RIḌĀ B. MUḤAMMAD MUḤSIN AL-HAMADĀNĪ:

Jihādiyya, Persian
MS: Majlis 927 Ṭabāṭabā'ī

AL-MUJĀHID:

Al-Jihādiyya
MSS: Raḍawī 2347, 2349-50 (cat., II, p.41; Bīnish, p.695)

2. ON BOOTY OF WAR

MĀJID B. FALĀḤ B. ḤASAN AL-SHAYBĀNĪ (late 10th century):

Risāla fī ḥurmat al-taṣarruf fi 'l-ājurr wa 'l-ḥijārāt al-mustakhraja min kharābāt al-Kūfa wa 'l-Ḥā'ir wa Ṭūs wa ghayrihā
MS: Marʿashī (AB, XI, p.172)

MUḤAMMAD B. ḤASAN AL-ʿĀMILĪ:

Risāla fi 'l-arḍ al-maftūḥa ʿanwatan
MS: Ḥusayniyyat Kāshif al-Ghiṭā' 55 (AB, XI, p.60)

MUḤAMMAD KĀẒIM B. MUḤAMMAD SHAFĪʿ AL-HAZĀRJARĪBĪ (mid-13th century):

Risāla fi 'l-arḍ al-maftūḥa ʿanwatan
MS: Millī 36 Arabic (cat., VII, pp.36-7)

MUḤAMMAD BĀQIR AL-KAZZĀZĪ AL-SAWIJBULĀGHĪ (d. after 1261):

Risāla fi 'l-arḍ al-maftūḥa ʿanwatan
MS: Millī 213 Arabic (cat., VII, pp.183-4)

MUḤAMMAD TAQĪ B. ABĪ ṬĀLIB AL-ARDAKĀNĪ AL-YAZDĪ (d. 1268):

Risāla dar aḥkām-o arāḍī-yi maftūḥ al-ʿanwa, Persian
MS: Millī 786f (cat., II, p.311)

MUḤAMMAD KĀẒIM B. RIḌĀ AL-ṬABARĪ (d. after 1267):

Risāla fi 'l-arḍ al-maftūḥa ʿanwatan
MS: Dānishgāh 3358/4 (cat., XI, p.2359)

ANONYMOUS:

Risāla fi 'l-arḍ al-maftūḥa ʿanwatan
MS: Sipahsālār 319/2 Mushīr (cat., III, p.111)

ĀL BAḤR AL-ʿULŪM:

Risāla fi 'l-arāḍī al-kharājiyya, included in his *Bulghat al-faqīh* (see above, chapter 5)

3. ON NON-MUSLIMS

ḤUSAYN AL-KHWĀNSĀRĪ:

Ḥall shakk fī kawn baʿḍ ahl al-balad kāfiran wa aktharahum Muslimūn
MS: Dānishgāh 6710/73 (cat., XVI, p.342)

AL-MAJLISĪ II:

Ṣawāʿiq al-Yahūd = Risāla dar aḥkām-i jizya, Persian
MSS: Marʿashī 187/26 (cat., I, p.214); Dānishgāh 5878/2 (cat., XVI, p.119); Fayḍiyya 1290/15 (cat., III, p.75)

ḤAYDAR ʿALĪ AL-SHĪRWĀNĪ:

Risāla fī wujūb qatl sābb al-Nabī
MS: Dānishgāh 4292/7 (cat., XIII, p.3263)

AL-BIHBAHĀNĪ:

Risāla fī anna inkār uṣūl al-madhhab lā jūjib al-kufr
MS: Gulpāyigānī 1870/16 (cat., III, p.92)

AL-QUMMĪ:

Aḥkām al-jizya fī zaman al-ghayba, included in his *al-Rasā'il* (see above, chapter 5)

MUḤAMMAD TAQĪ B. MUḤAMMAD ḤUSAYN AL-KĀSHĀNĪ (d. 1321):

Tawḍīḥ al-masā'il, Persian, on commercial relations between the Muslims and non-Muslims
MSS: Millī 765f (cat., II, p.293); Shīrāz, Fārs

ANONYMOUS:

Jawāz-i musāfirat-i Pādishāh bi-Farang, Persian
MS: Masjid-i Jāmiʿ 243 (cat., p.358)

ʿABD AL-RASŪL AL-FĪRŪZKŪHĪ:

Ḥukm taklīf al-kāfir bi 'l-qaḍā' maʿ suqūṭih bi 'l-Islām
Edition: Tehran, 1321

ʿABD ALLĀH AL-MĀMAQĀNĪ:

Kashf al-astār ʿan wujūb al-ghusl ʿala 'l-kuffār
Edition: Najaf, 1344 (in his *al-Ithnāʿashariyya*)

4. ON NON-SHĪʿĪS

AL-MAJLISĪ II:

Ḥukm-i māl-i Nāṣib-i, Persian
MSS: Marʿashī 187/15 (cat., I, p.211); Gulpāyigānī 1223/6 (cat., II, p.263)

JAMĀL AL-DĪN AL-KHWĀNSĀRĪ:

Risāla dar māl-i Nāṣibī, Persian
MS: Tabrīz, Qāḍī (*Nash.*, VII, p.522)

AL-KHWĀJŪ'Ī:

Risāla fī ḥaqīqat al-Nāṣib
MS: Mashhad, Adabiyyāt 25/8 Fayyāḍ (cat., p.212)

ANONYMOUS (written before 1169):

Rafʻ al-iltibās ʻan aḥkām al-nās
MS: Marʻashī 1965 (cat., V, pp.336-7)

ʻABBĀS ʻALĪ B. MUḤAMMAD AL-KAZZĀZĪ (d. after 1229):

Aḥkām al-mukhālifīn
MS: Marʻashī 2841/1 (cat., VIII, p.46)

AL-BALĀGHĪ:

ʻIqd fī ilzām ghayr al-Imāmī bi aḥkām niḥlatih
Edition: Tehran, 1378

ORDERING GOOD AND FORBIDDING EVIL

ḤASAN AL-KARAKĪ:

Al-Amr bi 'l-maʻrūf wa 'l-nahy ʻan al-munkar
MSS: Wazīrī 2077 (cat., IV, p.1150); Adabiyyāt 120/12 Ḥikmat (cat., p.42)

AL-AKHBĀRĪ:

K. al-Amr bi 'l-maʻrūf wa 'l-nahy ʻan al-munkar
MS: Dānishgāh 3341/9 (cat., XI, p.2330)

ANONYMOUS (belonging to 13th century):

K. al-Amr bi 'l-maʻrūf wa 'l-nahy ʻan al-munkar
MS: Gawharshād 1458/1 (cat., p.220)

AL-SHAFTĪ:

Iqāmat al-ḥudūd fī zaman al-ghayba, Persian
MSS: Fayḍiyya 138/2 (cat., I, p.20, II, p.72); Gulpāyigānī 435 (cat., II, p.103); Ustādī (cat., p.48)

C

ON CONTRACTS

1. GENERALITIES

AL-ḤURR AL-ʻĀMILĪ:

Risāla fī anna 'l-taṣarruf wa 'l-yad dalīl al-milkiyya
MS: Fayḍiyya 1910/3 (cat., III, p.148)

AL-BIHBAHĀNĪ:

Risāla fī anna 'l-aṣl fī 'l-muʻāmalāt al-ṣiḥḥa
MSS: Dānishgāh 713/3 (cat., V, p.1777); Ḥuqūq 247/4j (cat., p.348)

L-QUMMĪ:

Risāla fī jawāz taṣarruf al-mālik maʻ al-ʻilm bi-taḍarrur al-jār

Risāla fī 'l-sharṭ ḍimn al-ʻaqd

Both included in his *al-Rasā'il* and *Jawāmiʻ al-rasā'il* (see above, chapter 5)

ASAN ĀL KĀSHIF AL-GHIṬĀ':

Qawāʻid al-muʻāmalāt
MS: Dānishgāh 6906/1 (cat., XVI, p.411)

ḤMAD B. ʻALĪ MUKHTĀR AL-GULPĀYIGĀNĪ:

Aṣālat al-luzūm fī 'l-ʻuqūd
MS: Marʻashī 3494/1 (cat., IX, p.290)

UḤAMMAD TAQĪ AL-HARAWĪ:

Risāla fī 'l-sharṭ ḍimn al-ʻaqd
MS: Nūrbakhsh 559/1 (cat., II, p.203)

BU 'L-QĀSIM AL-KUJŪRĪ (d. after 1314):

Risāla fī qāʻidat kull mā yuḍman bi-ṣaḥīḥih yuḍman bi-fāsidih
Edition: Tehran, 1314

UḤAMMAD JAʻFAR B. MUḤAMMAD ʻALĪ AL-ḤUSAYNĪ AL-KĀSHĀNĪ (d. 1317):

Risāla fī 'l-shurūṭ
Edition: Tehran, 1315

L BAḤR AL-ʻULŪM:

Risāla fī 'l-qabḍ wa ḥaqīqatih

Risāla fī qāʻidat mā yuḍman bi-ṣaḥīḥih yuḍman bi-fāsidih

Risāla fī qāʻidat al-yad

Risāla fī ʻaqd al-fuḍūlī

All included in his *Bulghat al-faqīh* (see above, chapter 5)

AHDĪ AL-KHĀLIṢĪ:

Al-Qawāʻid al-fiqhiyya fī 'l-muʻāmalāt
Edition: Mashhad, 1343

ALĪ B. MUḤAMMAD ḤUSAYN AL-SHAHRASTĀNĪ:

Risāla fī 'l-iʻrāḍ ʻan al-māl
Edition: Tehran, 1320

L-BALĀGHĪ:

Risāla fī qāʻidat mā yuḍman bi-ṣaḥīḥih yuḍman bi-fāsidih
Edition: Najaf, 1343 (together with his *Ḥāshiyat al-Makāsib*)

L-ĪRAWĀNĪ:

Jumān al-silk fī 'l-iʻrāḍ ʻan al-milk
Edition: Tehran, 1379 (together with his *Ḥāshiyat al-Makāsib*)

AḤMAD B. ʿINĀYAT ALLĀH AL-ZANJĀNĪ:

Īḍāḥ al-aḥwāl fī aḥkām al-ḥālāt al-ṭāriya ʿala ʾl-māl
MS: Zanjānī 129 (cat., p.244)

2. ON FORMULAS

IBN ṬAYY:

Al-Durr al-manḍūd
MSS: Raḍawī 6496 (cat., V, p.420); Mashhad, Ilāhiyyāt 192 (cat., I p.113)

MUFLIḤ AL-ṢAYMARĪ:

Jawāhir al-kalimāt
MSS: Jaʿfariyya (Ṭuʿma II, p.31); Majlis 5405/5, 5354/4 (cat., XVI, pp.265, 310); Raḍawī 6464, 2326, 2596 (cat., II, pp.34-5, V, p.403); Mūza 4329 (cat., p.203); Marʿashī 2255/2, 3702, 133/2 (cat., I, p.153, VI, p.240, X, p.104); Gawharshād 1120 (cat., p.255); Millī 1668/5 Arabic (cat., X, p.250); Malik 2862 (cat., I, p.214); Dānishgāh 3702 (cat., XII, p.2706); Masjid-i Aʿẓam 965/2

ḤUSAYN AL-ṢAYMARĪ:

Maḥāsin al-kalimāt = al-Īqāẓāt
MS: Raḍawī 2596 (cat., II, pp.118-19)

AL-KARAKĪ:

- *Ṣiyagh al-ʿuqūd wa ʾl-īqāʿāt*
  Editions: Tehran, 1315 (in the collection of *Kalimāt al-muḥaqqiqīn*), 1318
  Selected MSS: Raḍawī 2488-9, 7094 (cat., II, p.86, V, p.465); Marʿashī 680/3, 22/4, 133/1 (cat., I, pp.34, 153, II, p.273); Majlis 4339/10, 5354/2 (cat., XII, pp.41-2, XVI, p.264); Millī 1957/6f, 1956/2 Arabic (cat., VI, pp.429-30, X, p.638); Dānishgāh 5397/2, 6963/10 (cat., XV, p.4239, XVI, p.413); Malik 647 (cat., I, p.487); Bengal 645 (cat., I, p.318)
  Translation: Persian, by Muḥammad Yūsuf al-Astarābādī (late 13th century), edited several times (e.g. Tabrīz, 1313)
- *Anīs al-tawwābīn*, his opinions on this topic compiled by Ḥāfiẓ al-Kāshānī

MS: Marʿashī 1003/4 (cat., III, p.199)

AL-SHAHĪD AL-THĀNĪ:

Ṣiyagh al-ʿuqūd
MSS: Jawādayn (AB, V, p.278, XV, p.109); Gulpāyigānī 682/2 (cat., II, p.201); Gharb 786/2 (cat., p.276)

AL-MINSHĀR - ʿAlī b. Aḥmad b. Hilāl al-ʿĀmilī (mid-10th century):

Ṣiyagh al-ʿuqūd wa ʾl-īqāʿat
MS: Majlis 7185

AL-MUKHTĀRĪ:

Maqālīd al-quṣūd
MSS: Gawharshād 1187/3, 1049.4 (cat., p.408); Gulpāyigānī (cat., II, p.217); Wazīrī 3250/3 (cat., V, p.1587)

A'FAR QULĪ B. 'ABD AL-'ALĪ (d. after 1246):

Ṣiyagh al-'uqūd
MS: Mar'ashī 2009.2 (cat., VI, p.12)

IUḤAMMAD JA'FAR AL-ASTARĀBĀDĪ:

Ṣiyagh al-'uqūd wa 'l-īqā'āt
Editions: Tabrīz, 1293: Tehran, 1333
MSS: Dānishgāh 4064/5 (cat., XIII, p.3047); Mar'ashī 1541/2 (cat., IV, p.343); Millī 1622 Arabic (cat., X, p.175); Raḍawī 5714, 7234 (Bīnish, p.907)
Translation: Persian, by Muḥammad Taqī b. Muḥammad muqīm al-Astarābādī al-Sārawī, MS: Gawharshād 1124/1 (cat., p.149)

L-MARĀGHĪ:

Ṣiyagh al-'uqūd wa 'l-īqā'āt
MS: Majlis 4368 (cat., XII, p.78)

ALĪ B. GUL MUḤAMMAD AL-QĀRPŪZĀBĀDĪ AL-ZANJĀNĪ (d. 1290):

Ṣiyagh al-'uqūd
Editions: Tabrīz, 1308 and others (see Mushār, cols. 595-6)

ABD AL-'ALĪ B. MUḤAMMAD AL-HARANDĪ (late 13th century):

Ṣiyagh al-'uqūd, Persian
MS: Gulpāyigānī 1151 (cat., II, p.127)

IUḤAMMAD HĀSHIM AL-KHWĀNSĀRĪ:

Ṣiyagh al-'uqūd
Editions: Iṣfahān, 1310, 1317
MS: Gulpāyigānī 1135/4 (cat., II, p.231)

ABD ALLĀH AL-MĀMAQĀNĪ:

Al-Durr al-manḍūd
Edition: Najaf, 1346

NONYMOUS:

Ṣiyagh al-'uqūd
MS: Mar'ashī 1149/2 (cat., III, p.323)

Nabdha fī ṣiyagh al-'uqūd
MS: Gharb 4712/8 (cat., p.381)

TRANSACTION

ĀSHIF AL-GHIṬĀ:

Sharḥ al-Qawā'id, a commentary on the chapter on transaction of al-'Allāma's *Qawā'id al-aḥkām*
MSS: Raḍawī 7747-8 (Bīnish, p.880); Malik 1106, 2656 (cat., I, p.431); Majlis 1308, 4330, 5147/1 (cat., IV, pp.80-1, XII, p.22, XV, p.217); Fayḍiyya 911 (cat., I, p.154); Gawharshād 741/1 (cat., p.330); Matḥaf 2960 (cat., I, p.246); Princeton 1345 New Series; Najaf, Madrasat al-Sayyid (AB, XIII, p.132); Ustādī (cat., p.24)

AL-AKHBĀRĪ:

K. al-Tijārāt wa 'l-manāfi' wa 'l-ṣinā'āt
MS: Dānishgāh 3341/10 (cat., XI, p.2330)

MUḤSIN AL-KHANFAR AL-NAJAFĪ (d. 1270):

K. al-Tijāra, his lectures compiled by Abū Ṭālib al-Qā'inī
MS: Mar'ashī 1520 (cat., IV, p.322)

AL-ANṢĀRĪ:

- *K. al-Makāsib = al-Matājir*
Editions: Tabrīz, 1375 and others
Autograph: Dānishgāh, microfilm 3642 (cat., II, p.208)
Commentaries: (1) by al-Rashtī, edited Tehran, 1317 (together with Muḥammad Ḥasan al-Māmaqānī's *Ghāyat al-āmāl*), MS: Gulpāyigānī 697 (cat., II, p.62); (2) by Riḍā b. Muḥammad Hādī al-Hamadānī, MS: Shīrāzī (AB, VI, p.219); (3) *Ghāyat al-āmāl*, by Muḥammad Ḥasan al-Māmaqānī, edited Tehran, 1317, MSS: Dānishgāh 752-4 (cat., V, pp.1948-51); (4) *Bughyat al-ṭālib*, by Abu 'l-Qāsim b. Ma'ṣūm al-Ḥusaynī al-Ishkawarī (da. 1324-5); edited Tehran, 1322; (5) by Muḥammad 'Alī b. Muḥammad Ṣādiq al-Khwānsārī, edited Tehran, 1324 (in the margin of al-Anṣārī's *al-Makāsib*); (6) by al-Khurāsānī, edited Tehran, 1319; (7) by al-Yazdī, edited Tehran, 1324, 1378; (8) by Muḥammad Taqī al-Shīrāzī, edited Tehran, 1323; (9) *Maqṣad al-Ṭālib*, by Abu 'l-Qāsim b. Zayn al-'Ābidīn al-Ḥusaynī Imām al-Jum'a (d. 1346), edited Tehran, 1314, 1368; (10) *Nihāyat al-āmāl*, by 'Abd Allāh al-Māmaqānī, edited Najaf, 1345; (11) by al-Balāghī, edited Najaf, 1343; (12) by al-Īrawānī, edited Tehran, 1365, 1379; (13) *Munyat al-ṭālib*, al-Nā'īnī's lectures on *al-Makāsib* compiled by Mūsā b. Muḥammad al-Khwānsārī, edited Najaf, 1357-8, Tehran, 1373; (14) a second collection of al-Nā'īnī's lectures on *al-Makāsib*, compiled by Muḥammad Taqī al-Āmulī, edited Tehran, 1372-3; (15) by Muḥammad Ḥusayn al-Iṣfahānī (d. 1361), edited Tehran, 1363; (16) *Bulghat al-ṭālib*, by Muḥammad Kāẓim al-Shīrāzī (d. 1367), edited Tehran, 1370; (17) *Hidāyat al-ṭālib*, by Fattāḥ b. Muḥammad 'Alī al-Shahīdī, edited Tabrīz, 1375; (18) *Nahj al-faqāha*, by al-Ḥakīm, edited Najaf, 1371; (19) *Miṣbāḥ al-faqāha*, al-Khu'ī's lectures on *al-Makāsib*, compiled by Muḥammad 'Alī al-Tawḥīdī, edited Najaf, 1374-82; (20) *al-Muḥāḍarāt fi 'l-fiqh al-Ja'farī*, another collection of al-Khu'ī's lectures on *al-Makāsib*, compiled by 'Alī al-Ḥusaynī al-Shāhrūdī, edited Najaf, 1373-84

- *Al-Bay' wa 'l-khiyārāt*, his lectures compiled by one of his pupils
MS: Mar'ashī 1795 (cat., V, p.181)

'ALĪ AL-KANĪ (d. 1306):

Aḥkām al-'uqūd wa 'l-khiyārāt
Editions: Tehran, 1304, 1317 (together with his *K. al-Qaḍā'*)

(a)

PROHIBITED BUSINESS

. GENERAL

L-KHUMAYNĪ:

Al-Makāsib al-muḥarrama
Edition: Tehran, 1381

URTAḌĀ AL-ḤĀ'IRĪ:

Ibtighā' al-faḍīla
Edition: Qum, 1383

. ON MUSIC

L-SABZAWĀRĪ:

Risāla fi 'l-ghinā'
MSS: Sipahsālār 8190/13 (cat., V, p.352); Dānishgāh 354/14 (cat., XII, p.2526); Masjid-i A'ẓam 3118; Majlis 3263/2 (cat., X, pp. 873-4)

Risāla fi 'l-ghinā', different from above
MS: Dānishgāh, microfilm 3653/2 from a private MS (cat., II, p.213)

ALĪ B. MUḤAMMAD AL-'ĀMILĪ:

Tanbīh al-ghāfilīn, in refutation of al-Sabzawārī's above-mentioned treatises
MS: Dānishgāh, microfilm 3653/1 from a private MS (cat., II, p.212)

ĪR LAWḤĪ - Muḥammad Hādī b. Muḥammad al-Ḥusaynī al-Sabzawārī (late 11th century):

I'lām al-aḥibbā'
MSS: Majlis 5672/1, 5511 (cat., XVI, p.410, XVII, pp.124-5)

ANONYMOUS (belonging to early 12th century):

Maqāmāt al-sālikīn, Persian
MS: Dānishgāh 5702 (cat., XVI, pp. 70-1)

ĀJID AL-BAḤRĀNĪ - Muḥammad b. Ibrāhīm al-Ḥusaynī (early 12th century):

Īqāẓ al-nā'imīn
MSS: Sipahsālār 8151/3 (cat., III, p.230); Tustariyya (AB, II, p.505)
Abridgement: by Mūsā b. Faḍl Allāh al-Ḥusaynī al-Hamadānī (late 13th century), MS: Fayḍiyya 1960/10 (cat., III, p.156)

ḤUSAYN AL-QAZWĪNĪ:

Risāla fī ḥall ḥadīth warad fi 'l-ṣawt al-ḥasan
MSS: Raḍawī 2505/6 (cat., II, p.118); Zanjānī 76/6 (cat., pp.220-1)

'ABD AL-ṢAMMAD AL-HAMADĀNĪ:

Risāla fi 'l-ghinā'
MSS: Millī 3029/7f (cat., VI, p.811); Nujūmī (cat., p.255)

AL-QUMMĪ:

Risāla fi 'l-ghinā', included in his *al-Rasā'il* (see above, chapter 5)

MUḤAMMAD JAʿFAR B. MUḤAMMAD ḤUSAYN AL-SHAHRASTĀNĪ (d.1260):

Risāla wajīza fi 'l-ghinā'
MS: Dānishgāh 1111/3 (cat., V, p.1896)

MAḤMŪD AL-KIRMĀNSHĀHĪ:

Risāla fī ḥurmat al-ghinā'
MS: Marʿashī 1537/2 (cat., IV, p.337)

MUḤAMMAD RASŪL AL-KĀSHĀNĪ (13th century):

Risāla fī ḥurmat al-ghinā'
MS: Sipahsālār 7564/5 (cat., V, p.353)

NAẒAR ʿALĪ B. SULṬĀN AL-ṬĀLIQĀNĪ (d. 1306):

Risāla fi 'l-ghinā'
Edition: Tehran, 1304

ABU 'L-MAJD:

Risāla fi 'l-ghinā'
Edition: an abridgement of it is edited Tehran, 1381 (in al-Khumaynī's *al-Makāsib al-muḥarrama*)
MS: Zanjānī 112 (cat., p.239)

3. ON BACKBITING

HĀDĪ AL-ṬIHRĀNĪ:

Risāla fi 'l-ghayba
MS: Majlis 5402/2 (cat., XVI, p.307)

4. ON WORKING FOR THE GOVERNMENT

AL-MURTAḌĀ:

Mas'ala fi 'l-ʿamal maʿ al-sulṭān
Edition: London, 1980 AD (in the *Bulletin of the School of Oriental and African Studies*, XLIII, pp.22-4)
MSS: Sipahsālār 2524 (cat., V, pp.557-9); Majlis 5187/3 (cat., XVI, p.6); Dānishgāh 6914/19 (cat., XVI, p.398); Princeton 2751 Yahuda (cat., p.137); Berlin Pet. 40 (cat., IV, pp.347-8); Ṣāḥib al-Dharīʿa (cat. of microfilms of Dānishgāh, I, p.575); Kāshān, ʿĀṭifī (*Nash.*, XI-XII, p.953)

5. ON TAX REVENUE AND GOVERNMENT'S GIFTS

AL-KARAKĪ:

Qāṭiʿat al-lajāj
Edition: Tehran, 1313 (in the collection of *al-Riḍāʿiyyāt wa 'l-kharājiyyāt*)
Selected MSS: Raḍawī 2527-8, 2798 (cat., II, p.99); Dānishgāh 872/2, 7202 (cat., V, p.1967, XVI, p.486); Majlks 5650 (cat., XVII, p.106); Millī 1906 Arabic (cat., X, p.566); al-Imām al-Mahdī (Maḥfūẓ II, p.212); Malik 597 (cat., I, p.559); Los Angeles M1283/4 (cat., p.722)

Translation: Persian, by Muḥammad Bāqir b. Abi 'l-Futūḥ al-Mūsawī (late 11th century), MS: Tabrīz, Thiqat al-Islām (*Nash.*, VII, p.532)

L-QAṬĪFĪ:

Al-Sirāj al-wahhāj
Edition: Tehran 1313 (in the above-mentioned collection)

USAYN B. ʿABD AL-ṢAMAD:

Risāla fī ḥilliyyat jawā'iz al-sulṭān
MS: Millī 1943/2 Arabic (cat., X, p.616); Ḥakīm 1506m (cat., I, pp.37-8)

L-ARDABĪLĪ:

Risāla fi 'l-kharāj

Risāla mukhtaṣara fi 'l-kharāj
Editions: Tehran, 1313 (in the above-mentioned collection), 1318 (in the margin of al-Khurāsānī's *Durar al-fawā'id*)
Selected MSS: Sipahsālār 1446/4-5 (cat., IV, p.364); Millī 1889 Arabic (cat., X, p.533); Dānishgāh 7387/99 (cat., XVI, p.534)

ĀJID AL-SHAYBĀNĪ:

Risāla fī ḥill al-kharāj
Edition: Tehran, 1313 (in the above-mentioned collection)
MS: Marʿashī (AB, XI, p.179)

ABD ALLĀH B. ʿĪSĀ AL-IṢFAHĀNĪ AL-AFANDĪ (d. around 1130):

Al-Kharājiyya
MS: Marʿashī (AB, XI, p.179)

ULLĀ KITĀB - Muḥammad Taqī b. Muḥammad al-Najafī (mid-13th century):

Al-Miṣbāḥ al-wahhāj
MSS: Gharb 5316 (cat., p.192); Sipahsālār 6113 (cat., IV, p.365)

(b)

SALE

. GENERAL

UḤAMMAD IBRĀHĪM B. QĀSIM AL-KĀẒIMĪ AL-NAJAFĪ (13th century):

K. al-Buyūʿ
MS: Majlis 4436 (cat., XII, pp.121-2)

ABD AL-KARĪM AL-QAZWĪNĪ AL-GĪLĀNĪ (late 13th century):

K. al-Bayʿ
MS: Marʿashī 2045 (cat., VI, p.55)

ANONYMOUS (belonging to late 13th century):

K. al-Bayʿ
MSS: Gulpāyigānī 697, 643 (cat., II, p.21); Fayḍiyya 1718

ḤASAN B. IBRĀHĪM AL-NAJMĀBĀDĪ:

K. al-Bayʿ
MSS: Tustariyya (AB, III, p.191); Dānishgāh 726 (cat., V, p.1938)

MUḤAMMAD B. ʿALĪ AL-ḤUJJA AL-KŪHKAMARĪ (d. 1373):

K. al-Bayʿ, his lectures compiled by Abū Ṭālib al-Tajlīl
Edition: Qum, 1373

AL-KHUMAYNĪ:

K. al-Bayʿ
Edition: Najaf, 1389-97

MUḤAMMAD RIḌĀ AL-GULPĀYIGĀNĪ:

K. al-Bayʿ, his lectures compiled by ʿAlī al-Ḥusaynī al-Mīlānī
Edition: Qum, 1400

2. SPECIFIC

MĀJID AL-SHAYBĀNĪ:

Risāla fī wujūb al-ittijār bi-māl al-ṣaghīr wa istinmāʾih lah
MS: Marʿashī (AB, XXV, p.29)

AL-MUKHTĀRĪ:

Al-ʿAyn fī taʿāruḍ ḥaqqay al-mutabāyaʿayn
MSS: Dānishgāh 1859/4 (cat., VIII, p.459); Marʿashī 3382/1 (cat., IX, p.158)

AL-QUMMĪ:

- *Risāla fi ʾl-muʿāṭāt*
- *Risāla fi ʾl-fuḍūlī*
- *Risāla fī annah hal yajūz li-man bāʿ silʿatah min ghayrih an yashtariyahā minh, maʿ al-sharṭ aw bi-dūnih*

All included in his *al-Rasāʾil* (see above, chapter 5)

MUḤAMMAD RASŪL B. ʿABD AL-ʿAZĪZ (mid-13th century):

Al-Tanbīh fī waẓāʾif al-faqīh
MS: Gulpāyigānī 1936

ABŪ ṬĀLIB AL-QĀʾINĪ:

Yanābīʿ al-wilāya
MS: Raḍawī 7170 (cat., V, p.531)

MUḤAMMAD RAḤĪM AL-BURŪJIRDĪ:

Risāla fi ʾl-bayʿ al-fuḍūlī
MS: Raḍawī 5849 (Bīnish, p.790)

MUḤAMMAD ʿALĪ B. MUḤAMMAD BĀQIR AL-MASJIDSHĀHĪ al-IṢFAHĀNĪ (d. 1318):

Risāla fi ʾl-wilāyāt
Edition: Tehran, 1312

AL BAḤR AL-ʿULŪM:

- *Risāla fī bayʿ al-muʿāṭāt*
- *Risāla fī talaf al-mabīʿ qabl qabḍih*
- *Risāla fi 'l-wilāyāt*

All included in his *Bulghat al-faqīh* (see above, chapter 5)

(c)

RIGHT OF CANCELLATION

1. GENERAL

ʿALĪ ĀL KĀSHIF AL-GHIṬĀʾ:

Sharḥ al-Lumʿa, as a commentary on the relevant chapter of al-Shahīd al-Awwal's *al-Lumʿa al-Dimashqiyya*
Edition: Tehran, 1319
MSS: Raḍawī 2388 (cat., II, p.54); Majlis 113 Khuʾī (cat., VII, pp.118-19)

HĀDĪ AL-ṬIHRĀNĪ:

Dhakhāʾir al-nubuwwa
Edition: Tabrīz, 1325
MSS: Dānishgāh 799 (cat., V, pp.1880-2); Majlis 2717/1, 2753/3 (cat., IX, pp.38, 139)

MURTAḌĀ B. AḤMAD AL-KHUSRAWSHĀHĪ (d. 1372):

Nithārāt al-kawākib, a commentary on the relevant chapter of al-Anṣārī's *al-Makāsib*
Edition: Tehran, 1370

2. SPECIFIC

AL-KARAKĪ:

- *Risāla fī taḥqīq al-bayʿ bi-sharṭ al-khiyār*
  MS: Dānishgāh 2888/2 (cat., X, p.1733)
- *Risāla fī taṣarruf al-mushtarī fī zaman al-khiyār*
  MSS: Majlis 3333/6 (cat., X, pp.1130-1; see also AB, XI, pp.148-9)

ANONYMOUS:

Fāʾida fī jawāz bayʿ al-sharṭ
MS: Majlis 5202/2 (cat., XVI, p.33)

MUḤAMMAD RIḌĀ B. MUḤAMMAD ʿALĪ AL-ISFARJĀNĪ AL-GULPĀYIGĀNĪ (d. after 1258)

Risāla fī jawāz akhdh al-arsh min ghayr al-nagdayn
MS: Dānishgāh 1953/6 (cat., VIII, p.568)

MUḤAMMAD B. ʿALĪ AL-KHUSRAWSHĀHĪ AL-TABRĪZĪ (d. around 1312):

Al-Risāla al-Bāqiriyya
Edition: Tabrīz, 1310 (together with his *Mishkāt al-maṣābīḥ*)

SHAYKH AL-SHARĪʿA:

Risāla fi 'l-khiyārāt
MS: Dānishgāh 2627/2 (cat., IX, p.1503)

(d)

LOAN AND INTEREST

AL-BIHBAHĀNĪ:

Risāla fī buṭlān al-qarḍ bi-sharṭ al-muʿāmala al-muḥābātiyya
MSS: Raḍawī 7197 (cat., V, pp.431-2); Sipahsālār 907/16 (cat., V, p.36); Millī 231/4 Arabic (cat., VII, p.203); Ḥuqūq 247/4j (cat., p.351); Ilāhiyyāt 385/4d (cat., I, p.291); Marʿashī 2115/4, 1470/4 (cat., IV, p.264, VI, p. 127); Gulpāyigānī 1870/14 (cat., III, p.92); Fayḍiyya 1189/2 (cat., III, p.65); Princeton 149/11 New Series; Zanjānī 76/1 (cat., p.221); Tabrīz, Qāḍī (*Nash.*, VII, p.521)

MUḤAMMAD MAHDĪ AL-ḤUSAYNĪ AL-MASHHADĪ:

Al-Ḥiyal al-sharʿiyya, in refutation of al-Bihbahānī's above-mentioned treatise
MS: Majlis 1804/4 (cat., IX, pp.318-19)

MUḤAMMAD ʿALĪ B. MUḤAMMAD KALĪL AL-ḤUSAYNĪ AL-MARʿASHĪ (early 13th century):

Khādimiyya dar ḥurmat-i ḥiyal-i sharʿiyya, Persian
MSS: Marʿashī 234 (cat., I, p.260); Dānishgāh 2695 (cat., X, p.1578)

AL-QUMMĪ:

Risāla fi 'l-muʿāmala al-muḥābātiyya bi-sharṭ al-qarḍ wa bi 'l-ʿaks, included in his *al-Rasā'il* (see above, chapter 5)

MUḤAMMAD B. MUḤAMMAD ṢĀDIQ AL-MŪSAWĪ AL-KHWĀNSĀRĪ (13th century):

Risāla fī ʿadam jawāz al-ḥiyal al-sharʿiyya
MS: Ustādī (cat., p.59)

MAḤMŪD B. ʿABD AL-ʿAẒĪM AL-MŪSAWĪ AL-KHWĀNSĀRĪ (13th century):

- *Risāla fī ḥukm al-muʿāmala al-muḥābātiyya*
  MS: Dānishgāh 1136/9 (cat., V, p.1890)
- *Risāla fī ḥiyal al-ribā*
  MS: Dānishgāh 1136/14 (cat., V, p.1893)

ĀL BAḤR AL-ʿULŪM:

Risāla fi 'l-qarḍ, included in his *Bulghat al-faqīh* (see above, chapter 5)

MUḤAMMAD HĀSHIM AL-KHURĀSĀNĪ:

Risāla-yi ribā'iyya, Persian
Edition: Mashhad, 1340; Tehran, 1352

MORTGAGE

ḤUSAYN B. ḤAYDAR AL-KARAKĪ:

Iṣābat al-ḥaqq = Risāla fī jawāz sharṭ al-murtahin al-wikāla li-nafsih fī bay' al-marhūn
MS: Malik (AB, XI, p.81)

ḤUSAYN QULĪ AL-HAMADĀNĪ:

K. al-Rahn
MS: Tustariyya (AB, XI, p.311)

SURETYSHIP

ANONYMOUS:

Risāla dar ḍamān, Persian
MS: Gawharshād 1685/5 (cat., p.149)

CONCILIATION

1. GENERAL

MUḤAMMAD TAQĪ AL-ARDAKĀNĪ:

Aḥkām-i ṣulḥ, Persian
MSS: Mar'ashī 3328/2 (cat., IX, pp.106-7); Fayḍiyya 991/1 (cat., III, p.46)

HĀDĪ AL-TIHRĀNĪ:

Al-Riḍwān = K. al-Ṣulḥ
MSS: Majlis 1950/1, 2753/1 (cat., IX, pp.138,661); Raḍawiyya 33 (cat., pp. 28-9)

2. SPECIFIC

AḤMAD AL-BAḤRĀNĪ:

Risāla fī taḥqīq mas'alat al-ṣulḥ 'ala 'l-majhūl
MS: Princeton 229/12 Yahuda (cat., p.139)

AL-SHAFTĪ:

Risāla fī ḥukm ṣulḥ ḥaqq al-rujū' fī 'l-ṭalāq al-raj'ī (see below, monographs on divorce)

MUḤAMMAD SHAFĪ' B. 'ABD AL-MAJĪD AL-MĀZANDARĀNĪ (d. after 1273):

Risāla fī ṣulḥ ḥaqq al-rujū' fī 'l-ṭalāq (see below, monographs on divorce)

MUḤAMMAD ḤUSAYN AL-KHWĀNSĀRĪ:

Risāla fī 'l-sharṭ ḍimn 'aqd al-ṣulḥ
MS: Mar'ashī 3041/5 (cat., VIII, p.243)

HIRE AND LEASE

1. GENERAL

AL-KIRMĀNSHĀHĪ:

K. al-Ijāra
MS: Raḍawī 6640 (cat., V, p.354)

ANONYMOUS:

K. al-Ijāra, a collection of lectures on this topic
MS: Majlis 4546/2 (cat., XII, p.219)

AL-RASHTĪ:

K. al-Ijāra
Edition: Tehran, 1298, 1316
MS: Masjid-i A'ẓam 11709

AL-KHURĀSĀNĪ:

K. al-Ijāra, his lectures compiled by his son, Muḥammad b. Kāẓim al-Khurāsānī
MS: Dānishgāh 1151/2 (cat., V, p.1832)

FAYYĀḌ AL-ZANJĀNĪ:

K. al-Ijāra
Edition: Tehran, 1343

MUḤAMMAD ḤUSAYN AL-IṢFAHĀNĪ:

K. al-Ijāra
Edition: Najaf, 1375

2. SPECIFIC

'ABD ALLĀH AL-TUSTARĪ:

Risāla fī tamalluk al-ajīr li 'l-ujra bi 'l-'aqd, included in his *al-Rasā'il* (see above, chapter 5)

AL-FAYḌ:

Risāla fī ḥukm akhdh al-ujra 'ala 'l-wājibāt
MSS: Mar'ashī 1401/8 (cat., IV, p.176); Majlis 3818/10 (cat., X, p.1843)

ANONYMOUS (belonging to early 14th century):

Risāla dar ajal-i ijāra, Persian
MS: Dānishgāh 4457/1 (cat., XIII, p.3414)

ĀL BAḤR AL-'ULŪM:

Risāla fī akhdh al-ujra 'ala 'l-wājibāt, included in his *Bulghat al-faqīh* (see above, chapter 5)

MUḤAMMAD ḤUSAYN AL-IṢFAHĀNĪ:

Risāla fī ḥukm akhdh al-ujra 'ala 'l-wājibāt
Edition: Tehran, 1363 (together with his *Ḥāshiyat al-Makāsib*)

PROCURATION

ABD ALLĀH AL-TUSTARĪ (d. 1021):

Risāla fī wakīl al-zawja
Translation: Persian, by Muḥammad Ṣādiq al-Sirkānī, MS: Wazīrī (cat. of microfilms of Dānishgāh, I, p.705)

L-QUMMĪ:

Ḥukm al-ṭalāq bi-da'wā al-wikāla 'an al-zawj ma' inkārih (see below, monographs on divorce)

NONYMOUS:

Risāla fī ṭalāq mudda'ī al-wikāla 'an al-zawj ma' inkār al-zawj (see below, monographs on divorce)

ABD ALLĀH AL-KIRMĀNSHĀHĪ:

Ta'āruḍ al-wakīl wa 'l-muwakkil fī mā law bā' rajul li-rajul shay'an wa sharaṭ li-nafsih al-khiyār
MS: Ilāhiyyāt 819/2d (cat., II, p.20)

L-SHAFTĪ:

Risāla fī ṭalāq mudda'ī al-wikāla 'an al-zawj ma' inkār al-zawj (see below, monographs on divorce)

ENDOWMENT

. GENERAL

ḤMAD B. 'ALĪ MUKHTĀR AL-GULPĀYIGĀNĪ:

K. al-Waqf
MS: Mar'ashī 3494/7 (cat., II, p.293)

UḤAMMAD KĀẒIM B. RIḌĀ AL-ṬABARĪ:

Risāla fī bayān ba'ḍ masā'il al-waqf
MS: Dānishgāh 3358/3 (cat., XI, p.2359)

L-ANṢĀRĪ:

K. al-Wuqūf wa 'l-ṣadaqāt
MS: Ma'had 1295 (cat. p.112)

K. al-Waqf, his lectures compiled by Muḥammad Ibrāhīm al-Rashtī
MS: Mar'ashī 1066 (cat., III, p.251)

ḤMAD B. MUḤAMMAD MUḤSIN AL-FAYḌĪ (late 13th century):

K. al-Waqf
MS: Gawharshād 38 (cat., p.361)

BŪ ṬĀLIB AL-QĀ'INĪ:

Ṣafwat al-maqāl
MS: Mar'ashī 3132 (cat., VIII, p.361)

AL-RASHTĪ:

K. al-Waqf
MSS: Tustariyya 622/1 (cat., p.869); Majlis 3275/2, 4312,
37 Ṭabāṭabā'ī (cat., X, pp.883-4, XII, p.5)

AL-KHURĀSĀNĪ:

Risāla fi 'l-waqf
Edition: Baghdad, 1331 (in his *Shadharāt*)
Commentary: by Mahdī al-Khāliṣī, edited Baghdad, 1331 (in his *al-Darārī al-lāmi'āt*)

MUḤAMMAD ṢĀLIḤ B. FAḌL ALLĀH AL-ḤĀ'IRĪ AL-SIMNĀNĪ (d. 1391):

K. al-Waqf
Edition: Tehran, 1377

2. SPECIFIC

AḤMAD B. ZAYN AL-'ĀBIDĪN AL-'ĀMILĪ:

Bayān al-ḥaqq wa tibyān al-ṣidq
MS: Raḍawī 2259 (cat., II, pp.15-16); Fayḍiyya 1961 (cat., I, p.36)

ḤUSAYN ĀL 'UṢFŪR:

Burhān al-ashrāf fī man' bay' al-awqāf
MS: Raḍawī 6462 (cat., V, pp.373-4)

AL-QUMMĪ:

Risāla fi 'l-waqf wa bayān ḥāl madrasa lā yu'lam wāqifuhā, included in his *al-Rasā'il* (see above, chapter 5)

AL-SHAFTĪ:

Risāla fī 'adam luzūm al-qabḍ idhā ja'al al-wāqif al-tawliya li-nafsih
MSS: Fayḍiyya 1089/3, 1373/2 (cat., III, p.54, 87); Mar'ashī 3192/1 (cat., VIII, pp.412-13)

ABU 'L-QĀSIM B. MUḤAMMAD MAHDĪ AL-NARĀQĪ (d. 1256):

Mulakhkhaṣ al-maqāl, in refutation of al-Shaftī's above-mentioned treatise
MS: Mar'ashī 3136 (cat., VIII, p.365)

MUḤAMMAD B. 'ĀSHŪR AL-KIRMĀNSHĀHĪ:

Risāla fī bay' al-waqf
MS: Mar'ashī 2575/fols. 12-14 (cat., VII, p.165)

LEGACIES

1. GENERAL

AL-ANṢĀRĪ:

K. al-Waṣāyā, as a commentary on the relevant chapter of al-'Allāma's *Irshād al-adhhān*
Editions: Tehran, 1305, 1325 (both together with his *al-Makāsib*)
MS: Fayḍiyya 993/1 (cat., III, p.47)

L-RASHTĪ:

K. al-Waṣāyā
MS: Dānishgāh 6711/1 (cat., XVI, p.343)

L BAḤR AL-ʿULŪM:

Risāla fi ʾl-waṣiyya, includee in his *Bulghat al-faqīh* (see above, chapter 5)

NONYMOUS:

Masāʾil-i waṣāyā, Persian
MS: Millī 2633/3f (cat., VI, p.191)

UẒAFFAR B. MUḤAMMAD ʿALĪ AL-ḤUSAYNĪ AL-RASHTĪ (early 14th century):

Al-Masāʾil al-Rashtiyya
MS: Marʿashī 1246/2 (cat., IV, pp.44-5)

. SPECIFIC

ASAN AL-GĪLĀNĪ (late 11th century):

Masʾlatān fi ʾl-waṣiyya
MS: Majlis 2773/3-4 (cat., IX, p.209)

L-QUMMĪ:

Risāla fī munajjazāt al-marīḍ, included in his *al-Rasāʾil* and his *Jawāmiʿ al-rasāʾil* (see above, chapter 5)

UḤAMMAD JAʿFAR B. MUḤAMMAD ḤUSAYN AL-ṬIHRĀNĪ (d. after 1256):

Risāla fī taṣarrufāt al-marīḍ
MS: Fayḍiyya 771/3 (cat., III, p.20)

ASHKŪR B. MUḤAMMAD AL-ḤAWLĀWĪ AL-NAJAFĪ (d. 1272):

Risāla fī munajjazāt al-marīḍ
Edition: Tehran, 1323

L-ANṢĀRĪ:

Risāla fī munajjazāt al-marīḍ
MS: Dānishgāh 6956/4 (cat., XVI, p.411)

UḤAMMAD ʿABBĀS AL-MŪSAWĪ AL-LAKNAWĪ:

Al-Rawḍ al-arīḍ fī munajjazāt al-marīḍ
MS: Marʿashī 2030 (cat., VI, p.36)

L BAḤR AL-ʿULŪM:

Risāla fī munajjazāt al-marīḍ, included in his *Bulghat al-faqīh* (see above, chapter 5)

UḤAMMAD ḤUSAYN AL-KHWĀNSĀRĪ:

Risāla fī munajjazāt al-marīḍ
MS: Marʿashī 3041/4 (cat., VIII, p.342)

AL-YAZDĪ:

Risāla fī munajjazāt al-marīḍ
Editions: Tehran, 1324, 1378 (together with his *Ḥāshiyat al-Makāsib*)

ABU 'L-QĀSIM B. ZAYN AL-ʿĀBIDĪN AL-ḤUSAYNĪ:

Risāla fī munajjazāt al-marīḍ
Edition: Tehran, 1323

MUḤSIN B. ʿABD AL-KARĪM AL-AMĪN AL-ʿĀMILĪ (d. 1373):

Al-Rawḍ al-arīḍ fī taṣarrufāt al-marīḍ
Edition: [Sidon?], n.d.

MUḤAMMAD ṢĀLIḤ AL-SIMNĀNĪ:

Risāla fī munajjazāt al-marīḍ
Edition: Tehran, 1377

MARRIAGE

1. GENERAL

ANONYMOUS (belonging to late 9th century):

Nuzhat al-arwāḥ
MSS: Bengal 647 (cat., I, p.320); Dānishgāh 6875, 882/6, 4989/3 (cat., V, pp.2085-7, XV, p.4077, XVI, p.387); Raḍawī 2853 (cat., V, p.527)

ʿIZZ AL-DĪN AL-ĀMULĪ (early 10th century):

Lumʿa dar nikāḥ-i dāʾim wa mutʿa, Persian
MSS: Raḍawī 2552 (cat., II, p.106); Fayḍiyya 1617/1 (cat., III, p.109); Malik 5445 (AB, XVIII, pp.353-4); Dānishgāh 3106/9 (cat., XI, p.2060); Majlis 843 (cat., III, p.74); Marʿashī 1667/5 (cat., V, p.62)

ʿALĪ B. IBRĀHĪM B. SULAYMĀN AL-BAḤRĀNĪ:

Sharḥ k. al-nikāḥ
MS: Dār al-Kutub 19178 (cat., I, p.289)

ʿABD AL-KARĪM AL-ḤĀʾIRĪ:

K. al-Nikāḥ, his lectures compiled by Maḥmūd al-Āshtiyānī
Edition: Tehran, n.d.

2. ON PROPRIETY BETWEEN THE SEXES

ʿAṬĀʾ ALLĀH B. MASĪḤ AL-ĀMULĪ (10th century):

Fāʾida fī ḥurmat simāʿ ṣawt al-marʾa li 'l-rajul
MS: Majlis 4339/3 (cat., XII, pp.38-9)

AL-KHWĀJŪʾĪ:

Risāla fī ḥukm al-naẓar ilā wajh al-ajnabiyya
MSS: Princeton 1317 New Series (fols. 47b-64a); Wazīrī 3742/4 (cat., V, p.1778)

3. ON FORMULA

AL-MURTAḌĀ:

Mas'ala fī iftiqār al-nikāḥ ila 'l-qabūl al-ṣarīḥ, included in his *Shatāt al-fawā'id* (see above, chapter 5)

IBN FAHD:

Aḥkām ʿaqd al-nikāḥ
MS: Majlis 2750/5 (cat., IX, p.126)

MUFLIḤ AL-ṢAYMARĪ:

Al-Nabdha al-ʿuqūdiyya fi 'l-ṣiyagh al-nikāḥiyya
MS: Majlis 5405/6 (cat., XVI, p.311)

MUḤAMMAD ʿALĪ AL-ASTARĀBĀDĪ (late 11th century):

- *Risāla dar ṣiyagh-i ʿaqd-i nikāḥ*, Persian
  MS: Dānishgāh 3514/24 (cat., XII, p.2528)

- *Ṣiyagh-i nikāḥ*, Persian
  MS: Dānishgāh 3514/25 (cat., XII, p.2528)

AL-MAJLISĪ II:

Nikāhiyya = Ṣiyagh-i nikāḥ, Persian
MSS: Millī 1261/2 Arabic (cat., IX, p.249); Dānishgāh 4064/7 (cat., XIII, pp.3047-8); Marʿashī 187/7, 602/3, 1683/2 (cat., I, p.207, II, p.196, V, p.78); Wazīrī 1318/3 (cat., III, p.927); Fayḍiyya 913/1 (cat., III, p.37); Gulpāyigānī 1046/1, 1416/2 (cat., II, pp.224, 258); Raḍawī 5714 (Bīnish, p.907)

ANONYMOUS (belonging to late 11th century):

Risāla fī ṣiyagh ʿaqd al-nikāḥ
MS: Majlis 83/1 Khu'ī (cat., VII, pp.183-4)

MUḤAMMAD BĀQIR B. ISMĀʿĪL AL-ḤUSAYNI AL-KHWĀTŪNĀBĀDĪ (d. 1127):

Ṣiyagh-i Nikāḥ, Persian
MS: Fayḍiyya 2020 (cat., II, p.80)

MUḤAMMAD B. MUḤAMMAD ZAMĀN AL-KĀSHĀNĪ:

- *Al-Ḥaqq al-ṣurāḥ fī mā lā budd minh fī Ījāb al-nikāḥ = al-Qawl al-sadīd*
  MSS: Marʿashī 1675 (cat., V, p.71); Majlis 1966/3 (cat., IX, p.678); Nūrbakhsh 108/5 (cat., I, p.131)

- *Ṣiyagh al-nikāḥ*
  MSS: Majlis 1966/1 (cat., IX, pp.674-6); Nūrbakhsh 108/6 (cat., I, p.132)

AL-KIRMĀNSHĀHĪ:

Ṣiyagh al-nikāh
MS: Majlis 5325/1 (cat., XVI, p.236)

MUḤAMMAD JAʿFAR AL-ASTARĀBĀDĪ:

Ṣiyagh al-nikāḥ
MSS: Dānishgāh 4064/4 (cat., XIII, p.3047); Marʿashī 1541/1 (cat.,

IV, p.343); Ḥujjatiyya 703/8 (cat., p.122); Gulpāyigānī 1416/1 (cat., II, p.258); Millī 1622 Arabic (cat., X, p.175)

4. ON LEGAL GUARDIANS

LUṬF ALLĀH AL-MAYSĪ:

Al-Wathā'iq wa 'l-'iqāl = Risāla fī faskh al-zawja al-ṣaghīra nikāḥ al-walī lahā ba'd kibarihā
MS: Amīr al-Mu'minīn (AB, XXV, p.26)

'ALĪ NAQĪ AL-KAMARA'Ī :

Risāla fī wilāyat al-ab wa 'l-jadd fī 'l-nikāḥ
MS: Majlis 333/4 (cat., X, p.1129)

AL-FAYḌ:

Risāla fi 'l-wilāya 'ala 'l-bikr fi 'l-tazwīj
MSS: Majlis 3818/11 (cat., X, p.1844); Mar'ashī 1401/9 (cat., IV, pp.176-7)

MUḤAMMAD JA'FAR B. 'ABD ALLĀH AL-ḤUWAYZĪ:

Risāla fi 'l-waṣiyya bi 'l-nikāḥ
MS: Adabiyyāt 275/3 Kirmān (cat., p.42)

KHALAF B. 'ABD AL-'ALĪ AL-BAḤRĀNĪ:

Risāla fī wilāyat al-mūṣā ilayh bi 'l-tazwīj fī 'l-nikāḥ
MS: Mar'ashī 3450/9 (cat., IX, p.245)

AL-SHARĪF AL-ḤUSAYNĪ (12th century):

Fā'ida fi wilāyat al-ab wa 'l-jadd 'ala 'l-bākira
MS: Dānishgāh 5590/2 (cat., XVI, p.41)

MUḤAMMAD MAHDĪ AL-ḤUSAYNĪ AL-MASHHADĪ:

Risāla fī wilāyat al-ab fi 'l-nikāḥ
MS: Majlis 1804/6 (cat., IX, p.321)

'ALĪ B. MUḤAMMAD ḤUSAYN AL-SHAHRASTĀNĪ:

Risāla fi 'l-wilāya 'ala 'l-bikr
Edition: Tehran, 1320

5. ON LEGAL OBSTACLES

AL-KARAKĪ:

Shurūṭ al-nikāḥ
MS: Mar'ashī 680/4 (cat., II, p.273)

ANONYMOUS (belonging to 10th century):

Risāla fi 'l-waṭy bi 'l-shubha
MS: Dānishgāh 6963/1 (cat., XVI, p.412)

AL-KHWĀJŪ'Ī:

Risāla fī 'adam jawāz tazwīj al-mu'mina bi 'l-mukhālif
MS: Mar'ashī 1142/3 (cat., III, p.316)

ṢĀḤIB AL-ḤADĀ'IQ:

- *Risāla fī ḥurmat al-umm bi 'l-'aqd 'ala 'l-bint*
  MS: Tustariyya (cat., VI, p.395)
- *Al-Ṣawārim al-qāṣima li-ẓuhūr al-jāmi'īn bayn bintayn min wuld Fāṭima*
  MSS: Mar'ashī 3450/8 (cat., IX, p.244); Nūrbakhsh 437/2 (cat., II, pp.132-3)

AL-BIHBAHĀNĪ:

- *Risāla fī jawāz al-jam' bayn Fāṭimiyyatayn*
  MSS: Raḍawī 8218 (cat., V, p.431); Rawḍātī (AB, XX, p.72)
- *Risāla fī buṭlān al-'aqd 'ala 'l-ṣaghīra li-ajl al-maḥramiyya*
  MSS: Dānishgāh 5418/11 (cat., XVI, p.5); Gulpāyigānī 1870.9 (cat., III, p.91); Zanjānī 76/2 (cat., p.222)

ḤUSAYN AL-QAZWĪNĪ:

- *Ghāyat al-ikhtiyār fī aḥkām munākaḥat al-kuffār*
  MS: Majlis 3781 (cat., X, p.1768)
- *Risāla fī ḥukm nikāḥ al-ṣaghīra li-gharaḍ maḥramiyyat ummihā*
  MSS: Raḍawī 2595/8 (cat., II, p.118); Zanjānī 76/8 (cat., pp.220-1)

AL-KIRMĀNSHĀHĪ:

Man' al-man' min al-jam' bayn Fāṭimiyyatayn, in refutation of Ṣāḥib al-Ḥadā'iq's above-mentioned treatise
MSS: Ilāhiyyāt 98/2 Āl Āqā, 828/2d (cat., I, p.714, II, p.22)

AL-QUMMĪ:

- *Risāla fi 'l-aqd 'ala 'l-ṣaghīra li-mujarrad al-maḥramiyya*, included in his *al-Rasā'il* (see above, chapter 5)
- *Risāla fī da'wā al-mar'a khuluwwahā 'an al-māni'*
  MSS: Gharb 646/22 (cat., p.257); Majlis 4298 (cat., XI, p.313); Burūjirdī (AB, XI, p.184)

'ALĪ B. MUḤAMMAD (early 13th century):

Qāṭi'at al-mirā' fī taḥqīq mujarrad al-iddi'ā'
MS: Mar'ashī 3133 (cat., VIII, p.362)

AL-SHAFTĪ:

- *Risāla fī jawāz al-ittikāl 'alā qawl al-nisā' fī intifā' mawāni' al-nikāḥ*
- *Risāla fī ḥurmat 'umm al-mawṭū' wa bintih wa ukhtih 'ala 'l-wāṭi'*

Both included in his *Su'āl wa jawāb* (see above, chapter 5)

'ABD ALLĀH AL-KIRMĀNSHĀHĪ:

Mas'ala fī imra'a i'taqadat anna zawjahā ṭallaqahā fa-tazawwajat thumma tabayyn 'adam al-ṭalāq
MS: Ilāhiyyāt 819/3d (cat., II, p.20)

AL-ANṢĀRĪ:

Al-Taḥrīm bi 'l-muṣāhara, as a commentary on the relevant discussion in al-'Allāma's *Irshād al-adhhān*
Editions: Tehran, 1305, 1326, Tabrīz, 1375 (all together with his *al-Makāsib*)

MS: Fayḍiyya 993/1 (cat., III, p.47)

ʿABD AL-RASŪL AL-FĪRŪZKŪHĪ:

Risāla fī ḥukm ʿaqd al-inqiṭāʿ ʿala ʾl-ṣaghīr aw al-ṣaghīra li ʾl-maḥramiyya
Edition: Tehran, 1321

RĀḤAT ḤUSAYN AL-GŪPĀLPŪRĪ:

Al-Wajīza al-ʿāṣima min shubhat ḥurmat al-jamʿ bayn thintayn min wuld Fāṭima
Edition: Locknow, 1372

AḤMAD AL-ZANJĀNĪ:

Muḥarramāt-i abadiyya, Persian
Edition: Qum, n.d.

6. ON FOSTER RELATIONSHIP

AL-KARAKĪ:

Risāla fi ʾl-riḍāʿ
Edition: Tehran, 1313 (in the collection of *al-Riḍāʿiyyāt wa ʾl-kharājiyyāt*)
Selected MSS: Marʿashī 680/7, 2773/2 (cat., II, p.274, VII, p.332); Majlis 4566/13 (cat., XII, p.264); Tustariyya (AB, XI, p.192); Sipahsālār 2533/10 (cat., V, p.54); Princeton 1399 New Series

AL-QAṬĪFĪ:

Risāla fi ʾl-riḍāʿ, in refutation of al-Karakī's above-mentioned treatise
Edition: Tehran, 1313 (in the above-mentioned collection)
MSS: Dānishgāh 7043/8 (cat., XVI, p.437); Raḍawī 7622 (Bīnish, p.826)

ANONYMOUS (written in 931-74):

Risāla fi ʾl-riḍāʿ
MS: Sinā 282/2 (cat., I, p.141)

ḤUSAYN B. ʿABD AL-ṢAMAD:

Risāla fi ʾl-riḍāʿ
MSS: Ḥakīm, 2226 (AB, XX, pp.6-7); Majlis 5168/2, 613 Ṭabāṭabāʾī (cat., XV, p.305); Fayḍiyya 1430/2 (cat., III, p.91)

MĀJID AL-SHAYBĀNĪ:

Risāla fi ʾl-riḍāʿ = Ithbāt al-ḥurma nasaban wa riḍāʿan
MSS: Dānishgāh 2105/4, 7043/7 (cat., VIII, p.740, XVI, p.437)

AL-DĀMĀD:

- *Ḍawābiṭ al-riḍāʿ*
  Edition: Tehran, 1313 (in the above-mentioned collection)
  Selected MSS: Raḍawī 2788 (cat., V, p.467); Mashhad, Ilāhiyyāt 219 (cat., I, p.130); Majlis 2724, 4900/19 (cat., IX, pp.53-4, XIV, p.61); Dānishgāh 6817/1 (cat., XVI, p.368); Mashhad, Adabiyyāt 59/2 Fayyāḍ (cat., p.193)
  Translation: Persian by Sulṭān Ḥusayn al-Wāʿiẓ al-Astarābādī (d. afte 1078), MS: Dānishgāh 5372 (cat., XV, pp.4223-4)
- *Al-Riḍāʿiyya = al-Radd ʿalā mā uʿturiḍ bih ʿalā Ḍawābiṭ al-riḍāʿ*
  MS: Baku M140/33 (*Nash.*, IX, p.241)

AL-MAJLISĪ I:

Riḍā'iyya, Persian
MSS: Dānishgāh 944/10 (cat., V, pp.1901-2); Majlis 4903/17, 5168/3 (cat., XIV, p.125, XV, pp.305-6); Raḍawī 6703 (cat., V, p.445); Malik 1752 (cat., II, p.411); Wazīrī 990/4 (cat., II, p.809); Fayḍiyya 346/3 (cat., III, p.9); Gulpāyigānī 686/3, 1046/2 (cat., II, pp.203, 224); Mar'ashī 70/4, 3719/3, 3034/4 (cat., I, p.84, VIII,p.2225, X, p.119); Millī 1598/3 Arabic (cat., X, p.129)

MUḤAMMAD FĀḌIL B. MUḤAMMAD MAHDĪ AL-MASHHADĪ (d. after 1086):

Mas'ala fi 'l-riḍā'
MS: Raḍawī 2783/2 (cat., V, p.456)

ḤUSĀM AL-DĪN B. JAMĀL AL-DĪN AL-ṬURAYḤĪ AL-NAJAFĪ (d. after 1094):

Al-Tabṣira al-jaliyya fi 'l-masā'il al-muhimma al-riḍā'iyya
MSS: Millī 1598/2 Arabic (cat., X, p.129); Ḥakīm (see also AB, III, p.317)

AL-MAJLISĪ II:

Riḍā'iyya, Persian
Edition: Tehran, 1313 (in the above-mentioned collection)
MSS: Los Angeles M587/2 (cat., p.682); Masjid-i A'ẓam 3147

MUḤAMMAD HĀDĪ B. MUḤAMMAD ṢĀLIḤ AL-MĀZANDARĀNĪ:

Risāla fī ma'rifat aḥkām al-riḍā'
MSS: Mar'ashī 1409/14, 3719/2 (cat., IV, p.190, X, p.119); Nawwāb 271/1 law (cat., p.473)

ABU 'L-ḤASAN B. MUḤAMMAD ṬĀHIR AL-SHARĪF AL-FUTŪNĪ AL-'ĀMILĪ (d. 1138):

Risāla fi 'l-riḍā'
MSS: Dār al-Kutub 3326j (cat., I, p.356); Dānishgāh 7135 (cat., XVI, p.463); Mar'ashī 3719/1 (cat., X, p.118)

ANONYMOUS (belonging to mid-12th century):

Masā'il al-riḍā'
MS: Wazīrī 1819/2 (cat., III, p.1064)

MUḤAMMAD B. 'ABD AL-KARĪM AL-ṬABĀṬABĀ'Ī AL-BURŪJIRDĪ (d. before 1168):

Risāla fī ma'rifat aḥhām al-riḍā'
MSS: Dānishgāh 1102/2, 1257/37 (cat., V, p.1902, VII, p.2677)

'ABD AL-NABĪ B. AḤMAD AL-BAḤRĀNĪ (d. after 1150):

Risāla fi 'l-riḍā'
MS: Burūjirdī (AB, XI, p.192)

AL-KHWĀJŪ'Ī:

Al-Riḍā'iyya
MSS: Masjid-i A'ẓam 3148; Mashhad, Adabiyyāt 25/3 Fayyāḍ (cat., p.211)

ṢĀḤIB AL-ḤADĀʾIQ:

Kashf al-qināʿ, in refutation of al-Dāmād's *Ḍawābiṭ al-riḍāʿ*
MSS: Dānishgāh 891/1 (cat., V, p.1988); Majlis 5434/22 (cat., XVI, p.339); Los Angeles M106/2 (cat., p.664)

AL-QUMMĪ

Risāla fī iḍrāʿ al-ukht ukhtahā al-ṣughrā, included in his *Jawāmiʿ al-rasāʾil* (see above, chapter 5)

MUḤAMMAD ʿALĪ AL-HAZĀRJARĪBĪ:

Al-Riḍāʿiyya
MS: Malik 2137 (cat., I, p.337)

ṢADR AL-DĪN MUḤAMMAD B. ṢĀLIḤ AL-ʿĀMILĪ AL-IṢFAHĀNĪ (d. 1263):

Sharḥ al-Urjūza al-riḍāʿiyya
MSS: Fayḍiyya 1105 (cat., I, p.135); Majlis 5459/2, 642 Ṭabāṭabāʾī (cat., XVI, p.364); Marʿashī 3724 (cat., X, p.122)

MUḤAMMAD TAQĪ AL-NŪRĪ:

Risāla dar riḍāʿ, Persian
MS: Burūjirdī (AB, XI, p.190)

AL-ANṢĀRĪ:

Risāla fi ʾl-riḍāʿ
Edition: Tabrīz, 1375 (together with his *al-Makāsib*)
MS: Fayḍiyya 993/1 (cat., III, p.47)

AḤMAD AL-FAYḌĪ:

Risāla fi ʾl-riḍāʿ
MS: Gawharshād 38 (cat., p.361)

ZAYN AL-ʿĀBIDĪN B. MUḤAMMAD ʿALĪ AL-SABZAWĀRĪ AL-IṢFAHĀNĪ (d. after 1312):

- *Durrat al-durrayn*
  MS: Marʿashī 2404/2 (cat., VII, p.6)
- *Tuḥfat al-albān*
  MS: Gulpāyigānī 1627 (cat., II, p.155)

HĀDĪ AL-ṬIHRĀNĪ:

Risāla fi ʾl-riḍāʿ
MSS: Majlis 2714/2 (cat., IX, pp.19-20); Tustariyya 344/2 (cat., pp.853-4)

ĀL BAḤR AL-ʿULŪM:

Risāla fi ʾl-riḍāʿ, included in his *Bulghat al-faqīh* (see above, chapter 5)

AL-KHURĀSĀNĪ:

Risāla fi ʾl-riḍāʿ
Edition: Baghdad, 1331 (in his *Shadharāt*)
Commentary: by Mahdī al-Khāliṣī, edited Baghdad, 1331 (in his *al-Darārī al-lāmiʿāt*)

MUḤAMMAD HĀSHIM AL-KHURĀSĀNĪ:

Risāla-yi riḍā'iyya, Persian
Edition: Mashhad, 1340; Tehran, 1352

'ABD AL-HĀDĪ B. ISMĀ'ĪL AL-ḤUSAYNĪ AL-SHĪRĀZĪ:

Al-Riḍā', his lectures compiled by Muḥammad Taqī al-Tabrīzī
Edition: Najaf, 1372

AḤMAD AL-ZANJĀNĪ:

Riḍā'iyya, Persian
Edition: Qum, 1368

ANONYMOUS:

Risāla dar riḍā', Persian
MS: Gawharshād 1187/1 (cat., p.123)

7. ON TEMPORARY MARRIAGE

AL-MUFĪD:

Al-Mūjaz fi 'l-mut'a
MSS: Raḍawī 2427 (cat., II, p.67); Vatican 720/2 Arabic (cat., I, p.68)
Abridgement: by al-Karakī (d. 940), MS: Dānishgāh 2888/4 (cat., X, p.1733)

AL-MURTAḌĀ:

Mas'ala fī nikāḥ al-mut'a, included in his *Shatāt al-fawā'id* (see above, chapter 5)

AL-KARAKĪ:

Fā'ida fi 'l-mut'a
MSS: Dānishgāh 2144 (cat., IX, p.806); Leiden 967/3 Warn. (cat., IV, p.117)

AL-KHWĀJŪ'Ī:

Risāla fī jawāz ḥaml al-zawja al-munqaṭi'a min balad ilā ākhir
MS: Mashhad, Adabiyyāt 25/5 Fayyāḍ (cat., pp.211-12)

AL-KHURĀSĀNĪ:

Mas'ala fi 'l-ikhlāl bi-dhikr al-ajal fi 'l-mut'a
Edition: Tehran, 1318 (together with his *Durar al-fawā'id*)

8. ON NUPTIAL GIFT

AL-MUFĪD:

Risāla fi 'l-mahr
MS: Tustariyya 78/2 (cat., p.831)

BAHĀ' AL-DĪN AL-'ĀMILĪ:

Risāla fī jawāz man' al-zawja nafsahā 'an al-zawj ḥattā taqbiḍ al-mahr
MSS: Majlis 1805/55, 4900/51 (cat., IX, pp.357-8, XIV, pp.75-6); Dānishgāh 918/5 (cat., V, p.1784); Gulpāyigānī 16 (cat., I, p.136)

AḤMAD AL-BAḤRĀNĪ:

Risāla fī tamalluk al-mahr ajmaʻ bi-mujarrad al-ʻaqd
MS: Princeton 229/9 Yahuda (cat., p.138)

AḤMAD B. IBRĀHĪM B. ʻĪSĀ B. DARWĪSH AL-BAḤRĀNĪ (d. after 1171):

Risāla fī istiḥqāq al-mahr idhā māt aḥad al-zawjayn qabl al-dukhūl
MS: Princeton 229/8 Yahuda (cat., p.138)

AL-QUMMĪ:

Risāla fī mas'alat al-shīrbahā, included in his *al-Rasā'il* and his *Jawāmiʻ al-rasā'il* (see above, chapter 5)

ʻABD ALLĀH AL-MĀMAQĀNĪ:

Ghāyat al-su'ūl fī intiṣāf al-mahr bi 'l-mawt qabl al-dukhūl
Edition: Najaf, 1344 (in his *al-Ithnāʻashariyya*)

MUḤSIN AL-AMĪN AL-ʻĀMILĪ:

Ḍiyā' al-ʻuqūl fī ḥukm al-mahr adhā māt aḥad al-zawjayn qabl al-dukhūl
Edition: Sidon, 1332

9. ON CHILDREN

ḤUSAYN AL-QAZWĪNĪ:

Risāla fī ḥukm mawt al-walad fī baṭn ummih wa ḥayātih maʻ mawt al-umm
MSS: Raḍawī 2595/7 (cat., II, p.118); Zanjānī 76/7 (cat., pp.220-1)

10. ON MAINTENANCE

AL-KIRMĀNSHĀHĪ:

Muẓhir al-mukhtār fī ḥukm al-nikāḥ maʻ al-iʻsār
MSS: Majlis 5325/2 (cat., XVI, p.2347); Ilāhiyyāt 98/3 Āl Āqā, 828/3d (cat., I, p.714, II, p.23); Zanjān (cat., p.143)

ʻABD ALLĀH AL-KIRMĀNSHĀHĪ:

Mas'ala fī nafaqat al-zawja al-mufḍaya
MS: Ilāhiyyāt 819/4d (cat., II, p.20)

MUḤAMMAD B. ʻĀSHŪR AL-KIRMĀNSHĀHĪ:

Risāla fī nafaqat al-zawja
MS: Marʻashī 2575/3 (cat., VII, p.164)

MUḤAMMAD BĀQIR B. MUḤAMMAD ḤASAN AL-BĪRJANDĪ (d. 1352):

Risāla fī iʻsār al-zawj
MS: Marʻashī 3410/1 (cat., IX, p.193)

D

ON UNILATERAL OBLIGATIONS

DIVORCE

AL-MURTAḌĀ:

Mas'ala fi 'l-ṭalāq al-thalāth bi-lafẓ wāḥid, included in his *Shatāt al-fawā'id* (see above, chapter 5)

AL-KARAKĪ:

Risāla fī ṭalāq al-ghā'ib
MS: Sipahsālār 2919/21 (cat., V, p.306); Shīrāz, Dānishgāh

AL-SHAHĪD AL-THĀNĪ:

Risāla fī ṭalāq al-ḥā'iḍ wa 'l-ghā'ib, included in his *Majmū'at al-ifādāt* (see above, chapter 5)

'ABD ALLĀH AL-TUSTARĪ:

Risāla fi 'l-ṭalāq al-rajʿī, included in his *al-Rasā'il* (see above, chapter 5)

AḤMAD AL-BAḤRĀNĪ (d. 1131):

Risāla fī anna 'l-ṭalqa wa 'l-ṭalqatayn hal tabqā bi 'l-taḥlīl aw tan'adim
MS: Princeton 229/18 Yahuda (cat., p.139)

AL-KHWĀJŪ'Ī:

- *Fā'ida fī ṭalāq al-walī*
  MS: Princeton 1317 New Series (fols. 45b-46a)

- *Al-Farq bayn al-ṭalāq al-rajʿī wa 'l-bā'in*
  MS: Mar'ashī 3112/2 (cat., VIII, p.337)

AL-QUMMĪ:

- *Risāla fī infirād al-ṭalāq bi-'iwaḍ 'an al-khul'*, included in his *al-Rasā'il* and *Jawāmi' al-rasā'il* (see above, chapter 5).

- *Ḥukm al-ṭalāq bi-da'wā al-wikāla 'an al-zawj ma' inkārih*
  MS: Mar'ashī 1259/9 (cat., IV, p.63); Zanjān (cat., p.142)

- *Risāla fī da'wā al-ṭalāq ma' inkār al-zawja*, included in his *al-Rasā'il* (see above, chapter 5)

- *Risāla fī iqrār al-rajul bi-ṭalāq zawjatih*
  MS: Mar'ashī 1259/8 (cat., IV, p.62)

ANONYMOUS (mid-13th century):

Risāla fī ḥukm ṭalāq mudda'ī al-wikāla 'an al-zawj ma' inkār al-zawj, as a commentary on al-Qummī's second treatise above
MS: Fayḍiyya 1373/1 (cat., III, p.87)

ṢĀḤIB AL-MAQĀBIS:

Mablagh al-naẓar wa natījat al-fikar = Risāla fī iqrār al-zawj bi-ṭalāq zawjatih
MSS: Dānishgāh 1827/2 (cat., VIII, p.424); Princeton 3737/1 New Series; Fayḍiyya 17/3 (cat., III, p.1); Burūjirdī (AB, XIX, p.57)

IBN ṬAWQ AL-BAḤRĀNĪ:

Mas'ala fī ṭalāq al-ḥā'iḍ,
MS: Marʿashī 2538/15 (cat., VI, p.339)

AL-SHAFTĪ:

- *Risāla fī ṭalāq muddaʿī al-wikāla ʿan al-zawj maʿ inkār al-zawj*
  MS: Fayḍiyya 1089/5 (cat., III, p.54)
- *Risāla fī ḥukm ṣulḥ ḥaqq al-rujūʿ fi 'l-ṭalāq al-rajʿī*
  MS: Marʿashī 3393/1 (cat., IX, p.179)

MUḤAMMAD SHAFĪʿ B. ʿABD AL-MAJĪD AL-MĀZANDARĀNĪ:

Risāla fī ṣulḥ ḥaqq al-rujūʿ fi 'l-ṭalāq
MS: Marʿashī 1798/2 (cat., V, p.184)

MUḤAMMAD TAQĪ AL-HARAWĪ:

- *Risāla fī ṭalāq al-zawja bi-ʿiwaḍ minhā*
  MS: Dānishgāh 3713/1 (cat., XII, p.2712)
- *Ḥāshiya ʿalā Risālat ṭalāq al-zawja bi-ʿiwaḍ minhā*, a commentary on al-Qummī's first treatise above
  MS: Dānishgāh 3713/2 (cat., XII, p.2713)

ʿABD AL-ḤUSAYN B. ʿALĪ AL-ṬIHRĀNĪ, SHAYKH AL-ʿIRĀQAYN (d. 1286):

Mas'ala fī tawkīl al-zawja fi 'l-ṭalāq ḍimn ʿaqd lāzim
MS: Dānishgāh 770/1 (cat., V, p.1798)

AL-KHURĀSĀNĪ:

Maqāla fi 'l-ṭalāq
Edition: Baghdad, 1331 (in his *Shadharāt*)

MUḤAMMAD BĀQIR AL-BĪRJANDĪ:

Risāla fi 'l-rujūʿ fi 'l-ṭalāq
MS: Marʿashī 3410/2 (cat., IX, p.194)

EXPIATION

AL-MAJLISĪ II:

Risāla dar kaffārāt, Persian
MSS: Marʿashī 187/4, 1683/3 (cat., I, p.206, V, p.78); Gulpāyigānī 1223/5 (cat., II, p.236)

MANUMISSION

MUḤAMMAD ṢĀLIḤ AL-KHWĀTŪNĀBĀDĪ:

Ādab-i saniyya, Persian
MS: Rawḍātī (cat., I, pp.72 ff)

MUḤAMMAD ASHRAF B. ʿABD AL-ḤASĪB AL-ḤUSAYNĪ:

Risāla dar tadbīr-i ʿabd, Persian
MS: Dānishgāh 5894/4 (cat., XVI, p.136)

AL-QUMMĪ:

Risāla fī mālikiyyat al-ʿabd, included in his *al-Rasāʾil* (see above, chapter 5)

AḤMAD B. ʿALĪ MUKHTĀR AL-GULPĀYIGĀNĪ:

Izāḥat al-shukūk fī tamalluk al-mamlūk
MS: Marʿashī 3401 (cat., IX, p.185)

MUḤAMMAD ʿALĪ AL-SHAFTĪ:

Risāla fī itlāf al-ʿabd māl al-mawlā wa jināyatih ʿalayh
MS: Marʿashī 1995/1 (cat., V, p.366)

CONFESSION

ḤUSAYN B. ʿABD AL-ṢAMAD:

Risāla fi ʾl-iqrār, as a commentary on the relevant chapter of al-ʿAllāma's *Qawāʿid al-aḥkām*
MSS: Dānishgāh 918/6 (cat., V, pp.1865-6); Majlis 4900/49 (cat., XIV, p.74)

AL-QUMMĪ:

Risāla fī iqrār al-rajul bi-ṭalāq zawjatih (see above, monographs on divorce)

ṢĀḤIB AL-MAQĀBIS:

Mablagh al-naẓar (see above, monographs on divorce)

AL-ANṢĀRĪ:

Risāla fī qāʿidat man malak shayʾan malak al-iqrār bih
Editions: Tabrīz, 1303 (together with his *K. al-Ṭahāra*), 1375 (together with his *al-Makāsib*)
Commentary: by ʿAbd Allāh al-Māmaqānī, edited Najaf, 1345 (in his *al-Qalāʾid al-thamīna*)

ʿABD ALLĀH AL-MĀMAQĀNĪ:

Risāla fī iqrār baʿḍ al-waratha bi-dayn wa inkār al-bāqī
Edition: Najaf, 1344 (in his *al-Ithnāʿashariyya*)

OATHS AND VOWS

1. GENERAL

ANONYMOUS (belonging to 10th century):

Aḥkām-i yamīn wa nadhr wa ʿahd, Persian
MS: Marʿashī 3048/6 (cat., VIII, p.267)

AL-MAJLISĪ II:

Risāla dar nadhr, Persian
MS: Gawharshād 1169 (cat., p.192)

RAḌĪ AL-DĪN B. MUḤAMMAD NABĪ AL-QAZWĪNĪ:

Risāla fī 'l-nadhr
MS: Zanjān (cat., p.130)

JAMĀL AL-DĪN AL-KHWĀNSĀRĪ:

Risāla fī 'l-nadhr
MS: Majlis 84/2 Khu'ī (cat., VII, p.388)

2. SPECIFIC

ʿABD ALLĀH AL-TUSTARĪ:

Risāla fī anna 'l-nadhr hal yataʿallaq bi 'l-mubāḥ, included in his *al-Rasā'il* (see above, chapter 5)

MUḤAMMAD RIḌĀ AL-MĀZANDARĀNĪ (early 12th century):

Risāla dar nadhr-i muʿallaq bi-baʿd az marg, Persian
MS: Marʿashī 3312/2 (cat., IX, p.93)

AL-MUKHTĀRĪ:

- *ʿUmdat al-nāẓir fī ʿuqdat al-nādhir - Risāla fī buṭlān al-nadhr al-muʿallaq bi-mā maʿd al-mawt*
  MS: Dānishgāh 4002 (cat., XII, p.2991)
- *Inārat al-ṭurūs*, a commentary on a sentence of the chapter on vow of al-Shahīd al-Awwal's *al-Durūs al-sharʿiyya*
  MS: Marʿashī 3382/3 (cat., IX, pp.159-60)

AL-SARĀB:

Risāla dar nadhr-i taṣadduq, Persian
MS: Dānishgāh 2091/9 (cat., VIII, p. 716)

E

ON 'RULES'

HUNTING AND SLAUGHTERING

. GENERAL

USAYN B. RŪḤ ALLĀH AL-ḤUSAYNĪ AL-ṬABASĪ (late 10th century):

Shikārnāma = Ṣayd wa dhabāḥa, Persian
MS: Āṣafiyya 155 Shīʿī law (cat., II, pp.254-5); Malik 1644 (AB, XV, p.105)

L-SHĪRWĀNĪ:

Risāla dar ṣayd wa dhabāḥa, Persian
MS: Fayḍiyya 1665/5 (cat., III, p.113); Iṣfahān, Adabiyyāt (*Nash.*, V, p.304)

UḤAMMAD B. MUḤAMMAD RIḌĀ AL-QUMMĪ (late 11th century):

K. al-Ṣayd wa 'l-dhabā'iḥ
MS: Masjid-i Aʿẓam 3134

ALĪ B. ḤUSAYN AL-KARBALĀ'Ī:

Aḥkām-i ṣayd wa dhabā'iḥ, Persian
MS: Marʿashī (AB, XV, p.106)

ABD AL-KARĪM B. MUḤAMMAD HĀDĪ AL-ṬABASĪ (early 12th century):

Tabṣirat al-Shīʿa fī aḥkām al-dhabīḥa, Persian
MS: Tiflis 440/2 (*Nash.*, VIII, p.221)

UḤAMMAD TAQĪ AL-NŪRĪ:

Risāla fi 'l-ṣayd wa 'l-dhabāḥa, Persian
MS: Ḥujjatiyya 612 (cat., p.25)

ALĪ AL-QĀRPŪZĀBĀDĪ:

K. al-Ṣayd wa 'l-dhabā'iḥ, Persian
Edition: Tehran, 1288

. SPECIFIC

L-MUFĪD:

Risāla fī taḥrīm dhabā'iḥ Ahl al-Kitāb
MSS: Sipahsālār 2533/7 (cat., IV, p.546); Dānishgāh 6914/21 (cat., XVI, p.398); Berlin 10276/fols. 43b-47 (Sezgin, I, p.550); Marʿashī 3694/1 (cat., X, p.92)

UḤAMMAD B. ḤĀRITH AL-MANṢŪRĪ AL-BAḤRĀNĪ (d. after 952):

Mas'ala fī ishtirāṭ istiqrār al-ḥayāt fi 'l-dhabīḥa
MS: Majlis 2761/7 (cat., IX, p.159)

L-ARDABĪLĪ:

Mas'ala fi 'l-dhibḥ = Risāla fī kifāyat basmalat al-dhābiḥ al-junub wa

in qaṣad qirāʾat iḥdā al-suwar al-ʿazāʾim
MS: Tabrīz, Qāḍī (*Nash.*, VII, p.522)

AL-MUJTAHID:

Risāla fī ḥukm dhabāʾiḥ Ahl al-Kitāb
MS: Majlis 3988/7 (cat., X, p.2165)

BAHĀʾ AL-DĪN AL-ʿĀMILĪ:

Risāla fī dhabāʾiḥ Ahl al-Kitāb
Edition: Tehran, 1315 (in the collection of *Kalimāt al-muḥaqqiqīn*)
Selected MSS: Gulpāyigānī 146/6, 245/3, 243/3 (cat., I, pp.136, 228, 229); Dānishgāh 944/8, 3119/5, 4448/1, 5873/5 (cat., V, pp.1879-80, XI, p. 2073, XIII, p.3406, XVI, p.117); Marʿashī 1003/6, 3667/2 (cat., III, p.195, X, p.59); Millī 1391 Arabic (cat., IX, p.401); Princeton 151/4 New Series; Baku M140.25 (*Nash.*, IX, p.240)

MUḤAMMAD TAQĪ B. ḤUSAYN AL-NAQAWĪ AL-NAṢĪRĀBĀDĪ (d. 1289):

Risāla fī dhabāʾiḥ Ahl al-Kitāb, Persian
Edition: Locknow (AB, XX, p.387)

BANDA ḤUSAYN B. MUḤAMMAD AL-NAQAWĪ AL-NAṢĪRĀBĀDĪ (d. 1295):

Risāla fī dhabāʾiḥ Ahl al-Kitāb, Urdu
Edition: Locknow (AB, XX, p.387)

ABU ʾL-QĀSIM AL-RAḌAWĪ AL-LĀHŪRĪ (early 14th century):

Al-Jawāb bi ʾl-ṣawāb fī ḥurmat dhabāʾiḥ Ahl al-Kitāb
Edition: Lahore, 1316

FOOD AND DRINK

1. GENERAL

ANONYMOUS (belonging to 8th-9th centuries):

Khulāṣat al-bayān, Persian
MS: Marʿashī 3008/16 (cat., VIII, p.192)

RAḌĪ AL-DĪN MUḤAMMAD B. ḤUSAYN AL-KHWĀNSĀRĪ (early 12th century):

Māʾida-yi samāwiyya, Persian
MSS: Marʿashī 204 (cat., I, p.234); Majlis 1048 (AB, XIX, p.10); Tabrīz, Millī (ibid.)

2. SPECIFIC

AL-SHAYKH

Masʾala fī taḥrīm al-fuqqāʿ
MSS: Bodleian Arab.f.64/fols. 92b-97b; Tustariyya 300/8 (cat., p.850); Ḥakīm 364; Rawḍātī (Ḥujjatī, p.627)

MĀJID AL-SHAYBĀNĪ:

Risāla fī ḥilliyyat al-ʿinab wa ʾl-zabīb al-mulqayayn fī ʾl-khill li-kasb al-ḥumūḍa
MS: Marʿashī (AB, XI, p.177)

AL-KHWĀJŪ'Ī:

Risāla fī jawāz al-tadāwī bi 'l-khamr
MS: Marʻashī 1142/4 (cat., III, p.316)

AL-QUMMĪ:

Risāla fī ḥukm al-anfiḥa al-ma'khūdha min al-mayta, included in his *Jawāmiʻ al-rasā'il* (see above, chapter 5)

ʻABD ALLĀH AL-KIRMĀNSHĀHĪ:

Risāla fī ḥukm al-safarjal al-mughlā fi 'l-ʻaṣīr al-ʻinabī qabl dhihāb al-thuluthayn
MS: Ilāhiyyāt 819/1d (cat., II, p.19)

3. ON TOBACCO

AL-ḤURR AL-ʻĀMILĪ:

Risāla fī ḥurmat shurb al-tutun wa 'l-qahwa, included in his *al-Fawā'id al-Ṭūsiyya* (edited Qum, 1404)
MSS: Majlis 1805/110, 4900/109 (cat., IX, pp.383-4, XIV, pp.104-5); Dānishgāh 1699/4 (cat., VIII, p.251)

AL-AKHBĀRĪ:

Risāla fī ḥurmat al-ghalyan, Persian
MS: Wazīrī 135/7 (cat., I, p.176)

ANONYMOUS (written before 1257):

Risāla fī ḥurmat al-tanbāk
MS: Marʻashī 750.8 (cat., II, p.355)

MUḤAMMAD B. ʻABD AL-WAHHĀB AL-KĀẒIMĪ:

Durrat al-aslāk fī ḥukm dukhān al-tanbāk
MS: Ḥakīm 386m

4. ON EPIDEMICS

NIʻMAT ALLĀH AL-JAZĀ'IRĪ:

Musakkin al-shujūn fī ḥukm al-firār min al-wabā' wa 'l-ṭāʻūn
MSS: Dānishgāh 587 (cat., V, pp.2042-3); Sipahsālār 5551 (cat., V, p.566); Malik 1868 (cat., I, p.674); Marʻashī 3442 (cat., IX, pp. 228-9)

BAḤR AL-ʻULŪM:

Risāla fī ḥukm al-firār min al-ṭāʻūn
MS: Tehran, Muḥīṭ (AB, XI, p.208)

MUḤAMMAD JAʻFAR AL-ASTARĀBĀDĪ:

Safīnat al-najāt fī ḥukm al-firār min al-wabā' wa 'l-ṭāʻūn
MS: Marʻashī 2437/2 (cat., VII, p.31)

USURPATION

1. GENERAL

AL-ANṢĀRĪ:

K. al-Ghaṣb
MS: Tustariyya (AB, XVI, p.57)

MUḤAMMAD JAʿFAR B. MUḤAMMAD ḤUSAYN AL-ṬIHRĀNĪ (late 13th century):

K. al-Ghaṣb
MS: Fayḍiyya (cat., III, p.20)

AḤMAD AL-FAYḌĪ:

K. al-Ghaṣb
MS: Tustariyya (AB., XVI, p.56)

AL-RASHTĪ:

K. al-Ghaṣb
Edition: Tehran, 1322
MSS: Malik 2398 (cat., I, p.527); Majlis 3352/1 (cat., X, pp.1175-6); Tustariyya (AB, XIII, p.319)

MUḤAMMAD TAQĪ B. MUḤAMMAD BĀQIR AL-MASJIDSHĀHĪ (d. 1332):

Risāla fī 'l-ghaṣb
Edition: Tehran, 1327

2. SPECIFIC

ANONYMOUS:

Risāla fī annah hal yaḍmin ghāṣib al-khamr
MS: Dānishgāh 1118/2 (cat., V, pp.1899-900)

PRE-EMPTION

AL-KHWĀJŪ'Ī:

Al-Fuṣūl al-khamsa fī 'l-shufʿa
MS: Dānishgāh 791/1 (cat., V, p.1961)

RECLAMATION

1. GENERAL

MUḤAMMAD SAʿĪD B. QĀSIM AL-ḤUSAYNĪ AL-ṬABĀṬABĀ'Ī AL-QUHPĀ'Ī (d. 1092):

Rawḍ al-jinān
MS: Fayḍiyya 2037 (cat., I, pp.120-1)

MUḤSIN AL-KHANFAR:

K. Iḥyā' al-mawāt, his lectures compiled by Abū Ṭālib al-Qā'inī
MS: Marʿashī 1520 (cat., IV, p.322)

L-RASHTĪ:

K. Iḥyā' al-mawāt
MS: Tustariyya 622/2 (cat., p.869)

SPECIFIC

L-KARAKĪ:

Risāla fi 'l-arḍ al-mundarisa
MSS: Raḍawī 2443, 7618 (cat., II, p.69; Bīnish, pp.784, 798); Dānishgāh 6958/1 (cat., XVI, p.411); Sipahsālār 3392/2 (cat., III, p.111); Majlis 3147/8 (cat., X, p.725); Mar'ashī 1409/3 (cat., IV, p.186); Gulpāyigānī 146 (cat., I, p.136); Fayḍiyya 1290/13 (cat., III, p.75)

L-SHAFTĪ:

Kārīziyya, Persian
MS: Gawharshād 1094 (cat., p.131)

UḤAMMAD BĀQIR B. ZAYN AL-'ĀBIDĪN AL-KHWĀNSĀRĪ (d. 1313):

Al-Nahriyya
Edition: Iṣfahān, 1377
MS: Dānishgāh 1836/2 (cat., VIII, p.431)

FOUND PROPERTY

L-ANṢĀRĪ:

K. al-Luqaṭa
MS: Ma'had 1295 (cat., p.112)

L-RASHTĪ:

K. al-Luqaṭa
MSS: Majlis 37 Ṭabāṭabā'ī; Masjid-i A'ẓam 11793

INHERITANCE

GENERAL

L-SHAYKH:

Al-Ījāz fi 'l-farā'iḍ
Edition: Najaf, 1383
MSS: Millī 1943/9 Arabic (cat., X, p.920); Raḍawī 6039 (cat., V, p.372); Ḥakīm 364 (cat., I, p.79); Tustariyya 300/10 (cat., p.850); Mar'ashī (Ḥujjatī, p.624); Burūjirdī 218/3, 646 (ibid.)

U'ĪN AL-DĪN AL-MIṢRĪ:

Al-Ma'ūna fī masā'il al-mīrāth
MS: Masjid-i A'ẓam 3085/2

NONYMOUS:

Risāla fi 'l-mawārīth
MS: Masjid-i A'ẓam 3085/4

NAṢĪR AL-DĪN AL-ṬŪSĪ - Abū Jaʿfar Muḥammad b. Muḥammad b. Ḥasan (d. 672):

- *Al-Bayyināt fī taḥrīr al-mawārīth*
  MS: Dānishgāh 7689/4 (cat., XVI, p.672)

- *Jawāhir al-ḥaqā'iq = al-Farā'iḍ al-Naṣīriyya*
  Selected MSS: Marʿashī 49/1, 2264/2, 3457/2 (cat., I, pp. 60-1, VI, p.248, IX, p.256); Millī 1247/2 Arabic, 795/2f (cat., II, p.322, IX, p.232); Raḍawī 2749, 5711 (cat., V, p.470); Masjid-i Aʿẓam 3085/5; Adabiyyāt 70/4d (cat., p.191); Dānishgāh 7684/3 (cat., XVI, p.670)
  Commentaries: (1) *al-Mas'ala al-nāfiʿa li 'l-mabāḥith al-jāmiʿa li-aqsā al-wārith*, by al-Sayyid ʿAmīd al-Dīn, edited Tehran, 1315 (in the collection of *Kalimāt al-muḥaqqiqīn*), 1318 (together with al-Khurāsānī's *Durar al-farā'id*), MSS: Millī 795/2f (cat., II, p.323); Majlis 2719/7 (cat., IX, pp.42-3); Gulpāyigānī 2397/2 (cat., III, p.245); Marʿashī 2362/3 (cat., VI, p.345); (2) *al-Durra al-durriyya*, by Fakhr al-Dīn Aḥmad b. Muḥammad al-Sabīʿī, MSS: Millī 795/5f (cat., II, p.324); Dār al-Kutub 20039 (cat., I, p.310); (3) by ʿAbd al-Ḥayy al-Ashraqī al-Jurjānī, MS: Millī 795/7f (cat., II, p.326); (4) by Abu 'l-Ḥasan b. Aḥmad al-Abīwardī (mid-10th century), MSS: Millī 795/8 (cat., II, pp.326-7); Wazīrī 1264/3, 1243/2 (cat., III, pp.904, 910); Tustariyya 857/9 (cat., p.877); Marʿashī 2264/3, 99/2, 2362/4, 478/5 (cat., II, pp.83, 117, VI, p.248, 345); Dānishgāh 781, 6262, 7176/11, 7171/3 (cat., V, pp.1936-8, XVI, pp.225, 474); Āṣafiyya 119 Shīʿī law (cat., II, pp.247-8); Sinā 225 (cat., I, p.105); Mashhad, Adabiyyāt 59/4 Fayyāḍ (cat., p.193); Raḍawī 6513 (cat., V, p.458); (5) Persian, anonymous, MSS: Sinā 225/6 (cat., I, p.106); Ilāhiyyāt 293/1 (cat., I, p.275); (6) by Bahā' al-Dīn al-ʿĀmilī, MS: Raḍawī 2359 (cat., II, pp.45-6); (7) by ʿAbd Allāh b. Khalīl (d. after 1006), MS: Sinā 225/8 (cat., I, p.106)

AL-ʿALLĀMA:

Risāla fi 'l-mawārīth
MS: Masjid-i Aʿẓam 3085/7

IBN AL-MUTAWWIJ:

Al-Farā'iḍ
MS: Iṣfahān, Adabiyyāt (*Nash.*, V, p.302)

ʿALĪ B. ḤASAN AL-KHAṬṬĪ (early 9th century):

Al-Farā'iḍ
MSS: Marʿashī 3457/3, 2005, 2362/2 (cat., IV, p.8, VI, pp.343-4, IX, p.256); Gulpāyigānī 1993/1 (cat., III, p.130); Iṣfahān, Dānishgāh 17058/1 (cat., p.928)

AL-KARAKĪ:

Sharḥ mabḥath al-mīrāth min al-Mukhtaṣar al-nāfiʿ (see AB, VI, pp. 193-4)
MSS: Dānishgāh 1643/4 (cat., VIII, p.220, see also XVI, pp. 369, 62 for MSS 6817/2, 7564/2); Majlis 5059/1 (cat., XV, pp.20-1)

AL-SHAHĪD AL-THĀNĪ:

Al-Ḥāshiya ʿalā k. al-farā'iḍ min al-Mukhtaṣar al-nāfiʿ
MS: Majlis 5340/1 (cat., XVI, p.251)

ONYMOUS (written before 924):

Risāla fi 'l-mīrāth
MS: Majlis 2719/6 (cat., IX, p.42)

JḤAMMAD B. AḤMAD B. ABĪ ṬĀLIB (9th-10th century):

Al-Farā'iḍ
MS: Tehran, Farhād Mu'tamid (cat., p.223)

ONYMOUS (written before 1039):

Risāla mukhtaṣara fi 'l-mawārīth
MS: Masjid-i A'ẓam 3085/3

JḤ ALLĀH AL-ḤĀFIẒ:

Mawārīth, Persian
MS: Millī 1966/4f (cat., IV, pp.453-4)

ONYMOUS (belonging to 10th century)

Sharḥ k. al-farā'iḍ min al-Muktaṣar al-nāfi'
MSS: Majlis 5340/4 (cat., XVI, p.252); Gawharshād 940/1, 1808/1 (cat., p.280); Burūjirdī, 2 MSS (AB, XIII, p.379, XIV, p.97)

BD ALLĀH B. KHALĪL:

Risāla fi 'l-mawārīth
MSS: Masjid-i A'ẓam 3085/6; Raḍawī 2757 (cat., V, p.445); Dānishgāh 7684 (cat., XVI, p.670); Sinā 225/7 (cat., I, p.106)

LĪ B. MUḤYĪ AL-DĪN AL-JĀMI'Ī AL-'ĀMILĪ (d. after 1008):

Risāla fi 'l-mīrāth
MSS: Adabiyyāt 243/8 Kirmān (cat., p.38); Wazīrī 2344/2 (cat., IV, p.1258); Fayḍiyya 1484/5 (cat., III, p.94)

AHĀ' AL-DĪN AL-'ĀMILĪ:

Al-Farā'iḍ al-bahā'iyya, the chapter on inheritance of his *al-Ḥabl al-matīn* (see above, chapter 5)
Commentary: by Muḥyī al-Dīn b. 'Abd al-Laṭīf al-Jāmi'ī (11th century), MSS: Mar'ashī 1118/4, 2362/10 (cat., III, pp.289-90, VI, p.346)

Risāla fi 'l-mawārīth
MSS: Gulpāyigānī 1114/2 (cat., II, p.227); Raḍawiyya 87/4 (cat., p.55); Wazīrī 1060/3 (cat., III, p.839)

UḤAMMAD QĀSIM AL-SĀWIJĪ, KHUDĀBAKHSH (d. after 1033):

Tuḥafa-yi Rafī'ī, Persian
Selected MSS: Dānishgāh 5822 (cat., XVI, pp.98-9); Millī 939/2f (cat., II, p.479); Majlis 7455, 9396; Fayḍiyya 935 (cat., II, p.11); Gulpāyigānī 95 (cat., I, p.95); Mar'ashī 99, 3100 (cat., I, p.117, VIII, p.323); Masjid-i A'ẓam 340, 16543

U'IZZ AL-DĪN AL-MŪSAWĪ:

Al-'Ashara al-kāmila
MS: Mar'ashī 3630/1 (cat., X, p.30)

ʻABD AL-ḤASĪB B. AḤMAD AL-ʻĀMILĪ (late 11th century):

Risāla dar irth, Persian
MS: Majlis 5213/1 (cat., XVI, p.44)

JAMĀL AL-DĪN B. ʻALĪJĀN AL-NAṬANZĪ (mid-11th century):

Ithnāʻashariyya, Persian
MS: Dānishgāh 723/2 (cat., V, p.1763)

MUḤAMMAD ṬĀHIR AL-QUMMĪ:

Tuḥfat al-dārayn
MS: Dānishgāh 3317/15 (cat., XI, p.2301)

ʻABD AL-SALĀM AL-ANṢĀRĪ (11th century):

Sharḥ-i mabḥath-i irth az Irshād al-adhhān, Persian
MS: Dānishgāh 4408 (cat., XIII, p.3368)

AL-ḤURR AL-ʻĀMILĪ:

Khulāṣat al-abḥāth
MSS: Majlis 4471/9, 109/1 Khu'ī (cat., VII, p.115, XII, p.147); Millī 795/6f (cat., II, p.395); Gulpāyigānī 327/6 (cat., I, p.282); Malik (AB, VII, p.209); Fayḍiyya 1493/3 (cat., III, p.94)

MUḤAMMAD ṢĀLIḤ AL-ASTARĀBĀDĪ (early 12th century):

Ḥāshiyat k. al-farā'iḍ min al-Sharā'iʻ
MS: Mahdawī 592/15 (cat., p.126)

AL-MUKHTĀRĪ:

- *Risāla dar irth*, Persian
  MS: Dānishgāh 1860 (cat., VIII, p.461)
- *Taqwīm al-mīrāth*
  MSS: Fayḍiyya 1417 (cat., II, p.38)

ṢADR AL-DĪN MUḤAMMAD AL-ṬABĀṬABĀ'Ī AL-YAZDĪ:

Al-Farā'iḍ
MS: Wazīrī 320/1 (cat., I, p.303)

ṢĀḤIB AL-ḤADĀ'IQ:

Al-Risāla al-Muḥammadiyya
MSS: Ḥakīm 242 (*Nawādir*, pp.43-5); Dānishgāh 7712/5 (cat., XVI, p.682); Majlis 337 Ṭabāṭabā'ī, 3341/2 (cat., X, pp.1139-40); Gulpāyigānī 307/2 (cat., I, p.267); Marʻashī 1670/1 (cat., V, p.67); Iṣfahān, Dānishgāh 16914/1 (cat., p.923); Raḍawī 6468 (cat., V, p.443)

ʻABD AL-ʻAẒĪM B. MUḤAMMAD MAʻṢŪM (12th/early 13th century):

Risāla dar mawārīth, Persian
MS: Burūjirdī (AB, XXIII, p.218)

AL-QUMMĪ:

Risāla fi 'l-mīrāth, included in his *al-Rasā'il* and his *Jawāmiʻ al-rasā'il* (see above, chapter 5)

UḤAMMAD SHAFĪʿ B. MUḤAMMAD AL-ĪRAWĀNĪ (d. after 1256):

Miṣbāḥ al-hidāya
MS: Marʿashī 2362/1 (cat., VI, p.343)

ASAN ĀL KĀSHIF AL-GHIṬĀʾ:

Al-Mawārīth
MSS: Mahdawī 810/3 (cat., p.128); Mashhad, Bāqiriyya (AB, I, p.443)

ABD AL-ʿALĪ B. MUḤAMMAD AL-HARANDĪ (late 13th century)

Ṣaḥīfat al-mīrāth
MS: Marʿashī 1810 (cat., V, p.195)

L-ANṢĀRĪ:

Fāʾida fi ʾl-mawārīth
Editions: Tabrīz, 1303 (together with his *K. al-Ṭahāra*), 1375 (together with his *al-Makāsib*)

UḤAMMAD TAQĪ B. ḤUSAYN AL-NAQAWĪ AL-NAṢĪRĀBĀDĪ (d. 1289):

Risāla-yi irth, Urdu
Edition: Locknow

UḤSIN B. MUḤAMMAD RAFĪʿ AL-RASHTĪ (late 13th century):

Madīnat al-abḥāth
MS: Marʿashī 1379/4 (cat., IV, p.153)

BU ʾL-QĀSIM B. MUḤAMMAD ʿALĪ AL-KALĀNTAR AL-ṬIHRĀNĪ (d. 1292):

Risāla fi ʾl-irth
MS: Sipahsālār 2426 (cat., I, p.419)

UḤAMMAD BĀQIR B. MURTAḌĀ AL-ṬABĀṬABĀʾĪ AL-YAZDĪ (d. 1298):

Sharḥ Urjūza fi ʾl-mawārīth
MS: Marʿashī 2128/5 (cat., VI, p.140)

UḤAMMAD TAQĪ AL-HARAWĪ:

Risāla fi ʾl-irth
Edition: Tehran, 1404
MSS: Marʿashī 2362/3 + 12 (cat., VI, pp.344, 347); Tustariyya (AB, I, p.442)

INĀYAT ALLĀH B. ABI ʾL-FATḤ (13th century):

Risāla fi ʾl-irth
MS: Marʿashī 2362/11 (cat., VI, p.347)

ALĪ NAQĪ B. MUḤAMMAD RIḌĀ AL-ANṢĀRĪ AL-TABRĪZĪ (d. after 1312):

Majmaʿ al-rashād
MSS: Marʿashī 2021 (cat., VI, pp.22-3); Dānishgāh 2723 (cat., X, p.1598)

AYN AL-ʿĀBIDĪN AL-SABZAWĀRĪ:

Thamarat al-fuʾād
MS: Marʿashī 2404/1 (cat., VII, p.5)

AL-RASHTĪ:

K. al-Irth
MS: Dānishgāh 6711/3 (cat., XVI, p.343)

MUḤAMMAD JAʿFAR AL-ḤUSAYNĪ AL-KĀSHĀNĪ:

Risāla fī 'l-farā'iḍ
Edition: Tehran, 1315

ḤASAN AL-ḤUSAYNĪ:

Risāla dar irth, Persian
MS: Marʿashī 3265/1 (cat., IX, pp.53-4)

HĀDĪ AL-ṬIHRĀNĪ:

Risāla fī 'l-irth
MS: Majlis 2755/1 (cat., IX, p.142)

ĀL BAḤR AL-ʿULŪM:

Risāla fī 'l-mawārīth, included in his *Bulghat al-faqīh* (see above, chapter 5)

MUḤAMMAD HĀSHIM AL-KHURĀSĀNĪ:

Risāla-yi irth, Persian
Editions: Mashhad, 1340; Tehran, 1352, 1381 (with al-Khumaynī's footnotes)

2. ON RIGHT OF PRIMOGENITURE

AL-SHAHĪD AL-THĀNĪ:

Risāla fī 'l-ḥabwa wa aḥkāmihā, included in his *Majmūʿat al-ifādāt* (see above, chapter 5)

AL-SHĪRWĀNĪ:

Risāla dar ḥabwa, Persian
MS: Fayḍiyya 1665/21 (cat., III, p.113); Iṣfahān, Adabiyyāt (*Nash.*, V, p.304); Dānishgāh 7008/20 (cat., XVI, p.427)

AL-KHWĀJŪ'Ī:

Risāla fī 'l-ḥabwa
MSS: Marʿashī 1142/2 (cat., III, p.315); Dānishgāh 7103/4 (cat., XVI, p.455)

IBN ṬAWQ AL-BAḤRĀNĪ:

Jawāb mas'ala ʿan al-ḥabwa
MS: Marʿashī 2358/14 (cat., VI, pp.338-9)

MUḤAMMAD B. ʿĀSHŪR AL-KIRMĀNSHĀHĪ:

Risāla fī 'l-ḥabwa
MS: Marʿashī 2575/2 (cat., VII, p.164)

ʿALĪ B. RIḌĀ ĀL BAḤR AL-ʿULŪM:

Risāla fī 'l-ḥabwa
Edition: Tehran, 1290-1 (together with his *al-Burhān al-qāṭiʿ*)

ḤAMMAD ṬĀHĀ NAJAF (d. 1323):

Risāla fi 'l-ḥabwa
Edition: Najaf, 1324 (together with his *al-Inṣāf*)

BD ALLĀH AL-MĀMAQĀNĪ:

Tuḥfat al-ṣafwa
Edition: Tabrīz, 1320

ON WIFE'S SHARE

-SHAHĪD AL-THĀNĪ:

Risāla fī mīrāth al-zawja, included in his *Majmūʿat al-ifādāt* (see above, chapter 5)

ḤAMMAD ʿALĪ AL-RAḌAWĪ (late 11th century):

Risāla dar irth al-zawja = Risāla fī ḥirmān al-zawja ʿan baʿḍ matrūkāt al-zawj, Persian
MS: Dānishgāh 3514/26 (cat., XII, p.2528)

-KHWĀJŪ'Ī:

Risāla fī irth al-zawja
MSS: Marʿashī 1142/1 (cat., III, p.315); Dānishgāh 7103/3 (cat., XVI, p.455)

ḤAMMAD TAQĪ AL-NŪRĪ:

Risāla dar irth al-zawja, Persian (see AB, XI, p.55)
MS: Ḥujjatiyya 612 (cat., p.25)

BAḤR AL-ʿULŪM:

Risāla fī irth al-zawja, included in his *Bulghat al-faqīh* (see above, chapter 5)

IAYKH AL-SHARĪʿA:

Ibānat al-mukhtār fī irth al-zawja min thaman al-ʿiqār baʿd al-akhdh bi 'l-khiyār
MSS: Dānishgāh 2627/1 (cat., IX, p.1502); Majlis 3255/1 (cat., X, pp.843-4)

Ṣiyānat al-Ibāna ʿan waṣmat al-riṭāna
MSS: Dānishgāh 2627/3 (cat., IX, p.1503); Majlis 3255/3 (cat., X, pp. 844-5)

BD ALLĀH AL-MĀMAQĀNĪ:

Al-Muḥākama bayn al-ʿalamayn fī farʿ ʿadam irth al-zawja min al-arāḍī
Edition: Najaf, 1344 (in his *al-Ithnāʿashariyya*)

MISCELLANY

BD AL-MALIK B. FATḤĀN:

Sharḥ al-mas'ala al-nahbiyya, a commentary on a question of the chapter on inheritance of al-ʿAllāma's *Qawāʿid al-aḥkām* (see above, chapter 5)

ANONYMOUS (written befor 1040):

Sharḥ mas'ala min masā'il mīrāth al-Qawāʿid, a commentary on another question of al-ʿAllāma's above-mentioned work (see above, chapter 5)

AL-QUMMĪ:

Risāla fī annah idhā māt aḥad wa ʿalayh dayn aw waṣiyya fa-hal yantaqil al-taraka ila 'l-waratha am lā, included in his *al-Rasā'il* and *Jawāmiʿ al-rasā'il* (see above, chapter 5)

ʿABD ALLĀH AL-KIRMĀNSHĀHĪ:

Mas'ala fī irth man qatal waladah khaṭa'an
MS: Ilāhiyyāt 819/5d (cat., II, p.21)

ARBITRATION

1. GENERAL

AL-QUMMĪ:

Risāla fi 'l-qaḍā', included in his *al-Rasā'il* and *Jawāmiʿ al-rasā'il* (see above, chapter 5)

AḤMAD AL-KIRMĀNSHĀHĪ:

Manāhij al-aḥkām (see AB, XXII, p.340)
MSS: Ilāhiyyāt 112-13 Āl Āqā (cat., I, p.804)

MUḤAMMAD B. MUḤAMMAD ʿALĪ AL-HARANDĪ AL-IṢFAHĀNĪ (d. 1243):

Qanādīl al-ʿasjadāt
MSS: Marʿashī 2355, 2600 (cat., VI, p.330, VII, p.185); Raḍawī 7038 (cat., V, p.475);

AL-MUJĀHID:

K. al-Qaḍā'
MS: Gawharshād 594 (cat., p.370)

AḤMAD AL-NARĀQĪ:

K. al-Qaḍā' wa 'l-shahādāt
MS: Bāqiriyya (AB, XVII, p.140)

MUḤAMMAD QULĪ B. MUḤAMMAD AL-KANTŪRĪ (d. 1260):

Aḥkām al-ʿidāla al-ʿAlawiyya, Persian
Edited (AB, I, pp.299-300)

ḤASAN ĀL KĀSHIF AL-GHIṬĀ':

Al-Silāḥ al-māḍī
MSS: Dānishgāh 7001/1 (cat., XVI, p.424); Raḍawī 8218 (Bīnish, p. 846); Adabiyyāt 139/1 Kirmān (cat., p.40); Mahdawī 810/2 (cat., p.128)

ANONYMOUS (belonging to mid-13th century):

Al-Yanābīʿ
MS: Dānishgāh 3054 (cat., X, p.1996)

MUḤAMMAD ḤASAN B. MUḤAMMAD TAQĪ (d. after 1267):

K. al-Qaḍā' wa 'l-shahādāt
MS: Los Angeles M904 (cat., p.321)

AL-ANṢĀRĪ:

K. al-Qaḍā'
MSS: Ma'had 1352 (cat., p.116); Fayḍiyya 993/1 (cat., III, p.47); Majlis 403 Ṭabāṭabā'ī; Gawharshād 785/1 (cat., p.369)

K. al-Qaḍā', his lectures compiled by Muḥammad Taqī al-Tunukābunī
MS: Mar'ashī 1992 (cat.,V, p.363)

K. al-Qaḍā', another collection of his lectures compiled by Ḥusayn b. Muḥammad Ḥasan al-Mūsawī al-Darb Imāmī
MSS: Raḍawī 2526 (cat., II, p.98); Majlis 169 Khu'ī (cat., VII, p.217)

AḤMAD AL-FAYḌĪ:

Al-Qaḍā' wa 'l-shahādāt
MS: Gawharshād 38 (cat., 361)

ANONYMOUS (belonging to late 13th century)

K. al-Qaḍā'
MS: Fayḍiyya 993/2 (cat., III, p.47)

'ALĪ AKBAR AL-QAZWĪNĪ:

Risāla fī bayān aḥkām al-qaḍā'
MS: Millī 1783/17 Arabic (cat., X, p.368)

'ALĪ AL-KANĪ:

K. al-Qaḍā' = Taḥqīq al-dalā'il
Editions: Tehran, 1304, 1317
MS: Gharb 1103/1 (cat., p.289)

AL-RASHTĪ:

K. al-Qaḍā'
Edition: Qum, 1401
MSS: Majlis 3275, 3352/2, 5309, 37 Ṭabāṭabā'ī, 45 Ṭabāṭabā'ī (cat., X, pp.883-4, 1175-6, XVI, p.225); 'Abd al-'Aẓīm 328 (cat., p.469); Dānishgāh 6711/2 (cat., XVI, p.343); Mashhad, Ilāhiyyāt 800 (cat., I, pp.221-2); Los Angeles M645 (cat., p.321); Ustadī (cat., p.29)

ḤUSAYN QULĪ AL-HAMADĀNĪ:

K. al-Qaḍā' wa 'l-shahādāt, his lectures compiled by one of his pupils
MS: Tustariyya (AB, IV, p.372)

AL-ĀSHTIYĀNĪ:

K. al-Qaḍā'
Edition: Tehran, 1327
MS: Fayḍiyya 1608 (cat., I, p.203)

AL-KHURĀSĀNĪ:

K. al-Qaḍā', his lectures compiled by his son, Muḥammad b. Muḥammad Kāẓim al-Khurāsānī

MSS: Dānishgāh 1511/1 (cat., V, p.1832); Ḥuqūq 273j (cat., p.160); Malik 6270 (cat., I, p.161); Raḍawī 8533 (Bīnish, p.953)

ḌIYĀ' AL-DĪN AL-'ARĀQĪ:

K. al-Qaḍā'
Editions: Najaf, 1357, 1361

AL-KHU'Ī:

Mabānī Takmilat al-Minhāj
Edition: Najaf, 1395-6

MUḤAMMAD RIḌĀ AL-GULPĀYIGĀNĪ:

K. al-Qaḍā', his lectures compiled by 'Alī al-Ḥusaynī al-Mīlānī
Edition: Qum, 1401-3

2. ON JUDICIAL PROCEDURE

AL-SHAHĪD AL-AWWAL:

Masā'il tazāḥum al-ḥuqūq
MS: Tehran, Mudarris Raḍawī (AB, XX, p.340)

ḤUSAYN B. 'ABD AL-ṢAMAD:

Risāla fi 'l-shiyā'
MSS: Tustariyya 300/15 (cat., p.851); Ṣāḥib al-Dharī'a (AB, XI, p.153)

AL-MUJTAHID:

Risāla fī tanāzu' al-zawjayn fī matā' al-bayt
MS: Mar'ashī 2785/3 (cat., VII, p.348)

AL-DĀMĀD:

Risāla fī tanāzu' al-zawjayn fī qadr al-mahr
MSS: Mar'ashī 2519/2 (cat., VII, pp.104-5); Raḍawī 2438, 7211 (cat., II, p.70, V, p.426); Majlis 4553/4 (cat., XII, p.236); Baku M140/69 (*Nash.*, IX, p.244); Āstāna 8353/3 (cat., pp.203-4); Dār al-Kutub 3326j (cat., I, p.401)
Commentary: by the author, MS: Raḍawī 229 law (cat., II, p.71)

AḤMAD AL-BAḤRĀNĪ:

Risāla fi 'l-da'wā 'ala 'l-mayyit
MS: Princeton 229/10 Yahuda (cat., p.138)

AL-KHWĀJŪ'Ī:

Risāla fī jawāz muqāṣṣat al-munkir law ḥalaf
MS: Mar'ashī 1987/2 (cat., V, p.358)

AL-QUMMĪ:

Risāla fī tanāzu' al-zawjayn fī matā' al-bayt, included in his *al-Rasā'il* and *Jawāmi' al-rasā'il* (see above, chapter 5)

NAẒAR 'ALĪ B. SULṬĀN AL-ṬĀLIQĀNĪ:

Risāla fī da'wā al-'ayn
Edition: Tehran, 1304

.L BAḤR AL-ʿULŪM:

Risāla fī aḥkām al-daʿāwī, included in his *Bulghat al-faqīh* (see above, chapter 5)

.IYĀ' AL-DĪN AL-ʿARĀQĪ:

Risāla fī taʿāqub al-ayādī
Editions: Najaf,1357, 1361 (together with his *K. al-Qaḍā'*)

Maqāla fī 'l-daʿāwī
Edition: Najaf, 1345 (together with his *Sharḥ Tabṣirat al-mutaʿallimīn*)

. ON WITNESS

.L-KARAKĪ:

Risāla fī 'l-ʿidāla = Risāla fī maʿrifat al-kabā'ir
MSS: Dānishgāh 5397/3, 2144/39, 6963/2, 2888/5, 1015/3 (cat., V, pp.1496-7, IX, p.828, X, p.1733, XV, p.4239, XVI, p.412); Majlis 4339/7 (cat., XII, p. 40); Raḍawī 3538, 7615 (cat., II, p.90, V, p.442); Marʿashī 1409/4 (cat., IV, p.186); Adabiyyāt 282/2 Kirmān (cat., p.43); Los Angeles M451 (cat., p.241)

.L-SHAHĪD AL-THĀNĪ:

Risāla fī 'l-ʿidāla
MSS: Sipahsālār 7461/2 (cat., V, p.314); Marʿashī 444/4, 1445/4 (cat., II, p.48, IV, p.232); Dānishgāh 7019/2 (cat., XVI, p.431); Ilāhiyyāt 561/5d (cat., I, p.329)

ʿABD AL-ʿĀLĪ AL-KARAKĪ:

Risāla fī 'l-kabā'ir
MS: Sipahsālār 2919/20 (cat., V, p.423)

.AHĀ' AL-DĪN AL-ʿĀMILĪ:

Risāla fī 'l-ʿidāla
MS: Dār al-Kutub 21230 (cat., I, p.376)

.MUḤAMMAD IBRĀHĪM B. MUḤAMMAD MAʿSŪM AL-QAZWĪNĪ:

Risāla fī 'l-farq bayn al-ṣaghā'ir wa 'l-kabā'ir
MS: Majlis 1803/12 (cat., IX, p.302)

ṢĀḤIB AL-ḤADĀ'IQ:

Risāla fī 'l-ʿidāla
MS: Los Angeles M106/3 (cat., p.664)

AL-QUMMĪ:

Risāla fī taḥqīq mā yuʿtabar fi 'l-shahāda
MS: Marʿashī 1259/7 (cat., IV, p.62)

MUḤAMMAD MAHDĪ B. MUḤAMMAD SHAFĪʿ AL-ASTARĀBĀDĪ:

Al-Muʿtadil fī bayān ḥaqīqat al-ʿidāla al-sharʿiyya
MS: Ustādī (cat., p.51)

AL-ANṢĀRĪ:

Risāla fī 'l-ʿidāla

Editions: Tabrīz, 1303 (together with his *K. al-Ṭahāra*), 1375 (together with his *al-Makāsib*)
MSS: Dānishgāh 6956/3 (cat., XVI, p.411); Millī 1945/8 Arabic (cat. X, p.627)
Commentaries: (1) by 'Abd Allāh al-Māmaqānī, edited Najaf, 1345 (in his *al-Qalā'id al-thamīna*); (2) by Fattāḥ al-Shahīdī, edited Tabrīz, 1375 (together with his *Hidāyat al-ṭālib*)

ANONYMOUS:

Risāla dar 'idālat, Persian
MS: Gawharshād 1685/4 (cat., p. 152)

NAẒAR 'ALĪ AL-ṬĀLIQĀNĪ:

Risāla fī ishtirāṭ ḥusn al-ẓāhir fī qabūl al-shahāda
Edition: Tehran, 1304

MUḤAMMAD ḤUSAYN AL-KHWĀNSĀRĪ:

Risāla fi 'l-'idāla
MS: Mar'ashī 3041/21 (cat., VIII, p.250)

AL-KHURĀSĀNĪ:

Maqāla fi 'l-'idāla
Edition: Baghdad, 1331 (in his *Shadharāt*)

PENAL LAW

AL-ABĪWARDĪ:

Risāla dar diyāt wa qiṣāṣ, Persian
MS: Dānishgāh 7242/5 (cat., XV, p.497)

AL-MAJLISĪ II:

Risāla dar ḥudūd wa diyāt, Persian
Edition: Tehran, 1262
MSS: Mar'ashī 2831, 496, 2513/3, 652 (cat., II, pp.105, 249, VII, p.99, VIII, p.36); Fayḍiyya 210/2 (cat., III, p.8); Gulpāyigānī, 3 MSS (cat., II, p.63); Millī 1854/9 (cat., IV, p.317)

AL-QUMMĪ:

Risāla fī man qutil 'an umm wa ṣabī faṭīm wa zawja wa lā yarḍī al-wālida illā bi 'l-qiṣāṣ, included in his *Jawāmi' al-rasā'il* (see above, chapter 5)

YŪSUF B. 'ABD AL-FATTĀḤ AL-ṬABĀṬABĀ'Ī AL-TABRĪZĪ (d. 1242):

Musawwid al-khudūd fī masā'il al-ḥudūd
MS: Mar'ashī 2513/1 (cat., VII, pp.98-9)

MUḤAMMAD JA'FAR AL-ASTARĀBĀDĪ:

Risāla dar ḥudūd wa qiṣāṣ wa diyāt, Persian
MS: Sinā 618 (cat., I, p.399)

AḤMAD B. MUṢṬAFĀ AL-KHU'AYNĪ:

Sharḥ al-Durar al-bahiyya

MS: Marʿashī 3100/2 (cat., VIII, p.323)

AL-KHUʾĪ:

Mabānī Takmilat al-Minhāj (see above, general works on arbitration)

AL-MUNTAẒIRĪ:

K. al-Ḥudūd
Edition: Qum, 1399

Bibliography

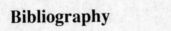

An asterisk beside the name of a book in the list below means that wherever the name of its author is given in a reference without mentioning a specific work by him, it refers to this particular work marked with the asterisk.

ʿABBĀSIYYA = al-Maktaba al-ʿAbbāsiyya, Basra
Catalogue: *Makhṭūṭāt al-Maktaba al-ʿAbbāsiyya fi 'l-Baṣra*, by ʿAlī al-Khāqānī, in *Majallat al-Majmaʿ al-ʿIlmī al-ʿIrāqī*, VIII-X (1961-3)

ʿABBĀS AL-QUMMĪ (d. 1359/1941):
- *Al-Fawā'id al-Raḍawiyya*, Tehran, 1367 q
- *Al-Kunā wa 'l-alqāb*, Sidon, 1357-8 q
- *Safīnat al-biḥār*, Najaf, 1352-5 q

ʿABD ALLĀH AL-JAZĀ'IRĪ (d. 1173/1759-60):
Al-Dhakhīra al-bāqiya, MS 1916/29, Majlis Library, Tehran

ʿABD ALLĀH AL-TŪNĪ (d. 1071/1660-1):
Risāla fī ṣalāt al-jumʿa, MS 128 Khu'ī, Majlis Library, Tehran (pp. 12-97)

ʿABD AL-ʿAẒĪM = Kitābkhāna-yi Āstāna-yi Ḥaḍrat-i ʿAbd al-ʿAẓīm, Rayy
Catalogue: *Fihrist-i nuskhahāy-i khaṭṭī-yi Kitābkhāna-yi Āstāna-yi imāmzāda ʿAbd al-ʿAẓīm-i Ḥasanī dar shahr-i Rayy*, by M.T. Dānishpazhūh, in *Nashriyya-yi Kitābkhāna-yi Markazī-yi Dānishgāh-i Tehran dar bāra-yi nuskhahāy-i khaṭṭī*, III (Tehran, 1964), pp. 61-83, 427-80

ʿABD AL-JALĪL AL-QAZWĪNĪ (6th/12th century):
Al-Naqḍ, ed. J. Muḥaddith Urmawī, Tehran, 1358 sh

ʿABD AL-MAJĪD MAḤMŪD ʿABD AL-MAJĪD:
Al-Ittijāhāt al-fiqhiyya ʿind Aṣḥāb al-Ḥadīth fi 'l-qarn al-thālith al-hijrī, Cairo, 1979

ʿABD AL-NABĪ AL-JAZĀ'IRĪ (d. 1021/1709-10):
Al-Iqtiṣād fī sharḥ al-Irshād, MS 5886/2, Majlis Library, Tehran

ABU 'L-ʿABBĀS AL-ḤARRĀNĪ (d. 745/1344-5):
Al-Musawwada fī uṣūl al-fiqh, ed. M.M. ʿAbd al-Ḥamīd, Cairo, 1964

ABŪ ʿALĪ = Muḥammad b. Ismāʿīl al-Māzandarānī al-Ḥā'irī (d. 1215/1800-1):
Muntahā al-maqāl fī ʿilm al-rijāl, Tehran, 1300 q

ABU 'L-ḤUSAYN AL-BAṢRĪ (d. 436/1044):
Al-Muʿtamad fī uṣūl al-fiqh, ed. M. Hamīd Allāh, Damascus, 1964-5

ABŪ MANṢŪR AL-ṬABRISĪ (early 6th/12th century):
Al- Iḥtijāj ʿalā ahl al-lajāj, ed. M.B. al-Kharsān, Najaf, 1966

ABU 'L-QĀSIM B. ḤASAN AL-YAZDĪ (mid-13th/19th century):
Tarjama-yi fārsī-yi Sharā'iʿ al-Islām, ed. M.T. Dānishpazhūh, Tehran 1346-53 sh

ADABIYYĀT = Kitābkhāna-yi Dānishkada-yi Adabiyyāt wa ʻUlūm-i Insānī-yi Dānishgāh-i Tehran, Tehran
Catalogues:
- *Fihrist-i nuskhahāy-i khaṭṭī-yi Kitābkhāna-yi Dānishkada-yi Adabiyyāt*, by M.T. Dānishpazhūh, Tehran, 1960
- *Fihrist-i nuskhahāy-i khaṭṭī-yi Kitābkhāna-yi Dānishkada-yi Adabiyyāt, majmūʻa-yi Imām Jumʻa-yi Kirmān*, by M.T. Dānishpazhūh, Tehrna, 1965
- *Fihrist-i nuskhahāy-i khaṭṭī-yi Kitābkhāna-yi Dānishkada-yi Adabiyyāt, majmūʻa-yi waqfī-yi ʻAlī Aṣghar Ḥikmat*, Tehran, 1341 sh

AFANDĪ = ʻAbd Allāh b. ʻĪsā al-Iṣfahānī (d. around 1130/1718):
Riyāḍ al-ʻulamā', Qum, 1401 q -

ĀGHĀ BUZURG AL-ṬIHRĀNĪ (d. 1389/1970):
Al-Dharīʻa ilā taṣānīf al-Shīʻa, Tehran and Najaf, 1353-98 q

AḤMAD = Aḥmad b. Muḥammad b. Ḥanbal (d. 241/855):
Al-Musnad, Cairo, 1313 q

ʻALĪ B. MUḤAMMAD AL-ʻĀMILĪ (d. 1103/1691-2):
- *Al-Durr al-manthūr*, ed. A. al-Ḥusaynī, Qum, 1398 q
- *Al-Sihām al-māriqa*, MS 1576, Marʻashī Library, Qum

ʻALLĀMA = Jamāl al-Dīn Ḥasan b. Yūsuf b. al-Muṭahhar al-Ḥillī (d. 726/1325):
- *Īḍāḥ al-ishtibāh*, Tehran, 1319 q
- *Khulāṣat al-aqwāl = Rijāl al-ʻAllāma al-Ḥillī*, Najaf, 1961
- *Mabādi' al-wuṣūl ilā ʻilm al-uṣūl*, ed. ʻA.M.ʻA. al-Baqqāl, Najaf, 1970
- *Mukhtalaf al-Shīʻa*, Tehran, 1324 q
- *Muntahā al-maṭlab*, Tehran, 1333 q
- *Nihāyat al-wuṣūl ilā ʻilm al-uṣūl*, MS 1908 Marʻashī Library, Qum
- *Tabṣirat al-mutaʻallimīn*, ed. A. al-Ḥusaynī and H. al-Yūsufī, Qum, n.d.
- *Tahdhīb al-uṣūl*, Tehran, 1308 q
- *Taḥrīr al-aḥkām al-sharʻiyya*, Tehran, 1314 q

AMBROSIANA = Biblioteca Ambrosiana, Milano
Catalogue: *Catalogue of the Arabic Manuscripts in the Biblioteca Ambrosiana*, by Oscar Löfgren and Renato Traini, Vicenza, 1975-81

AMĪN AL-ASTARĀBĀDĪ = Muḥammad Amīn b. Muḥammad Sharīf (d. 1036/1626-7):
- *Dānishnāma-yi shāhī*, MS 4668/11, Central Library, University of Tehran
-* *Al-Fawā'id al-Madaniyya*, Tabrīz, 1321 q
- *Jawāb masā'il al-shaykh Ḥusayn al-Ẓahīrī al-ʻĀmilī*, MS 1067/4, Central Library, University of Tehran

AMĪR AL-MU'MINĪN = Maktabat al-Imām Amīr al-Mu'minīn al-ʻĀmma, Najaf
Catalogue: *(Chand nuskha-yi khaṭṭi az) Maktabat al-Imām Amīr al-Mu'minīn al-ʻĀmma dar Najaf*, by M.T. Dānishpazhūh, in *Nashriyya-yi Kitābkhāna-yi Markazī-yi Dānishgāh-i Tehran dar bāra-yi nuskhahāy-i khaṭṭī*, V (Tehran, 1968), pp.409-19

ANJUMAN-I TARAQQĪ-YI URDŪ, Karachi
Catalogue: *Makhṭūṭāt-i Anjuman-i Taraqqī-yi Urdū*, by S.F.ʻA. Raḍawī, Karachi, 1967

ANṢĀRĪ = Murtaḍā b. Muḥammad Amīn al-Tustarī (d. 1281/1864):
Al-Rasā'il = Farā'id al-uṣūl, Tehran, 1296 q

ARDABĪLĪ = Aḥmad b. Muḥammad, al-Muqaddas (d. 993/1585):
Majmaʿ al-fā'ida wa 'l-burhān, Tehran, 1272 q

ĀṢAFIYYA = Aṣafiyya Library, Hyderabad, Deccan
Catalogue: *Fihrist-i Kutub-i ʿArabī wa Fārsī wa Urdū makhzūna-yi Āṣafiyya*, by Taṣadduq Ḥusayn al-Mūsawī al-Naysābūrī al-Kantūrī, Hyderabad, 1347-57 q

ĀSHNĀ'Ī = Āshnā'ī bā chand nuskha-yi khaṭṭī, by H. Mudarrisī Ṭabāṭabā'ī and R. Ustādī, Qum, 1396 q

ʿASQALĀNĪ = Shihāb al-Dīn Aḥmad b. ʿAlī b. Ḥajar (d. 852/1449):
Al-Maṭālib al-ʿāliya, ed. H. al-Aʿẓamī, Kuwait, 1971 -

ĀSTĀNA = Kitābkhāna-yi Āstāna-yi Muqaddasa-yi Qum, Qum
Catalogue: *Fihrist-i nusakh-i khaṭṭī-yi Kitābkhāna-yi Āstāna-yi Muqaddasa-yi Qum*, by M.T. Dānishpazhūh, Qum, 1355 sh

BAGHAWĪ = Abū Muḥammad Ḥusayn b. Masʿūd al-Farrā' (d. 510/1117):
Maṣābīḥ al-sunna, Cairo, 1318 q

BAGHDĀDĪ = the private collection of Sayyid Muḥammad al-Baghdādī, Najaf
Catalogue: *Makhṭūṭāt maktabat . . . al-sayyid Muḥammad al-Baghdādī al-Ḥasanī*, by M.H. al-Amīnī, Najaf, 1964

BAHĀ' AL-DĪN AL-ʿĀMILĪ (d. 1030/1621):
- *Mashriq al-shamsayn*, Tehran, 1321 q (together with the author's *al-Ḥabl al-matīn*)
- *Al-Wajīza*, Qum, 1396 q
- *Zubdat al-uṣūl*, Tehran, 1319 q

BAḤRĀNĪ = Yūsuf b. Aḥmad b. Ibrāhīm, Ṣāḥib al-Ḥadā'iq (d. 1186/1772):
- *Al-Ḥadā'iq al-nāḍira*, ed. M.T. al-Īrawānī, Najaf, 1377 q -
- *Al-Kashkūl = Anīs al-musāfir wa jalīs al-ḥāḍir*, Bombay, 1291-2 q
- *Lu'lu'at al-baḥrayn*, Bombay, n.d.

BAḤR AL-ʿULŪM = Muḥammad Mahdī b. Murtaḍā al-Ṭabāṭabā'ī (d. 1212/1797):
Al-Fawā'id al-rijāliyya = Rijāl al-sayyid Baḥr al-ʿUlūm, Najaf, 1965-7

BĀJŪRĪ = Ibrāhīm b. Muḥammad (d. 1277/1860-1):
Ḥāshiyat Fatḥ al-qarīb = Ḥāshiya ʿalā sharḥ al-ʿallāma Ibn Qāsim al-Ghazzī ʿalā matn al-shaykh Abī Shujāʿ, Cairo, 1285 q

BANKIPORE = Oriental Public Library, Bengal
Catalogues:
- Arabic: *Miftāḥ al-kunūz al-khafiyya*, by Mawlawī ʿAbd al-Ḥamīd, Patna 1918-22
- Persian: *Mir'āt al-ʿulūm*, by Mawlawī ʿAbd al-Khallāq Ṣāḥib, Patna, 1925

BĀQIRIYYA = Kitābkhāna-yi Madrasa-yi Bāqiriyya, Mashhad

BARQĪ = Abu Jaʿfar Aḥmad b. Muḥammad b. Khālid al-Qummī (d. 274-80/

889-94):
* *Al-Maḥāsin*, ed. J. Muḥaddith Urmawī, Tehran, 1370 q
Al-Rijāl, ed. J. Muḥaddith Urmawī, Tehran, 1342 sh (together with Ibn Dāwūd's *K. al-Rijāl*)

BAYHAQĪ = Abū Bakr Aḥmad b. Ḥusayn al-Naysābūrī (d. 458/1065):
Al-Sunan, Hyderabad, 1354-6 q

BAZANṬĪ = Abū Ja'far Aḥmad b. Muḥammad b. Abī Naṣr (d. 221/836):
Jāmi' al-bazanṭī, a part of it which is inserted in Ibn Idrīs's *al-Sarā'ir*, pp. 477-8 (Tehran, 1270 q)

BENGAL = The Royal Asiatic Society, Bengal
Catalogue: *Catalogue of the Arabic Manuscripts in the Collection of the Royal Asiatic Society of Bengal*, by W.Ivanow and others, Calcutta, 1939-51

BERLIN = Staat Bibliothek, Berlin
Catalogue: *Verzeichniss der Arabischen Handschriften der Königlichen Bibliothek zu Berlin*, by W. Ahlwardt, Berlin, 1887-99

BIBLIOTHÈQUE NATIONALE (Paris):
Catalogue:
(I) *Catalogues des manuscrits Arabes*, by M. Le Baron de Slane, Paris, 1883-95
(II) *Catalogue des manuscrits Arabes des novelles acquisitions*, by E. Blochet, Paris, 1924

BIHBAHĀNĪ = Muḥammad Bāqir b. Muḥammad Akmal, al-Waḥīd (d. 1205/1791):
- *Al-Fawā'id al-'atīqa*, Tehran, 1279 q (together with Muḥammad Ḥusayn al-Iṣfahānī's *al-Fuṣūl al-Gharawiyya*, pp.431-66)
- *Taḥqīq fi 'l-qiyās*, MS 458/3, Mar'ashī Library, Qum
- *Ta'līqāt manhaj al-maqāl*, Tehran, 1307 q (together with Muḥammad b. 'Alī al-Astarābādī's *Manhaj al-maqāl*)

BĪNISH, T:
Fihristi-i alifbā'ī-yi nuskhahāy-i khaṭṭī-yi Kitābkhāna-yi Āstāna-yi Mashhad, Tehran, 1351 sh (in *Fihrist-i nuskhahāy-i khaṭṭī-yi du kitābkhāna-yi Mashhad*, the second volume of *Majmū'a-yi fihrist-i nuskhahāy-i khaṭṭī-yi kitābkhānahāy-i shahrastānhāy-i Iran*, pp. 563-1080)

BODLEIAN = The Bodleian Library, Oxford
Catalogues:
- (I) *Bibliothecae Bodleianae Codicum Manuscriptorum Orientalum . . . Catalogus*, by J. Uri, Oxford, 1787;
- (II) *Catalogi Codicum Manuscriptorum Orientalium Bibliothecase Bodleianae, Pars Secunda, Arabicos Complectens*, by Alexander Nicoll, Oxford, 1835
- (III) *Catalogue of the Persian,Turkish,Hindûstânî, and Pushtû Manuscripts in the Bodleian Library*, by Ed. Sachau and Hermann Ethé, Part I (the Persian Manuscripts), Oxford, 1889

BRITISH LIBRARY (London):
Catalogues:
- (Rieu) *Supplement to the Catalogue of the Arabic Manuscripts in the British Museum*, by Charles Rieu, London, 1894

- (II) *A Discriptive List of the Arabic Manuscripts Acquired by the Trustees of the British Museum since 1895*, by A.G. Elliss and E. Edwards, London, 1912

BRUNSCHVIG, R.:
'Les *uṣūl al-fiqh* Imamites a leur stade ancien (X^{e} et XIe siècles)', in *Le Shī'isme Imamate* (Paris, 1970), pp.201-13

BŪHĀR = the Būhār Library, Imperial Library, Calcutta
Catalogue: *Catalogue of the Arabic Manuscripts in the Būhār Library*, by Shams al-'Ulamā' M. Hidāyat Ḥusayn Khān Bahādur, Calcutta, 1923

BURŪJIRDĪ = Maktabat Madrasat al-sayyid al-Burūjirdī, Najaf
Catalogue: *Makhṭūṭāt Maktabat Madrasat al-sayyid al-Burūjirdī*, by A. al-Ḥusaynī, in his *Dalīl al-Makhṭūṭāt* (Qum, 1397 q), pp.4-43

CAMBRIDGE = the University Library, Cambridge
A Descriptive Catalogue of the Oriental Manuscripts belonging to the Late E.G. Browne, by Edward G. Browne and Reynold A. Nicholson, Cambridge, 1932

CONGRESS = the Library of Congress, Washington
Catalogue: *Fihris al-makhṭūṭāt al-'Arabiyya fī Maktabat al-kunghress*, by Ṣ. al-Munajjid, Beirut, 1969

DACCA = the Dacca University Library, Dacca
Catalogue: *The Persian, Urdu and Arabic Manuscripts in the Dacca University Library*, by A.B.M. Habibullah, Dacca, 1966-8

DĀMĀD = Muḥammad Bāqir b. Shams al-Dīn Muḥammad al-Ḥusaynī al-Astarābādī (d. 1040/1630-1):
Al-Rawāshiḥ al-samāwiyya, Tehran, 1311 q

DĀNISHGĀH = Kitābkhāna-yi Markazaī wa Markaz-i Asnād-i Dānishgāh-i Tehran, Tehran
- Catalogue: *Fihrist-i nuskhahāy-i khaṭṭī-yi Kitābkhāna-yi Markazī-yi Dānishgāh-i Tehran*, by M.T. Dānishpazhūh and 'A.N. Munzawī, Tehran, 1330-57 sh
- Microfilms: *Fihrist-i mīkrufīlmhāy-i Kitābkhāna-yi Markazī-yi Dānishgāh-i Tehran*, by M.T. Dānishpazhūh, Tehran, 1348 sh -

DĀNISHPAZHŪH, M.T.:
His introduction to the 4th volume of Abu 'l-Qāsim b. Ḥasan al-Yazdī's *Tarjama-yi Sharā'i' al-Islām*, Tehran, 1353 sh

DĀR AL-KUTUB (Cairo):
- Catalogue: *Fihrist al-makhṭūṭāt*, by Fu'ād Sayyid, Cairo, 1961-2
- General catalogue: *Fihris al-kutub al-'Arabiyya*, Cairo, 1924-59

DĀRIMĪ = Abū Muḥammad 'Abd Allāh b. 'Abd al-Raḥmān al-Tamīmī al-Samarqandī (d. 255/869):
Sunan, Damascus, 1349 q

DIHKHUDĀ = Sāzmān-i Lughatnāma-yi Dihkhudā, Tehran
Catalogue: *Fihrist-i kitābkhāna-yi Sāzmān-i Lughatnāma-yi Dihkhudā*, by M.T. Dānishpazhūh, in *Nashriyya-yi Kitābkhānā-yi Markazī-yi Dānishgāh-i Tehran dar bāra-yi nuskhahāy-i khaṭṭī*, III (Tehran, 1964) pp. 1-59, 387-426

IZFŪLĪ = Muḥammad b. Faraj Allāh al-Qāḍī (13th/19th century):
Fārūq al-ḥaqq, Tehran, 1316 q (together with Kāshif al-Ghiṭā''s *al-Ḥaqq al-mubīn*)

URUST B. ABĪ MANṢŪR AL-WĀSIṬĪ (2nd/8th century):
Kitāb Durust b. Abī Manṣūr, Tehran, 1371 q (in the collection of *al-Uṣūl al-sittat ʿashar*, pp. 158-69)

ARHĀD MUʿTAMID = the private collection of Farhād Muʿtamid, Tehran
Catalogue: *Fihrist-i kitābkhāna-yi Farhād Muʿtamid*, by M.T. Dānishpazhūh and Gh. R. Farzānapūr, in *Nashriyya-yi Kitābkhāna-yi Markazī-yi Dānishgāh-i Tehran dar bāra-yi nuskhahāy-i khaṭṭī*, III (Tehran, 1964), pp.141-276

ARHANG = Kitābkhāna-yi ʿUmūmī-yi Farhang wa Hunar, Mashhad
Catalogue: *Fihrist-i kutub-i khaṭṭī-yi Kitābkhāna-yi Farhang wa Hunar*, by R. Shākirī, Mashhad, 1348 sh

AYḌ = Muḥammad b. Murtaḍā al-Kāshānī, known as Muḥsin al-Fayḍ (d. 1091/1680):
Al-Ḥaqq al-mubīn, ed. J. Muḥaddith Urmawī, Tehran, 1390 q (together with the author's *al-Uṣūl al-aṣīla*)
Mafātīḥ al-sharāʾiʿ, ed. ʿI. al-Musawī al-Baḥrānī, Vol.1, Beirut, 1969
Al-Maḥajja al-bayḍāʾ, ed. ʿA.A. al-Ghaffārī, Tehran, 1339-42 sh
Al-Uṣūl al-aṣīla, ed. J. Muḥaddith Urmawī, Tehran, 1390 q
Al-Wāfī, Tehran, 1323 q

AYḌIYYA = Kitābkhāna-yi Madrasa-yi Fayḍiyya, Qum
Catalogue: *Fihrist-i nuskhahāy-i khaṭṭī-yi Kitābkhāna-yi Madarasa-yi Fayḍiyya*, by R. Ustādī, Qum, 1396q

U'ĀD SAYYID:
Fihris al-makhṭūṭāt al-muṣawwara, Maʿhad Iḥyāʾ al-Makhṭūṭāt al-ʿArabiyya, Cairo, 1954 -

UṢŪL = Fuṣūl khaṭar bi 'l-bāl ḥīn muṭālaʿat kitāb al-ṭahāra, MS 2647, Marʿashī Library, Qum

UTŪNĪ = Abu 'l-Ḥasan b. Muḥammad Ṭāhir al-Sharīf al-Nabāṭī al-ʿĀmilī (d. 1138/1725-6):
Tanzīh al-Qummiyyīn min al-maṭāʿin, Qum, 1328 sh

AWHARSHĀD = Kitābkhāna-yi Masjid-i Gawharshād, Mashhad
Catalogue: *Fihristi-i Kitābkhāna-yi Jāmiʿ-i Gawharshād*, by ʿA. Nūrānī and K.M. Shānachī, in *Fihrist-i nuskhahāy-i khaṭṭī-yi chahār kitābkhāna-yi Mashhad*, the first volume of *Majmūʿa-yi fihrist-i nuskhahāy-i khaṭṭī-yi kitābkhānahāy-i shahrastānhāy-i Iran* (Tehran, 1351 sh), pp.57-435

HARB = Kitābkhāna-yi Gharb, Hamadān
Catalogue: *Fihrist-i nuskhahāy-i khaṭṭī-yi Kitābkhāna-yi Gharb*, by J. Maqṣūd, Tehran, 1397 q

HAZĀLĪ = Abū Ḥāmid Muḥammad b. Muḥammad al-Ṭūsī (d. 505/1111):
Iḥyāʾ ʿulūm al-dīn, Cairo, 1312 q
Al-Mustaṣfā, Cairo, 1356 q

GHAZZĪ = Shams al-Dīn Muḥammad b. Qāsim, Ibn al-Gharābīlī (d. 918/1512):
Fatḥ al-Qarīb al-Mujīb fī sharḥ alfāẓ al-Taqrīb, ed. L.W.C. Van Denberg, Leiden, 1894

GULPĀYIGĀNĪ = Kitābkhāna-yi Madrasa-yi Gulpāyigānī, Qum
Catalogue: *Fihrist-i nuskhahāy-i khaṭṭī-yi Kitābkhāna-yi ʿUmūmī-yi . . . Gulpāyigānī*, by A. Ḥusaynī and R. Ustādī, Qum, 1357-61 sh

ḤAKĪM = Maktabat al-Imām al-Ḥakīm al-ʿĀmma, Najaf
Catalogues:
- *Fihrist makhṭūṭāt Maktabat al-Imām al-Ḥakīm al-ʿĀmma*, by M.M. Najaf, Najaf, 1969
- *Fihrist makhṭūṭāt al-shaykh Muḥammad al-Rashtī al-muhdāt ilā Maktabat al-Imām al-Ḥakīm al-ʿĀmma*, by A. al-Ḥusaynī, Najaf, 1971

ḤĀKIM AL-NAYSĀBŪRĪ = Abū ʿAbd Allāh Muḥammad b. ʿAbd Allāh (d. 405/1014-15)
Al-Mustadrak ʿala ʾl-Ṣaḥīḥayn, Hyderabad, 1340 q

ḤAKĪM AL-TIRMIDHĪ = Abū ʿAbd Allāh Muḥammad b. ʿAlī b. Ḥasan (d. around 320/932):
Nawādir al-uṣūl, Beirut, n.d.

ḤALABĪ = Abu ʾl-Ṣalāḥ Taqī al-Dīn b. Najm al-Dīn (d. 447/1055-6):
- *Al-Kāfī*, MS 441/1, Marʿashī Library, Qum
- *Taqrīb al-maʿārif*, MS 2263, Marʿashī Library, Qum

ḤASAN AL-ṢADR (d. 1354/1935):
Taʾsīs al-Shīʿa li-funūn al-Islām, Baghdad, 1951

ḤAYDAR, ʿALĪ:
Durar al-ḥukkām, sharḥ Majallat al-aḥkām, translated from Turkish into Arabic by Fahmī al-Ḥusaynī, Baghdad and Beirut, n.d.

ḤAYDARIYYA = Khizānat al-Rawḍa al-Ḥaydariyya, Najaf
Catalogue: *Fihrist makhṭūṭāt Khizānat al-Rawḍa al-Ḥaydariyya*, by A. al-Ḥusaynī, Najaf, 1971

HAYTHAMĪ = Nūr al-Dīn ʿAlī b. Abī Bakr (d. 807/1404-5):
Majmaʿ al-zawāʾid, Cairo, 1352-3 q

ḤIMYARĪ = Abu ʾl-Qāsim ʿAbd Allāh b. Jaʿfar al-Qummī (3rd/9th century
Qurb al-isnād, Tehran, n.d.

ḤUJJATĪ, M.B.:
Barrasī-yi āthār-i Shaykh-i Ṭūsī wa guzārish-i nuskhahāy-i khaṭṭī-yi ānhā, in *Yādnāma-yi Shaykh-i Ṭūsī*, III (Mashhad, 1976), pp.590-676

ḤUJJATIYYA = Kitābkhāna-yi Madrasa-yi Ḥujjatiyya, Qum
Fihrist-i nuskhahāy-i khaṭṭī-yi Kitābkhāna-yi Madrasa-yi Ḥujjatiyya, by R. Ustādī, Qum, 1354 sh

ḤUQŪQ = Kitābkhāna-yi Dānishkada-yi Ḥuqūq wa ʿUlūm-i Sīyāsī wa Iqtiṣādī-yi Dānishgāh-i Tehran, Tehran
Catalogue: *Fihrsit-i nuskhahāy-i khaṭṭī-yi Kitābkhāna-yi Dānishkada-Ḥuqūq . . .*, by M.T. Dānishpazhūh, Tehran, 1961

URR AL-ʿĀMILĪ (d. 1104/1693):
Amal al-āmil, ed. A. al-Ḥusaynī, Baghdad, 1965
* *Wasāʾil al-Shīʿa*, ed. ʿA.R. al-Rabbānī and M. al-Rāzī, Tehran, 1376-89 q

USAYN B. ʿABD AL-ṢAMAD AL-ʿĀMILĪ (d. 984/1576):
Al-ʿIqd al-Ḥusaynī, ed. J. al-Mudarrisī, Yazd, n.d.
Maqāla fī wujūb al-iftāʾ wa bayān al-ḥaqq ʿalā kull man ʿalim bih, MS 1686/3, Fayḍiyya Library, Qum
Risāla fī ḥukm al-ḥuṣr wa ʾl-bawārī, MS 1836/12, Majlis Library, Tehran
Risāla fī taḥqīq baʿḍ al-masāʾil al-fiqhiyya, MS 5960/3, Majlis Library, Tehran
Tisʿa masāʾil, MS 1805/53, Majlis Library, Tehran
Wuṣūl al-akhyār ilā uṣūl al-akhbār, Tehran, 1309 q

USAYN AL-KARAKĪ (d. 1076/1665-6):
Hidāyat al-abrār ilā ṭarīq al-Aʾimma al-aṭhār, MS 3278/1, Marʿashī Library, Qum

USAYNIYYAT KĀSHIF AL-GHIṬĀʾ, Najaf

BN ʿASĀKIR = Abu ʾl-Qāsim ʿAlī b. Ḥasan b. Hibat Allāh al-Dimashqī (d. 573/1177-8):
Tarjimat al-Imām ʿAlī b. Abī Ṭālib ʿalayh al-salām min Taʾrīkh madīnat Dimashq, ed. M.B. al-Maḥmūdī, Beirut, 1975

BN AL-ATHĪR = Majd al-Dīn Mubārak b. Muḥammad al-Jazarī al-Shaybānī (d. 606/1210):
Jāmiʿ al-uṣūl, Cairo, 1368 q

BN AL-BARRĀJ = Qāḍī ʿAbd al-ʿAzīz b. Niḥrīr al-Shāmī (d. 481/1088):
Al-Muhadhdhab, MS 441/2, Marʿashī Library, Qum
Sharḥ Jumal al-ʿIlm wa ʾl-ʿamal, ed. K.M. Shānachī, Mashhad, 1974

BN DĀWŪD = Taqī al-Dīn Ḥasan b. ʿAlī b. Dāwūd al-Ḥillī (d. after 707/1307):
K. al-Rijāl, ed. J. Muḥaddith Urmawī, Tehran, 1342 sh

BN FAHD = Abu ʾl-ʿAbbās Aḥmad b. Muḥammad b. Fahd al-Asadī al-Ḥillī (d. 841/1437-8):
Al-Muhadhdhab al-bāriʿ, MS 275, Marʿashī Library, Qum
Al-Muqtaṣar min sharḥ al-Mukhtaṣar, MS 2524, Marʿashī Library, Qum

BN ḤAZM = Abū Muḥammad ʿAlī b. Aḥmad al-Qurṭubī (d. 456/1064):
Al-Iḥkām fī uṣūl al-aḥkām, ed. A.M. Shākir, Cairo, 1345-8 q
Mulakhkhaṣ ibṭāl al-qiyās wa ʾl-raʾy wa ʾl-istiḥsān wa ʾl-taqlīd wa ʾl-taʿlīl, ed. S. al-Afghānī, Damascus, 1960

BN IDRĪS = Abū ʿAbd Allāh Muḥammad b. Manṣūr b. Aḥmad b. Idrīs al-ʿIjlī al-Ḥillī (d. 598/1202):
Al-Sarāʾir al-ḥāwī li-taḥrīr al-fatāwī, Tehran, 1270 q

BN AL-JAWZĪ = Abu ʾl-Faraj ʿAbd al-Raḥmān b. ʿAlī al-Qurashī al-Baghdādī (d. 597/1201):
Manāqib al-Imām Aḥmad b. Ḥanbal, Cairo, 1979

IBN AL-NADĪM = Abu 'l-Faraj Muḥammad b. Isḥāq al-Warrāq al-Baghdādī (late 4th/10th century):
Al-Fihrist, ed. R. Tajaddud, Tehran, [1971]

IBN QUDĀMA = Muwaffaq al-Dīn 'Abd Allāh b. Aḥmad al-Maqdisī (d. 620/1223-4):
Taḥrīm al-naẓar fī kutub ahl al-kalām, ed. G. Makdisi, London, 1962

IBN SA'D = Abū 'Abd Allāh Muḥammad b. Sa'd Kātib al-Wāqidī (d. 230/844-5):
K. al-Ṭabaqāt al-kabīr, ed. E. Sachau and others, Leiden, 1904-15

IBN SHAHRĀSHŪB = Rashīd al-Dīn Muḥammad b. 'Alī al-Sarawī (d. 588/1192):
- *Ma'ālim al-'ulamā'*, ed. 'A. Iqbāl, Tehran, 1353 q
- *Mathālib al-Nawāṣib*, MS Nāṣiriyya Library, Lucknow
- *Mutashābih al-Qur'ān*, ed. Ḥ. al-Muṣṭafawī, Tehran, 1369 q

IBN ṬĀWŪS = Raḍī al-Dīn 'alī b. Mūsā al-Ḥasanī al-Ḥusaynī al-Ḥillī (d. 664/1265-6):
- *Al-Iqbāl bi-ṣālih al-a'māl*, Tehran, 1320 q
- *Kashf al-maḥajja*, Najaf, 1950

IBN AL-TURKUMĀNĪ = 'Alā' al-Dīn 'Alī b. 'Uthmān al-Mārdīnī (d. 750/1349-50):
Al-Jawhar al-naqī fi 'l-radd 'ala 'l-Bayhaqī, Hyderabad, 1354-6 q (together with al-Bayhaqī's *al-Sunan al-kubrā*)

IBN ZUHRA = Abu 'l-Makārim Ḥamza b. 'Alī b. Zuhra al-Ḥalabī (d. 585/1189-90):
Ghunyat al-nuzū', Tehran, 1276 q (in the collection of *al-Jawāmi' al-fiqhiyya*, pp. 523-626)

ILĀHIYYĀT = Kitabkhāna-yi Dānishkada-yi Ilāhiyyāt wa ma'ārif-i Islāmī-yi Dānishgāh-i Tehran, Tehran
Catalogue: *Fihrist-i nuskhahāy-i khaṭṭī-yi Kitābkhāna-yi Dānishkada-yi Ilāhiyyāt wa Ma'ārif-i Islāmī*, by M.T. Dānishpazhūh and M.B. Ḥujjatī, Tehran, 1345-8 sh

AL-IMĀM AL-MAHDĪ = Maktabat al-Imām al-Mahdī, Sāmarrā' (Iraq)

INDIA OFFICE, London:
Catalogues:
- *A Catalogue of the Arabic Manuscripts in the Library of the India Office*, by O. Loth and R. Levy, London, 1937
- (Ashburner) *Catalogue of Two Collections of Persian and Arabic Manuscripts Preserved in the India Office Library*, by E.D. Ross and E.G. Browne, London, 1902

IQBĀL, 'A.:
Khānidān-i Nawbakhtī, Tehran, 1345 sh

IṢFAHĀN, DĀNISHGĀH = Kitābkhāna-yi Dānishgāh-i Iṣfahān, Iṣfahān
Catalogue: *Fihrist-i nuskhahāy-i khaṭṭī-yi Kitābkhāna-yi Dānishgāh-i Iṣfahān*, by I. Afshār and M.T. Dānishpazhūh, in *Nashriyya-yi Kitābkhāna-yi Markazī-yi Dānishgāh-i Tehran dar bāra-yi nuskhahāy-i khaṭṭī*, XI-XII (Tehran, 1362 sh), pp.880-950

ṢFAHĀN, ʻUMŪMĪ = Kitābkhāna-yi ʻUmūmī-yi Iṣfahān, Iṣfahān
Catalogue: *Fihrist-i nuskhahāy-i khaṭṭī-yi Kitābkhāna-yi ʻUmūmī-yi Iṣfahān*, by J. Maqṣūd, Tehran, 1349 sh

A ʻFARIYYA = al-Maktaba al-Jaʻfariyya, Madrasat al-Hindī, Karbalā'
Catalogue: *(Chand nusha-yi khaṭṭī az) Kitābkhāna-yi Jaʻfariyya*, by M.T. Dānishpazhūh, in *Nashriyya-yi Kitābkhāna-yi Markazī-yi Dānishgāh-i Tehran dar bāra-yi nuskhahāy-i khaṭṭī*, V (Tehran, 1968), pp. 434-7

ĀMIʻ AḤĀDĪTH AL-SHĪʻA, Qum, 1399 q (Vol. I)

AWĀD AL-ʻĀMILĪ (d. 1226/1811):
Miftāḥ al-karāma, ed. M. al-Amīn al-ʻĀmilī, Cairo-Sidon-Tehran, 1324 q

AWĀDAYN = Maktabat al-Jawādayn, Kāẓimiyya (Iraq)

AZĀ'IRĪ = Niʻmat Allāh b. ʻAbd Allāh al-Mūsawī (d. 1112/1710):
-* *Al-Anwār al-Nuʻmāniyya*, ed. M.ʻA. al-Qāḍī al-Ṭabāṭabā'ī, Tabrīz, 1382 q
- *Manbaʻ al-ḥayāt fī ḥujjiyyat qawl al-mujtahidīn min al-amwāt*, MS 2761/4, Majlis Library, Tehran

KALBĀSĪ = Muḥammad Ibrāhīm b. Muḥammad Ḥasan al-Iṣfahānī (d. 1262/1846):
Shawāriʻ al-hidāya, MS $\frac{5082}{174}$ (temporary), Marʻashī Library, Qum

KAMARA'Ī = ʻAlī Naqī b. Muḥammad Hāshim al-Iṣfahānī (mid-11th/17th century):
Risāla dar ithbāt-i luzūm-i wujūd-i mujtahid dar zamān-i ghaybat-i Imām, MS 3813, Majlis Library, Tehran

KARĀJAKĪ = Abu 'l-Fatḥ Muḥammad b. ʻUthmān (d. 449/1057-8):
Kanz al-fawā'id, Tabrīz, 1322 q

KARAKĪ = Nūr al-Dīn ʻAlī b. ʻAbd al-ʻĀlī al-ʻĀmilī (d. 940/1534):
Ṭarīq istinbāṭ al-aḥkām, ed. ʻA. al-Faḍlī, Najaf, 1971

KĀSHĀN, RAḌAWĪ = Kitābkhāna-yi Āyat Allāh Raḍawī, Kāshān
Catalogue: *Nuskhahāy-i khaṭṭī-yi Kitābkhāna-yi Āyat Allāh Raḍawī dar shahr-i Kāshān*, by M.T. Dānishpazhūh, in *Nashriyya-yi Kitābkhāna-yi Markazī-yi Dānishgāh-i Tehran dar bāra-yi nuskhahāy-i khaṭṭī*, VII (Tehran, 1353 sh), pp. 29-94

KĀSHĀNĪ = Maktabat al-sayyid ʻAbbās al-Kāshānī, Karbalā'
Catalogue: *Makhṭūṭāt Maktabat . . . al-sayyid ʻAbbās al-Ḥusaynī al-Kāshānī fī Karbalā'*, by Ḥ.M. Haddū, Karbalā', 1966

KĀSHIF AL-GHIṬĀ' = Jaʻfar b. Khiḍr al-Najfī (d. 1228/1813):
- *Al-Ḥaqq al-mubīn*, Tehran, 1316 q
- *Sharḥ al-Qawā'id*, MS, private collection of R. Ustādī, Qum (now in Marʻashī Library, Qum)

KASHSHĪ = Abū ʻAmr Muḥammad b. ʻUmar b. ʻAbd al-ʻAzīz (eartly 4th/10th century):
Rijāl al-Kashshī, abridged by al-Shaykh al-Ṭūsī as *Ikhtiyār maʻrifat al-rijāl*, ed. Ḥ. al-Muṣṭafawī, Mashhad, 1348 sh

KĀẒIMĪ = Asad Allāh b. Ismāʿīl al-Tustarī (d. 1234/1818-19):
- * *Kashf al-qināʿ*, Tehran, 1317 q
- *Maqābis al-anwār*, Tehran, 1322 q

KHĀLIṢĪ = Maktabat Madrasat Madīnat al-ʿIlm, Kāẓimiyya (Iraq)
Catalogue: *Makhṭūṭat khizānat Jāmiʿat Madīnat al-ʿilm*, by Ḥ.M. Haddū Baghdad, 1972

KHALKHĀLĪ, M.M.:
Fiqh al-Shīʿa, Tehran, 1393 q (Vol. 3)

KHALLĀF, ʿAbd al-Wahhāb:
ʿIlm uṣūl al-fiqh, Kuwait, 1968

KHAṬĪB = Abū Bakr Aḥmad b. ʿAlī b. Thābit al-Baghdādī (d. 463/1072):
Mishkāt al-maṣābīḥ, ed. M.N. al-Albānī, Damascus, 1962

KHUMAYNĪ = Rūḥ Allāh b. Muṣṭafā al-Mūsawī:
Risāla fī 'l-ijtihād wa 'l-taqlīd, Qum, 1385 q (in a collection of his treatises entitled *al-Rasā'il*)

KHWĀJŪ'Ī = Muḥammad Ismāʿīl b. Muḥammad Ḥusayn al-Iṣfahānī (d. 1173/1759-60):
Risāla fī wujūb ittibāʿ al-mujtahid li-ẓannih, MS 1317/5 New Series, Princeton University Library

KHWĀNSĀRĪ = Muḥammad Bāqir b. Zayn al-Ābidīn al-Mūsawī (d. 1313/1395):
Rawḍāt al-jannāt, ed. M.T. al-Kashfī and A. Ismāʿīliyān, Tehran-Qum, 1390-2 q

KHAYRĀT KHĀN = Kitābkhāna-yi Madrasa-yi Khayrāt Khān, Mashhad
Catalogue: *Fihrist-i nuskhahāy-i khaṭṭī-yi Madrasa-yi Khayrāt Khān*, by M. Fāḍil, in the third volume of *Majmūʿa-yi fihrist-i nuskhahāy-i khaṭṭī-yi kitābkhānahāy-i shahrastānhāy-i Iran* (Tehran, 1353 sh), pp. 1717-97

KULAYNĪ = Abū Jaʿfar Muḥammad b. Yaʿqūb al-Rāzī (d. 329/941):
Al-Kāfī, ed. ʿA. A. al-Ghaffārī, Tehran, 1377-9 q

LEIDEN = Biblioteek Rijkauniversitat, Leiden
Catalogus codicum Orientalium, by R.P.A. Dozy and others, Leiden, 1851-77

LOS ANGELES = University Research Library, University of California, Los Angeles
Catalogue: *Fihrist-i nuskhahāy-i khaṭṭī-yi Dānishgāh-i Los Angeles*, by M.T. Dānishpazhūh, in *Nashriyya-yi Kitābkhāna-yi Markazī-yi Dānishgāh-i Tehran dar bāra-yi nuskhahāy-i khaṭṭī*, XI-XII (Tehran, 1362 sh), pp. 1-772

MAʿĀRIF = Kitābkhāna-yi ʿUmūmī-yi Maʿārif (= Kitābkhāna-yi Millī), Tehran
Catalogue: *Fihrist-i kutu-i khaṭṭī-yi Kitābkhāana-yi ʿUmūmī-yi Maʿārif*, by ʿA. Jawāhir Kalām, Tehran, 1934-5

McDERMOTT, M.J.:
The Theology of al-Shaykh al-Mufīd, Beirut, 1978

[M]A'HAD = Ma'had al-Dirāsāt al-Islāmiyya al-'Ulyā', Baghdad
Catalogue' *al-Makhṭūṭāt al-'Arabiyya fī Ma'had al-Dirāsāt al-Islāmiyya al-'Ulyā'*, by Ṣ.A. al-'Alī, Baghdad, 1968

[M]AHDAWĪ = the private collection of A. Mahdawī, Tehran
Catalogue: *Fihrist-i nuskhahāy-i khaṭṭī-yi kitābkhāna-yi khuṣūṣī-yi Dr. Aṣghar Mahdawī*, by M.T. Dānishpazhūh, in *Nashriyya-yi Kitāb-Khāna-yi Markazī-yi Dānishgāh-i Tehran dar bāra-yi nuskhahāy-i khaṭṭī*, II (Tehran, 1962), pp.59-181

[M]AḤFŪẒ, Ḥ.'A.:
(I) *Nafā'is al-makhṭūṭāt al-'Arabiyya fī Iran*, in *Majallat Ma'had al-Makhṭūṭāt al-'Arabiyya*, III (1957), pp.3-78
(II) *Al-Makhṭūṭāt al-'Arabiyya fi 'l-'Irāq*, in the above-mentioned periodical, IV (1958), pp.195-258

[M]AḤMAṢĀNĪ, Ṣ.:
Falsafat al-tashrī' fi 'l-Islām, Beirut, 1961

[M]ĀḤŪZĪ = Sulaymān b. 'Abd Allāh al-Baḥrānī (d. 1121/1709-10):
Al-'Ashara al-kāmila, MS 3866, Majlis Library, Tehran

[M]AJLIS = Kitābkhāna-yi Majlis, Tehran
Catalogue: *Fihrist-i Kitābkhāna-yi Majlis-i Shūrāy-i Millī*, by 'A. Ḥā'irī and others, Tehran, 1305-57 sh

[M]AJLISĪ I = Muḥammad Taqī b. Maqṣūd 'Alī al-Iṣfahānī (d. 1070/1659-60):
Lawāmi'-i Ṣāḥibqarānī, Tehran, 1331 q
Rawḍat al-muttaqīn, Tehran, 1393-9 q

[M]AJLISĪ II = Muḥammad Bāqir b. Muḥammad Taqī al-Iṣfahānī (d. 1110/1699):
* *Biḥār al-anwār*, Tehran, 1376 q -
Mir'āt al-'uqūl, Tehran, 1321-5 q
Sayr wa sulūk, MS 880, Mar'ashī Library, Qum (fols. 52a-56a)
Zād al-ma'ād, Iṣfahān, 1311 q

[M]ALIK = Kitābkhāna-yi Millī-yi Malik, Tehran
Catalogue: *Fihrist-i kitābhāy-i khaṭṭī-yi Kitābkhāna-yi Millī-yi Malik*, by A. Afshār and M.T. Dānishpazhūh, Tehran, 1352-61 sh

[M]ĀMAQĀNĪ = 'Abd Allāh b. Muḥammad Ḥasan (d. 1351/1932-3);
Miqbās al-hidāya, Tehran, 1345 q
Tanqīḥ al-maqāl, Najaf, 1350-2 q

[M]ANCHESTER = the John Rylands Library, Manchester
Catalogue: *Catalogue of the Arabic Manuscripts in the John Rylands Library*, by A. Mingana, Manchester, 1934

[M]AQRĪZĪ = Taqī al-Dīn Aḥmad b. 'Alī (d. 845/1441-2):
Ma'rifat mā yajib li-Āl al-Bayt al-Nabawī min al-ḥaqq 'alā man 'adāhum, ed. M.A. 'Āshūr, Cairo, 1392 q

[M]AR'ASHĪ = Kitābkhāna-yi 'Umūmī-yi . . . Mar'ashī, Qum
Catalogue: *Fihrist-i nuskhahāy-i khaṭṭī-yi Kitābkhāna-yi 'Umūmī-yi . . . Mar'ashī*, by A. Ḥusaynī, Qum, 1395 q -

[A]L-MASĀ'IL AL-MUHANNĀ'IYYA = Ajwibat al-masā'il allatī sa'alahā

Muhannā b. Sinān ʿan al-ʿAllāma wa Fakhr al-Muḥaqqiqīn, MS 1474 Central Library, University of Tehran (fols. 79b-103b)

MASJID-I AʿẒAM = Kitābkhāna-yi Masjid-i Aʿẓam, Qum

MASJID-I JĀMIʿ = Kitābkhāna-yi Masjid-i Jāmiʿ, Tehran
Catalogue: *Fihrist-i nuskhahāy-i khaṭṭī-yi Kitābkhāna-yi Madrasa-yi Chihilsutūn-i Masjid-i Jāmiʿ-i Tehran*, by R. Ustādī, in *Āshnāʾī bā chand nuskha-yi khaṭṭī* (Qum, 1396q), pp.305-88

MASHHAD, ADABIYYĀT = Kitābkhāna-yi Dānishkada-yi Adabiyyāt wa ʿUlūm-i Insānī-yi Dānishgāh-i Firdawsī, Mashhad
Catalogue: *Fihrist-i nuskhahāy-i khaṭṭī-yi Kitābkhāna-yi Dānishkada-yi Adabiyyāt*. . ., by M. Fāḍil, Mashhad, 1976 -

MASHHAD, ILĀHIYYĀT = Kitābkhāna-yi Dānishkada-yi Ilāhiyyāt wa Maʿārif-i Islāmī, Mashhad
Catalogues:
- *Fihrist-i nuskhahāy-i khaṭṭī-yi Kitābkhāna-yi Dānishkada-yi Ilāhiyyāt* . . ., by M. Fāḍil, Mashhad, 1976 -
- (Microfilms) *Fihrist-i mīkrufīlmhāy-i Kitābkhāna-yi Dānishkada-yi Ilāhiyyāt* . . ., by M. Fāḍil, in *Nashriyya-yi Dānishkada-yi Ilāhiyyāt wa maʿārif-i Islāmī-yi Mashhad*, XII (1974), pp.193-234, XV (1975), pp.157-201

MATḤAF = Maktabat al-Matḥaf al-ʿIrāqī, Baghdad
Catalogue: *Makhṭūṭāt Maktabat al-Matḥaf al-ʿIrāqī*, by U.N. al-Naqshbandī andʿA.A. al-Qashṭīnī, Baghdad, 1975 (Vol. 1)

MIFTĀḤ = the private collection of Ḥ. Miftāḥ, Tehran
Catalogue: *Fihrist-i nuskhahāy-i khaṭṭī-yi Kitābkhāna-yi Dr. Ḥusayn Miftāḥ*, by M.T. Dānishpazhūh, in *Nahriyya-yi Kitābkhāna-yi Markazī-yi Dānishgāh-i Tehran dar bāra-yi nuskhahāy-i khaṭṭī*, VII (Tehran, 1353 sh), pp.95-511

MILLĪ = Kitābkhāna-yi Millī, Tehran
Catalogue: *Fihrist-i nusakh-i khaṭṭī-yi Kitābkhāna-yi Millī*, by ʿA. Anwār, Tehran, 1344-58 sh

MIQDĀD = Jamāl al-Dīn Miqdād b. ʿAbd Allāh al-Suyūrī al-Ḥillī (d. 826/1423):
Al-Tanqīḥ al-rāʾiʿ, MS 1725, Marʿashī Library, Qum

MĪR ḤAMĪD ḤUSAYN B. MUḤAMMAD QULĪ AL-LAKNAWĪ (d. 1306/1888-9)
ʿAbaqāt al-anwār, translated into Arabic by ʿAlī al-Ḥusaynī al-Mīlānī Qum, 1398 q (Vol. I)

MĪRZĀ JAʿFAR = Kitābkhāna-yi Madrasa-yi Mīrzā Jaʿfar, Mashhad
Catalogue: *Fihrist-i nuskhahāy-i khaṭṭī-yi Kitābkhāna-yi Madrasa-yi Mīrzā Jaʿfar*, by ʿA. Nūranī and K.M. Shānachī, in *Fihrist-i nuskhahāy-i khaṭṭī-yi chahār kitābkhāna-yi Mashhad*, the first volume of *Majmūʿa-yi fihrist-i nuskhahāy-i khaṭṭī-yi kitābkhānahāy-i shahrastānhāy-i Iran* (Tehran, 1351 sh), pp.25-43

MUʿALLIM = Muḥammad ʿAlī Muʿallim Ḥabībābādī:
Makārim al-āthār, Iṣfahān, 1337 sh -

MUDARRIS = Muḥammad ʿAlī b. Muḥammad Ṭāhir al-Tabrīzī (d. 1373/1954

Rayḥānat al-adab, Tehran, Vol. 1, 1335 sh; Vols. 2-6, 1328-33 sh

UFĪD = Abū ʻAbd Allāh Muḥammad b. Muḥammad b. Nuʻmān al-Baghdādī, Ibn al-Muʻallim (d. 413/1022):
Awā'il al-maqālāt, ed. ʻA.W. Charandābī and F. al-Zanjānī, Tabrīz, 1364 q
Al-Fuṣūl al-mukhtāra min al-ʻUyūn wa 'l-maḥāsin, Najaf, n.d. (2nd edition)
Il-Ifṣāḥ fi 'l-imāma, Najaf, 1950
Al-Ikhtiṣāṣ, ed. M.M. al-Kharsān, Najaf, 1971
Jawāb ahl al-Ḥā'ir fī mā sa'alū ʻanh min sahw al-Nabī, Qum, 1398 q (in ʻAlī b. Muḥammad al-ʻĀmilī's *al-Durr al-Manthūr*, I, pp.111-20)
Al-Masā'il al-Ṣāghāniyya, Najaf, n.d.
Al-Masā'il al-Sarawiyya, Qum., n.d. (in the collection of *ʻIddat rasā'il li 'l-Shaykh al-Mufīd*, pp. 207-232)
al-Masā'il al-ʻUkbariyya, MS 2313, Central Library, University of Tehran (fols. 58b-69b)
Al-Radd ʻala aṣḥāb al-ʻadad, Qum, 1398 q (in ʻAlī b. Muḥammad al-ʻĀmilī's *al-Durr al-Manthūr*, I, pp.122-34)
Al-Tadhkira bi-uṣūl al-fiqh, Tabrīz, 1322 q (in al-Karājakī's *Kanz al-fawā'id*, pp. 186-94)
Taṣḥīḥ al-iʻtiqād, ed. ʻA.W. Charandābī, Tabrīz, 1364 q (together with the author's *Awā'il al-maqālāt*)

UḤAMMAD AL-ĀMULĪ = Shams al-Dīn Muḥammad b. Maḥmūd (8th/14th century):
Nafā'is al-funūn, Tehran, 1377-9 q

UḤAMMAD AL-ARDABĪLĪ (d. 1101/1689-90):
Jāmiʻ al-ruwāt, Tehran, 1331 sh

UḤAMMAD BĀQIR AL-ṢADR:
Durūs fī ʻilm al-uṣūl, Beirut, 1978
Al-Fatāwā al-wāḍiḥa, Najaf, 1396 q

UḤAQQIQ = Najm al-Dīn Abu 'l-Qāsim Jaʻfar b. Ḥasan al-Ḥillī (d. 676/1277):
Maʻārij al-uṣūl, Tehran, 1310 q
al-Muʻtabar, Tehran, 1318 q
Nukat al-Nihāya, Tehran, 1276 q (in the collection of *al-Jawāmiʻ al-fiqhiyya*, pp. 373-470)
Sharā'iʻ al-Islām, Beirut, n.d.

UNDHIRĪ = Zakī al-Dīn ʻAbd al-ʻAẓīm b. ʻAbd al-Qawī (d. 656/1258):
Mukhtaṣar Ṣaḥīḥ Muslim, ed. M.N. al-Albānī, Kuwait, 1969

URTAḌĀ = Abu 'l-Qāsim ʻAlī b. Ḥusayn al-Mūsawī, ʻAlam al-Hudā (d. 436/1044):
Al-Dharīʻz ilā uṣūl al-sharīʻa, ed. A. Gurjī, Tehran, 1346-8 sh
Ibṭāl al-ʻamal bi-akhbār al-āḥād, microfilm 1162, Central Library, University of Tehran (fols. 142b-143a)
Al-Intiṣār, Najaf, 1971
Jawābāt al-masā'il al-mawṣiliyya al-thālitha, the above-mentioned microfilm (fols. 36-56a)
Jawābāt al-masā'il al-mawṣiliyya al-thāniya, the above-mentioned microfilm (fols. 31-5)
Jawābāt al-masā'il al-Tabbāniyyāt, microfilm 1255, Central Library, University of Tehran

- *Jawābāt al-masāʾil al-Ṭarābulusiyyāt*, microfilm 1162, Central Library, University of Tehran
- *Al-Shāfī*, Tehran, 1302 q

MURTAḌĀ AL-RĀZĪ = Jamāl al-Dīn Abū ʿAbd Allāh Muḥammad b. Ḥusayn b. Ḥasan (6th/12th century):
Tabṣirat al-ʿawāmm, ed. ʿA. Ḥāʾirī, Tehran, n.d.

MUSHĀR, Khānbābā:
Fihrist-i kitābhāy-i chāpī-yi ʿArabī, Tehran, 1344 q

MUSLIM = Abu ʾl-Ḥusayn Muslim b. Ḥajjāj al-Qushayrī al-Naysābūrī (d. 261/875):
Saḥīḥ Muslim, Cairo, 1290 q

MUTTAQĪ = ʿAlāʾ al-Dīn ʿAlī b. Ḥusām al-Dīn al-Burhānpūrī (d. 975/1567):
Kanz al-ʿummāl, Hyderabad, 1945-75

MUẒAFFAR, Muḥammad Riḍā:
Uṣūl al-fiqh, Najaf, 1967

MŪZA = Mūza-yi Iran-i Bāstān, Tehran
Catalogue: *Fihrist-i nuskhahāy-i khaṭṭī-yi kitābkhāna-yi Mūza-yi Iran-i Bāstān*, by M.T. Dānishpazhūh, in *Nashriyya-yi Kitābkhāna-yi Markazī-yi Dānishgāh-i Tehran dar bāra-yi nuskhahāy-i khaṭṭī*, II (Tehran, 1962), pp.199-218

NĀʾĪNĪ = Muḥammad Ḥusayn b. ʿAbd al-Raḥīm (d. 1355/1936):
Munyat al-ṭālib, a collection of al-Nāʾīnī's lectures compiled by Mūsā al-Najafī al-Khwānsārī, Tehran, 1373 q

NAJAFĪ = Muḥammad Ḥasan b. Muḥammad Bāqir, Ṣāḥib al-Jawāhir (d. 1266/1850):
Jawāhir al-kalām, ed. ʿA. al-Qūchānī and others, Najaf-Tehran, 1377-1401 q

NAJĀSHĪ = Abu ʾl-ʿAbbās Aḥmad b. ʿAlī al-Asadī al-Ṣayrafī (d. 450/1058-9):
Rijāl al-Najāshī, Tehran, 1337 sh

NASĀʾĪ = Abū ʿAbd al-Raḥmān Aḥmad b. ʿAlī b. Shuʿayb (d. 303/915):
Sunan, Cairo, 1312 q

NASHRIYYA = Nashriyya-yi Kitābkhāna-yi Markazī-yi Dānishgāh-i Tehran dar bāra-yi nuskhahāy-i khaṭṭī, Tehran, 1340 sh -

NAṢĪR AL-DĪN AL-ṬŪSĪ (d. 672/1274):
Akhlāq-i Nāṣirī, ed. M. Mīnuwī and ʿA.R. Ḥaydarī, Tehran, 1356 sh

NAWĀDIR = Min nawādir makhṭūṭāt Maktabat Āyat Allāh al-Ḥakīm al-ʿĀmm
Najaf, 1962

NAWWĀB = Kitābkhāna-yi Madrasa-yi Nawwāb, Mashhad
Catalogue: *Fihrist-i nuskhahāy-i khaṭṭī-yi kitābkhāna-yi Madrasa-yi Nawwāb*, by ʿA. Nūrānī and K.M. Shānachī, in *Fihrist-i nuskhahāy-i khaṭṭī-yi du kitābkhāna-yi Mashhad*, the second volume of *Majmūʿa-yi fihrist-i nuskhahāy-i khaṭṭī-yi kitābkhānahāyi shahrastānhāy-i Iran*

(Tehran, 1351 sh), pp.437-562

UJŪMĪ = the private collection of M. Nujūmī, Kirmānshāh (Iran)
Catalogue: *Makhṭūṭāt maktabat al-sayyid Murtaḍā al-Nujūmī*, by A. al-Ḥusaynī, in his *Dalīl al-makhṭūṭāt* (Qum, 1397 q), pp.214-97

U'MĀNĪ = Abū 'Abd Allāh Muḥammad b. Ibrāhīm al-Kātib, Ibn Abī Zaynab (d. around 350/961):
Tafsīr al-Nu'mānī, Tehran, 1387 q (in al-Majlisī II's *Biḥār al-anwār*, XCIII, pp.1-97)

ŪRBAKHSH = Kitābkhāna-yi Nūrbakhsh, Khāniqāh-i Ni'mat Allāhī, Tehran
Catalogue: *Fihrist-i nuskhahāy-i khaṭṭī-yi Kitābkhāna-yi Nūrbakhsh* . . ., by I. Dībājī, Tehran, 1970-3

ŪRĪ = Ḥusayn b. Muḥammad Taqī (d. 1320/1902):
Mustadrak al-Wasā'il, Tehran, 1382 q

ĀḌĪ NU'MĀN = Abū Ḥanīfa Nu'mān b. Muḥammad al-Tamīmī al-Maghribī (d. 363/974):
Ikhtilāf uṣūl al-madhāhib, ed. M. Ghālib, Beirut, 1973

ĀDIRIYYA = al-Maktabat al-Qādiriyya, Jāmi' al-Shaykh 'Abd al-Qādir al-Gīlānī, Baghdad
Catalogue: *al-Āthār al-khaṭṭiyya fi 'l-Maktabat al-Qādiriyya* . . ., by 'I. 'A. Ra'ūf, Baghdad, 1974-7

AFFĀL = Sayf al-Dīn Muḥammad b. Aḥmad al-Shāshī (d. 507/1113-14):
Ḥilyat al-'ulamā' = al-Mustaẓharī, ed. Y.A.I. Darādka, Beirut, 1980

ASṬALĀNĪ = Shihāb al-Dīn Aḥmad b. Muḥammad al-Khaṭīb (d. 923/1517):
Al-Mawāhib al-ladunniyya, Cairo, 1325-8 q

AWĀM AL-DĪN AL-WISHNAWĪ:
Ḥadīth al-Thaqalayn, Cairo, 1374 q

UHPĀ'Ī = 'Ināyat Allāh b. 'Alī (d. after 1016/1607-8):
Majma' al-rijāl, ed. Ḍ. al-'Allāma, Iṣfahān, 1387 q

AḌAWĪ = Kitābkhāna-yi Āstān-i Quds-i Raḍawī, Mashhad
Catalogue: *Fihrist-i kutub-i Kitābkhāna-yi mubāraka-yi Āstān-i Quds-i Raḍawī*, Mashhad, 1305 sh -

AḌAWIYYA = Kitābkhāna-yi Madrasa-yi Raḍawiyya, Qum
Catalogue: *Fihrist-i nuskhahāy-i khaṭṭī-yi Kitābkhāna-yi Madrasa-yi Raḍawiyya*, by Ḥ. Mudarrisī Ṭabāṭabā'ī, Qum, 1355 sh

AḌĪ AL-DĪN AL-QAZWĪNĪ (d. 1096/1685):
Ḍiyāfat al-ikhwān, ed. A. al-Ḥusaynī, Qum, 1397 q
Tārīkh-i mashāhīr-i Imāmiyya, MS 3514/1, Central Library, University of Tehran (pp. 327-8)

ĀHNIMĀY-I KITĀT, Persian periodical, Tehran, 1337-57 sh

ASHT = Kitabkhāna-yi 'Umūmī-yi, Rasht
Catalogue: *Fihrist-i nuskhahāy-i khaṭṭī-yi kitābkhāna-yi Jam'iyyat-i Nashr-i Farhang-i shahr-i Rasht*, by M. Rawshan, in the thrid volume

of *Majmūʿa-yi fihrist-i nuskhahāy-i khaṭṭī-yi kitābkhānahāy-i shahrastānhāy-i Iran* (Tehran, 1351), pp.1081-238

RĀWANDĪ = Quṭb al-Dīn Saʿīd b. Hibat Allāh (d. 573/1178):
Fiqh al-Qurʾān, ed. A. al-Ḥusaynī, Qum, 1397-9 q

RAWḌĀTĪ = the private collection of M.ʿA. Rawḍātī, Iṣfahān
Catalogue: *Fihrist-i kutub-i khaṭṭī-yi kitābkhānahāy-i Iṣfahān*, by M.ʿA. Rawḍātī, Iṣfahān, 1377 q

RIḌĀ AL-QAZWĪNĪ = Riḍā b. Muḥammad ʿAlī al-Ḥusaynī (mid-13th/19th century):
Al-Farq bayn al-Akhbāriyyīn wa ʾl-Uṣūliyyīn, MS 3720, Marʿashī Library, Qum

RISĀLA FI ʾL-ṬAHĀRA WA ʾL-ṢALĀT (belonging to the 12th/18th century), MS 307/1, Gulpāyigānī Library, Qum

ṢADŪQ = Abū Jaʿfar Muḥammad b. ʿAlī al-Qummī, Ibn Bābawayh (d. 381/991-2):
- *ʿIlal al-sharāʾiʿ*, ed. F. al-Ṭabāṭabāʾī al-Yazdī, Qum, 1377-8 q
- *Al-Iʿtiqādāt*, Tehran, 1379 q (together with al-Miqdād's *al-Nāfiʿ yawm al-ḥashr fī sharḥ al-bāb al-ḥādīʿashr*, pp. 66-115)
-* *Man lā yaḥḍuruh al-faqīh*, ed. Ḥ.M. al-Kharsān, Najaf, 1957
- *Al-Muqniʿ*, ed. M. Wāʿiẓzāda, Tehran, 1377 q
- *Al-Tawḥīd*, ed. H.Ḥ. al-Ṭihrānī, Tehran, 1387 q

ṢAFĀʾĪ, A.:
Hishām b. al-Ḥakam, Tehran, 1342 sh

ṢAFFĀR = Abū Jaʿfar Muḥammad b. Ḥasan b. Farrukh al-Qummī (d. 290/902-3):
Baṣāʾir al-darajāt, ed. M. Kūchabāghī, Tabrīz, 1381 q

ṢĀḤIB AL-DHARĪʿA = Maktabat Ṣāḥib al-Dharīʿa al-ʿĀmma, Najaf

ṢĀḤIB AL-MAʿĀLIM = Ḥasan b. Zayn al-Dīn al-ʿĀmilī (d. 1011/1602):
Maʿālim al-dīn, Tehran, n.d.

ṢĀḤIB AL-MADĀRIK = Muḥammad b. ʿAlī al-Mūsawī al-ʿĀmilī (d. 1009/1600):
- *Hidāyat al-ṭālibīn*, MS 4641, Majlis Library, Tehran
-* *Madārik al-aḥkām*, Tehran, 1322 q

SALLĀR = Abū Yaʿlā Ḥamza b. ʿAbd al-ʿAzīz al-Daylamī (d. 448/1056-7):
Al-Marāsim, ed. M. al-Bustānī, Beirut, 1980

SALṬANATĪ = Kitābkhāna-yi Salṭanatī, Tehran
Catalogue: *Fihrist-i kutub-i dīnī wa madhhabī-yi khaṭṭī-yi Kitābkhāna-yi Salṭanatī*, by Badrī Ātābāy, Tehran, 1352 sh

SAMĀHĪJĪ = ʿAbd Allāh b. Ṣāliḥ al-Baḥrānī (d. 1135/1723):
Munyat al-mumārisīn, MS 1916/27, Majlis Library, Tehran

SARYAZDĪ = Kitābkhāna-yi Saryazdī, Madrasa-yi Khān, Yazd
Catalogue: *[Fihrist-i nuskhahāy-i khaṭṭī-yi] Kitābkhāna-yi Saryazdī*, by M.T. Dānishpazhūh, in *Nashriyya-yi Kitābkhāna-yi Markazī-yi Dānishgāh-i Tehran dar bāra-yi nuskhahāy-i khaṭṭī*, IV (Tehran, 196

pp. 417-32

SHAHĪD I = Shams al-Dīn Muḥammad b. Makkī al-ʿĀmilī (d. 786/1384):
- *Dhikrā al-Shīʿa*, Tehran, 1271 q
- *Al-Durūs al-sharʿiyya*, Tehran, 1269 q
- *Al-Qawāʿid wa ʾl-fawāʾid*, Tehran, 1308 q

SHAHĪD II = Zayn al-Dīn b. ʿAlī b. Aḥmad al-ʿĀmilī (d. 966/1559):
- *Al-Dirāya*, ed. M.J. Āl Ibrāhīm, Najaf, n.d.
- *Masālik al-afhām*, Tehran, 1273 q
- *Al-Rawḍa al-bahiyya*, Najaf, 1386-90 q

SHAHRASTĀNHĀ = *Majmūʿa-yi fihrist-i nuskhahāy-i khaṭṭī-yi kitābkhāna-hāy-i shahrastānhāy-i Iran*, Tehran, 1351-3 sh

SHAHRASTĀNĪ = Abu ʾl-Fatḥ Muḥammad b. ʿAbd al-Karīm (d. 548/1153); *Al-Milal wa ʾl-niḥal*, ed. A.M. al-ʿĪd, Cairo, 1977

SHARAF AL-DĪn, ʿAbd al-Ḥusayn:
Al-Murājaʿāt, Beirut, n.d.

SHARḤ QAṬRAT AL-BAḤRAYN (early 11th/17th century), MS 1843, Marʿashī Library, Qum

SHARĪF AL-JURJĀNĪ (d 816/1413):
Sharḥ al-Mawāqif, Constantinople, 1286 q

SHĀṬIBĪ = Abū Isḥāq Ibrāhīm b. Mūsā al-Gharnāṭī (d. 790/1388):
Al-Muwāfaqāt, Cairo, 1344 q

SHAYKH = Abū Jaʿfar Muḥammad b. Ḥasan al-Ṭūsī (d. 460/1067):
- *Al-Fihrist*, ed. M.Ṣ. Āl Baḥr al-ʿUlūm, Najaf, 1937
- *Al-Ghayba*, Tabrīz, 1323 q
- *Al-Istibṣār*, ed. Ḥ.M. al-Kharsān, Najaf, 1375-6 q
- *Tahdhīb al-aḥkām*, ed. Ḥ M. al-Kharsān, Najaf, 1958-62
- *ʿUddat al-uṣūl*, Tehran, 1314 q

SHĪRĀZĪ = Maktabat Madrasat al-Shīrāzī, Sāmarrāʾ (Iraq)

SHUBBAR = ʿAbd Allāh b. Muḥammad Riḍā al-Ḥusaynī (d. 1242/1826):
Bughyat al-ṭālibīn, MS 3972, Majlis Library, Tehran

SINĀ = Kitābkhāna-yi Majlis-i Sinā, Tehran
Catalogue: *Fihrist-i kitābhāy-i khaṭṭī-yi Kitābkhāna-yi Majlis-i Sinā*, by M.T. Dānishpazhūh and B. ʿIlmī Anwārī, Tehran, 1356-9 sh

SIPAHSĀLĀR = Kitābkhāna-yi Madrasa-yi Sipahsālār, Tehran
Catalogue: *Fihrist-i Kitābkhāna-yi Madrasa-yi ʿAlī-yi Sipahsālār*, by Ibn Yūsuf Shīrāzī and others, Tehran, 1315-56 sh

SULAYMĀN KHĀN = Kitābkhāna-yi Madrasa-yi Sulaymān Khān, Mashhad
Catalogue: *Fhrist-i nuskhahāy-i khaṭṭī-yi Kitābkhāna-yi Madrasa-yi Sulaymān Khān*, by ʿA. Nūrānī and K.M. Shānachī, in *Fihrist-i nuskhahāy-i khaṭṭī-yi chahār kitābkhāna-yi Mashhad*, the first volume of *Majmūʿa-yi fihrist-i nuskhahāy-i khaṭṭī-yi kitābkhānahāy-i shahrastānhāy-i Iran* (Tehran, 1351 sh), pp.1-24

SUYŪṬĪ = Jalāl al-Dīn 'Abd al-Raḥmān b. Abī Bakr (d. 911/1505):
Iḥyā' al-mayt, Najaf, n.d.

ṬABARĀNĪ = Abu 'l-Qāsim Sulaymān b. Aḥmad b. Ayyūb (d. 360/970-1):
Al-Mu'jam al-ṣaghīr, ed. 'A.M. 'Uthmān, Madina, 1968

ṬABRISĪ = Abū 'Alī Faḍl b. Ḥasan, Amīn al-Islām (d. 548/1154):
Majma' al-bayān, Tehran, 1379-82 q

TABRĪZ, MILLĪ = Kitābkhāna-yi Millī, Tabrīz
Catalogue: *Fihrist-i Kitābkhāna-yi Millī-yi Tabrīz*, by W. Sayyid Yūnusī, Tabrīz, 1345 sh

TAḤĀWĪ = Abū Ja'far Aḥmad b. Muḥammad al-Azdī (d. 321/933):
Mushkil al-āthār, Hyderabad, 1333 q

ṬAḤṬĀWĪ = Aḥmad b. Muḥammad b. Ismā'īl (d. 1231/1816):
Ḥāshiyat al-Durr al-mukhtār, Cairo, 1254 q

TARBIYAT = Kitābkhāna-yi Tarbiyat, Tabrīz
Catalogue: *Fihrist-i Kitabkhāna-yi Dawlatī-yi Tarbiyat*, by M. Nakhjawānī, Tabrīz, 1329 sh

TIRMIDHĪ = Abū 'Īsā Muḥammad b. 'Īsā al-Sulamī (d. 279/892-3):
Sunan, Beirut, 1394 q

TOPKAPI SERAYI = Topkapi Serayi Müzesi Kütüphanesi, Istanbul
Catalogue: *Arapça yazmalar kataloğu*, by F.E. Karatay, Istanbul, 1964

ṬU'MA, S.H.:
- *Makhṭūṭāt Karbalā'*, Najaf, 1973
- *Khazā'in kutub Karbalā' al-ḥāḍira*, Najaf, 1977

TUNUKĀBUNĪ = Muḥammad b. Sulaymān (d. 1302/1884-5):
Qiṣaṣ al-'ulamā', Tehran, n.d.

ṬURAYḤĪ = Fakhr al-Dīn b. Muḥammad 'Alī (d. 1085/1674-5)
Jāmi' al-maqāl, Tehran, 1374 q

TUSTARĪ, Muḥammad Taqī
- *Qāmūs al-rijāl*, Tahran, 1379 q -
- *Risāla fī sahw al-Nabī*, Tehran, 1349 sh (together with Vol. 11 of the author's *Qāmūs al-rijāl*)

TUSTARIYYA = Maktabat al-Ḥusayniyya al-Tustariyya, Najaf
Catalogue: *Fihrist-i nuskhahāy-i khaṭṭī-yi Kitābkhāna-yi Ḥusayniyya-yi Shūshtarīhā*, by A. Ismā'īliyān and R. Ustādī, in *Nashriyya-yi Kitābkhāna-yi Markazī-yi Dānishgāh-i Tehran dar bāra-yi nuskhahāy-i khaṭṭī*, XI-XII (Tehran, 1362 sh), pp. 787-879

USTĀDĪ = the private collection of R. Ustādī, Qum (now in Mara'ashī Library, Qum)
Catalogue: *Ṣad wa shaṣt nuskha-yi khaṭṭī az yak kitābkhāna-yi shakhṣī*, by R. Ustādī, Qum, 1354 sh

VATICAN = Biblioteca Vaticana
Catalogue: *Elenco munscritt arabi Islamici della Biblioteca Vaticana*, by G. Levi della vida, Rome, 1935-65

WAḤĪD, Perisan periodical,Tehran, 1342-59 sh

WAZĪRĪ = Kitābkhāna-yi Wazīrī, Yazd
Catalobue: *Fihrist-i nuskhahāy-i khaṭṭī-yi Kitābkhāna-yi Wazīrī*, by M. Shīrwānī, Tehran, 1350 sh -

YĀDNĀMA-YI SHAYKH-I ṬŪSĪ, ed. M. Wā'iẓzāda, Mashhad, 1972-6

YAḤYĀ AL-BAḤRĀNĪ = Sharaf al-Dīn Yaḥyā b. Ḥusayn b. 'Ashīra al-Muftī (d. after 967/1559-60):
Risāla fī ma'rifat mashā'ikh al-Shī'a, ed. M.T. Dānishpazhūh, in *Majalla-yi Dānishkada-yi Adabiyyāt-i Tabrīz*, XIX (1345 sh), pp.306-19

YAḤYĀ B. SA'ĪD = Najīb al-Dīn Yaḥyā b. Aḥmad b. Sa'īd al-Hudhalī al-Ḥillī (d. 689/1290):
Nuzhat al-nāẓir, ed. A. al-Ḥusaynī and N. al-Wā'iẓī, Najaf, 1386 q

ZANJĀN = the private collection of 'Izz al-Dīn al-Ḥusaynī, Zanjān
Catalogue: *Makhṭūṭāt maktabat Imām al-Jum'a*, by A. al-Ḥusaynī, in his *Dalīl al-makhṭūṭāt* (Qum, 1397 q), pp. 88-170

ZANJĀNĪ = the private collection of A. Zanjānī, Qum
Catalogue: *Fihrist-i nuskhahāy-i khaṭṭī-yi kitābkhāna-yi shakhṣī-yi . . . Zanjānī*, by R. Ustādī and Ḥ. Mudarisī Ṭabāṭabā'ī, in *Āshnā'i bā chand nuskha-yi khaṭṭī* (Qum, 1396 q), pp. 155-304

ZARQĀ', M.A.:
Al-Madkhal al-fiqhī al-'āmm, Damascus, 1959

ZUḤAYLĪ, W.:
Al-Wasīṭ, Damascus, 1969

Index

Special abbreviation:

M. = Muḥammad

1 - AUTHORS

A

ʿAbbās Abū Turābī 158
ʿAbbās ʿAlī al-Kazzāzī 170
ʿAbbās al-Jaṣānī 69
ʿAbbās al-Qazwīnī 75
ʿAbbās al-Tūnī 135
ʿAbd al-ʿĀlī al-Harandī 173, 207
ʿAbd al-ʿAlī al-Jāpalaqī 123, 133, 146
ʿAbd al-ʿĀlī al-Karakī 51, 66, 71, 120, 135, 213
ʿAbd al-ʿAlī al-Rashtī 68
ʿAbd Allāh al-Afandī 177
ʿAbd Allāh b. ʿAlībābā 88
ʿAbd Allāh al-Hazārjarībī 82
ʿAbd Allāh al-Jazā'irī 86, 87, 109
ʿAbd Allāh b. Khalīl 204, 205
ʿAbd Allāh al-Kirmānshāhī 82, 127, 183, 189, 194, 201, 210
ʿAbd Allāh al-Māmaqānī 70, 112-13, 118, 121, 128, 154, 159, 169, 173, 174, 194, 197, 209, 214
ʿAbd Allāh al-Māzandarānī 156
ʿAbd Allāh al-Ṣaymarī 162
ʿAbd Allāh Shubbar 87, 98
ʿAbd Allāh al-Tūnī 8, 147
ʿAbd Allāh al-Tustarī 51, 85, 96, 106, 126, 133, 143, 145, 146, 154, 162, 163, 166, 182, 183, 195, 198
ʿAbd al-ʿAẓīm b. M. Maʿṣūm 206
ʿAbd al-ʿAzīz b. al-Barrāj 43, 63, 121
ʿAbd al-Ghanī 83
ʿAbd al-Ghanī al-Kishmīrī 67
ʿAbd al-Hādī al-Dilījānī 135
ʿAbd al-Hādī al-Shīrāzī 157, 193
ʿAbd al-Ḥasīb al-ʿĀmilī 122, 206
ʿAbd al-Ḥayy al-Jurjānī 133, 135, 204
ʿAbd al-Ḥusayn al-Aʿsam 68
ʿAbd al-Ḥusayn al-Aṣbaghī 88
ʿAbd al-Ḥusayn al-ʿĀṣī 81
ʿAbd al-Ḥusayn al-Baraghānī 72, 74
ʿAbd al-Ḥusayn al-Ḥillī 122
ʿAbd al-Ḥusayn al-Kāẓimī 135
ʿAbd al-Ḥusayn al-Qazwīnī 69
ʿAbd al-Ḥusayn al-Ṭihrānī 196
ʿAbd al-Karīm al-Ḥā'irī 11, 58, 138, 186
ʿAbd al-Karīm al-Īrawānī 91
ʿAbd al-Karīm al-Jurjānī 77
ʿAbd al-Karīm al-Qazwīnī 177
ʿAbd al-Karīm al-Ṭabasī 199
ʿAbd al-Malik b. Fatḥān 72, 209
ʿAbd al-Nabī al-Baḥrānī 191
ʿAbd al-Nabī al-Jazā'irī 53, 71
ʿAbd al-Nabī al-Qazwīnī 151
ʿAbd al-Qādir al-Māzandarānī 82
ʿAbd al-Raḥmān al-ʿAtā'iqī 71
ʿAbd al-Raḥmān al-Qazwīnī 68
ʿAbd al-Raḥīm b. Maʿrūf 95
ʿAbd al-Raḥīm al-Qazwīnī 68
ʿAbd al-Rashīd al-Tustarī 89
ʿAbd al-Rasūl al-Fīrūzkūhī 120, 131, 169, 190
ʿAbd al-Ṣāḥib al-Narāqī 118
ʿAbd al-Salām al-Anṣārī 72, 206
ʿAbd al-Ṣamad al-Hamadānī 66, 68, 97, 175
ʿAbd al-Ṣamad al-Tabrīzī 67
ʿAbd al-Wahhāb al-Baraghānī 87
ʿAbd al-Wahhāb al-Maḥallātī 69
ʿAbd al-Wāḥid al-Ḍarīr 155
Al-Ābī 58, 70
ʿĀbid Ḥusayn al-Anṣārī 67
Abū ʿAbd Allāh al-Anṣārī 131
Abū ʿAlī al-Ḥā'irī 98
Abu 'l-Fatḥ al-Sharīfī 115
Abu 'l-Ḥasan al-Abīwardī 204, 214
Abu 'l-Ḥasan al-Angajī 142
Abu 'l-Ḥasan al-Futūnī 86, 191
Abu 'l-Ḥasan al-Iṣfanānī 58, 94, 100
Abu 'l-Ḥasan b M. Kāẓim 168
Abu 'l-Ḥasan al-Mūsawī 100
Abu 'l-Ḥasan al-Shahrastānī 90
Abu 'l-Ḥasan al-Tunukābunī 68
Abu 'l-Maʿālī al-Astarābādī 134
Abu 'l-Majd al-Iṣfahānī 11, 93, 131, 176

Abu 'l-Makārim al-Zanjānī 131
Abu 'l-Qāsim b. ʿAbbās 87
Abu 'l-Qāsim al-Gulpāyigānī 114
136
Abu 'l-Qāsim al-Ḥusaynī 174,
186
Abu 'l-Qāsim al-Ishkawarī 176
Abu 'l-Qāsim al-Kalāntarī al-Ṭihrānī 11, 207
Abu 'l-Qāsim al-Khwānsārī 155,
156
Abu 'l-Qāsim al-Kujūrī 171
Abu 'l-Qāsim al-Lāhūrī 200
Abu 'l-Qāsim al-Mūsawī 161
Abu 'l-Qāsim al-Narāqī 184
Abu 'l-Qāsim al-Yazdī 67
Abū Ṭālib al-Findiriskī 81
Abū Ṭālib al-Hamadānī 99
Abū Ṭālib al-Qā'inī 156, 178,
183
Abū Ṭālib al-Qummī 137
Abū Ṭālib al-Tajlīl 178
Abū Ṭālib al-Zanjānī 166
Abū Turāb al-Khwānsārī 93
Abū Turāb al-Qazwīnī 90
Abū Yaʿlā 102
Aḥmad al-Aḥsā'ī 75
Aḥmad b. ʿAlī Mukhtār al-Gulpāyigānī 71, 157, 171,
183, 197
Aḥmad al-ʿĀmilī 129, 184
Aḥmad al-Baḥrānī 108, 129,
137, 144, 181, 194, 195, 212
Aḥmad al-Bihbahānī 130
Aḥmad al-Fayḍī 183, 192, 202,
211
Aḥmad b. Ibrāhīm b. ʿĪsā al-Baḥrānī 194
Aḥmad al-Iṣfahānī 133
Aḥmad al-Jazā'irī 116, 123
Aḥmad al-Khu'aynī 155, 214
Aḥmad al-Khwānsārī 94
Aḥmad al-Kirmānshāhī 151, 210
Aḥmad al-Malāyirī 70
Aḥmad b. al-Najjār 73
Aḥmad al-Narāqī 57, 92-3, 98,
111, 117, 210
Aḥmad al- Rashtī 92
Aḥmad al-Sabīʿī 132, 204
Aḥmad al-Tabrīzī 165
Aḥmad al-Tūnī 81
Aḥmad al-Zanjānī 114, 172, 193
Al-Akhbārī 143, 157, 160, 165,
168, 170, 174, 201
ʿAlā' Burhān al-Tabrīzī 96
ʿAlā' al-Mulk Fāḍil Khān 139
Āl Baḥr al-ʿUlūm 112, 118, 168,
171, 179, 180, 182, 185, 192,
208, 209, 213
ʿAlī b. ʿAbd al-Ghaffār 69
ʿAlī b. ʿAbd al-Ṣamad al-ʿĀmilī
132
ʿAlī b. Aḥmad b. Abī Jāmiʿ 74
ʿAlī Akbar b. ʿAlī 82
ʿAlī Akbar al-Khwānsārī 72, 135
ʿAlī Akbar al-Qazwīnī 92, 114,
127, 211
ʿAlī Āl Baḥr al-ʿUlūm 66, 140,
208
ʿAlī b. ʿAlī b. Ḥusayn al-ʿĀmilī
66
ʿAlī Āl Kāshif al-Ghiṭā' 68, 111,
168, 179
ʿAlī al-ʿAlyārī 83, 140, 162
ʿAlī al-Anṣārī 133
ʿAlī al-Aʿrajī 83
ʿAlī al-Baḥrānī 186
ʿAlī al-Baraghānī 66
ʿAlī al-Burūjinī 93
ʿAlī al-Duzdarī 69
ʿAlī al-Gharawī 124
ʿAlī b. Hilāl al-Jazā'irī 50, 73
ʿAlī al-Ḥusaynī al-Astarābādī
135
ʿAlī al-Ḥusaynī al-Mīlānī 178, 212
ʿAlī b. Ḥusayn al-Mūsawī al-ʿĀmilī 122
ʿAlī al-Kanī 174, 211
ʿAlī al-Karbalā'ī 114, 199
ʿAlī al-Khaṭṭī 204
ʿAlī al-Khwānsāri 69
ʿAlī al-Khwātūnābādī 69
ʿAlī al-Maqābī 144
ʿAlī al-Maysī 134
ʿAlī al-Māzraʿī 104
ʿAlī al-Minshār 172
ʿAlī b. Muḥammad 189
ʿAlī b. M. al-ʿĀmilī 67, 74, 81,
133, 175
ʿAlī Muḥammad al-Ḥusaynī 69
ʿAlī al-Muḥammadī 157
ʿAlī b. M. Jaʿfar al-Astarābādī
75, 77, 90
ʿAlī b. Muḥyī al-Dīn al-Jāmiʿī
205
ʿAlī al-Naḥārīrī 134
ʿAlī al-Nahāwandī 11
ʿAlī Naqī al-Kamara'ī 142, 188
ʿAlī Naqī al-Ṭabāṭabā'ī 69, 78
ʿAlī Naqī al-Tabrīzī 207
ʿAlī al-Qārpūzābādī 74, 173, 199
ʿAlī Riḍā al-Tajallī 147
ʿAlī al-Ṣā'igh 71
ʿAlī al-Sāwijī 99
ʿAlī al-Shahrastānī 138, 141,
171, 188

ʿAlī al-Shūlastānī 138
ʿAlī al-Ṭihrānī 69, 76
ʿAlī al-Tustarī 99
ʿAlī al-ʿUṣfūrī 151
ʿAlī al-Yazdī al-Mudarris 72
ʿAlī al-Zawārī 134
ʿAlī b. Zayn al-ʿĀbidīn 69
Al-ʿAllāma 8, 23, 47-9, 70-6, 103, 152, 204
Amīn al-Astarābādī 52, 54, 129
Amīn al-Islām al-Tabrisī 45, 114
Amīn al-Tūnī 149
Amjad Ḥusayn Allāhābādī 83
Al-Anṣārī 9, 11, 57, 99, 112, 118, 124, 137, 154, 156, 157, 158, 160, 174, 183, 184, 185, 189, 192, 197, 202, 203, 207, 211, 213
Āqā al-Darbandī 90
Al-Ardabīlī 51-3, 83, 95, 115, 164, 177, 199
Asad Allāh al-Shaftī 69, 130
Al-Āshtiyānī 11, 112, 118, 131, 141, 144, 153, 211
ʿAṭā' Allāh al-Āmulī 186
Awrang Zib al-Qājār 66
ʿAzīz Allāh al-Khalkhālī 132

B

Badr al-Dīn al-Naysābūrī 150
Bahā' al-Dīn al-ʿĀmilī 51, 71, 74, 85, 96, 106, 117, 122, 125, 136, 140, 141, 143, 145, 146, 155, 159, 193, 200, 204, 205, 213
Bahā' al-Dīn al-Mashriqī 147
Baḥr al-ʿUlūm 56, 89-90, 156, 165, 201
Al-Balāghī 121, 131, 132, 141, 170, 171, 174
Banda Ḥusayn al-Naqawī 200
Bāyazīd al-Thānī 123, 138, 145
Al-Bihbahānī 9, 55, 56, 81, 83, 84, 85, 86, 87, 89, 97, 110, 120, 124, 130, 151, 161, 169, 170, 180, 189
Al-Burūjirdī 11, 58, 100, 138, 152, 156, 158

D

Al-Dāmād 51, 67, 72, 74, 78, 96, 107, 123, 124, 133, 146, 158, 190, 212
Dāwūd al-Burūjirdī 68
Dhu 'l-Majdayn 75
Ḍiyā' al-Dīn al-Aʿrajī 73
Ḍiyā' al-Dīn al-ʿArāqī 9, 11, 58, 94, 121, 141, 212, 213
Ḍiyā' al-Dīn al-Ḥusaynī 133
Ḍiyā' al-Dīn al-Jurjānī 95
Ḍiyā' al-Dīn al-Marʿashī 84

F

Al-Fāḍil al-Hindī 51, 71, 88, 109, 149, 165
Al-Fāḍil al-Jawād 116, 135
Al-Fāḍil al-Miqdād = al-Miqdād
Faḍl Allāh al-Astarābādī 104
Fakhr al-Dīn al-Mūsawī 81
Fakhr al-Dīn al-Narāqī 74, 92
Fakhr al-Dīn al-Sabīʿī 132, 204
Fakhr al-Dīn al-Ṭurayḥī 66, 123
Fakhr al-Muḥaqqiqīn 48, 49, 76, 103, 119, 152, 163
Fattāḥ al-Shahīdī 118, 174, 214
Al-Fayḍ 5, 16, 18, 52, 55, 86-7, 128, 148, 153, 182, 188
Fayḍ Allāh al-Tafrīshī 136
Fayḍ Ḥusayn 75
Fayyāḍ al-Zanjānī 158, 182

G

Ghulām Ḥusayn al-Darbandī 92

H

Ḥabīb Allāh al-Kāshānī 66, 92, 118
Hādī al-Kirmānshāhī 69
Hādī al-Ṭihrānī 11, 93, 112, 118, 157, 176, 179, 181, 192, 208
Ḥāfiẓ al-Kāshānī 172
Al-Ḥakīm 58, 92, 94, 174
Al-Ḥalabī 13, 43, 63
Ḥāmid al-Budalā' 107
Hārūn al-Jazā'irī 122
Ḥasan b. ʿAbd al-Ghaffār 134
Ḥasan b. ʿAlī al-Ḥusaynī 100
Ḥasan ʿAlī al-Ṭihrānī 157
Ḥasan ʿAlī al-Tustarī 85, 147
Ḥasan Āl Kāshif al-Ghiṭā' 57, 91, 93, 98, 171, 207, 210
Ḥasan al-Aʿrajī 69
Ḥasan al-Bujnūrdī 119
Ḥasan b. Ghiyāth al-Astarābādī 134-5
Ḥasan al-Gīlānī 185

Ḥasan al-Ḥā'irī al-Yazdī 98
Ḥasan b. al-Ḥusām 77
Ḥasan al-Ḥusaynī 208
Ḥasan al-Ḥusaynī al-Gīlānī 83
Ḥasan al-Ḥusaynī al-Kāshānī 70, 83
Ḥasan Isfandiyārī 73
Ḥasan b. Ismā'īl al-Qummī 118
Ḥasan al-Karakī 146, 170
Ḥasan b. M. al-Astarābādī 115
Ḥasan al-Najmābādī 153, 160, 178
Ḥasan b. Rāshid al-Ḥillī 132
Ḥasan al-Ṣadr 131
Ḥasan al-Yazdī al-Mudarris 68
Hāshim 167
Hāshim al-Ḥusaynī 128
Ḥaydar 'Alī al-Shīrwānī 81, 143, 153, 155, 165, 167, 169
Hidāyat Allāh al-Qummī 110
Al-Ḥurr al-'Āmilī 5, 55, 87, 88, 156, 170, 201, 206
Ḥusayn b. 'Abd al-Ṣamad 51, 52, 71, 75, 106, 120, 122, 133, 139, 146, 177, 197, 212
Ḥusayn al-Ardabīlī 95
Ḥusayn al-A'sam 68
Ḥusayn b. Abi 'l-Qāsim al-Khwānsārī 82, 130
Ḥusayn 'Alī al-Muntaẓirī 11, 152, 158, 215
Ḥusayn Āl 'Uṣfūr 86, 87, 88, 90, 97, 137, 184
Ḥusayn al-Dāmghānī 135
Ḥusayn al-Darb Imāmī 211
Ḥusayn al-Hamadānī 75
Ḥusayn b. Ḥaydar al-Karakī 162
Ḥusayn al-Ḥillī 113
Ḥusayn al-Karakī 181
Ḥusayn al-Khwānsārī 51, 87, 107, 158, 169
Ḥusayn b. M. al-Ḥusaynī 166
Ḥusayn al-Naqawī 137
Ḥusayn al-Qazwīnī 67, 71, 82, 128, 130, 141, 142 175, 189, 195
Ḥusayn Qulī al-Hamadānī 153, 156, 181, 211
Ḥusayn al-Ṣaymarī 67, 166, 172
Ḥusayn al-Ṭabasī 199
Ḥusayn al-Uwālī 135
Ḥusayn al-Wā'iẓ 98
Ḥusām al-Dīn al-Ṭurayḥī 191

I

Ibn Abī Jumhūr 117,119, 132, 134
Ibn Abi 'l-Majd 45, 64
Ibn al-Barrāj 43, 63, 121
Ibn Dāwūd al-Ḥillī 65, 76, 103
Ibn Fahd 50, 78-9, 104, 119, 128, 133, 152, 162, 163, 187
Ibn Fahd al-Aḥsā'ī 79
Ibn Ḥamza 45, 65
Ibn Hilāl 50, 73
Ibn Idrīs 38, 46, 65, 102
Ibn al-Mutawwij 49, 73, 78, 204
Ibn al-Najjār 73
Ibn Najm al-Dīn 103
Ibn Shahrāshūb 45, 46, 102
Ibn Ṭawq al-Baḥrānī 111, 117, 120, 127, 138, 144, 145, 167, 196, 208
Ibn Ṭayy 79, 172
Ibn Zuhra 8, 46, 65
Ibrāhīm al-Dizfūlī 89
Ibrāhīm al-Kaf'amī 159
Ibrāhīm Khalīfa Sulṭān 81, 84
Ibrāhīm al-Lāhījī 68
Ibrāhīm b. Layth al-Ḥusaynī 134
Ibrāhīm al-Qazwīnī 9, 68
Ibrāhīm al-Shīrāzī 82
Ibrāhīm al-Warrāq 114
'Imad al-Ṭabarī 45, 95
'Imād al-Dīn Yūsuf 146
'Ināyat Allāh b. Abi 'l-Fatḥ 207
'Ināyat Allāh al-Lārījānī 90
Al-Īrawānī 121, 141, 171, 174
Ismā'īl al-Hazarjarībī 82
Ismā'īl al-Marandī 92
Ismā'īl al-Nūrī 93
Ismā'īl al-Urmawī 75
'Izz al-Dīn al-Āmulī 186
'Izz al-Dīn Baḥr al-'Ulūm 113

J

Ja'far al-Ḥuwayzī 81, 86
Ja'far al-Khwānsārī 155
Ja'far al-Sabzawārī 69
Ja'far al-Subḥāni 12
Ja'far Qulī b. 'Abd al-'Alī 173
Ja'far al-Zahdazī 67
Jamāl al-Dīn al-Khwānsārī 51, 107, 149, 169, 198
Jamāl al-Dīn al-Mūsawī 66, 69, 90
Jamāl al-Dīn b. al-Najjār 73
Jamāl al-Dīn al-Naṭanzī 206
Jawād al-'Āmilī 56, 90
Jawād al-Karakī 71
Jawād al-Maysī 67, 133
Jawād al-Najafī 83

K

Kamāl al-Dīn al-Astarābādī 115
Al-Karakī 50, 51, 65, 72, 75, 79-80, 95, 104-5, 117, 126, 129, 134-5, 139, 144, 145, 152, 155, 158, 159, 163, 172, 176, 179, 188, 190, 193, 195, 203, 204, 213
Kāshif al-Ghiṭā' 56, 91, 97, 117, 124, 127, 128, 130, 142, 160, 167, 173
Khalaf al-Baḥrānī 188
Khalaf al-Ḥā'irī 68
Khālid - Sayyid Mīrzā 115
Khalīl al-Qazwīnī 55, 147
Khiḍr al-ʿAfkāwī 77, 99
Al-Khu'ī 11, 58, 121, 124, 125, 142, 174, 212, 215
Al-Khumaynī 12, 58, 94, 100, 119, 125, 154, 175, 178
Al-Khurāsānī 9, 11, 57, 94, 112, 127, 174, 182, 184, 192, 193, 196, 211, 214
Al-Khwājū'ī 84, 109, 122, 126, 127, 128, 141, 142, 144, 150, 157, 158, 166, 167, 170, 186, 188, 191, 193, 195, 201, 202, 208, 209, 212
Al-Kirmānshāhī 82, 90, 110, 126, 157, 159, 182, 187, 189, 194

L

Luṭf ʿAlī al-Tabrīzī 91
Luṭf Allāh al-Maysī 80, 163, 188

M

Mahdī al-Futūnī 56
Mahdī al-Ḥakīm 70
Mahdī al-Khāliṣī 70, 125, 128, 171
Mahdī al-Narāqī 89, 97
Mahdī al-Qumsha'ī 69
Mahdī al-Ṭabāṭabā'ī 87
Maḥmūd al-Āshtiyānī 138, 186
Maḥmūd al-Burūjirdī 90
Maḥmūd al-Hāshimī 12
Maḥmūd al-Kāẓimī 158
Maḥmūd al-Khwānsārī 180
Maḥmūd al-Khu'ī 92
Maḥmūd al-Kirmnshāhī 111, 165, 176
Maḥmūd al-Marʿashī 92
Maḥmūd al-Maythamī 112
Maḥmūd al-Najafī al-Kāshānī 112
Maḥmūd al-Shāhrūdī 166
Maḥmūd al-Shūlastānī 139
Al-Māḥūzī 55, 71, 125, 129, 136, 138, 144
Mājid al-Baḥrānī 123
Mājid al-Ḥusaynī al-Baḥrānī 175
Mājis al-Shaybānī 168, 177, 178, 190, 200
Al-Majlisī I 54, 96, 107, 164, 191
Al-Majlisī II 5, 52, 54, 97, 107-8, 124, 136, 138, 148, 153, 164, 169, 187, 191, 196, 198, 214
Malik M. al-Tūnī 116
Al-Marāghī 117, 173
Mashkūr al-Ḥawlāwī 185
Masīḥ al-Ṭihrānī 66, 74, 78, 82
Masʿūd al-Bihbahānī 125
Al-Maysī 71, 134, 135
Al-Miqdād 15, 38, 49, 78, 115, 116
Mīrak Mūsā al-Tūnī 124
Mīr Fattāḥ 117, 173
Mīr Lawḥī 175
Muhadhdhab al-Dīn al-Nīlī 46, 102-3
Muḥyī al-Dīn al-Jāmiʿī 205
Muḥyī al-Kirmānī 75
Muʿizz al-Dīn al-Ḥusaynī 114
Muʿizz al-Dīn al-Mūsawaī 85, 116, 136, 205
Al-Mufīd 7, 34, 37-43, 62, 100-1, 114, 161, 193, 199
Mufliḥ al-Ṣaymarī 50, 79, 104, 152, 172, 187
M. ʿAbbās al-Laknawī 83, 127, 185
M. b. ʿAbd al-Karīm al-Burūjirdī 191
M. b. ʿAbd al-Wahhāb al-Kāẓimī 124, 201
M. b. Abī Ṭālib al-Astarābādī 135
M. b. Aḥmad b. Abī Ṭālib 205
M. b. Aḥmad al-Baḥrānī 144, 155
M. b. Aḥmad b. Khwātūn al-ʿĀmilī 71
M. Amīn al-Aharī 69
M. b. ʿAlī al-Ardakānī 90
M. b. ʿAlī al-Astarābādī 115
M. ʿAli al-Astarābādī 115
M. ʿAlī al-Gīlānī 83, 140
M. b. ʿAlī b. Ḥaydar al-ʿĀmilī 116, 165
M. ʿAlī al-Hazārjarībī 74, 82, 192
M. ʿAlī al-Kāẓimī 11
M. ʿAlī al-Khusrawshāhī 179
M. ʿAlī al-Khwānsārī 174

M. b. ʿAlī b. Khwātūn al-ʿĀmilī 96, 133
M. ʿAlī al-Marʿashī 180
M. ʿAlī al-Masjidshāhī 178
M. ʿAlī al-Māzandarānī 68
M. b. ʿAlī b. Mu'min 66
M. ʿAlī al-Nūrī 72
M. ʿAlī al-Qarāchadāghī 83
M. ʿAlī al-Raḍawī 70, 82, 209
M. b. ʿAlī al-Raḍawī 78
M. ʿAlī al-Shaftī 69, 78, 142, 197
M. ʿAlī al-Sirkānī 64
M. ʿAlī al-Tabrīzī al-Mudarris 75
M. ʿAlī al-Tawḥīdī 174
M. ʿAlī al-Yazdī 99
M. ʿAlī al-Yūzbāshī 112
M. ʿAlī al-Zanjānī 161
M. al-Amrūhawī 143
M. al-Aʿrajī 69
M. Ashraf al-Ḥusaynī 153, 197
M. al-Ashrafī 100
M. b. ʿĀshūr al-Kirmānshāhī 69, 151, 187, 194, 208
M. b. Bahrām 76
M. Bāqir al-Bīrjandī 194, 196
M. Bāqir al-Gulpāyigānī 69, 82, 88
M. Bāqir al-Kazzāzī 168
M. Bāqir al-Khwānsārī 203
M. Bāqir al-Khwātūnābādī 187
M. Bāqir al-Lāhījī 91
M. Bāqir al-Marāghī 69
M. Bāqir b. M. Taqī 65
M. Bāqir al-Mūsawī 177
M. Bāqir al-Ṣadr 12
M. Bāqir al-Sharīf al-Qummī 88
M. Bāqir al-Ṭabāṭabā'ī al-Yazdī 72, 207
M. Bāqir al-Tabrīzī 160
M. Bāqir al-Yazdī 69
M. Fāḍil al-Mashhadī 191
M. al-Fīrūzābādī 141
M. al-Fishārakī 153
M. Hādī al-Astarābādī 213
M. Hādī al-Ḥusaynī 132
M. Hādī al-Māzandarānī 74, 142, 161, 191
M. Hādī al-Mīlānī 158
M. Hādī al-Sabzawārī 175
M. Hādī al-Khu'ī 71
M. al-Harawī 210
M. al-Ḥarfūshī 117
M. b. Ḥārith al-Astarābādī 121
M. b. Hārith al-Baḥrānī 135, 199
M. Ḥasan Adīb 67
M. b. Ḥasan al-ʿĀmilī 81, 136, 168
M. Ḥasan al-Baraghānī 72
M. Ḥasan al-Bārfurūshī 83
M. Ḥasan al-Harawī 88
M. Ḥasan al-Khurāsānī 110
M. Ḥasan al-Māmaqānī 94, 174
M. Ḥasan b. M. Taqī 211
M. Ḥasan al-Muẓaffar 74
M. Ḥasan al-Nūrbakhshī 110
M. Ḥasan al-Qazwīnī 88
M. Ḥasan al-Qummī 123
M. Ḥasan al-Shīrāzī 57, 118
M. b. Ḥasan al-Tabrīzī 131
M. Hāshim al-Khurāsānī 140, 173, 180, 193, 208
M. Hāshim al-Khwānsārī 130, 160
M. Hāshim al-Ṭasūjī 70
M. al-Ḥujja al-Kūhkamarī 178
M. Ḥusayn Āl Kāshif al-Ghiṭā' 113
M. Ḥusayn al-ʿArab al-Dāmād 70
M. Ḥusayn al-Basṭāmī 133
M. al-Ḥusaynī 136
M. al-Ḥusaynī al-Lāhījī 108
M. al-Ḥusaynī al-Qummī 110
M. Ḥusayn al-Iṣfahānī 9, 11, 58, 174, 182
M. Ḥusayn al-Kāẓimī 69-70
M. Ḥusayn al-Khwānsārī 75, 118, 126, 143, 154, 159, 166, 167, 181, 185, 214
M. Ḥusayn al-Khwātūnābādī 97, 129
M. Ḥusayn al-Qumsha'ī 83, 93
M. b. Ḥusayn al-Raḍawī 66
M. Ḥusayn al-Raḍawī 69, 74, 78
M. Ḥusayn al-Raḍawī al-Kāshānī 70
M. Ḥusayn al-Shahrastānī 70
M. Ḥusayn al-Ṭabīb al-Ṭihrānī 69
M. Ibrāhīm al-Ḥā'irī al-Qazwīnī 77
M. Ibrāhīm al-Ḥusaynī al-Qazwīnī 81, 84, 115, 213
M. Ibrāhīm al-Kalbāsī 86, 93, 99
M. Ibrāhīm al-Kāẓimī 177
M. Ibrāhīm al-Kharaqānī 68
M. Ibrāhīm al-Mūsawī 111
M. Ibrāhīm al-Qishlāqī 66, 83
M. Ibrāhīm al-Rashtī 183
M. Isḥāq al-Fayyāḍ 11
M. Ismāʿīl al-Fadā'i 75, 135
M. Ismāʿīl al-Khwātūnābādī 148
M. b. Ismāʿīl al-Māzandarānī 98
M. Jaʿfar al-Ābāda'ī 83, 99
M. Jaʿfar al-Ardastānī 151
M. Jaʿfar al-Astarābādī 74, 75, 77, 82, 84, 91, 117, 133, 140 163, 173, 187, 201, 214

M. Jaʿfar al-Farāhī 88
M. Jaʿfar al-Hamadānī 82, 84, 86
M. Jaʿfar al-Ḥusaynī al-Kāshānī 171, 208
M. Jaʿfar al-Ḥuwayzī 188
M. Jaʿfar al-Kalbāsī 72
M. Jaʿfar al-Khabūshānī 107
M. Jaʿfar al-Kirmānshāhī 75, 87, 111
M. Jaʿfar b. M. Ṭāhir 83
M. Jaʿfar al-Sabzawārī 133, 144, 161
M. Jaʿfar al-Sharastānī 176
M. Jaʿfar al-Shīrāzī 142
M. Jaʿfar al-Ṭihrānī 185, 202
M. Jawād Mullā Kitāb 78
M. Jawād al-Narāqī 91
M. Kāẓim 67
M. Kāẓim al-Hamadānī 68
M. Kāẓim al-Hazārjarībī 168
M. Kāẓim al-Langrūdī 66, 69
M. Kāẓim al-Sabzawārī 108
M. Kāẓim al-Shīrāzī 152, 174
M. Kāẓim al-Ṭabarī 71, 168, 183
M. Kāẓim al-Tūysirkānī 149
M. al-Khwātūnābādī 82
M. al-Langrūdī 69
M. Mahdī al-Gīlānī 68
M. Mahdī al-Ḥusaynī al-Mashhadī 72, 86, 180, 188
M. Mahdī al-Kalbāsī 72, 78, 93, 111
M. Mahdī al-Khwānsārī 132
M. Mahdī al-Kujūrī 69
M. Mahdī al-Maḥallātī 99
M. Mahdī al-Mūsawī 82
M. Mahdī al-Qazwīnī 69
M. Mahdī al-Raḍawī 135
M. al-Maqābī 89
M. al-Mashriqī 147
M. Maʿṣūm al-Hāshimī 132
M. b. Maʿsūm al-Raḍawī 77
M. b. M. b. ʿAbd Allāh 73
M. b. M. ʿAlī al-Kāshānī 66
M. b. M. Kāẓim al-Khurāsānī 182, 211
M. b. M. Maʿṣūm al-Mashhadī 86
M. b. M. Muḥsin al-Kāshānī 86
M. b. M. Riḍā al-Qummī 199
M. b. M. Ṣādiq al-Khwānsārī 180
M. b. M. Zamān al-Kāshānī, 140, 156, 187
M. Muḥsin al-Kāshānī 86
M. Muʾmin al-Ḥusaynī 143
M. Muqīm al-Bārfurūshī 82
M. Muqīm al-Yazdī 147
M. Murād al-Kishmīrī 88
M. al-Muwaḥḥidī 138
M. al-Nāʾīnī 82
M. al-Naraqī 151
M. Naṣīr al-Bārfurūshī 142, 152
M. b. Naṣṣār al-Ḥuwayzī 133
M. b. Niẓām al-Dīn al-Astarābādī 133
M. b. Qāsim 147
M. b. Qāsim al-Iṣfahānī 81
M. Qāsim al-Māzandarānī 165
M. Qāsim al-Sāwijī 205
M. Qulī al-Kantūrī 210
M. al-Raḍawī al-Ṭūsī 69
M. Rafīʿ b. Faraj al-Gīlānī 82, 115, 150
M. Rafīʿ al-Gīlānī al-Iṣfahānī 84
M. Raḥīm al-Burūjirdī 70, 74, 159, 178
M. Raḥīm al-Sabzawārī 161
M. Rasūl b. ʿAbd al-ʿAzīz 178
M. Rasūl al-Kāshānī 176
M. Riḍā Āl Baḥr al-ʿUlūm 77, 82
M. Riḍā al-Astarābādī 87, 130
M. Riḍā b. ʿAlī Sharīf al-Gulpāyigānī 82
M. Riḍā al-Hamadānī 168
M. Riḍā al-Isfarjānī 179
M. Riḍā al-Māzandarānī 198
M. Riḍā al-Mūsawī al-Gulpāyigānī 160, 178, 212
M. Riḍā al-Muẓaffar 12
M. Riḍā al-Shīrāzī 66
M. Riḍā al-Tabrīzī 71
M. al-Ruḥafzāʾī 151
M. Ṣādiq 82
M. Ṣādiq al-Ḥillī al-Shīrāzī 144
M. Ṣādiq al-Kishmīrī 67
M. Ṣādiq b. Muḥammad 67
M. Ṣādiq al-Rūḥānī 75
M. Ṣādiq al-Sirkānī 104, 139, 183
M. Saʿīd 85
M. Saʿīd al-Quhpāʾī 115, 202
M. Ṣāliḥ al-Astarābādī 67, 86, 207
M. Ṣāliḥ al-Baraghānī 71, 72
M. Ṣāliḥ al-Dāmād 83, 92
M. Ṣāliḥ al-Farāhānī 65
M. Ṣāliḥ al-Khalkhālī 82, 140
M. Ṣāliḥ al-Khwātūnābādī 142, 161, 197
M. Ṣāliḥ al-Simnānī 184, 186
M. Sarwar al-Bihsūdī 11-12
M. Shafīʿ al-Īrawānī 207
M. Shafīʿ al-Fūmanī 124
M. Shafīʿ al-Māzandarānī 181, 196
M. Shafīʿ b. M. Ḥusayn 77
M. al-Shahshahānī 91
M. Ṭāhā Najaf 93, 125, 209

M. Ṭāhir al-Dizfūlī 83
M. Ṭāhir al-Harawī 88
M. Ṭāhir al-Ḥusaynī 137
M. Ṭāhir al-Qummī 145, 148, 153, 156, 206
M. Ṭāhir al-Rānakū'ī 69
M. Taqī al-Āmulī 94, 138, 174
M. Taqī al-Ardakānī 168, 181
M. Taqī al-Astarābādī 67, 107
M. Taqī al-Barghānī 68
M. Taqī al-Burūjirdī 11
M. Taqī al-Harawī 83, 92, 99, 130, 171, 196
M. Taqī al-Iṣfahānī al-Mudarris 118
M. Taqī al-Kāshānī 169
M. Taqī al-Kishmīrī 148
M. Taqī al-Khishtī 66
M. Taqī al-Masjidshāhī 202
M. Taqī b. M. Raḥīm al-Iṣfahānī 9, 124
M. Taqī Mulā Kitāb 177
M. Taqī al-Naqawī 200, 207
M. Taqī al-Nūrī 160, 162, 192, 199, 207, 209
M. Taqī al-Qā'inī 149
M. Taqī al-Shīrāzī 58, 152, 154, 174
M. Taqī al-Ṭabasī 71
M. Taqī al-Tabrīzī 193
M. Taqī al-Ṭāliqānī 68
M. Taqī al-Tunukābunī 211
M. al-Tunukābunī 72
M. al-Turkābādī 110
M. al-Ṭūsī al-Mashhadī 90
M. Yaḥyā al-Sāwijī 140
M. Yūsuf al-Astarābādī 129
M. Yūsuf al-Gīlānī 133
M. Yūsuf al-Lāhījī 86
Al-Muḥaqqiq 8, 14, 18, 23, 47, 48, 64, 65-70, 102, 139
Muḥsin al-Amīn 75, 186, 194
Muḥsin al-A'rajī 86, 89, 91, 151
Muḥsin al-Ardabīlī 158
Muḥsin al-A'sam 68
Muḥsin al-Khanfar 174, 202
Muḥsin al-Rashtī 127, 207
Al-Mujāhid 9, 57, 87, 92, 98, 111, 210
Al-Mujtahid 120, 128, 131, 139, 146, 168, 200, 212
Mu'īn al-Dīn al-Miṣrī 46, 126, 203
Al-Mukhtārī 77, 127, 138, 138, 145, 172, 178, 198, 206
Mullā Mu'min 131
Mu'min al-Ardabīlī 71
Munīr al-Dīn al-Burūjirdī 121
Muntajab al-Dīn al-Rāzī 154
Murād al-Tafrishī 125
Al-Murtaḍā 7, 34, 41-3, 45, 46, 63, 101-2, 121, 161, 176, 187, 193, 195
Murtaḍā al-Ḥā'irī 175
Murtaḍā al-Khusrawshāhī 179
Murtaḍā al-Sārawī 146
Murtaḍā al-Sidihī 83
Mūsā Āl Kāshif al-Ghiṭā' 82, 123
Mūsā b. Faḍl Allāh al-Hamadānī 69, 175
Mūsā al-Khwānsārī 174
Mūsā al-Kirmānshāhī 75
Muṣṭafā al-Khu'ī 68
Muẓaffar al-Rashtī 70, 185

N

Al-Nā'īnī 9, 11, 58, 119, 138, 141, 174
Naṣīr al-Dīn al-Narāqī 82-3
Naṣīr al-Dīn al-Ṭūsī 204
Naṣr Allāh al-Astarābādī 71, 154
Naẓar 'Alī al-Ṭāliqānī 176, 212, 214
Ni'mat Allāh b. 'Abd Allāh 68
Ni'mat Allāh al-Jazā'irī 55, 123, 201
Niẓām al-Dīn al-Sāwijī 96
Nūr Allāh al-Tustarī 84, 125, 141, 146
Nūr al-Dīn al-Akhbārī 86

Q

Qāsim al-Najafī 69
Al-Qaṭīfī 50, 66, 71, 73, 119, 132, 152, 159, 177, 190
Al-Qaṭṭān 50, 79
Qawām al-Dīn al-Qazwīnī 67
Querry, A. 67
Al-Qummī 9, 57, 92, 98, 110, 133, 157, 160, 162, 165, 167, 169, 171, 176, 178, 180, 183, 184, 185, 189, 190, 192, 194, 195, 197, 201, 206, 210, 212, 213, 214

R

Raḍī al-Dīn al-Khwānsārī 77, 107, 200
Raḍī al-Dīn b. M. Nabī al-Qazwīnī 120, 198

Raḍī al-Dīn M. b. Ḥasan al-Qazwīnī 162
Rafīʿ al-Dīn al-Nāʾīnī 72, 84, 96, 107
Rāḥat Ḥusayn al-Gūpalpūrī 159,190
Al-Rashtī 57,125,156,157,174,182, 184,185,202,203,208,211
Al-Rāwandī 45, 46, 102, 115
Riḍā al-Hamadānī 57, 94, 174
Riḍā al-Luṭfī 121
Riḍā al-Tabrīzī 69
Rūḥ Allāh al-Ḥāfiẓ 205

S

Al-Sabzawārī 52, 81, 85, 96, 117, 147, 164, 175
Ṣādiq al-Tabrīzī 11, 112
Ṣadr al-Dīn al-ʿĀmilī 192
Ṣadr al-Dīn al-Hamadānī 56, 89, 125
Ṣadr al-Dīn M. al-Raḍawī al-Kāshānī 155
Ṣadr al-Dīn al-Ṭabāṭabāʾī al-Yazdī 82, 150, 155, 206
Al-Ṣadūq 4, 33, 40-1, 62
Ṣafī al-Dīn al-Ṭurayḥī 129
Ṣāḥib al-Fuṣūl 9, 99
Ṣāḥib al-Ḥadāʾiq 55, 56, 84, 89, 109-10, 126, 137, 189, 192, 206, 213
Ṣāḥib al-Jawāhir 57, 93, 99, 111
Ṣāḥib al-Maʿālim 8, 51, 53, 84, 106, 136, 164
Ṣāḥib al-Madārik 23, 24, 51, 52-3, 84, 133
Ṣāḥib al-Maqābis 57, 74, 92, 98, 126, 154, 196, 197
Ṣāḥib al-Riyāḍ 56, 77, 87, 91, 98, 110, 165, 167
Al-Sahrashtī 45, 64
Sallār b. ʿAbd al-ʿAzīz 14, 43, 63
Al-Samāhījī 55, 97, 108-9, 149
Al-Sarāb 115, 142, 148-9, 161, 198
Al-Sayyid ʿAmīd al-Dīn 48, 76, 204
Shādhān b. Jibriʾīl 139
Al-Shaftī 56, 99, 111, 130, 137, 165, 170, 181, 183, 184, 189, 196,203
Shāh Ṭāhir al-Dakanī 135
Al-Shahīd al-Awwal 8, 14, 15, 18, 23, 24, 38, 48, 49, 76-8, 104, 116, 119, 132, 152, 162, 163, 212
Al-Shahīd al-Thānī 50, 52, 66, 71, 80-3, 105, 120, 122, 125, 126, 129, 132, 133, 145-6, 152, 155, 163-4, 172, 195, 204, 208, 209, 213
Shams al-Dīn al-Astarābādī 128
Shams al-Dīn M. Mitqālbāf 105
Sharaf al-Dīn ʿAlī al-Astarābādī 135
Al-Sharīf al-Ḥusaynī 188
Shāriḥ al-Wāfiya 56, 89, 125
Al-Shaykh 4, 7, 18, 23, 44-8, 63, 102, 121, 122, 200, 203
Shaykh al-Sharīʿa 131, 180, 209
Al-Shīrwānī 67, 74, 107, 128, 153, 199, 208
Shubbar b. M. al-Najafī 127, 155, 162
Shukr Allāh al-Ḥusaynī 127
Sulṭān M. al-Kāshānī 133
Sulṭān al-ʿUlamāʾ 8, 107, 164

T

Ṭāhir al-Ḥusaynī al-Dakanī 135
Al-Tuwalānī 134

Y

Yaḥyā b. Saʿīd 18, 47, 70, 102
Yaʿqūb al-Bārfurūshī 124
Al-Yazdī 58, 94, 100, 112, 154, 174, 186
Yūsuf al-Gīlānī 70
Yūsuf al-Tabrīzī 214

Z

Ẓahīr al-Dīn al-Nīlī 76
Zayn al-ʿĀbidīn al-Ṭabāṭabāʾī 68
Zayn al-ʿĀbidīn al-Ḥusaynī 96
Zayn al-ʿĀbidīn al-Lārījānī 142
Zayn al-ʿĀbidīn al-Sabzawārī 192, 207
Zayn al-ʿĀbidīn al-Tabrīzī 129
Zayn al-ʿĀbidīn al-Ṭabāṭabaʾī 68
Zayn al-Dīn al-Ḥillī 103

2 - TITLES

A

Al-ʿĀbidiyya 135
Abwāb al-jinān 148
Ādāb al-ṣalāt 136
Ādāb-i saniyya 197
Ādāb al-tijāra 97
Adillat al-rashād 93
Afʿāl-i ḥajj 164
Aḥkām ʿaqd al-nikāḥ 187
Aḥkām al-amwāt 128
Aḥkām al-ʿidāla al-ʿAlawiyya 210
Aḥkām al-ḥajj 165
Aḥkām al-janā'iz 128
Aḥkām al-jizya 169
Aḥkām al-khalal 154
Aḥkām al-mukhālifīn 170
Aḥkām-i nijāsāt 129
Aḥkām al-nisā' 114
Aḥkām ṣalāt al-jumʿa 151
Aḥkām-i ṣayd wa dhabā'iḥ 199
Aḥkām-i shakk wa sahw 153
Aḥkām-i ṣulḥ 181
Aḥkām al-ṭawāf 166
Aḥkām al-ʿumra 167
Aḥkām al-ʿuqūd 174
Aḥkām-i yamīn 198
Al-Aḥmadī 36
Ajwad al-taqrīrāt 11
Ajwibat al-masā'il 107, 109, 110, 112
Ajwibat al-masā'il al-fiqhiyya 103, 104, 107, 109
Ajwibat masā'il al-Ḥusayn b. Rabīʿa al-Madanī 105
Ajwibat masā'il Ibn Farrūj 105
Ajwibat masā'il Ibn Zuhra 103
Ajwibat masā'il mawlānā Yūsuf al-Māzandarānī 104
Ajwibat masā'il al-mawlā Majd al-Dīn 107
Ajwibat al-masā'il al-Māziḥiyya 105
Ajwibat masā'il al-Miqdād 104
Ajwibat masā'il M. b. Juwaybar 106
Ajwibat masā'il M. b. Mujāhid 104
Ajwibat al-masā'il al-muhannā'iyya 103
Ajwibat al-masā'il al-Najafiyya 105
Ajwibat al-masā'il al-Ṣaymariyya 104
Ajwibat masā'il al-sayyid ʿAbd Allāh 108, 110
Ajwibat masā'il al-sayyid Ḥusayn 111
Ajwibat masā'il al-sayyid Sharaf al-Dīn al-Samākī 105
Ajwibat masā'il al-sayyid Yaḥyā 108
Ajwibat al-masā'il al-Shāmiyya 105
Ajwibat masā'il al-shaykh ʿAbd Allāh 108
Ajwibat masā'il al-shaykh ʿAlī al-Baḥrānī 108
Ajwibat masā'il al-shaykh Ṭāhir 106
Ajwibat masā'il al-shaykh M. al-Darāzī 111
Ajwibat masā'il al-shaykh Nāṣir al-Khaṭṭī 108
Ajwibat masā'il al-shaykh Ṣāliḥ al-Jazā'irī 106
Ajwibat masā'il al-shaykh Sulaymān 108
Ajwibat masā'il Shukr b. Ḥamdān 105
Ajwibat al-masā'il al-thalāth 109, 111
Ajwibat masā'il waradat . . . ʿan al-sāda al-ʿulamā' 104
Al-Aʿlām al-jaliyya 133
Al-Alfiyya 132
ʿAmal al-yawm wa 'l-layla 122
Al-Amr bi 'l-maʿrūf 170
Al-ʿAnāwīn 117
Anīs al-Tawwābīn 172
Anīs al-tujjār 97
Al-Anwār al-ʿaliyya 132
Al-Anwār al-bahiyya 122
Anwār al-dirāya 88
Anwār al-faqāha 93
Al-Anwār al-Gharawiyya 78
Al-Anwār al-Ḥīriyya 109
Al-Anwār al-jaliyya 109
Al-Anwār al-lawāmiʿ 87
Al-Anwār al-qamariyya 136
Al-Anwār al-Raḍawiyya 66
Anwār al-riyāḍ 91
ʿAqd al-kisā' 114
Al-Aqṭāb al-fiqhiyya 117
Arbaʿ masā'il fiqhiyya 104
Aṣālat al-luzūm 171
Al-ʿAshara al-kāmila 205
Al-Ashiʿʿa al-badriyya 135
ʿAwā'id al-ayyām 117
Al-ʿAwīṣ 100
Awqāt-i namāz 138

Awqāt al-ṣalāt 138
Awthaq al-wasā'il 91
Ayādī sabā 107
Al-Āya al-mubṣira 75
Āyāt al-aḥkām 115, 116
Āyāt al-jihād 168
Al-ʿAyn 178

B

Bāb-i jinān 144
Al-Badr al-zāhir 152, 156
Baḥr al-fawā'id 11
Al-Baḥr al-zākhir 125
Baḥr al-ḥaqā'iq 68
Baḥr al-jawāhir 93
Al-Baḥr al-lāmiʿ 66
Al-Bayān 76
Bayān al-ḥaqq 184
Al-Bayyināt 204
Bidāyat al-hidāya 87
Bughyat al-rāghibīn 152
Bughyat al-ṭālib 97, 174
Buḥūth fiqhiyya 113
Al-Bulgha 146
Bulghat al-faqīh 112
Bulghat al-ṭālib 174
Burhān al-ashrāf 184
Al-Burhān al-qāṭiʿ 66
Burhān al-sadād 71
Bushrā al-muḥaqqiqīn 47

D

Dalā'il al-aḥkām 68, 69, 74
Dalīl al-nāsik 166
Daqā'iq al-afhām 69
Ḍawābiṭ al-khams 153
Dawābiṭ al-riḍāʿ 190
Al-Dhahabiyya 141
Al-Dhahab al-masbūk 141
Dhakhā'ir al-imāma 158
Dhakhā'ir al-nubuwwa 179
Dhakhā'ir al-ʿuqbā 85
Al-Dhakhīra al-abadiyya 109
Al-Dhakhīra al-bāqiya 109
Dhakhīrat al-badā'iʿ 68
Dhakhīrat al-maʿād 72, 85
Dhakhīrat al-jazā' 85
Al-Dharā'iʿ 68
Dharā'iʿ al-aḥlām 94
Dharā'iʿ al-anām 70
Dhikrā al-Shīʿa 76
Dhikrā dhawi 'l-nuhā 131
Al-Dhukhr al-lāmiʿ 86
Al-Ḍiyā' al-lāmiʿ 66
Ḍiyā' al-ʿuqūl 194
Droit Musulman 67
Durar al-fawā'id 11
Al-Durar al-ghawālī 121
Al-Durar al-manẓūma 72
Durar al-niqād 71
Al-Durra 89
Al-Durra al-durriyya 204
Al-Durra al-Ḥā'iriyya 69, 78
Al-Durra al-Najafiyya 110
Al-Durra al-ṣafiyya 132
Durrat al-aslāk 201
Durrat al-durrayn 192
Al-Durr al-manḍūd 172, 173
Al-Durūs 76
Durūs fī fiqh al-Shīʿa 125
Durūs fī ʿilm al-uṣūl 12

F

Fā'ida fī ḥurmat ṣalāt al-jumʿa 150
Fā'ida fī ḥurmat simāʿ ṣawt al-mar'a 186
Fā'ida fī jawāz bayʿ al-sharṭ 179
Fā'ida fi 'l-mawārīth 207
Fā'ida fi 'l-mutʿa 193
Fā'ida fī ṭalāq al-walī 195
Al-Fdhālik 90
Al-Fakhriyya 119
Al-Fākiha al-Kāẓimiyya 108
Al-Fakhriyya 123
Al-Farā'iḍ 204, 206
Al-Farā'iḍ al-Bahā'iyya 205
Al-Farā'iḍ al-Naṣīriyya 204
Farā'id al-uṣūl 11
Farā'iḍ-i yawmiyya 132
Al-Farq bayn al-farīḍa wa 'l-nāfila 121
Al-Farq bayn al-ṭalāq al-rajʿī wa 'l-bā'in 195
Farq-i miyān mard wa zan 114
Al-Faṣīḥ al-munhij 47
Faṣl al-khiṭāb 129
Faṣl al-khiṭāb al-Ibrāhīmiyya 82
Fatāwā 105
Al-Fatāwā al-Ḥusayniyya 97
Fatḥ al-mafātīḥ 86
Fattāḥ al-majāmiʿ 90
Al-Fawā'id 68, 112
Al-Fawā'id al-ʿaliyya 122, 135
Fawā'id fī ṣalāt al-musāfir 155
Al-Fawā'id al-Gharawiyya 136
Fawā'id al-marām 67
Fawā'id mutafarriqa 105
Fawā'id al-Qawāʿid 80
Al-Fawā'id al-sariyya 136

awā'id al-Sharā'i' 79
awā'id al-uṣūl 11
iqh al-Qur'ān 115
iqh al-Ṣādiq 75
iqh-i shāhī 95, 123
l-Fīrūzajāt al-Ṭūsiyya 90
l-Fiṭra al-malakūtiyya 122
l-Fuṣūl al-khamsa 202
uṣūṣ fīrūzajāt khafiyya 90

G

l-Ghāliya 131
hanā'im al-ayyām 92
hanīmat al-ma'ād 71
hāyat al-āmāl 174
hāyat al-ījāz 133
hāyat al-ikhtiyār 189
hāyat al-marām 79
hāyat al-murād 77, 167
hāyat al-su'ūl 194
l-Gharawiyya 135
hunyat al-nuzū' 65
hurar al-majāmi' 66
l-Ghurra 90
l-Ghurra al-Gharawiyya 78
l-Ghurra al-Ḥanafiyya 90

H

add al-masāfa 155
l-Hādī ila 'l-rashād 71
l-Ḥabl al-matīn 85
l-Hadā'iq al-nāḍira 89
ādī al-muḍillīn 135
l-Ḥadīqa al-Najafiyya 83
adīqat al-muttaqīn 91, 96
adiqat al-Rawḍa 83
adiyyat al-ikhwān 123
adiyyat al-mu'minīn 123
l-Ḥajj wa 'l-'umra 164
all al-'asīr 130
all 'ibāra mu'ḍala 74
all shakk 169
all al-'uqūd 108
l-Ḥaqā'iq 69
aqq al-qaḍā' 112
l-Ḥaqq al-ṣurāḥ 187
l-Ḥā'iriyya 141
l-Ḥāshiya 'alā k. al-farā'iḍ 204, 206
āshiya 'alā Risālat al-ṭalāq 196
āshiya 'alā risālat al-Tūnī 149
āshiyat al-Irshād 76
-Ḥāshiya al-raḍiyya 83
āshiyat al-Sharā'i' 80
Ḥāwī al-marām 69
Al-Ḥaydariyya 135
Al-Hidāya 62, 134
Hidāyat al-aḥkām 88
Hidāyat al-akhyār 99
Hidāyat al-a'lām 86
Hidāyat al-anām 69, 159
Hidāyat al-ikhwān 107
Al-Hidāya al-Mahdiyya 77
Hidāyat al-sā'il 108
Hidāyat al-Shī'a 92
Hidāyat al-ṣirāṭ 149
Hidāyat al-ṭalib 174
Hidāyat al-ṭālibīn 84, 100
Hidāyat al-umma 88
Ḥisān al-yawāqīt 138
Al-Ḥiyal al-shar'iyya 180
Al-Ḥujja 147
Ḥukm al-ḥākim 161
Ḥukm-i māli-i Nāṣibī 169
Ḥukm mulāqī al-najis 129
Ḥukm al-musāfara 163
Ḥukm ru'yat al-hilāl 161
Ḥukm taklīf al-kāfir 169
Ḥukm al-ṭalāq 183, 195
Ḥurmat al-mashāhid 167
Ḥurmat ṣalāt al-jum'a 150

I

Al-Ibāna al-marḍiyya 82, 140
Ibānat al-mukhtār 209
Ibtighā' al-faḍīla 175
Īḍāḥ al-aḥwāl 172
Īḍāḥ al-fawā'id 76
Īḍāḥ al-kalām 68
Īḍāḥ al-Nāfi' 66
Īḍāḥ al-Riyāḍ 92
Al-I'ḍālāt al-'awīṣāt 107
'Iddat masā'il 112
Idrāk al-rak'a 138
Al-Ifāda al-ijmāliyya 120
Ifāḍat al-Qadīr 131
Al-Iḥtiyāṭāt al-fiqhiyya 109
Al-'Ijāla al-mūjaza 165
Al-Ījāz 203
I'lām al-aḥibba 175
Al-I'lām 101
Imāṭat al-lithām 116
Imlā' fī waṣf dīn al-Imāmiyya 62
Inārat al-ṭurūs 77, 198
Īnās sulṭān al-mu'minīn 116
Al-'Ināya al-Ilāhiyya 90
Al-Inṣāf 93
Al-Intiṣār 63
Iqāmat al-ḥudūd 170
Īqāẓ al-nā'imīn 175

ʿIqd fi 'l-ʿilm al-ijmālī 121
ʿIqd fī ilzām ghayr al-Imāmī 170
Al-ʿIqd al-Ḥusaynī 120
ʿIqd al-jawāhir 103
ʿIqd al-la'ālī 121
Al-Iqtiṣād 71, 121
Al-Iqtiṣād wa 'l-irshād 122
Irshād al-adhhān 71
Irshād al-mustarshidīn 99
Irshād al-ṣāliḥīn 137
Irshād al-sālik 165
Al-Irtimās fi 'l-ṣawm 162
Iṣābat al-ḥaqq 181
Iṣbāḥ al-Shīʿa 64
Ishārāt al-fiqh 82
Ishārat al-sabq 64
Al-Ishrāf 62
Ishtiraṭ ṣiḥḥat al-ṣawm 162
Iṣlāḥ al-ʿamal 98
Al-Isṭanbuliyya 123
Istiḥbāb al-tayāsur 139
Ishiqṣā' al-naẓar 89
Ithbāt al-siyāda 158, 159
Al-Ithnāʿashariyya 107, 136, 206
Al-Ithnāʿashariyyāt 122
Al-Iʿtikāfiyya 163
Izāḥat al-ʿilla 139
Izāḥat al-iltibās 142
Izāḥat al-shukūk 141, 142, 197
Izāḥat al-waswasa 167
Iẓhār mā ʿindī 165
Al-ʿIzziyya 102

J

Al-Jaʿfariyya 134
Jā' al-ḥaqq 148
Jalā' al-shubahāt 151
Jamʿa 146
Jāmiʿ-i ʿAbbāsī 96
Jāmiʿ al-aḥkām 69
Jāmiʿ al-aqwāl 92
Jāmiʿ al-fawā'id 73, 85, 116
Jāmiʿ-i Jaʿfarī 67
Jāmiʿ-i Raḍawī 67
Jāmiʿ al-jawāmiʿ 66, 69
Al-Jāmiʿ al-kabīr 91
Jāmiʿ al-kalim 141
Jāmiʿ al-khilāf 70
Jāmiʿ al-madārik 94
Jāmiʿ al-maqāṣid 80
Jāmiʿ al-sharā'iʿ 70
Jāmiʿ al-shatāt 110
Jannat al-khuld 99
Jawābāt al-masā'il al-Mawṣiliyya 101
Jawābāt masā'il Mayyāfāriqīn 101
Jawābāt al-masā'il al-Rāziyyāt 101
Jawābāt masā'il al-sharīf al-Rassī 101
Jawābāt al-masā'il al-Tabbāniyyāt 101
Jawābāt al-masā'il al-Ṭarābulusiyyāt 101
Al-Jawāb bi 'l-ṣawāb 200
Jawāb-i masā'il-i Khurāsān 107
Jawāb-i masā'il-i mīrzā sayyid ʿAlī 107
Jawāb-i masā'il-i Shāh ʿAbbās 106
Jawāb mas'ala ʿan al-ḥabwa 208
Jawāhir al-fiqh 63
Jawāhir al-ḥaqā'iq 116, 204
Jawāhir al-kalām 93
Jawāhir al-kalimāt 172
Jawāhir al-masā'il 99
Jawāmiʿ al-kalām 74
Jawāmiʿ al-rasā'il 110
Jawāz ibdāʿ al-safar 162
Jawāz-i musāfirat-i pādishāh 169
Al-Jihādiyya 167, 168
Jumal al-ʿilm wa 'l-ʿamal 121
Al-Jumal wa 'l-ʿuqūd 63
Al-Jumāna al-bahiyya 132
Jumān al-silk 171

K

K. al-Amr bi 'l-maʿrūf 170
K. al-Bayʿ 177, 178
K. al-Buyūʿ 177
K. fi 'l-fiqh 62
K. al-Ghaṣb 202
K. al-Ḥajj 166
K. al-Ḥudūd 215
K. Iḥyā' al-mawāt 202, 203
K. al-Ijāra 182
K. al-Irth 208
K. al-Jihād 168
K. al-Khalal fi 'l-ṣalāt 154
K. al-Khums 158
K. al-Luqaṭa 203
K. al-Nikāḥ 186
K. al-Qaḍā' 210, 211, 212
K. al-Rahn 181
K. al-Ṣalāt 137, 138
K. al-Ṣawm 160
K. al-Ṣayd wa 'l-dhabā'iḥ 199
K. al-Ṣulḥ 181
K. al-Ṭahāra 124, 125
K. al-Tijāra 174
K. al-Waqf 183, 184

. al-Waṣāyā 184, 185
. al-Wuqūf wa 'l-ṣadaqāt 183
. al-Zakāt 157
l-Kafāf 163
l-Kāfī 63
anz al-durar al-aytām 77
anz al-fawā'id 71, 76
anz al-ʿirfān 115
anz al-Shīʿa 143
ārīziyya 203
ashf al-astār 199, 169
ashf al-awhām 162
ashf al-dirāya 88
ashf al-fawā'id 73
ashf al-ghiṭā' 91
ashf al-ḥaqā'iq 76
ashf al-ibhām 68, 69
ashf al-iltibās 79, 127
ashf al-lithām 88
ashf al-madārik 84
ashf al-maṭlūb 142
ashf al-niqāb 78
ashf al-qināʿ 68, 70, 192
ashf al-rayb 128
ashf al-rayba 151
ashf al-rayn 151
ashf al-rumūz 70
ashf al-rumūz al-khafiyya 81
ashf al-ẓalam 68
l-Kawākib al-durriyya 135
hādimiyya 180
l-Khalal fi 'l-ṣalāt 152, 153, 154
l-Kharājiyya 177
haṣā'iṣ al-aʿlām 68
hayr al-ʿamal 143
hazā'in al-aḥkām 76, 90
l-Khilāf 64
hilāfiyya 96
hulāṣat al-abḥāth 206
hulāṣat al-bayān 200
hulāṣat al-iʿtibār 163
hulāṣat al-tanqīḥ 79
ifāyat al-aḥkām 85
ifāyat al-muḥaṣṣilīn 75
ifāyat al-muhtadī 134
ifāyat al-muḥtāj 163
ifāyat al-ṭālibīn 78
ifāyat al-uṣūl 11
itābat bar kafan 129
l-Kurriyya 125

L

l-La'ālī al-zawāhir 110
amaʿāt 82
Al-Lamaʿāt al-nayyira 94
Al-Lawāmiʿ 82, 104
Lawāmiʿ al-aḥkām 89
Lawāmiʿ al-nikāt 112
Lu'lu' al-aḥkām 77
Al-Lu'lu' al-masjūr 126
Lumʿa 146, 151, 186
Al-Lumʿa al-Dimashqiyya 77
Al-Lumʿa al-jaliyya 108

M

Maʿālim al-dīn 79, 84
Maʿānī afʿāl al-ṣalāt 135
Maʿārif al-aḥkām 70
Maʿārij al-aḥkām 67
Maʿārij al-su'ūl 115
Maʿārij al-taḥqīq 123
Mabānī Takmilat al-Minhāj 212, 215
Mablagh al-naẓar 156, 196, 197
Al-Mabsūṭ 64
Madārik al-aḥkām 69, 84
Madīnat al-abḥath 207
Maʿdin al-ʿirfān 114
Mafātīḥ al-aḥkām 115
Mafātīḥ al-sharā'iʿ 86
Mā' al-ḥayāt 163
Mā'ida-yi samāwiyya 200
Majārī al-aḥkām 88
Majmaʿ al-aḥkām 69, 89
Majmaʿ al-ārā' 82
Majmaʿ al-bayān 71
Majmaʿ al-fā'ida wa 'l-burhān 83
Majmaʿ al-gharā'ib 78
Majmaʿ al-masā'il 66
Majmaʿ al-rashād 207
Mafātīḥ al-sharā'iʿ 52
Majmuʿat al-ifādāt 105
Al-Makāsib 174
Al-Makāsib al-muḥarrama 175
Makhāzin al-aḥkām 69
Makhzan al-asrār al-fiqhiyya 82
Makhzan al-la'ālī 121
Al-Manāfiʿ 66
Maʿnā qawl al-ʿAllāma 73
Manāhij al-aḥkām 68, 74, 92, 117, 210
Al-Manāhij al-sawiyya 88
Manāhij al-tadqīq 137
Al-Manāhil 92
Manāsik al-ḥajj 99, 163-6
Manhaj al-ijtihād 68
Manhaj al-rashād 72
Manhaj al-sadād 71
Manhaj al-salāma 159
Manhaj al-taḥqīq 154

Mandūb al-ṣawm 162
Maqābis al-anwār 92
Maqāla fi 'l-ḥath ʿalā ṣalāt al-jumʿa 145
Maqāla fi 'l-ʿidāla 214
Maqāla fi ṣalāt al-jumʿa 150
Maqāla fi 'l-ṭalāq 196
Maqāla fī wujūh al-Baḥth ʿan ṣalāt al-jumʿa 146
Al-Maqālāt al-Ghariyya 11
Maqālāt al-uṣūl 11
Al-Maqālīd al-Jaʿfariyya 117
Maqālīd al-quṣūd 172
Maqāmāt al-sālikīn 175
Maqāmiʿ al-faḍl 110
Al-Maqāṣid al-ʿaliyya 83, 109, 132
Maqṣad al-ṭālib 174
Al-Marāsim 63
Al-Marghūb 68
Al-Maṣābīḥ 87, 90
Maṣābīḥ al-aḥkām 90
Maṣābīḥ al-asrār 133
Maṣābīḥ al-hidāya 88
Al-Maṣābīḥ al-lawāmiʿ 86
Maṣābīḥ al-qulūb 97
Maṣābīḥ al-ẓalām 87, 89
Masā'il 102,107
Al-Masā'il al-akhbāriyya 89
Al-Masā'il al-Āmuliyya 103
Al-Masā'il al-arabaʿūn al-ʿĀmiliyya 113
Masā'il baʿḍ al-ajilla 103
Masā'il baʿḍ al-fuḍalā' 103
Al-Masā'il al-Baghdādiyya 102, 112
Al-Masā'il al-Baḥriyya 104
Al-Masā'il al-Baṣriyya 112
Al-Masā'il al-Bihbahāniya 108, 110
Masā'il fī abʿāḍ al-fiqh 102
Al-Masā'il al-fiqhiyya 79, 103, 106
Al-Masā'il al-Ḥā'iriyyāt 102
Al-Masā'il al-Hindiyya 108
Al-Masā'il al-Ḥusayniyya 108
Masā'il Ibn Najm 103
Masā'il-i waṣāyā 185
Al-Masā'il al-Kamāliyya 102
Al-Masā'il al-Kāzirūniyyāt 108
Al-Masā'il al-hkamsa 137
Al-Masā'il al-Khu'iyya 112
Al-Masā'il al-Khwāriyyāt 102
Al-Masā'il al-Madaniyyāt 106
Al-Masā'il al-Maẓāhiriyya 103
Al-Masā'il al-Miṣriyya 64, 102
Al-Masā'il al-Muḥammadiyya 109
Masā'il mutafarriqa 96, 102
Al-Masā'il al-Nāṣiriyyāt, 63, 103, 109
Al-Masā'il al-Naysābūriyya 101
Al-Masā'il al-Nīliyyāt 101
Al-Masā'il al-Ramliyyāt 101
Al-Masā'il al-Rashtiyya 185
Al-Masā'il al-Rassiyyāt 101
Masā'il al-riḍāʿ 191
Masā'il al-shaykh Abī Jaʿfar al-Ṭūsī 101
Masā'il al-shaykh Ẓahīr al-Dīn b. al-Ḥusām 104
Al-Masā'il al-Shāmiyya 104
Al-Masā'il al-Ṭabariyya 102
Masā'il tazāḥum al-ḥuqūq 212
Masā'il al-tilmīdh 105
Al-Masā'il al-Wāsiṭiyyāt 101
Mas'ala fi 'l-ʿamal maʿ al-sulṭān 176
Al-Mas'ala al-nāfiʿa 204
Mas'alat al-shaykh ʿAbd Allāh 109
Mas'alatān 106, 185
Al-Masālik 136
Masālik al-afhām 81, 116
Al-Masālik al-Jāmiʿiyya 132
Maslak al-rāshidīn 72
Mashāriq al-aḥkām 118
Mashāriq al-anwār 66
Mashāriq al-muhtadīn 88
Mashāriq al-shumūs 87
Mashriq al-shamsayn 85
Al-Masmūʿa 105
Al-Matājir 174
Maṭāliʿ al-anwār 137
Al-Maṭālib al-Muẓaffariyya 135
Maṭāriḥ al-anẓār 11
Al-Maʿūna 203
Mawāhib al-afhām 69
Al-Mawāhib al-Gharawiyya 69
Al-Mawāhib al-saniyya 75, 90
Al-Mawārīth 205, 207
Miftāḥ al-kalām 70
Miftāḥ al-karāma 90
Miftāḥ al-Riyāḍ 92
Minhāj al-hidāya 93
Minhāj al-milla 140
Minhāj al-najāt 83, 97, 162
Minhāj al-qibla 140
Minhāj al-umma 82
Miʿrāj al-sharīʿa 93
Mir'āt al-akhyār 155
Mir'āt al-muṣallīn 152
Mir'āt al-ʿuqūl 52
Miṣbāḥ al-faqāha 123, 174
Miṣbāḥ al-faqīh 94
Miṣbāḥ al-hidāya 207
Miṣbāḥ al-hudā 94

Miṣbāḥ al-ijtihād 68
Miṣbāḥ al-mubtadī 134
Al-Miṣbāḥ al-munīr 91
Al-Miṣbāḥ al-sāṭiʿ 87
Miṣbāḥ al-ṭarīq 98
Miṣbāḥ al-uṣūl 11
Al-Miṣbāḥ al-Wahhāj 177
Al-Mishkāt 124
Mishkāt al-anwār al-Ḥusayniyya 77
Al-Mishkāt al-Gharawiyya 78
Mishkāt al-hudāt 157
Mishkāt al-warā 133
Al-Mufradāt al-fāriqa 82
Muḥāḍarāt fi 'l-fiqh al-Jaʿfarī 174
Muḥāḍarāt fi uṣūl al-fiqh 11
Al-Muḥākama 209
Al-Muhadhdhab 63
Al-Muhadhdhab al-bāriʿ 78
Al-Muḥarrar 79
Muʿīn al-khawāṣṣ 98
Al-Mūjaz 79, 193
Mujlī al-sharīʿa 155
Mukhtalaf al-Shīʿa 72
Mukhtār al-madhhab 141
Al-Mukhtār 105
Al-Mukhtaṣar al-nāfiʿ 65
Mulakhkhaṣ al-maqāl 184
Munāqashāt fiqhiyya 107
Muntahā maqāṣid al-anām 70
Muntahā al-marām 153
Muntahā al-maṭlab 72
Muntakhab al-fawā'id 74
Muntakhab al-hidāya 88
Muntaqad al-manāfiʿ 66
Munyat al-albāb 78
Munyat al-rāghib 123
Munyat al-ṭālib 174
Al-Muqaddama al-farʿiyya 134
Al-Muqniʿ 67
Al-Muqniʿa 62
Al-Muqtaṣar 79
Al-Murshid 75
Murshid al-ʿawamm 98
Musakkin al-shujūn 201
Musawwid al-khudūd 214
Al-Muṣṭalaḥāt al-fiqhiyya 102
Mustamsak al-ʿUrwa al-wuthqā 94
Mustanad al-Shīʿa 93
Mustaqṣā al-ijtihād 71
Al-Mutʿa 115
Al-Muʿtabar 66
Muʿtaḍid al-Shīʿa 72
Al-Muʿtadil 213
Mutafarridāt al-Imāmiyya 101
Muʿtamad al-aḥkām 68
Muʿtamad al-anām 67
Muʿtamad al-Shīʿa 90
Al-Mutamassik bi-ḥabl Āl Rasūl 35
Muʿtaqad al-Imāmiyya 95
Mutashābih al-Qur'ān 102
Muẓhir al-mukhtār 194

N

Nabdha fī ṣiyagh al-ʿuqūd 173
Al-Nabdha al-ʿuqūdiyya 187
Naḍd al-qawāʿid al-fiqhiyya 116
Al-Nafḥa al-ʿanbariyya 109
Al-Nafḥa al-qudsiyya 137
Nafaḥāt al-ilhām 69
Nafy al-ḥaraj 118
Nahj al-faqāha 174
Nahj al-ʿirfān 47
Nahl al-sadād 71
Al-Najāt 132
Najāt al-ʿibād 99
Najāt al-mu'minīn 67
Najāt al-niswān 127
Al-Nahriyya 203
Al-Najmiyya 135
Najm al-mu'min 111
Natā'ij al-afkār 155
Nayl al-marām 95
Naẓm al-la'ālī 108
Nibrās al-hidāya 86
Al-Nihāya 64
Nihāyat al-afkār 11
Nihāyat al-āmāl 174
Nihāyat al-dirāya 11
Nihāyat al-iḥkām 84
Nihāyat al-iqdām 84
Nihāyat al-marām 87
Nihāyat al-muqtaṣid 86
Nihāyat al-taqrīr 138
Nihāyat al-uṣūl 11
Nikāḥiyya 187
Nithārāt al-kawākib 179
Niẓām al-farā'id 74
al-Niẓāmiyya 135
Nukat al-Nihāya 67
Al-Nukhba 87
Nukhbat al-wājibāt 97
Nūr al-hudā 156
Al-Nūr al-sāṭiʿ 68
Nūr-i sāṭiʿ 88
Nuzhat al-arwāḥ 186
Nuzhat al-nāẓir 47

Q

Qalā'id al-durar 116

Al-Qalāʼid al-saniyya 117
Al-Qāmiʻa li ʼl-bidʻa 149
Qanādīl al-ʻasjadāt 210
Qāṭiʻat al-lajāj 176
Qāṭiʻat al-mirāʼ 189
Qāṭiʻat al-qāl wa ʼl-qīl 126
Qaṭʻ al-maqāl 126
Al-Qaṭra 157
Qawāʻid al-aḥkām 73
Al-Qawāʻid al-Bāqiriyya 118
Al-Qawāʻid al-fiqhiyya 119, 171
Qawāʻid al-muʻāmalāt 171
Al-Qawāʻid al-sharʻiyya 117
Al-Qawāʻid wa ʼl-fawāʼid 116
Al-Qawl al-faṣl 127
Qiblat Irāq al-ʻAjam wa Khurāsān 139
Qibla-yi Ithnāʻashariyya 140
Qinṭār al-waẓāʼif 133
Qubāla qabaliyya 122
Qurrat al-ʻayn al-nāẓira 75

R

Al-Radd ʻalā aṣḥāb al-ʻadad 161
Al-Radd ʻalā iʻtirāḍāt 81
Rāfiʻ al-ibhām 159
Rafʻ al-iltibās 170
Al-Rasāʼil 11, 12, 106,109, 110
Al-Rasāʼil wa ʼl-masāʼil 111
Rawāʼiʻ al-aḥkām 67
Rawāʼiʻ al-amālī 121
Rawāshiḥ al-ʻināya al-Rabbāniyya 86
Al-Rawḍ al-arīḍ 185, 186
Al-Rawḍa al-bahiyya 81
Rawḍ al-jinān 81, 202
Rawḥ al-nasīm 145
Rayḥānat al-ṣudūr 161
Al-Riḍāʻiyya 190-3
Al-Riḍwān 181
Al-Risāla al-Bāqiriyya 179
Al-Risāla al-Barmakiyya 134
Al-Risāla al-Fahliyāniyya 109
Al-Risāla al-Ḥāʼiriyya 121
Al-Risāla al-maʻnawiyya 136
Al-Risāla al-Muḥammadiyya 206
Al-Risāla al-Najafiyya 152
Al-Risāla al-Raḍawiyya 69
Al-Risāla al-Sayfiyya 109
Risāla-yi sahla 82
Riyāḍ al-masāʼil 91
Al-Rūmiyya 122
Ruʼyat al-hilāl 161

S

Sadād al-ʻibād 90
Ṣafāʼ al-Rawḍa 83
Ṣafḥat almām 127
Safīnat al-najāt 201
Safīna-yi tawfīq 67
Ṣafwat al-maqāl 183
Ṣaḥīfat al-mīrāth 207
Al-Sahwiyya 152
Al-Salāmiyya 145
Al-Sarāʼir 65
Ṣawāʻiq al-Yahūd 169
Al-Sawāniḥ al-naẓariyya 88
Al-Ṣawārim al-qāṣima 189
Al-Ṣawmiyya 159-60
Al-Sayfiyya 135
Shaʻāʼir al-Islām 100
Shadhrat al-naḍīd 134
Shāfī al-ʻalīl 126
Sharāʼiʻ al-Islām 67
Sharḥ al-Durra al-bahiyya 214
Sharḥ ʻibāra mushikla 82
Sharḥ khuṭbat al-Jaʻfariyya 135
Sharḥ khuṭbat al-Sharāʼiʻ 67
Sharḥ K. al-Nikāḥ 186
Sharḥ al-Lumʻa 179
Sharḥ al-masʼala al-nahbiyya 73, 209
Sharḥ muqaddamat al-Ḥadāʼiq 89
Sharḥ Qaṭrat al-baḥrayn 85
Sharḥ al-Qawāʻid 173
Sharḥ Risālat al-ṣalāt 137
Sharḥ Tabṣirat al-mutaʻallimīn 94
Sharḥ Urjūza fi ʼl-mawārīth 207
Sharḥ al-Urjūza al-riḍāʻiyya 192
Al-Sharīʻa al-Nabawiyya 77
Shāriʻ al-najāt 96
Shatāt al-fawāʼid 101
Shawāriʻ al-aʻlām 70
Shawāriʻ al-anām 74
Shawāriʻ al-hidāya 86
Shawāriʻ al-Sharāʼiʻ 68
Al-Shihāb al-thāqib 148
Shikārnāma 199
Shurūṭ al-nikāḥ 188
Al-Silāḥ al-māḍī 210
Sirāj al-umma 83
Al-Sirāj al-wahhāj 177
Ṣirāṭ al-najāt 99
Ṣirāṭ al-yaqīn 75
Ṣiyagh-i nikāḥ 187
Ṣiyagh al-ʻuqūd 172-3
Siyānat al-Ibāna 209
Suʼāl wa jawāb 108, 110, 111, 112

ubul al-rashād 93
ulaymāniyya 114

T

'a'āruḍ al-adilla 12
a'āruḍ al-wakīl wa 'l-muwakkil 183
.l-Tabā'ud bayn al-bi'r wa al-bālū'a 125
.l-Tabṣira al-jaliyya 191
'abṣirat al-mubtadi'īn 123
'abṣirat al-muta'allimīn 74
'abṣirat al-Shī'a 199
'adāruk al-Madārik 84
.l-Tadhkira 75
'adhkirat al-fuqahā' 75
'adhkirat al-wadād 144
'afsīr-i Shāhī 115
'aḥammul al-'ibāda 119
'ahdhīb al-uṣūl 12
.l-Tahlīliyya 142
'aḥrīr al-aḥkām 75
'aḥrīr al-majalla 113
'aḥrīr al-Taḥrīr 73
'aḥrīr al-Wasīla 94, 100
'aḥqīq al-dalā'il 211
'aḥqīq fi 'l-qiyās 85
'aḥqīq al-ḥaqq 151
.l-Taḥrīm bi 'l-muṣāhara 189
'aḥṣīl al-iṭmīnān 115
'aḥṣīl al-manāfi' 65
.l-Takbīrāt al-sab' 144
.l-Taklīfiyya 119
.l-Takmila 75
.l-Takmila li 'l-Tabṣira 75
'akmilat Mashāriq al-shumūs 77
'akmilat al-Qawā'id 74
'akmilat al-Tabṣira 94
.l-Ta'līqa al-anīqa 83
'a'līq al-Irshād 80
.l-Ta'līqāt fi 'l-ṭahāra 124
'alkhīṣ al-aḥkām 160
'alkhīṣ al-marām 75
'amhīd al-Qawā'id 116
.l-Tanbīh 104, 105, 178
'anbīh al-anām 130
'anhīh al-ghāfilīn 175
.l-Tanqīḥ 124
'anqīḥ al-bayān 71
.l-Tanqīḥ al-rā'i' 78
.l-Taqiyya 118
.l-Taqrīrāt 111, 124
'aqwīm al-mīrāth 206
'aqwīm al-ṣalāt 137
'arā'iq al-Riyāḍ 92
'arīq al-rashād 71
'ashīl al-masālik 118
'ashrīḥ al-uṣūl 11
Taṭawwu' al-sawm 162
Ṭawāli' al-lawāmi' 66
Tawḍīḥ al-masā'il 100, 169
Tawḍīḥ al-mushkilāt 77
Tawfīr al-khums 158
Thamarat al-fu'ād 207
Thamarat al-jinān 71
Al-Tibyān 85
Al-Tuḥfa al-'Abbāsiyya 167
Tuḥfat al-abrār 99, 111
Tuḥfat ahl al-īmān 139
Tuḥfat al-albān 192
Tuḥfat al-dārayn 206
Al-Tuḥfa al-Gharawiyya 77
Tuḥfat al-ḥujjāj 166
Al-Tuḥfa al-Ḥusayniyya 97, 133
Al-Tuḥfa al-jaliyya 119
Al-Tuḥfa al-marḍiyya 145
Tuḥfat al-muṣallīn 98
Tuḥfat al-nisā' 114
Al-Tuḥfa al-Qawāmiyya 77
Al-Tuḥfa al-Raḍawiyya 97
Tuḥfat al-rāghib 98
Tuḥfat al-Riḍā 136
Tuḥfat al-ṣafwa 209
Al-Tuḥfa al-saniyya 76, 87
Tuḥfat al-sarā'ir 164
Al-Tuḥfa al-shahīdiyya 97
Tuḥfa-yi Rafī'ī 205
Al-Tusā'iyya 106
Al-Tuwalāniyya 134

U

'Uddat al-musāfirīn 155
'Umdat al-nāẓir 198
Urjūza ri 'l-zakāt 156
Al-'Urwat al-wuthqā 94, 100, 148
Al-'Uṣra 154
Al-Uṣūl 'ala 'l-nahj al-ḥadīth 11
Uṣūl al-dīn wa furū'uh 95
Uṣūl al-fiqh 12
'Uyūn al-masā'il al-fiqhiyya 107

W

Wadā'i' al-aḥkām 68
Wadā'i' al-nubuwwa 93
Wājibāt al-ḥajj 163
Wājibāt-i namāz 95, 96
Al-Wājibāt al-malikiyya 122
Wājibāt al-ṣalāt 134, 136
Al-Wajīza 98, 99, 135, 150
Al-Wajīza al-'āṣima 190
al-Waqt wa 'l-qibla 140
Wasā'il al-Shī'a 91
Al-Wasīla 65

Wasīlat al-maʿād 93
Wasīlat al-najāt 94, 98, 100
Wasīlat al-Qāṣid 73
Al-Waṣiyya bi 'l-ḥajj 166
Al-Wathā'iq wa 'l-ʿiqāl 188
Wathīqat al-wasā'il 92
Wiqāyat al-adhhān 11

Y

Al-Yanābīʿ 210
Yanābīʿ al-ḥikma 77
Yanābīʿ al-wilāya 178
Al-Yanbūʿ al-Munbajis 129
al-Yūsufiyya 123

Z

Al-Zahra 165
Zahr al-riyāḍ 92, 98
Al-Zahrāt al-zawiyya 81
Zakātiyya 124, 156
Zayniyya 132
Zubda 95
Zubdat al-bayān 115
Zubdat al-dalīl 98
Zubdat al-maqāl 158